Real-time Systems

Prentice Hall International Series in Computer Science

C.A.R. Hoare, Series Editor

Series listing continued at back of book

Real-time Systems
Specification, Verification and Analysis

edited by
Mathai Joseph

Prentice Hall

London   New York   Toronto   Sydney   Tokyo   Singapore
Madrid   Mexico City   Munich

First published 1996 by
Prentice Hall International (UK) Limited
Campus 400, Maylands Avenue
Hemel Hempstead
Hertfordshire, HP2 7EZ
A division of
Simon & Schuster International Group

© Prentice Hall International (UK) Ltd 1996

Printed at Redwood Books, Trowbridge, Wiltshire.

Library of Congress Cataloging-in-Publication Data

Available from the publisher

British Library Cataloguing in Publication Data

A catalogue record for this book is available from
the British Library

ISBN 0-13-455297-0

1   2   3   4   5   00   99   98   97   96

Contents

Preface

The field of real-time systems has not traditionally been hospitable to newcomers: on the one hand there are experts who seem to rely on experience and a few specialized documents and, on the other, there is a vast and growing catalogue of technical papers. There are very few textbooks and the most successful publications are probably collections of past papers carefully selected to cover different views of the field. As interest has grown, so has the community, and the more recent papers are spread over a large range of publications. This makes it particularly difficult to keep in touch with all the new developments.

If this is distressing to the newcomer, it is of no less concern to anyone who has to teach a course on real-time systems: one has only to move a little beyond purely technical concerns to notice how quickly the teachable material seems to disappear in a cloud of opinions and a range of possibilities. It is not that the field lacks intellectual challenges or that there is not enough for a student to learn. On the contrary, the problem seems to be a question of where to start, how to relate practical techniques with methods of analysis, analytical results with theories and, more crucially, how to decide on the objectives of a course.

This book provides a detailed account of three major aspects of real-time systems: program structures for real-time, timing analysis using scheduling theory and specification and verification in different frameworks. Each chapter focuses on a particular technique: taken together, they give a fairly comprehensive account of the formal study of real-time systems and demonstrate the effectiveness and applicability of mathematically based methods for real-time system design. The book should be of interest to computer scientists, engineers and practical system designers as it demonstrates also how these new methods can be used to solve real problems.

Chapters have different authors and each focuses on a particular topic, but the material has been written and edited so that the reader should notice no abrupt changes when moving from one chapter to another. Chapters are linked with cross-references and through their description and analysis of a common example: the mine pump (Burns & Lister, 1991; Mahony & Hayes, 1992). This allows the reader to compare the advantages and limitations of different techniques. There are a number of small examples in the text to illustrate the theory and each chapter ends with a set of exercises.

The idea for the book came originally from material used for the M.Sc. module on real-time systems at the University of Warwick. This module has now been taught by several of the authors over the last three years and has been attended by both students and visiting participants. However, it was planned that the book would contain a more comprehensive treatment of the material than might be used in a single course. This allows teachers to draw selectively on the material, leaving some parts out and others as further reading for students. Some possible course selections are outlined in Chapter 1 but many more are possible and the choice will be governed by the nature of the course and the interests and preparation of the students. Part of the material has been taught by the authors in advanced undergraduate courses in computer science, computer engineering and related disciplines; selections have also been used in several different postgraduate courses and in short courses for industrial groups. So the material has been used successfully for many different audiences.

The book draws heavily on recent research and can also serve as a source book for those doing research and for professionals in industry who wish to use these techniques in their work. The authors have many years of research experience in the areas of their chapters and the book contains material with a maturity and depth that would be difficult for a single author to achieve, certainly on a short time-scale.

Acknowledgements

Each chapter has been reviewed by another author and then checked and re-drafted by the editor to make the style of presentation uniform. This procedure has required a great deal of cooperation and understanding from the authors, for which the editor is most grateful. Despite careful scrutiny, there will certainly be inexcusable errors lurking in corners and we would be very glad to be informed of any that are discovered.

We are very grateful to the reviewers for comments on the draft and for providing us with the initial responses to the book. Anders Ravn read critically through the whole manuscript and sent many useful and acute observations and corrections. Matthew Wahab pointed out a number of inconsistencies and suggested several improvements. We are also glad to acknowledge the cooperation of earlier 'mine pump' authors, Andrew Lister, Brendan Mahony and Ian Hayes.

In addition, particular thanks are due to many other people for their comments on different chapters.

Chapters 1, 2: Tomasz Janowski made several useful comments, as did students of the M.Sc. module on real-time systems and the Warwick undergraduate course, *Verification and Validation*. Steve Schneider's specification in Z of the mine pump was a useful template during the development of the specification in Chapter 1.

Chapter 4: Gerhard Fohler, Swamy Kutti and Arcot Sowmya commented on an earlier draft. Thanks are also due to the present and past members of the real-time group at the University of Massachusetts.

Chapter 5: Jan Vitt read through the chapter carefully and made several suggestions for improvement.

Chapter 6: Jim Davies, Bruno Dutertre, Gavin Lowe, Paul Mukherjee, Justin Pearson, Ken Wood and members of the ESPRIT Basic Research Action CONCUR2 provided comments at various stages of the work.

Chapter 7: Zhou Chaochen was a source of encouragement and advice during the writing of this chapter.

The book was produced using LATEX2e, aided by the considerable ingenuity, skill and perseverance of Steven Haeck, with critical tips from Jim Davies and with help at many stages from Jeff Smith.

Finally, the book owes a great deal to Jackie Harbor of Prentice Hall International, who piloted the project through from its start, and to Alison Stanford, who was Senior Production Editor. Their combined efforts made it possible for the writing, editing and reviewing of the book to be interleaved with its production so that the whole process could be completed in 10 months.

The Series editor, Tony Hoare, encouraged us to start the book and persuaded us not to be daunted by the task of editing it into a cohesive text. All of us, editor and authors, owe a great deal for this support.

Department of Computer Science   Mathai Joseph
University of Warwick

Contributors

Professor Alan Burns   *burns@minster.cs.york.ac.uk*
Department of Computer Science
University of York
York YO1 5DD, U.K.

Dr. Jozef Hooman   *wsinjh@win.tue.nl*
Department of Mathematics and Computing Science
Eindhoven University of Technology
P.O. Box 513
5600 MB Eindhoven, The Netherlands

Professor Mathai Joseph   *mathai.joseph@dcs.warwick.ac.uk*
Department of Computer Science
University of Warwick
Coventry CV4 7AL, U.K.

Dr. Zhiming Liu   *zl2@mcs.le.ac.uk*
Department of Mathematics and Computer Science
University of Leicester
Leicester LE1 7RH, U.K.

Professor Krithi Ramamritham   *krithi@nirvan.cs.umass.edu*
Department of Computer and Information Science
University of Massachusetts at Amherst
Amherst MA 01003, U.S.A.

Dr. Ir. Henk Schepers   *schepers@prl.philips.nl*
Philips Research Laboratories
Information and Software Technology
Building WL-1
Prof. Holstlaan 4
5656 AA Eindhoven, The Netherlands

Dr. Steve Schneider   *steve@dcs.rhbnc.ac.uk*
Department of Computer Science
Royal Holloway, University of London
Egham
Surrey TW20 0EX, U.K.

Dr. Andy Wellings   *andy@minster.cs.york.ac.uk*
Department of Computer Science
University of York
York YO1 5DD, U.K.

Chapter 1

Time and Real-time

Mathai Joseph

Introduction

There are many ways in which we alter the disposition of the physical world. There are obvious ways, such as when a car moves people from one place to another. There are less obvious ways, such as a pipeline carrying oil from a well to a refinery. In each case, the purpose of the 'system' is to have a physical effect within a chosen time-frame. But we do not talk about a car as being a real-time system because a moving car is a *closed system* consisting of the car, the driver and the other passengers, and it is controlled from within by the driver (and, of course, by the laws of physics).

Now consider how an external observer would record the movement of a car using a pair of binoculars and a stopwatch. With a fast moving car, the observer must move the binoculars at sufficient speed to keep the car within sight. If the binoculars are moved too fast, the observer will view an area before the car has reached there; too slow, and the car will be out of sight because it is ahead of the viewed area. If the car changes speed or direction, the observer must adjust the movement of the binoculars to keep the car in view; if the car disappears behind a hill, the observer must use the car's recorded time and speed to predict when and where it will re-emerge.

Suppose the observer replaces the binoculars by an electronic camera which requires *n* seconds to process each frame and determine the position of the car. As when the car is behind a hill, the observer must predict the position of the car and point the camera so that it keeps the car in the frame even though it is 'seen' only at intervals of *n* seconds. To do this, the observer must model the movement of the car and, based on its past behaviour, predict its future movement. The observer may not have an explicit 'model' of the car and may not even be conscious of doing the modelling; nevertheless, the accuracy of the prediction will depend on how faithfully the observer models the actual movement of the car.

Finally, assume that the car has no driver and is controlled by commands radioed by the observer. Being a physical system, the car will have some inertia and a reaction time, and the observer must use an even more precise model if the car is to be controlled success-

1

fully. Using information obtained every n seconds, the observer must send commands to adjust throttle settings and brake positions, and initiate changes of gear when needed. The difference between a driver in the car and the external observer, or remote controller, is that the driver has a continuous view of the terrain in front of the car and can adjust the controls continuously during its movement. The remote controller gets snapshots of the car every n seconds and must use these to plan changes of control.

1.1 Real-time computing

A real-time computer controlling a physical device or process has functions very similar to those of the observer controlling the car. Typically, sensors will provide readings at periodic intervals and the computer must respond by sending signals to actuators. There may be unexpected or irregular events and these must also receive a response. In all cases, there will be a time-bound within which the response should be delivered. The ability of the computer to meet these demands depends on its capacity to perform the necessary computations in the given time. If a number of events occur close together, the computer will need to schedule the computations so that each response is provided within the required time-bounds. It may be that, even so, the system is unable to meet all the possible unexpected demands and in this case we say that the system lacks sufficient resources (since a system with unlimited resources and capable of processing at infinite speed could satisfy any such timing constraint). Failure to meet the timing constraint for a response can have different consequences: in some cases, there may be no effect at all; in other cases, the effects may be minor and correctable; in yet other cases, the results may be catastrophic.

Looking at the behaviour required of the observer allows us to define some of the properties needed for successful real-time control. A real-time program must

- *interact with an environment which has time-varying properties,*
- *exhibit predictable time-dependent behaviour, and*
- *execute on a system with limited resources.*

Let us compare this description with that of the observer and the car. The movement of the car through the terrain certainly has time-varying properties (as must any movement). The observer must control this movement using information gathered by the electronic camera; if the car is to be steered safely through the terrain, responses must be sent to the car in time to alter the setting of its controls correctly. During normal operation, the observer can compute the position of the car and send control signals to the car at regular intervals. If the terrain contains hazardous conditions, such as a flooded road or icy patches, the car may behave unexpectedly, e.g. skidding across the road in an arbitrary direction. If the observer is required to control the car under all conditions, it must be possible to react in time to such unexpected occurrences. When this is not possible, we can conclude that the real-time demands placed on the observer may, under some conditions, make it impossible to react in time to control the car safely. In order for a real-time system to manifest predictable time-dependent behaviour it is thus necessary for the environment to make predictable demands.

With a human observer, the ability to react in time can be the result of skill, training, experience or just luck. How do we assess the real-time demands placed on a computer system and determine whether they will be met? If there is just one task and a single processor computer, calculating the real-time processing load may not be very difficult. As the number of tasks increases, it becomes more difficult to make precise predictions; if there is more than one processor, it is once again more difficult to obtain a definite prediction.

There may be a number of factors that make it difficult to predict the timing of responses.

- A task may take different times under different conditions. For example, predicting the speed of a vehicle when it is moving on level ground can be expected to take less time than if the terrain has a rough and irregular surface. If the system has many such tasks, the total load on the system at any time can be very difficult to calculate accurately.
- Tasks may have dependencies: Task *A* may need information from Task *B* before it can complete its calculation, and the time for completion of Task *B* may itself be variable. Under these conditions, it is only possible to set minimum and maximum bounds within which Task *A* will finish.
- With large and variable processing loads, it may be necessary to have more than one processor in the system. If tasks have dependencies, calculating task completion times on a multi-processor system is inherently more difficult than on a single-processor system.
- The nature of the application may require distributed computing, with nodes connected by communication lines. The problem of finding completion times is then even more difficult, as communication between tasks can now take varying times.

1.2 Requirements, specification and implementation

The demands placed on a real-time system arise from the needs of the application and are often called the *requirements*. Deciding on the precise requirements is a skilled task and can be carried out only with very good knowledge and experience of the application. Failures of large systems are often due to errors in defining the requirements. For a safety-related real-time system, the operational requirements must then go through a hazard and risk analysis to determine the safety requirements.

Requirements are often divided into two classes: *functional requirements*, which define the operations of the system and their effects, and *non-functional requirements*, such as timing properties. A system which produces a correctly calculated response but fails to meet its timing-bounds can have as dangerous an effect as one which produces a spurious result on time. So, for a real-time system, the functional and non-functional requirements must be precisely defined and together used to construct the specification of the system.

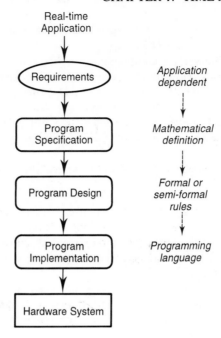

Figure 1.1 Requirements, specification and implementation

A *specification* is a mathematical statement of the properties to be exhibited by a system. A specification should be abstract so that

- it can be checked for conformity against the requirement, and
- its properties can be examined independently of the way in which it will be implemented, i.e. as a program executing on a particular system.

This means that a specification should not enforce any decisions about the structure of the software, the programming language to be used or the kind of system on which the program is to be executed: these are properly *implementation* decisions. A specification is transformed into an application by taking design decisions, using formal or semi-formal rules, and converted into a program in some language (see Figure 1.1).

In the next section, and in later chapters of this book, we shall study a simple but realistic problem and consider how a real-time system can be specified and implemented to meet the requirements. Different notations will be used for the specification and it will be shown how the properties of the implementation can be checked. This serves two purposes: first, using a common example allows us to compare different specification methods and see where they are most effective; second, it will be noticed as the specifications unfold that there are many hidden complexities in even apparently simple real-time problems. This is why mathematical description and analysis have an important role to play, as they help to deal with this complexity.

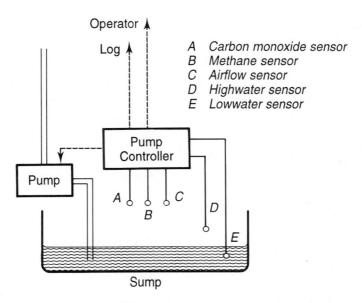

Figure 1.2 Mine pump and control system (adapted from Burns and Lister, 1991)

1.3 The mine pump

Water percolating into a mine is collected in a sump to be pumped out of the mine (see Figure 1.2). The water level sensors D and E detect when water is above a high and a low level respectively. A pump controller switches the pump on when the water reaches the high water level and off when it goes below the low water level. If, due to a failure of the pump, the water cannot be pumped out, the mine must be evacuated within one hour.

The mine has other sensors (A, B, C) to monitor the carbon monoxide, methane and airflow levels. An alarm must be raised and the operator informed within one second of any of these levels becoming critical so that the mine can be evacuated within one hour. To avoid the risk of explosion, the pump must be operated only when the methane level is below a critical level.

Human operators can also control the operation of the pump, but within limits. An operator can switch the pump on or off if the water is between the low and high water levels. A special operator, the supervisor, can switch the pump on or off without this restriction. In all cases, the methane level must be below its critical level if the pump is to be operated.

Readings from all sensors, and a record of the operation of the pump, must be logged for later analysis.

Safety requirements
From the informal description of the mine pump and its operations we obtain the following safety requirements:

1. The pump must not be operated if the methane level is critical.
2. The mine must be evacuated within one hour of the pump failing.
3. Alarms must be raised if the methane level, the carbon monoxide level or the air-flow level is critical.

Operational requirement
The mine is normally operated for three shifts a day, and the objective is for no more than one shift in 1000 to be lost due to high water levels.

Problem
Write and verify a specification for the mine pump controller under which it can be shown that the mine is operated whenever possible without violating the safety requirements.

Comments
The specification is to be the conjunction of two conditions: the mine must be operated when possible, and the safety requirements must not be violated. If the specification read 'The mine must not be operated when the safety requirements are violated', then it could be trivially satisfied by not operating the mine at all! The specification must obviate this easy solution by requiring the mine to be operated when it is safely possible.

Note that the situation may not always be clearly defined and there may be times when it is difficult to determine whether operating the mine would violate the safety requirements. For example, the pump may fail when the water is at any level; does the time of one hour for the evacuation of the mine apply to all possible water levels? More crucially, how is pump failure detected? Is pump failure always complete or can a pump fail partially and be able to displace only part of its normal output?

It is also important to consider under what conditions such a specification will be valid. If the methane or carbon monoxide levels can rise at an arbitrarily fast rate, there may not be time to evacuate the mine, or to switch off the pump. Unless there are bounds on the rate of change of different conditions, it will not be possible for the mine to be operated and meet the safety requirements. Sensors operate by sampling at periodic intervals and the pump will take some time to start and to stop. So the rate of change of a level must be small enough for conditions not to become dangerous during the reaction time of the equipment.

The control system obtains information about the level of water from the *Highwater* and *Lowwater* sensors and of methane from the *Methane* sensor. Detailed data is needed about the rate at which water can enter the mine, and the frequency and duration of methane leaks; the correctness of the control software is predicated on the accuracy of this information. Can it also be assumed that the sensors always work correctly?

The description explains conditions under which the mine must be evacuated but does not indicate how often this may occur or how normal operation is resumed after an evacuation. For example, can a mine be evacuated more than once in a shift or, following an evacuation, is the shift considered to be lost? If the mine is evacuated, it would be normal for a safety procedure to come into effect and for automatic and manual clearance to be needed before operation of the mine can resume. This information will make it possible to decide on how and when an alarm is reset once it has been raised.

1.3.1 Developing a specification

The first task in developing a specification is to make the informal description more precise. Some requirements may be very well defined but it is quite common for many requirements to be stated incompletely or with inconsistencies between requirements. For example, we have seen that there may be conditions under which it is not possible to meet both the safety requirements and the operational requirement; unfortunately, the description gives us no guidance about what should be done in this case. In practice, it is then necessary to go back to the user or the application engineer to ask for a more precise definition of the needs and to resolve inconsistencies. The process of converting informally stated requirements into a more precise form helps to uncover inconsistencies and inadequacies in the description, and developing a specification often needs many iterations.

We shall start by trying to describe the requirements in terms of some properties, using a simple mathematical notation. This is a first step towards making a formal specification and we shall see various different, more complete, specifications of the problem in later chapters.

Properties will be defined with simple predicate calculus expressions using the logical operators $\land$ *(and)*, $\lor$ *(or)*, $\Rightarrow$ *(implies)* and $\Leftrightarrow$ *(iff)*, and the universal quantifier $\forall$ *(for all)*. The usual mathematical relational operators will be used and functions, constants and variables will be typed. We use

$$F : T_1 \rightarrow T_2$$

for a function F from type T_1 (the *domain* of the function) to type T_2 (the *range* of the function) and a variable V of type T will be defined as $V : T$. An interval from C_1 to C_2 will be represented as $[C_1, C_2]$ if the interval is closed and includes both C_1 and C_2, as $(C_1, C_2]$ if the interval is half-open and includes C_2 and not C_1 and as $[C_1, C_2)$ if the interval is half-open and includes C_1 and not C_2.

Assume that time is measured in seconds and recorded as a value in the set *Time* and the depth of the water is measured in metres and is a value in the set *Depth*; *Time* and *Depth* are the set of real numbers.

S1: Water level
The depth of the water in the sump depends on the rate at which water enters and leaves the sump and this will change over time. Let us define the water level *Water* at any time to be a function from *Time* to *Depth*:

$$Water : Time \rightarrow Depth$$

Let *Flow* be the *rate of change* of the depth of water measured in metres per second and be represented by the real numbers; *WaterIn* and *WaterOut* are the rates at which water enters and leaves the sump and, since these rates can change, they are functions from *Time* to *Flow*:

rates : $WaterIn, WaterOut : Time \rightarrow Flow$

The depth of water in the sump at time t_2 is the sum of the depth of water at an earlier time t_1 and the difference between the amount of water that flows in and out in the time interval $[t_1, t_2]$. Thus $\forall t_1, t_2 : Time \cdot$

$$Water(t_2) = Water(t_1) + \int_{t_1}^{t_2} (WaterIn(t) - WaterOut(t))\, dt$$

HighWater and *LowWater* are constants representing the positions of the high and low water level sensors. For safe operation, the pump should be switched on when the water reaches the level *HighWater* and the level of water should always be kept below the level *DangerWater*:

$$DangerWater > HighWater > LowWater$$

If $HighWater = LowWater$, the high and low water sensors would effectively be reduced to one sensor.

S2: Methane level

The presence of methane is measured in units of pascals and recorded as a value of type *Pressure* (a real number). There is a critical level, *DangerMethane*, above which the presence of methane is dangerous.

The methane level is related to the flow of methane in and out of the mine. As for the water level, we define a function *Methane* for the methane level at any time and the functions *MethaneIn* and *MethaneOut* for the flow of methane in and out of the mine:

$Methane : Time \rightarrow Pressure$
$MethaneIn, MethaneOut : Time \rightarrow Pressure$

and $\forall t_1, t_2 : Time \cdot$

$$Methane(t_2) = Methane(t_1) + \int_{t_1}^{t_2} (MethaneIn(t) - MethaneOut(t))\, dt$$

S3: Assumptions

1. There is a maximum rate *MaxWaterIn* : *Flow* at which the water level in the sump can increase and at any time t, $WaterIn(t) \leq MaxWaterIn$.
2. The pump can remove water with a rate of at least *PumpRating* : *Flow*, and this must be greater than the maximum rate at which water can build up: *MaxWaterIn* < *PumpRating*.

3. The operation of the pump is represented by a predicate on *Time* which indicates when the pump is operating:

   Pumping : *Time* → *Bool*

   and at any time *t* if the pump is operating it will produce an outflow of water of at least *PumpRating*:

   $$(Pumping(t) \wedge Water(t)) > 0 \Rightarrow WaterOut(t) \geqslant PumpRating$$

4. The maximum rate at which methane can enter the mine is *MaxMethaneRate*. If the methane sensor measures the methane level periodically every t_M units of time, and if the time for the pump to switch on or off is t_P, then the reaction time $t_M + t_P$ must be such that normally, at any time *t*,

   $$(Methane(t) + MaxMethaneRate \cdot (t_M + t_P) + MethaneMargin)$$
   $$\leqslant DangerMethane$$

   where *MethaneMargin* is a safety limit.

5. The methane level does not reach *DangerMethane* more than once in 1000 shifts; without this limit, it is not possible to meet the operational requirement. Methane is generated naturally during mining and is removed by ensuring a sufficient flow of fresh air, so this limit has some implications for the air circulation system.

S4: Pump controller

The pump controller must ensure that, under the assumptions, the operation of the pump will keep the water level within limits. At all times when the water level is high and the methane level is not critical, the pump is switched on, and if the methane level is critical the pump is switched off. Ignoring the reaction times, this can be specified as follows:

$$\forall t : Time \cdot (Water(t) > HighWater \wedge Methane(t) < DangerMethane) \Rightarrow Pumping(t)$$
$$\wedge (Methane(t) \geq DangerMethane) \Rightarrow \neg Pumping(t)$$

Now let us see how reaction times can be taken into account. Since t_P is the time taken to switch the pump on, a properly operating controller must ensure that

$$Methane(t) < DangerMethane \wedge \neg Pumping(t) \wedge Water(t) \geqslant HighWater$$
$$\Rightarrow Pumping(t + t_P)$$

So if the operator has not already switched the pump on, the pump controller must do so when the water level reaches *HighWater*.

Similarly, the methane sensor may take t_M units of time to detect a methane level and the pump controller must ensure that

$$\forall t \in Time \cdot Pumping(t) \wedge (Methane(t) + MethaneMargin) = DangerMethane$$
$$\Rightarrow \neg Pumping(t + t_M + t_P)$$

S5: Sensors

The high water sensor provides information about the height of the water at time t in the form of predicates $HW(t)$ and $LW(t)$ which are true when the water level is above *HighWater* and *LowWater* respectively. We assume that at all times a correctly working sensor gives some reading (i.e. $HW(t) \vee \neg HW(t)$) and, since *HighWater* > *LowWater*, $HW(t) \Rightarrow LW(t)$.

The readings provided by the sensors are related to the actual water level in the sump:

$$\forall t \in Time \cdot \quad Water(t) \geqslant HighWater \Leftrightarrow HW(t)$$
$$\wedge \ Water(t) \geqslant LowWater \ \Leftrightarrow LW(t)$$

Similarly, the methane level sensor reads either $DML(t)$ or $\neg DML(t)$:

$$\forall t \in Time \cdot \quad Methane(t) \geqslant DangerMethane \Leftrightarrow DML(t)$$
$$\wedge Methane(t) < DangerMethane \Leftrightarrow \neg DML(t)$$

S6: Actuators

The pump is switched on and off by an actuator which receives signals from the pump controller. Once these signals are sent, the pump controller assumes that the pump acts accordingly. To validate this assumption, another condition is set by the operation of the pump. The outflow of water from the pump sets the condition *PumpOn*; similarly, when there is no outflow, the condition is *PumpOff*.

The assumption that the pump really is pumping when it is on and is not pumping when it is off is specified below:

$$\forall t \in Time \cdot \quad PumpOn(t) \Rightarrow Pumping(t)$$
$$\wedge \ PumpOff(t) \Rightarrow \neg Pumping(t)$$

The condition *PumpOn* is set by the actual outflow and there may be a delay before the outflow changes when the pump is switched on or off. If there were no delay, the implication $\Rightarrow$ could be replaced by the two-way implication *iff*, represented by $\Leftrightarrow$, and the two conditions *PumpOn* and *PumpOff* could be replaced by a single condition.

1.3.2   Constructing the specification

The simple mathematical notation used so far provides a more abstract and a more precise description of the requirements than does the textual description. Having come so far, the next step should be to combine the definitions given in **S1–S6** and use this to prove the safety properties of the system. The combined definition should also be suitable for transformation into a program specification which can be used to develop a program.

Unfortunately, this is where the simplicity of the notation is a limitation. The definitions **S1–S6** can of course be made more detailed and perhaps taken a little further towards what could be a program specification. But the mathematical set theory used for the specification is both too rich and too complex to be useful in supporting program development. To develop a program, we need to consider several levels of specification (and so far we have just outlined the beginnings of one level) and each level must be shown to preserve the properties of the previous levels. The later levels must lead directly to a program and an implementation and there is nothing so far in the notation to suggest how this can be done.

What we need is a specification notation that has an underlying computational model which holds for all levels of specification. The notation must have a calculus or a proof system for reasoning about specifications and a method for transforming specifications to programs. That is what we shall seek to accomplish in the rest of the book. Chapters 5–7 contain different formal notations for specifying and reasoning about real-time programs; in Chapter 8 this is extended to consider the requirements of fault-tolerance in the mine pump system. Each notation has a precisely defined computational model, or semantics, and rules for transforming specifications into programs.

1.3.3 Analysis and implementation

The development of a real-time program takes us part of the way towards an implementation. The next step is to analyze the timing properties of the program and, given the timing characteristics of the hardware system, to show that the implementation of the program will meet the timing constraints. It is not difficult to understand that for most time-critical systems, the speed of the processor is of great importance. But how exactly is processing speed related to the statements of the program and to timing deadlines?

A real-time system will usually have to meet many demands within limited time. The importance of the demands may vary with their nature (e.g. a safety-related demand may be more important than a simple data-logging demand) or with the time available for a response. So the allocation of the resources of the system needs to be planned so that all demands are met by the time of their deadlines. This is usually done using a scheduler which implements a scheduling policy that determines how the resources of the system are allocated to the program. Scheduling policies can be analyzed mathematically so the precision of the formal specification and program development stages can be complemented by a mathematical timing analysis of the program properties. Taken together, specification, verification and timing analysis can provide accurate timing predictions for a real-time system.

Scheduling analysis is described in Chapters 2–4; in Chapter 3 it is used to analyze an Ada 95 program for the mine pump controller.

1.4 How to read the book

The remaining chapters of this book are broadly divided into two areas: (a) scheduling theory and (b) the specification and verification of real-time and fault-tolerant properties of systems. The book is organized so that an interested reader can read chapters in the order in which they appear and obtain a good understanding of the different methods. The fact that each chapter has a different author should not cause any difficulties as chapters have a very similar structure, follow a common style and have cross-references.

Readers with more specialized interests may wish to focus attention on just some of the chapters and there are different ways in which this may be done:

- *Scheduling theory*: Chapters 2, 3 and 4 describe different aspects of the application of scheduling theory to real-time systems. Chapter 2 has introductory material which should be readily accessible to all readers and Chapter 3 follows on with more advanced material and shows how a mine pump controller can be programmed in Ada 95; these chapters are concerned with methods of analysis for fixed priority scheduling. Chapter 4 introduces dynamic priority scheduling and shows how this method can be used effectively when the future load of the system cannot be calculated in advance.

- *Scheduling and specification*: Chapters 2, 3 and 4 provide a compact overview of fixed and dynamic priority scheduling. Chapters 5, 6 and 7 are devoted to specification and verification using assertional methods, a real-time process calculus and the duration calculus respectively; one or more of these chapters can therefore be studied to understand the role of specification in dealing with complex real-time problems.

- *Specification and verification*: any or all of Chapters 5, 6 and 7 can be used; if a choice must be made, then using either Chapters 5 and 6, or Chapters 5 and 7, will give a good indication of the range of methods available.

- *Timing and fault-tolerance*: Chapter 8 shows how reasoning about fault-tolerance can be done at the specification level; it assumes that the reader has understood Chapter 5 as it uses very similar methods.

- *The mine pump*: Different treatments of the mine pump problem can be found in Chapters 1, 3, 5, 6, 7 and 8; though they are based on the description in this chapter, subtle differences may arise from the nature of the method used, and these are pointed out.

Each chapter has a section describing the historical background to the work and an extensive bibliography is provided at the end of the book to allow the interested reader to refer to the original sources and obtain more detail.

Examples are included in most chapters, as well as a set of exercises at the end of each chapter. The exercises are all drawn from the material contained in the chapter and range from easy to relatively hard.

1.5   Historical background

Operations research has been concerned with problems of job sequencing, timing, scheduling and optimization for many decades. Techniques from operations research provided the basis for the scheduling analysis of real-time systems and the paper by Liu and Lay-land (1973) remained influential for well over a decade. This was also the time of the development of axiomatic proof techniques for programming languages, starting with the classic paper by Hoare (1969). But the early methods for proving the correctness of programs were concerned only with their 'functional' properties and Wirth (1977) pointed out the need to distinguish between this kind of program correctness and the satisfaction of timing requirements; axiomatic proof methods were forerunners of the assertional method described and used in Chapters 5 and 8. Mok (1983) pointed out the difficulties in relating work in scheduling theory with assertional methods and with the needs of practical, multi-process programming; it is only recently that some progress has been made in this direction: e.g. see Section 5.7.1 and Liu *et al.* (1995).

There are many ways in which the timing properties of programs can be specified and verified. The methods can be broadly divided into three classes.

1. Real-time without time: Observable time in a program's execution can differ to an arbitrary extent from universal or absolute time and Turski (1988) has argued that time is an issue to be considered at the implementation stage but not in a specification; Hehner (1989) shows how values of time can be used in assertions and for reasoning about simple programming constructs, but also recommends that where there are timing constraints it is better to construct a program with the required timing properties than to try to compute the timing properties of an arbitrary program. For programs that can be implemented with fixed schedules on a single processor, or those with very restricted timing requirements, these restrictions make it possible to reason about real-time programs without reasoning about time.

2. Synchronous real-time languages: The *synchrony hypothesis* assumes that external events are ordered in time and the program responds as if instantaneously to each event. The synchrony hypothesis has been used in the ESTEREL (Berry & Gonthier, 1992), LUSTRE and SIGNAL family of languages, and in *Statecharts* (Harel, 1987). Treating a response as 'instantaneous' is an idealization that applies when the time of response is smaller than the minimum time between external events. External time is given a discrete representation (e.g. the natural numbers) and internal actions are deterministic and ordered. Synchronous systems are most easily implemented on a single processor. *Strong synchrony* is a more general form of synchrony applicable to distributed systems where nondeterminism is permitted but events can be ordered by a global clock.

3. Asynchronous real-time: In an asynchronous system, external events occur at times that are usually represented by a dense domain (such as the real numbers), and the system is expected to provide responses within time-bounds. This is the most general model of real-time systems and is applicable to single-processor, multi-processor and distributed systems. With some variations, this is the model we shall use for much of this book. As we shall see, restrictions must be imposed (or further assumptions made) to enable the timing properties of an asynchronous model to be fully determined: e.g. using discrete rather than dense time, imposing determinism, and approximating cyclic behaviour and aperiodicity by periodic behaviours. Few of these restrictions are really compatible with the asynchrony model but they can be justified because without them analysis of the timing behaviour may not be possible.

The *mine pump* problem was first presented by Kramer *et al.* (1983) and used by Burns and Lister (1991) as part of the description of a framework for developing safety-critical systems. A more formal account of the mine pump problem was given by Mahony and Hayes (1992) using an extension of the Z notation. The description of the mine pump in this chapter has made extensive use of the last two papers, though the alert reader will notice some changes. The first descriptions of the mine pump problem, and the description given here, assume that the requirements are correct and that the only safety considerations are those that follow from the stated requirements. The requirements for a practical mine pump system would need far more rigorous analysis to identify hazards and check on safety conditions under all possible operating conditions (see e.g. Leveson, 1995). Use of the methods described in this book would then complement this analysis by providing ways of checking the specification, the program and the timing of the system.

1.6   Exercises

Exercise 1.1   Define the condition *Alarm* which must be set when the water, methane or airflow levels are critical. Recall that, according to the requirements, *Alarm* must be set within one second of a level becoming critical. Choose an appropriate condition under which *Alarm* can be reset to permit safe operation of the mine to be resumed.

Exercise 1.2   Define the condition *Operator* under which the human operator can switch the pump on or off. Define a similar condition *Supervisor* for the supervisor and describe where the two conditions differ.

Exercise 1.3   In **S4**, separate definitions are given for the operation of the pump controller and for the delays, t_P to switch the pump on and t_M for the methane detector. Construct a single definition for the operation of the pump taking both these delays into account.

Exercise 1.4   Suppose there is just one water level sensor *SW*. What changes will need to be made in the definitions in **S1** and **S5**? (*N.B.*: in Chapter 7 it is assumed that there is one water level sensor.)

Exercise 1.5   Suppose a methane sensor can fail and that following a failure, a sensor does not resume normal operation. Assume that it is possible to detect this failure. To continue to detect methane levels reliably, let three sensors DML_1, DML_2 and DML_3 be used and assume that at most one sensor can fail. If the predicate MOK_i is *true* when the ith methane sensor is correct, i.e. operating according to the definition in **S6**, and *false* if the sensor has failed, define a condition which guarantees that the methane level sensor reading *DML* is always correct. (*Hint*: Since at most one sensor can fail, the correct reading is the same as the reading of any two equal sensor readings. *N.B.*: Chapter 8 examines the reliability of the mine pump controller in greater detail.)

Chapter 2

Fixed Priority Scheduling – A Simple Model

Mathai Joseph

Introduction

Consider a simple, real-time program which periodically receives inputs from a device every T units of time, computes a result and sends it to another device. Assume that there is a deadline of D time units between the arrival of an input and the despatch of the corresponding output.

For the program to meet this deadline, the computation of the result must take always place in less than D time units: in other words, for every possible execution path through the program, the time taken for the execution of the section of code between the input and output statements must be less than D time units.

If that section of the program consists solely of assignment statements, it would be possible to obtain a very accurate estimate of its execution time as there will be just one path between the statements. In general, however, a program will have a control structure with several possible execution paths.

For example, consider the following structured **if** statement:

```
1    Sensor_Input.Read(Reading);
2    if Reading $=$ $5$ then Sensor_Output.Write($20$)
3      elseif Reading $<$ $10$ then Sensor_Output.Write($25$)
4            else   ...
5                Sensor_Output.Write( ...)
6    end if;
```

There are a number of possible execution paths through this statement: e.g. there is one path through lines 1, 2 and 6 and another through lines 1, 2, 3 and 6. Paths will generally differ in the number of boolean tests and assignment statements executed and so, on most computers, will take different execution times.

In some cases, as in the previous example, the execution time of each path can be computed statically, possibly even by a compiler. But there are statements where this is not possible:

```
Sensor_Input.Read(Reading);
while X $>$ Reading $+$ Y loop
    . . .
end
```

Finding all the possible paths through this statement may not be easy: even if it is known that there are *m* different paths for any one iteration of this **while** loop, the actual number of iterations will depend on the input value in Reading. But if the range of possible input values is known, it may then be possible to find the total number of paths through the loop. Since we are concerned with real-time programs, let us assume that the program has been constructed so that all such loops will terminate and therefore that the number of paths is finite.

So, after a simple examination of alternative and iterative statements, we can conclude that:

- it is not possible to know in advance exactly how long a program execution will take, but
- it may be possible to find the range of possible values of the execution time.

Rather than deal with all possible execution times, one solution is to use just the longest possible, or *worst-case*, execution time for the program. If the program will meet its deadline for this worst-case execution, it will meet the deadline for any execution.

Worst-case
Assume that the worst-case upper bound to the execution time can be computed for any real-time program.

2.1   Computational model

We can now redefine the simple real-time program as follows: program P receives an event from a sensor every T units of time (i.e. the *inter-arrival time* is T) and in the worst case an event requires C units of computation time (Figure 2.1).

Assume that the processing of each event must always be completed before the arrival of the next event (i.e. there is no buffering). Let the deadline for completing the computation be D (Figure 2.2).

Figure 2.1 Computer and one sensor

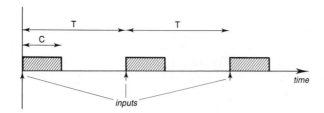

Figure 2.2 Timing diagram 1

If $D < C$, the deadline cannot be met. If $T < D$, the program must still process each event in a time $\leq T$ if no events are to be lost. Thus the deadline is effectively bounded by T and we need to handle only those cases where

$$C \leq D \leq T$$

Now consider a program which receives events from *two* sensors (Figure 2.3). Inputs from Sensor 1 come every T_1 time units and each needs C_1 time units for computation; events from Sensor 2 come every T_2 time units and each needs C_2 time units. Assume the deadlines are the same as the periods, i.e. T_1 time units for Sensor 1 and T_2 time units for Sensor 2. Under what conditions will these deadlines be met?

More generally, if a program receives events from n such devices, how can it be determined if the deadline for each device will be satisfied?

Before we begin to analyze this problem, we first define a program model and a system model. This allows us to study the problem of timing analysis in a limited context. We consider simple models in this chapter; more elaborate models will be considered in Chapters 3 and 4.

Program model
Assume that a real-time program consists of a number of *independent tasks* that do not share data or communicate with each other. A task is periodically invoked by the occurrence of a particular event.

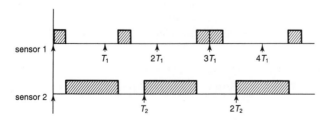

Figure 2.3 Timing diagram 2

System model

Assume that the system has one processor; the system periodically receives events from the external environment and these are not buffered. Each event is an invocation for a particular task. Note that events may be periodically produced by the environment or the system may have a timer that periodically creates the events.

Let the tasks of program P be $\tau_1, \tau_2, \ldots, \tau_n$. Let the inter-arrival time, or *period*, for invocations to task τ_i be T_i and let the computation time for each such invocation be C_i.

We shall use the following terminology:

- A task is *released* when it has a waiting invocation.
- A task is *ready* as long as the processing associated with an invocation has not been completed.
- A processor is *idle* when it is not executing a task.

2.2   Static scheduling

One way to schedule the program is to analyze its tasks statically and determine their timing properties. These times can be used to create a fixed scheduling table according to which tasks will be despatched for execution at run-time. Thus, the order of execution of tasks is fixed and it is assumed that their execution times are also fixed.

Typically, if tasks $\tau_1, \tau_2, \ldots, \tau_n$ have periods of $T_1, T_2, \ldots, T_n$, the table must cover scheduling for a length of time equal to the *least common multiple* of the periods, i.e. $LCM(\{T_1, T_2, \ldots, T_n\})$, as that is the time in which each task will have an integral number of invocations. If any of the T_i are co-primes, this length of time can be extremely large so where possible it is advisable to choose values of T_i that are small multiples of a common value.

Static scheduling has the significant advantage that the order of execution of tasks is determined 'off-line', before the execution of the program, so the run-time scheduling overheads can be very small. But it has some major disadvantages:

- There is no flexibility at run-time as all choices must be made in advance and must therefore be made conservatively to cater for every possible demand for computation.
- It is difficult to cater for sporadic tasks which may occur occasionally, if ever, but which have high urgency when they do occur.

For example, an alarm condition which requires a system to be shut down within a short interval of time may not occur very often but its task must still be accommodated in the scheduling table so that its deadline will be met if the alarm condition does occur.

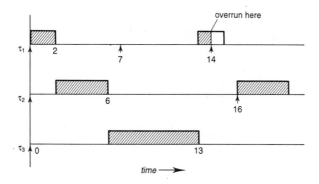

Figure 2.4 Priorities without pre-emption

2.3 Scheduling with priorities

In scheduling terms, a *priority* is usually a positive integer representing the urgency or importance assigned to an activity. By convention, the urgency is in inverse order to the numeric value of the priority and priority 1 is the highest level of priority. We shall assume here that a task has a single, fixed priority. Consider the following two simple scheduling disciplines:

Priority-based execution
When the processor is idle, the ready task with the highest priority is chosen for execution; once chosen, a task is run to completion.

Pre-emptive priority-based execution
When the processor is idle, the ready task with the highest priority is chosen for execution; at any time execution of a task can be pre-empted if a task of higher priority becomes ready. Thus, at all times the processor is either idle or executing the ready task with the highest priority.

Example 2.1 Consider a program with 3 tasks, τ_1, τ_2 and τ_3, that have the priorities, repetition periods and computation times defined in Figure 2.4. Let the deadline D_i for each task τ_i be T_i. Assume that the tasks are scheduled according to priorities, with no pre-emption.

	Priority	Period	Comp.time
τ_1	1	7	2
τ_2	2	16	4
τ_3	3	31	7

If all three tasks have invocations and are ready at *time*=0, task τ_1 will be chosen for execution as it has the highest priority. When it has completed its execution, task τ_2 will be executed until its completion at *time*=6.

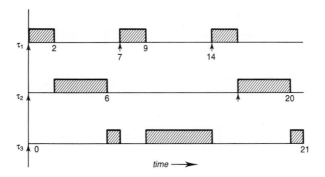

Figure 2.5 Priorities with pre-emption

At that time, only task τ_3 is ready for execution and it will execute from *time*=6 to *time*=13, even though an invocation comes for task τ_1 at *time*=7. So there is just one unit of time for task τ_1 to complete its computation requirement of two units and its next invocation will arrive before processing of the previous invocation is complete.

In some cases, the priorities allotted to tasks can be used to solve such problems; in this case, there is no allocation of priorities to tasks under which task τ_1 will meet its deadlines. But a simple examination of the timing diagram shows that between *time*=15 and *time*=31 (at which the next invocation for task τ_3 will arrive) the processor is not always busy and task τ_3 does not need to complete its execution until *time*=31. If there were some way of making the processor available to tasks τ_1 and τ_2 when needed and then returning it to task τ_3, they could all meet their deadlines.

This can be done using priorities with pre-emption: execution of task τ_3 will then be pre-empted at *time*=7, allowing task τ_1 to complete its execution at *time*=9 (Figure 2.5). Process τ_3 is pre-empted once more by task τ_1 at *time*=14 and this is followed by the next execution of task τ_2 from *time*=16 to *time*=20 before task τ_3 completes the rest of its execution at *time*=21.

2.4   Simple methods of analysis

Timing diagrams provide a good way to visualize and even to calculate the timing properties of simple programs. But they have obvious limits, not least of which is that a very long sheet of paper might be needed to draw some timing diagrams! A better method of analysis would be to derive conditions to be satisfied by the timing properties of a program for it to meet its deadlines.

Let an *implementation* consist of a hardware platform and the scheduler under which the program is executed. An implementation is called *feasible* if every execution of the program will meet all its deadlines.

Using the notation of the previous section, in the following sections we shall consider a number of conditions that might be applied. We shall first examine conditions that are *necessary* to ensure that an implementation is feasible. The aim is to find necessary conditions that are also *sufficient*, so that if they are satisfied an implementation is guaranteed to be feasible.

2.4.1 Necessary conditions

Condition C1

$$\forall i \cdot C_i < T_i$$

It is obviously necessary that the computation time for a task is smaller than its period, as, without this condition, its implementation can be trivially shown to be infeasible.

However, this condition is not sufficient, as can be seen from the following example.

Example 2.2

	Priority	Period	Comp.time
τ_1	1	10	8
τ_2	2	5	3

At *time=0*, execution of task τ_1 begins (since it has the higher priority) and this will continue for eight time units before the processor is relinquished; task τ_2 will therefore miss its first deadline at *time=5*.

Thus, under Condition C1, it is possible that the total time needed for computation in an interval of time is larger than the length of the interval. The next condition seeks to remove this weakness.

Condition C2

$$\sum_{j=1}^{i} (C_j/T_j) \leq 1$$

C_i/T_i is the utilization of the processor in unit time at level i. Condition C2 improves on Condition C1 in an important way: not only is the utilization C_i/T_i required to be less than 1 but the sum of this ratio over all tasks is also required not to exceed 1. Thus, taken over a sufficiently long interval, the total time needed for computation must lie within that interval.

This condition is necessary but it is not sufficient. The following example shows an implementation which satisfies Condition C2 but is infeasible.

Example 2.3

	Priority	*Period*	*Comp.time*
τ_1	1	6	3
τ_2	1	9	2
τ_3	2	11	2

Exercise 2.4.1 Draw a timing diagram for Example 2.3 and show that the deadline for τ_3 is not met.

Condition C2 checks that over an interval of time the arithmetic sum of the utilizations C_i/T_i is ≤ 1. But that is not sufficient to ensure that the total computation time needed for each task, *and for all those of higher priority*, is also smaller than the period of each task.

Condition C3
$$\forall i \cdot \sum_{j=1}^{i-1} \left(\frac{T_i}{T_j} \times C_j \right) \leq T_i - C_i$$

Here, Condition C2 has been strengthened so that, for each task, account is taken of the computation needs of all higher priority tasks. Assume that T_i/T_j represents integer division:

- Processing of all invocations at priority levels $1 \ldots i-1$ must be completed in the time $T_i - C_i$, as this is the 'free' time available at that level.
- At each level j, $1 \leq j \leq i-1$, there will be T_i/T_j invocations in the time T_i and each invocation will need a computation time of C_j.

Hence, at level j the total computation time needed is

$$\frac{T_i}{T_j} \times C_j$$

and summing this over all values of $j < i$ will give the total computation needed at level i. Condition C3 says that this must be true for all values of i.

This is another necessary condition. But, once again, it is not sufficient: if $T_j > T_i$, Condition C3 reduces to Condition C1 which has already been shown to be not sufficient.

There is another problem with Condition C3. It assumes that there are T_i/T_j invocations at level j in the time T_i. If T_i is not exactly divisible by T_j, then either $\lceil T_i/T_j \rceil$ is an overestimate of the number of invocations or $\lfloor T_i/T_j \rfloor$ is an underestimate. In both cases, an exact condition will be hard to define.

To avoid the approximation resulting from integer division, consider an interval M_i which is the least common multiple of all periods up to T_i:

$$M_i = LCM(\{T_1, T_2, \ldots, T_i\})$$

Since M_i is exactly divisible by all T_j, $j < i$, the number of invocations at any level j within M_i is exactly M_i/M_j.

This leads to the next condition.

Condition C4

$$\sum_{j=1}^{i} \left(C_j \times \frac{M_i/T_j}{M_i} \right) \leq 1$$

Condition C4 is the *Load Relation* and must be satisfied by any feasible implementation. However, this condition averages the computational requirements over each LCM period and can easily be shown to be not sufficient.

Example 2.4

	Priority	Period	Comp.time
τ_1	1	12	5
τ_2	2	4	2

Since the computation time of task τ_1 exceeds the period of task τ_2, the implementation is infeasible, though it does satisfy Condition C4.

Condition C4 can, moreover, be simplified to

$$\sum_{j=1}^{i} \left(C_j/T_j \right) \leq 1$$

which is Condition 2 and thus is necessary but not sufficient.

Condition C2 fails to take account of an important requirement of any feasible implementation. Not only must the *average* load be smaller than 1 over the interval M_i, but the load must at all times be sufficiently small for the deadlines to be met. More precisely, if at any time T there are t time units left for the next deadline at priority level i, the total computation requirement at time T for level i and all higher levels must be smaller than t. Since it *averages* over the whole of the interval M_i, Condition C2 is unable to take account of peaks in the computational requirements.

But while on the one hand it is necessary that at every instant there is sufficient computation time remaining for all deadlines to be met, it is important to remember that once a deadline at level i has been met there is no further need to make provision for computation at that level up to the end of the current period. Conditions which average over a long interval may take account of computations over the whole of that interval, including the time after a deadline has been met. For example, in Figure 2.5, task τ_2 has met its first deadline at *time*=6 and the computations at level 1 from *time*=7 to *time*=9 and from *time*=14 to *time*=16 cannot affect τ_2's response time, even though they occur before the end of τ_2's period at *time*=16.

2.4.2 A sufficient condition

So far, we have assumed that priorities are assigned to tasks in some way that characterizes their urgency, but not necessarily in relation to their repetition periods (or deadlines).

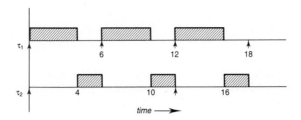

Figure 2.6 Timing diagram for Example 2.5

Consider, instead, assigning priorities to tasks in *rate-monotonic order*, i.e. in the inverse order to their repetition periods. Assume that task deadlines are the same as their periods. It can then be shown that if under a rate-monotonic allocation an implementation is infeasible then it will be infeasible under all other similar allocations.

Let *time*=0 be a *critical instant*, when invocations to all tasks arrive simultaneously. For an implementation to be feasible, the following condition must hold.

Condition C5

- The first deadline for every task must be met.
- This will occur if the following relation is satisfied:

$$n\left(2^{1/n} - 1\right) \geq \sum_{i=1}^{n} C_i/T_i$$

For $n = 2$, the upper bound to the utilization $\sum_{i=1}^{n} C_i/T_i$ is 82.84%; for large values of n the limit is 69.31%.

This bound is conservative: it is sufficient but not necessary. Consider the following example.

Example 2.5

	Priority	Period	Comp.time
τ_1	1	6	4
τ_2	2	12	4

In this case (Figure 2.6), the utilisation is 100% and thus fails the test. On the other hand, it is quite clear from the graphical analysis that the implementation is feasible as all deadlines are met.

2.5 Exact analysis

Let the *worst-case response time* be the maximum time between the arrival of an invocation and the completion of computation for that invocation. Then an implementation

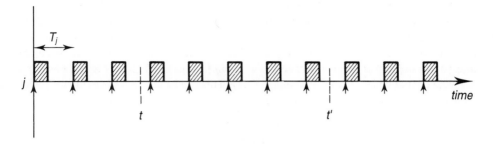

Figure 2.7 *Inputs*$(([t,t'),j) = 5$

is feasible if at each priority level i, the worst-case response time r_i is less than or equal to the deadline D_i. As before, we assume that the critical instant is at *time*=0.

If every task $\tau_j, j < i$, has higher priority than τ_i, the worst-case response time R_i is

$$R_i = C_i + \sum_{j=1}^{i-1} \lceil \frac{R_i}{T_j} \rceil \times C_j$$

In this form, the equation is hard to solve (since R_i appears on both sides).

2.5.1 Necessary and sufficient conditions

In this section, we show how response times can be calculated in a constructive way which illustrates how they are related to the number of invocations in an interval and the computation time needed for each invocation.

For the calculation, we shall make use of *half-open* intervals of the form $[t,t')$, $t < t'$, which contain all values from t up to, but not including, t'.

We first define a function *Inputs*$([t,t'),j)$, whose value is the number of events at priority level j arriving in the half-open interval of time $[t,t')$ (see Figure 2.7):

$$Inputs([t,t'),j) = \lceil t'/T_j \rceil - \lceil t/T_j \rceil$$

The computation time needed for these invocations is

$$Inputs([t,t'),j) \times C_j$$

So, at level i the computation time needed for all invocations at levels higher than i can be defined by the function *Comp*$([t,t'),i)$:

$$Comp([t,t'),i) = \sum_{j=1}^{i-1} Inputs([t,t'),j) \times C_j$$

Let the response time at level i in the interval $[t, t')$ be the value of the function $R(t, t', i)$. Let the computation time needed at level i in the interval $[t, t')$ be $t' - t$. The total computation time needed in this interval for all higher levels $0 \ldots i - 1$ is $Comp([t, t'), i)$; if this is zero, the processor will not be pre-empted in the interval and the whole of the time will be available for use at level i. Now suppose that the total computation time needed in the interval for the higher levels is not zero, i.e. $Comp([t, t'), i) > 0$. Then the response time at level i cannot be less than $t' + Comp([t, t'), i)$. This can be generalized to the following recursive definition of the function $R(t, t', i)$:

$$R(t, t', i) = \texttt{if } Comp([t, t'), i) = 0 \texttt{ then } t'$$
$$\texttt{else } R(t', t' + Comp([t, t'), i), i)$$

Another way to explain this is to note that in the interval $[t, t')$, the computation still to be completed at time t' (which is just outside the interval) is

$$(t' - t) - ((t' - t) - Comp([t, t'), i)) = Comp([t, t'), i)$$

The value of the function R at level i is the time when there is no computation pending at level i or any higher level, i.e. $Comp([t, t'), i) = 0$, and the whole of the interval $[t, t')$ has been used for computation.

The worst-case response time at level i can then be defined as

$$R_i = R(0, C_i, i)$$

If no computation is needed at levels $0 \ldots i - 1$, then the response time at level i is the computation time C_i; otherwise, add to C_i the amount of time needed at the higher levels. The object is to 'push' the estimated response time forward in decreasing jumps until eventually $Comp([t, t'), i) = 0$. Computation of R_i will terminate, i.e. the jumps are guaranteed to be diminishing, if the average load relation (Condition C4) is satisfied, i.e.

$$\sum_{j=1}^{i} \left(C_j \times \frac{M_i / T_j}{M_i} \right) \leq 1$$

2.5.2 Proof of correctness

We now show that the solution to the equation

$$R_i = C_i + \sum_{j=1}^{i-1} \lceil \frac{R_i}{T_j} \rceil \times C_j$$

given in terms of the function R is correct.

First observe that since the function $Comp$ has been defined over intervals, there is some t_2 such that

$$Comp([t_1, t_3), i) = Comp([t_1, t_2), i) + Comp([t_2, t_3), i), \ t_1 \leq t_2 \leq t_3$$

Proof: Let the sum of the computation time needed in the interval $[0,t)$ at the levels $0 \dots i-1$ plus the time needed at level i be t'. Then an invariant *INV* for the recursive equation R is

$$INV : Comp([0,t),i) + C_i = t'$$

Step 1: the initial condition $R(0, C_i, i)$ satisfies the invariant.
Step 2: by the induction hypothesis, $R(t', t' + Comp([0,t),i), i)$ satisfies the invariant. Further,

$$Comp([0,t'),i) + C_i = t' + Comp([t,t'),i)$$

Since for $0 \le t \le t'$, using interval arithmetic,

$$Comp([0,t'),i) = Comp([0,t),i) + Comp([t,t'),i)$$

we can substitute and simplify this to

$$Comp([0,t),i) + C_i = t'$$

This proves the induction step.
Step 3: on termination, $R_i = t'$ and

$$INV \wedge Comp([t,t'),i) = 0$$

Substituting for *INV* gives

$$Comp([0,t'),i) + C_i = t' \wedge R_i = t'$$

and substituting for *Comp* gives

$$\left(\sum_{j=1}^{i-1} \lceil \frac{R_i}{T_j} \rceil \times C_j \right) + C_i = t' \wedge R_i = t'$$

$\square$

A necessary and sufficient condition for feasibility for a system with n priority levels can now be defined.

Condition 6
$$\forall i \cdot 1 \le i \le n, R_i \le T_i$$

Note that unlike the sufficient Condition C5, this condition does not only apply to a rate-monotonic order of task priorities; it can be used to check all deadlines D_i where $C_i \le D_i \le T_i$.

The last two formulae can be shown to give Condition C4 by substituting M_i for t':

$$\sum_{j=1}^{i-1} (M_i/T_j) \times C_j + (M_i/T_i) \times C_i < M_i$$

or

$$\sum_{j=1}^{i} (C_j/T_j) \le 1$$

2.5.3 Calculating response times

The function R can also be evaluated by rewriting it as a recurrence relation:

$$R_i^{n+1} = C_i + \sum_{j=1}^{i-1} \left\lceil \frac{R_i^n}{T_j} \right\rceil \times C_j$$

where R_i^n is the response time in the nth iteration and the required response time is the smallest value of R_i^{n+1} to solve this equation. In Chapter 3, the tasks τ_j of higher priority than i will be collectively described by defining them as members of the set $hp(i)$ and the equation becomes

$$R_i^{n+1} = C_i + \sum_{j \in hp(i)} \left\lceil \frac{R_i^n}{T_j} \right\rceil \times C_j$$

To use the recurrence relation to find response times, it is necessary to compute R_i^{n+1} iteratively until the first value m is found such that $R_i^{m+1} = R_i^m$; then the response time is R_i^m.

Programs can be written to use either the recursive or iterative way to find response times. In the following examples we show how response times can be found by hand calculation using the recursive definition.

Example 2.6 For the following task set, find the response time for task τ_4.

	Priority	Period	Comp.time
τ_1	1	10	1
τ_2	2	12	2
τ_3	3	30	8
τ_4	4	600	20

Substitution shows that the task set satisfies Condition C4:

$$\sum_{j=1}^{i} \left(C_j \times \frac{600/T_j}{600} \right) \leq 1$$

The response time R_4 is therefore

$$
\begin{aligned}
R(0,20,4) \quad &= if\, Comp([0,20),4) = 0\, then\, 20 \\
&\quad else\, R(20, 20 + Comp([0,20),4)) \\
Comp([0,20),4) \quad &= Inputs([0,20),1) \times 1 \\
&\quad + Inputs([0,20),2) \times 2 \\
&\quad + Inputs([0,20),3) \times 8 \\
&= 2 \times 1 + 2 \times 2 + 1 \times 8 \\
&= 14
\end{aligned}
$$

Repeat this calculation for $R(20,34,4)$ by first computing

$$Comp([20,34),4) = Inputs([20,34),1) \times 1$$
$$+ Inputs([20,34),2) \times 2$$
$$+ Inputs([20,34),3) \times 8$$
$$= 2 \times 1 + 1 \times 2 + 1 \times 8$$
$$= 12$$

Calculation of the function *Comp* must be therefore be repeated to obtain $R(34,46,4)$:

$$Comp([34,46),4) = Inputs([34,46),1) \times 1$$
$$+ Inputs([34,46),2) \times 2$$
$$+ Inputs([34,46),3) \times 8$$
$$= 1 \times 1 + 1 \times 2$$
$$= 3$$
$$Comp([46,49),4) = 2$$
$$Comp([49,51),4) = 1$$
$$Comp([51,52),4) = 0$$

Thus the response time $R(0,20,4) = R(0,52,4)$ for task τ_4 is 52.

2.6 Extending the analysis

The rate-monotonic order provides one way of assigning priorities to tasks. It is easy to think of other ways: e.g. in deadline-monotonic order (if deadlines are smaller than periods). Priorities can also be assigned to tasks in increasing order of *slack time*, where the slack time for task τ_i is the difference $T_i - C_i$ between its period and its computation time. All these methods of assignment are *static* as the priority of a task is never changed during execution. The method of analysis described in this chapter can be used for any static assignment of priorities, but it does not provide a way of choosing between them.

So far, we have considered a very simple program model with independent tasks that do not inter-communicate. This has made it possible to schedule tasks without regard to any dependencies between them: any task with some incomplete computation is ready and it can be scheduled whenever it is ready and the processor is free. This type of model can be used for simple data-logging programs but most real-time programs have a more complex structure. If tasks can communicate with each other, using shared memory or by message passing, scheduling becomes far more complicated as it is not only time-driven. A task can receive a message only after the message has been sent, so a receiving task τ_2 will not be ready to be scheduled until the corresponding sending task τ_1 has been scheduled, even if τ_1 is of lower priority than τ_2.

When analysis shows that no allocation of priorities to tasks is feasible, it may mean that the single available processor is not sufficient to meet the processing load. Solutions are then either to obtain a faster processor (thereby effectively reducing the computation time for each task) or to add one or more processors. With multiple processors, there is the question of exactly how the processing load is divided between the processors. When tasks are statically assigned to processors, the analysis described here can be used for each processor. But two difficult problems are introduced: first, to find a good assignment of tasks to processors so that response time requirements are met, noting that finding the 'best' assignment of tasks to processors is in general an NP-complete problem; second, to account for communication between tasks over multiple processors, and without some constraints this can make the analysis very difficult.

In Chapter 3, we shall consider a more elaborate program model which takes task communication into account. And in Chapter 4, dynamic task priorities are introduced and it is seen that their use permits more flexibility and better utilization of resources.

2.7   Historical background

The problem of assigning resources to tasks is old and has been studied using the techniques of operations research (e.g. linear programming, dynamic programming). In this context, its best-known form is job-shop scheduling, where components are processed through a factory floor consisting of a number of machines. Effective job-shop scheduling requires generating schedules to meet hard deadlines using some form of priorities.

The first important results in the scheduling of hard-real-time systems are usually attributed to the classic paper by Liu and Layland (1973), which considered the question of determining feasibility for a fixed set of independent, periodic tasks and identified the *critical instant* at which all tasks are ready to start computation. Their method of analysis and their proof of the optimality of the rate-monotonic order resulted in much subsequent work being focussed on rate-monotonic scheduling (though, as we have seen here, other fixed priority scheduling methods are also of importance).

Necessary tests (e.g. Joseph, 1985) for feasibility were replaced by necessary and sufficient tests, together with a proof of correctness, in Joseph and Pandya (1986) where response time analysis was used to determine the feasibility of any fixed priority order with task deadlines $C_i \leq D_i \leq T_i$. Harter (1987), working with a simple temporal logic proof system, studied response time analysis for a program model that allowed procedure calls between tasks at different priority levels. Lehoczky *et al.* (1989) studied systems where $D_i = T_i$ (i.e. the Liu and Layland model) and developed a necessary and sufficient condition for feasibility using workloads, in terms of processor utilization; Nassor and Bres (1991) extended this to allow $D_i \leq T_i$. Audsley *et al.* (1991) defined response times using a recurrence relation, in which form it was used in other work (e.g. Audsley *et al.* 1993a) and also in what is now commonly called the *Rate Monotonic Book* (Klein *et al.*, 1993). Lehoczky (1990) used workload analysis to provide two ways to deal with cases where $D_i > T_i$, and Tindell (1993) provided a more general analysis using response times.

An excellent survey of work on fixed priority scheduling appeared in Audsley *et al.* (1995).

2.8 Exercises

Exercise 2.1 A real-time program has four tasks with the following characteristics:

	Priority	Period	Comp.time
τ_1	1	5	1
τ_2	2	15	2
τ_3	3	60	3
τ_4	4	200	7

(a) Determine using a graphical method whether the program will meet its deadlines if scheduled according to priorities but with no pre-emption.

(b) If scheduled with priorities and pre-emption, what is the response time for task τ_2?

Exercise 2.2 Given the following task set with priorities assigned in rate-monotonic order, check that task τ_3 meets its deadline of 36.

	Priority	Period	Comp.time
τ_1	1	6	2
τ_2	2	18	4
τ_3	3	36	6

Exercise 2.3 In the following task set, the response time for task τ_4 is smaller than for task τ_3:

	Period	Comp.time	Resp. limit
τ_1	10	1	10
τ_2	12	2	12
τ_3	40	8	40
τ_4	600	20	30

Choose a suitable allocation of priorities to the tasks and show that the response time limits for all tasks can be met.

Exercise 2.4 For the following task set:

	Period	Comp.time
τ_1	100	1
τ_2	10	4
τ_3	14	6
τ_4	50	8

check whether there is an assignment of priorities to tasks under which each task will meet its deadlines.

Chapter 3

Advanced Fixed Priority Scheduling

Alan Burns and Andy Wellings

Introduction

In this chapter, we consider an extended computational model and describe some of the more advanced methods of analysis that can be used. The features of the extended model permit efficient resource sharing at run-time and the methods of analysis allow effective prediction of the worst-case timing behaviour of an application.

The resources of a system include processors and communication media; on some systems there will also be disks and specialized hardware devices. Chapter 2 considered ways in which a single processor could be shared between simple processes using different scheduling techniques. In a similar way, run-time scheduling can be used to share other resources. There are two aspects to the use of any scheduling technique: the run-time behaviour it produces, and the methods of analysis available for predicting timing properties. As before, the computational model will be defined independently of the scheduling technique. The model defines the real-time software structure while the scheduling technique defines how this is mapped onto the system at run-time. Not all scheduling techniques can be used if accurate predictions of the resulting timing properties are needed.

3.1 Computational model

Most embedded real-time systems are inherently parallel in nature and the extended computational model allows the definition of concurrent tasks, each of which can be invoked repeatedly. Tasks may be *periodic* or *sporadic*. A periodic task is released by a timer event and a sporadic task by an event originating either from another task or from the environment of the system (typically as an interrupt). In Chapter 2, we considered events to be unbuffered and to be lost if they were not processed in time. Here we assume invocation events to be *persistent*: a periodic task that overruns into its next release period can continue directly with its next invocation.

32

Periodic and sporadic tasks have a minimal inter-arrival time T. Sporadic tasks may also have global constraints, such as the maximum number of invocations in a period. For example, a sporadic task may have an inter-arrival time of 1 ms and the restriction that no more than four invocation events occur in any 10 ms interval. As before, we shall be concerned with the worst-case response time R of a task. For a given scheduling technique, R represents the predicted latest possible task completion time, relative to its invocation event. We shall assume that the number N of tasks is fixed. In a distributed system with many processing nodes, each task is statically allocated to one node. Tasks may communicate with each other asynchronously through a *protected shared object* (PSO) which ensures mutual exclusion over the shared data. Tasks effectively perform atomic read and write operations on the shared object; we shall see later how this can be assured by a scheduling technique. This form of asynchronous communication ensures that a task's behaviour is simple (and hence predictable). Apart from waiting for access to PSOs, a task will proceed from its invocation event to the completion of that invocation in a straightforward way. The scheduling technique will ensure that tasks are blocked for the minimum time when attempting to access PSOs. A task execution must not voluntarily suspend itself during an invocation. For example, a task which sets up an input operation from an external device, and which must wait for a minimum time before reading the input value, cannot delay itself. Instead, the operation must be implemented using two tasks with the delay represented by setting a time offset between their executions. An alternative to asynchronous communication would be to allow tasks to exchange data directly, e.g. using an Ada `rendezvous` so that a PSO would then not be needed. As a task can always be used to implement a PSO, it is clear that there is no fundamental distinction between the two approaches. But we shall show that asynchronous communication allows enough flexibility in program design and permits efficient scheduling.

A software system therefore consists primarily of tasks and PSOs; like tasks, PSOs may be distributed over the nodes of a distributed system. To deal with the typical timing requirements of real-time systems we add the mechanism of a *transaction* to link input and output activities that have associated deadlines. A transaction may be periodic, with a deadline relative to some initial timing event, or sporadic, with a deadline relative to an input event. Transactions will be used to reflect end-to-end properties, i.e. from an input event to an output response. In a distributed system, input and output may be on different nodes and an end-to-end property may therefore cross node boundaries.

3.1.1 Example of transactions

Transactions are implemented using tasks and PSOs. A simple (non-distributed) transaction may be implemented as a single task but, more typically, a transaction will involve a number of tasks related in some precedence order.

For example, consider a simple periodic transaction consisting of three tasks, τ_1, τ_2 and τ_3. Assume that data is processed by the tasks in the order τ_1, τ_2 and τ_3. Let the precedence order over the tasks be represented by the operator $\prec$.

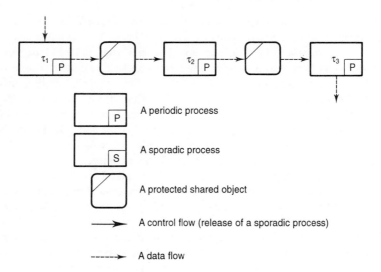

Figure 3.1 First implementation (with key)

Then, for the ith invocation of each task,

$$\forall i \cdot (\tau_1, i) \prec (\tau_2, i) \prec (\tau_3, i) \tag{3.1}$$

Thus the ith invocation of τ_1 is completed before the ith invocation of τ_2 begins, and likewise for τ_2 and τ_3. Invocation numbers can often be omitted for straightforward relations.

Figures 3.1, 3.2 (and 3.3) and 3.4 represent three different ways of implementing this transaction within the computational model.

In all three implementations, τ_1 is a periodic task (since the transaction is periodic); in Figure 3.1, τ_2 and τ_3 are also periodic and have the same period as τ_1 but their releases are offset in time. Let these offset values be represented as O_2 and O_3. In order for (3.1) to be satisfied, the scheduling technique must ensure

$$R_1 < O_2 \tag{3.2}$$

and

$$R_2 + O_2 < O_3 \tag{3.3}$$

For the deadline D of the transaction to be met:

$$O_3 + R_3 < D \tag{3.4}$$

In Figure 3.2, τ_2 and τ_3 are sporadic tasks released by τ_1 and τ_2 respectively. τ_1 writes to PSO_1 and then sends an event to τ_2 as its final action for that invocation. This is a

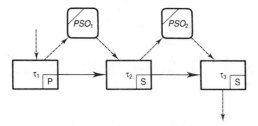

Figure 3.2 Second implementation (showing PSOs)

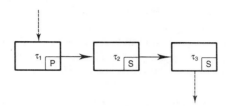

Figure 3.3 Second implementation (PSOs not shown)

commonly needed pair of operations and there is therefore an advantage in combining them into a single operation; we shall see in Section 3.3 that this has been done in Ada 95. We shall use a combined operation in subsequent diagrams, for example by redrawing Figure 3.2 as Figure 3.3; note that the arrow denoting control flow now also implies a possible data flow.

Relation 3.1 is satisfied by definition in this second implementation. To meet the transaction requirement, the following condition must be met:

$$R_1 + R_2 + R_3 < D \tag{3.5}$$

The second implementation has the advantage that its overall worst-case response time is likely to be less than that provided by the first implementation. This is because the timer events are spread out (e.g. because the hardware platform may not be able to support the release of periodic tasks at arbitrary times). Hence O_2 may be somewhat larger than R_1, and the scheduling technique may be able to guarantee (3.5) but not (3.4).

There is another property of the second implementation which may, or may not, be an advantage. Not only may the worst-case response time be less but the average- and best-case response times may also be less. Response times are calculated for the maximum load, and for certain patterns of invocation the load may be much less than the maximum. Hence, in the second implementation, data could ripple quickly through the system.

It is not always possible to guarantee that timing properties are strictly met. For example, a periodic event may in fact occur at times either a little before or a little later than its strict period. This *jitter* can have many effects and certain control applications may

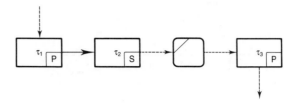

Figure 3.4 Third implementation

become unstable if results are output too early. So, in addition to a deadline, a transaction may need to have a maximum output jitter defined: e.g. to produce output within the interval $[D - J, D]$, where J is a jitter constant.

Assume, for illustration, that the minimum response time of all tasks is 0. Then the second implementation has an output bound of $[0, R_1 + R_2 + R_3]$, while the first implementation has a much tighter bound of $[O_3, O_3 + R_3]$ and this may make it conform more closely to the requirements.

The third implementation (Figure 3.4) attempts to combine the best features of the two earlier attempts by keeping the end-to-end response time small without making the timing conditions too rigid. Here τ_2 is sporadic but τ_3 is periodic. This implementation has the same bound on its output as for the second implementation (i.e. $[O_3, O_3 + R_3]$) but has a potentially lower value for O_3:

$$R_1 + R_2 < O_3 \tag{3.6}$$

The advantages of the third implementation increase with the number of tasks in the transaction. For example, if there are ten tasks it is still only the first and last tasks that need to be periodic.

In general, tasks may be associated with more than one transaction and the precedence relations between tasks can include branching and joining. Even with the simple example described above, it is clear that there are a number of design choices to be made. It is the role of a design method to provide the means by which a task set corresponding to a computational model is obtained from the system specification. Design methods will not be considered here in detail but some references can be found in Section 3.5.

3.1.2   Allocation

To prevent a task from suspending itself while accessing PSOs, the computational model must impose restrictions on remote actions (i.e. actions from one processing node to another): a task may read or write from a local PSO, may write to a remote PSO but may not read from a remote PSO.

To read from a remote PSO would involve suspending the task and would require the underlying execution environment to support a remote procedure call (RPC) mechanism. Unfortunately, RPC mechanisms are not usually amenable to timing analysis because of

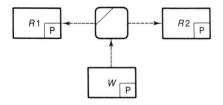

Figure 3.5 Centralized readers and writer

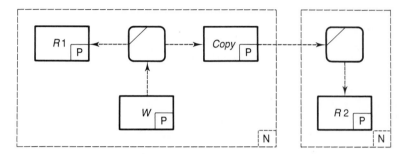

Figure 3.6 Distributed readers and writer

the effects of the communications network and the remote processor. By restricting the model, all that is required from the execution environment is an asynchronous message transfer feature that can place data in a remote PSO or release a remote sporadic task for execution.

The disadvantage of this restriction is that it may be difficult to distribute a program across a set of nodes. For example, to take an extreme case, if all the tasks in a program read from one PSO, they would all need to be located on the same node as the PSO. However, in practice, programs are not often so centralized and simple transformations to the program structure can usually make distributed allocation possible.

Consider a program with one PSO that is read by two tasks (R1 and R2) that must be allocated to different nodes because they interact directly with devices on these nodes. Clearly, the PSO can only be in one place and so the program structure must be changed to use two PSOs. Then data can be copied from the original PSO to one that is local to the task that does not have direct access. The copying can be done in a number of ways. If the two tasks are periodic, an additional periodic task can be used with a release time, period and deadline chosen so that data will appear in the second PSO in time for it to be read (locally). This transformation of the program is illustrated in Figures 3.5 and 3.6. where the outer box depicts a node boundary.

The restriction over remote access forces all significant computational events to be explicitly represented in the system description. Analysis can then be applied to all the relevant components and the effect of the addition of a new periodic task is easily analyzed.

It is not easy to analyze the timing properties of an operating system's RPC mechanism which automatically generates task stubs.

3.1.3   Summary

We have informally introduced a computational model that is appropriate for resource sharing in distributed real-time systems. The main features of this model are summarized below.

Extended program model
- A program consists of tasks and Protected Shared Objects (PSOs).
- Tasks and PSOs may be distributed over a physical system.
- The important timing properties of tasks and PSOs are known.
- A task's behaviour consists of a potentially unbounded series of invocations, each released by an invocation event. A task must not voluntarily suspend itself during an invocation.
- Periodic tasks are released by local timer events.
- Sporadic tasks are released by events originating in either another (possibly remote) task, or from the environment of the system.
- PSOs provide mutually exclusive access to the data shared between tasks.
- Tasks may write to any PSO, but can only read from local PSOs.
- Transactions are defined using precedence relations between tasks and are used to represent end-to-end timing properties.

3.2   Advanced scheduling analysis

In Chapter 2, the exact analysis was based on fixed priority pre-emptive scheduling and tasks were independent and periodic. Many of these restrictions will now be relaxed.

For the simple model, the timing attributes of a task consisted of its period T, its worst-case execution time C, a deadline D and its priority P. A recurrence relationship was defined for the worst-case response time (or completion time) R for each task, assuming that a fixed number N of tasks were executed on the processing node. The recurrence relation for task τ_i was:

$$R_i^{n+1} = C_i + \sum_{j \in hp(i)} \lceil \frac{R_i^n}{T_j} \rceil \times C_j \tag{3.7}$$

where $hp(i)$ is the set of tasks of higher priority than τ_i, and R^0 is given an initial value of C_i (although more efficient initial values can be found). The value R can be considered to be a 'computational window' into which C must be accommodated. When R_i^n is equal to R_i^{n+1}, then this value is the worst-case response time, R_i, and the goal is to ensure that this is less than D_i.

We shall now generalize equation (3.7) so that it can be used for the computational model described in the previous section:

- Tasks interact through PSOs (this requires the use of a 'priority ceiling' protocol).
- Tasks may have sporadic (non-periodic) executions.
- There may be jitter over the release time of a task.
- Task deadlines may take any values – including $D > T$.
- A task may have internal deadlines and external deadlines that occur before execution of the task is completed.
- Task priorities should be assigned optimally (even when $D > T$).
- Account must be taken of the execution time overheads.

Each of these issues is considered in the following sections.

3.2.1 Worst-case execution time

We have already seen that it is necessary to find the worst-case execution time of a task. In addition to processing time, it may also be necessary to estimate the time for delays in communication and disk access.

The worst-case execution time C can be found either by measurement or by analysis. Measurement is most useful to validate figures obtained by analysis but when used on its own it is hard to be sure when the worst-case has been observed. The difficulty in using analysis is that an accurate model of the processor (including caches, pipelines, memory wait states, etc.) must be available.

Techniques used for timing analysis usually require two steps: first decompose the code of a task into a directed graph of basic blocks which represent straightline code, then use the processor model to estimate the worst-case execution time.

Once the times for all the basic blocks are known, the directed graph can be collapsed. For example, for a simple alternative statement, the two basic blocks can be reduced to a single value (i.e. the larger of the two values for the alternative blocks). Similarly, loops can be collapsed using knowledge about maximum repetition bounds. More sophisticated graph reduction techniques can be used if sufficient semantic information is available. For a simple example, consider the following code:

```
for I in 1..10 loop
  if Cond then
    -- 100 time unit basic block
  else
    -- 10 time unit basic block
  end if
end loop
```

With no further information, the total timing 'cost' of this fragment would be $10 \times 100 + loop\, overhead$, giving a total of over 1000. But static analysis of the code may show that Cond is only true for, at most, three iterations, leading to a less pessimistic timing cost.

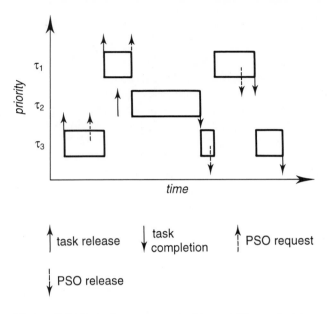

Figure 3.7 Execution sequence without ceiling priorities

3.2.2   Task interactions and ceiling priority algorithms

When tasks interact through PSOs, fixed priority scheduling can give rise to the phenomenon of *priority inversion*. Consider three tasks τ_1, τ_2 and τ_3 and assume that τ_1 has the highest priority and τ_3 the lowest. Assume also that τ_1 and τ_3 communicate through PSO_1. However rarely τ_1 and τ_3 may compete for access to PSO_1, there will be occasions for which τ_3 has gained access to the shared object just as τ_1 is released for execution. τ_1 will pre-empt τ_3 because of its higher priority but it will also be *blocked* as τ_3 has already obtained exclusive access to PSO_1.

This blocking is unavoidable but it is important to bound the delay and, ideally, to make it short. If τ_2 is released during the execution of τ_1, then we have a situation in which τ_1 is blocked by τ_3, and τ_3 is pre-empted by τ_2. The blocking will last for the entire execution time of τ_2. The condition under which a lower priority process is executing (i.e. τ_2) when a higher priority process (i.e. τ_1) is blocked is called *priority inversion*. This is illustrated in Figure 3.7. A scheduling technique must aim to minimize the time during which priority inversion occurs.

The solution is to adopt some form of *priority inheritance*; we describe one method in this section and refer to others in Section 3.5.

The method considered here is known as Immediate Ceiling Priority Inheritance (ICPI). With ICPI, all PSOs are assigned a priority equal to the maximum priority of any task that uses it. This is its *ceiling priority*. Whenever a task accesses a PSO, its priority

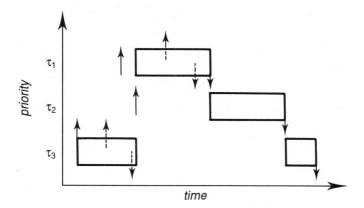

Figure 3.8 Execution sequence with ceiling priorities

is immediately raised to this ceiling level. Where a PSO is accessed externally (from a remote node), the priority assigned by the execution environment (the operating system) must be used and, typically, this will be higher than any local task priority.

As a task cannot be pre-empted by another task of equal or lower priority, only one task can ever be executing within a PSO.[1] Thus mutual exclusion, the fundamental property of a PSO, is guaranteed for single processor systems by this inheritance protocol. In addition, ICPI has another important property:

- A task may be blocked when it is released but only by a single lower priority task; once it has started executing it will not be blocked again (although it may, of course, be pre-empted by a higher priority task).

When a task is released, there may be a lower priority task currently executing with a ceiling priority of equal or higher priority. When this task has left the PSO and had its priority returned to a lower value, the released task will pre-empt it and start executing. As a task does not voluntarily suspend itself during its execution, no further lower priority task can gain access to any PSOs that the released task may require. Hence it proceeds through its execution without further blocking. This is illustrated in Figure 3.8 which represents the same behaviour as Figure 3.7, but with ICPI.

---

[1]To ensure this safety property, a pre-empted task must be placed at the front of the run queue (for its processor and its priority) if it must give way to a higher priority task. This ensures that it will run before any other task of the same priority. An alternative is to give the PSO a ceiling priority higher than any calling task.

As a task is only blocked at the beginning of its invocation it is only blocked once. And as a task does not start executing before it is blocked, the context switching overheads of the protocol are low. Other protocols involve executing the task, context switching to the blocking task, executing it and then context switching back again.

The final key property of ICPI is that it ensures that use of PSOs by tasks is deadlock free. As a task is not blocked more than once, no circular blocking dependencies can exist. It is not possible to write a program that will deadlock when executed with fixed priorities and ICPI.

In the analysis that follows, the maximum blocking factor will be denoted by B, which is easily calculated: it is the maximum time for which any lower priority task can execute with a ceiling priority equal to or greater than that of the task under consideration:

$$B_i = \max_{\tau_j \in lp(i)} (\max_{obj \in pso(i)} (usage(\tau_j, obj))) \tag{3.8}$$

where $lp(i)$ is the set of tasks with lower priority than τ_i, $pso(i)$ is the set of PSOs with a ceiling priority greater than or equal to the priority of τ_i and $usage$ gives the worst-case execution time of task τ_j in object obj.

Recall that the only way a task can obtain a ceiling priority is to access a PSO. The basic recurrent equation of Chapter 2 can easily be modified to include the blocking value:

$$R_i^{n+1} = B_i + C_i + \sum_{j \in hp(i)} \left\lceil \frac{R_i^n}{T_j} \right\rceil C_j \tag{3.9}$$

Note that while interference increases as you go down the priority order, blocking does not: a task can be blocked at most once.

3.2.3   Sporadic tasks and release jitter

In the simple model all tasks were assumed to be periodic and to be released with perfect periodicity: i.e. if task τ_i has period T_i then it was assumed to be released with exactly that frequency. Sporadic tasks can be incorporated into the model by assuming that they have some minimum inter-arrival interval. However, this is not a realistic assumption. Consider a sporadic task τ_s that is released by a remote periodic task τ_p and $\tau_p \prec \tau_s$; e.g. the first two tasks in Figures 3.3 and 3.4 could have this relationship. The period of the first task is T_p and the sporadic task will have the same period, but it is incorrect to assume that the maximum load (or interference) that τ_s exerts on low priority tasks can be represented in equations (3.7) or (3.9) as that of a periodic task with period $T_s = T_p$.

To understand the reason for this, consider two consecutive executions of τ_p. Assume that the event that releases τ_s occurs at the end of the periodic task's execution. On the first execution of τ_p, assume that the task does not complete until its latest possible time, i.e. R_p. However, on the next invocation assume there is no interference on τ_p so it completes within C_p. As this value could be arbitrarily small, let it be equal to zero. The two executions of the sporadic task are then separated not by T_p but by $T_p - R_p$. Figure 3.9

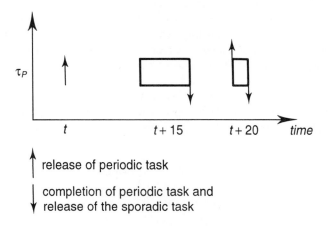

release of periodic task

completion of periodic task and
release of the sporadic task

Figure 3.9 Releases of sporadic tasks

illustrates this behaviour for T_p equal to 20, R_p equal to 15 and minimum C_p equal to 1 (i.e. two sporadic tasks released within six time units). Note that this phenomenon is of interest only if τ_p is remote as, otherwise, the variations in the release of τ_s could be accounted for by the standard equations.

To represent the interference caused by sporadic tasks upon other tasks correctly, the recurrence relation must be modified. Let the maximum variation in a task's release be called its *jitter*, represented by J. (In the example above, τ_s has a jitter of 15.) Examination of Figure 3.7 and the way the recurrence relation was derived suggests that it should be changed to the following:

$$R_i^{n+1} = B_i + C_i + \sum_{j \in hp(i)} \left\lceil \frac{R_i^n + J_j}{T_j} \right\rceil C_j \tag{3.10}$$

In general, periodic tasks do not suffer release jitter. An implementation may, however, restrict the granularity of the system timer which releases periodic tasks. In this situation a periodic task may also suffer release jitter. For example, a period of 10 with a system granularity of 8 will lead to a jitter value of 6, i.e. the periodic task will be released for its *time*=10 invocation at *time*=16. If response time R_i^* is to be measured relative to the real release time, then the jitter value must be added to the previous response time:

$$R_i^* = R_i + J_i \tag{3.11}$$

This assumes that the response time is smaller than T_i.

3.2.4   Arbitrary deadlines

When D_i, and hence possibly R_i, can be greater than T_i, the analysis must be changed again. When $D_i \leq T_i$, it is only necessary to consider a single release of each task. The critical instant, when all higher priority tasks are released at the same time, represents the maximum interference and hence the response time following a release at the critical instant must be the worst-case response time. However, when $D_i > T_i$, a number of releases must be considered.

Assume that the release of a task is delayed until all previous releases of the same task have been completed. For each potentially overlapping release, define a separate window $w(q)$, where q is the serial number of the window (i.e. $q = 0, 1, 2, ...$). Equation (3.9) can then be extended (ignoring jitter) as follows:

$$R_i^{n+1}(q) \;=\; B_i + (q+1)C_i + \sum_{j \in hp(i)} \left\lceil \frac{R_i^n(q)}{T_j} \right\rceil C_j \tag{3.12}$$

For example, with $q = 2$, three releases of task τ_i will occur in the window. For each value of q, a stable value of $w(q)$ can be found by iteration – as in equation (3.7). The response time is

$$R_i(q) \;=\; R_i^n(q) - qT_i \tag{3.13}$$

e.g. with $q = 2$ the task started $2T_i$ into the window and hence the response time is the size of the window minus $2T_i$.

The number of releases that need to be considered is bounded by the lowest value of q for which the following relation is true:

$$R_i(q) \;\leqslant\; T_i \tag{3.14}$$

At this point, the task completes execution before its next release and the succeeding windows do not overlap. The worst-case response time is then the maximum value found for each q:

$$R_i \;=\; \max_{q=0,1,2,...} R_i(q) \tag{3.15}$$

Note that for $D \leqslant T$, relation (3.14) is true for $q = 0$ and equations (3.12)and (3.13) can be simplified into their original form.

To combine the use of arbitrary deadlines with the effect of release jitter, two alterations must be made to this analysis. First, as before, the extent of interference must be increased if any higher priority tasks have release jitter:

$$R_i^{n+1}(q) \;=\; B_i + (q+1)C_i + \sum_{j \in hp(i)} \left\lceil \frac{R_i^n(q) + J_j}{T_j} \right\rceil C_j \tag{3.16}$$

The other change is in the structure of the task: if it is subject to release jitter then two consecutive windows will overlap if its response time plus the extent of jitter is greater than the period. To accommodate this, equation (3.13) must be altered:

$$R_i(q) \;=\; R_i^n(q) - qT_i + J_i \tag{3.17}$$

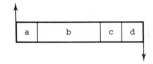

Figure 3.10 Task execution phases

3.2.5   Internal deadlines

As we shall see shortly (Section 3.2.7), it may be necessary for the model to take account of the overheads of context switching between tasks and to 'charge' this to some task. With realistic (i.e. non-zero) context switch times, the 'deadline' may well then not be at the end of the context switch. Moreover, the last observable event may not be at the end of the task execution and there may be a number of internal actions after the last output event.

Figure 3.10 gives a block representation of a task execution (excluding pre-emptions for higher priority tasks). Phase a is the initial context switch to begin the execution of the task, phase b is the task's actual execution time up to the last observable event, phase c represents the internal actions of the task following the last observable event and, finally, phase d is the cost of the context switch at the end of the task execution. The 'real' deadline of the task is at the end of phase b.

Let C^D be the computation time required before the real internal deadline (i.e. phases a + b only), and C^T the total computation time of the task in each period (i.e. all four phases). Note there is no requirement to complete C^T by T as long as C^D is completed by D. Hence, an adaptation of the analysis for arbitrary deadlines is required. If we include the two phases of computation into equation (3.16) we obtain:

$$R_i^{n+1}(q) \;=\; B_i \;+\; qC_i^T \;+\; C_i^D \;+\; \sum_{j \in hp(i)} \left\lceil \frac{R_i^n(q)+J_j}{T_j} \right\rceil C_j^T \qquad (3.18)$$

Combined with equations (3.17), (3.14) and (3.15), this allows the worst-case response time (R_i^D) for C_i^D to be calculated (assuming the maximum C_i^T interference from early releases of the task). It can be shown, trivially, that when the utilization of the processor is less than 100% the response times for all tasks are bounded.[2] What is important is that R_i^D is less than D_i.

3.2.6   Priority assignment

One of the consequences of having arbitrary or internal deadlines is that simple algorithms, such as those using rate-monotonic or deadline-monotonic assignment for de-

---

[2]Consider a set of periodic tasks with 100% utilization; let all tasks have deadlines equal to the LCM of the task set. Clearly, within the LCM period, no idle time occurs and no task executes for more than it needs, and hence all deadlines must be met.

riving priority orderings are no longer optimal. In this section we state a theorem and provide an algorithm for assigning priorities in these situations.

Theorem 3.1 If task τ is assigned the lowest priority and is feasible then, if a feasible priority ordering exists for the complete task set, an ordering exists with τ assigned the lowest priority.

If such a task τ is found, then the same reasoning can be applied to the task with the lowest but one priority, etc., and a complete priority ordering is obtained (if one exists).

An implementation in Ada of the priority assignment algorithm is given below. `Set` is an array of tasks that is ordered by priority, `Set(1)` being the highest and `Set(N)` the lowest priority. The procedure `Task_Test` tests whether task `K` is feasible at the current position in the array. The nested loops work by first putting a task into the lowest position and checking whether a feasible result is obtained. If this fails, the next higher priority position is then considered, and so on. If at any time the inner loop fails to find a feasible task, the whole procedure is abandoned. (Observe that a more compact algorithm can be used if an extra `Swap` is performed.) If the test of feasibility is exact (necessary and sufficient), then the priority ordering is optimal. Thus for arbitrary deadlines and internal deadlines (without blocking), an optimal ordering can be found.

```
procedure Assign_Pri (Set : in out Process_Set; N : Natural;
                      Ok : in out Boolean) is
begin
   for K in reverse 1..N loop
      for Next in reverse 1..K loop
         Swap(Set,K,Next);
         Task_Test(Set,K,Ok);
         Set(K).P := K;
         exit when Ok;
      end loop;
      exit when not Ok;
   end loop;
end Assign_Pri;
```

3.2.7 Overheads

Simple scheduling analysis usually ignores context switch times and queue manipulations but the time for this is often significant and cannot realistically be assumed to be negligible.

If a second processor is used to perform context switches (in parallel with the application/host processor) there will still be some context switch overhead. And when a software kernel is used, if the actual timing of operations models is not known a safely large overhead must be assumed. In addition, the interrupt handler for the clock will usually also manipulate the delay queue. When there are no tasks in the delay queue the cost may be only a few microseconds but if an application has, say, 20 periodic tasks that have a common release, the cost of moving all 20 tasks from the delay queue to the run queue may take hundreds of microseconds.

Context switch times can be accounted for by adding these times to the task that causes the context switch. For periodic tasks, the worst-case time for returning a task to the delay queue and switching back to a lower priority task may depend on the longest possible size of the delay queue (i.e. on the number of periodic tasks in the application). In most execution environments, the context switching will be performed by a non-pre-emptable section of code and will therefore itself give rise to blocking. For example, if a clock interrupt occurs once a low priority task has begun to suspend itself then the interrupt will be delayed. If this interrupt leads to a high priority task being released then it will also be delayed. Equation (3.8) should therefore have the form:

$$B_i = \max(\max_{\tau_j \in lp(i)} (\max_{obj \in pso(i)} (usage(\tau_j, obj))), C_E) \tag{3.19}$$

where C_E is the maximum non-pre-emptible execution time in the kernel.

To take account of the delay queue manipulations that occur in the clock interrupt handler (i.e. at one of the top priority levels) adequately, the overheads caused by each periodic task must be computed directly. It may be possible to model the clock interrupt handler using two parameters, C_{CLK} (the overhead occurring on each interrupt assuming that tasks are on the delay queue but none are removed), and C_{PER} (the cost of moving one task from the delay queue to the run-queue). Equation (3.7) thus becomes:

$$R_i^{n+1} = C_i + \Sigma_{j \in hp(i)} \left\lceil \frac{R_i^n}{T_j} \right\rceil C_j + \left\lceil \frac{R_i^n}{T_{CLK}} \right\rceil C_{CLK}$$
$$+ \Sigma_{f \in pts} \left\lceil \frac{R_i^n}{T_f} \right\rceil C_{PER} \tag{3.20}$$

where pts is the set of periodic tasks.

For a sporadic task (released by an interrupt), it is necessary to account for the interrupt handler's execution time. For most hardware systems, this handler will execute with a priority higher than the released sporadic task. In fact, it may well be higher than any application task. To account for this extra overhead, equation (3.20) must have an additional term included:

$$R_i^{n+1} = C_i + \Sigma_{j \in hp(i)} \left\lceil \frac{R_i^n}{T_j} \right\rceil C_j + \left\lceil \frac{R_i^n}{T_{CLK}} \right\rceil C_{CLK}$$
$$+ \Sigma_{f \in pts} \left\lceil \frac{R_i^n}{T_f} \right\rceil C_{PER} + \Sigma_{g \in sts} \left\lceil \frac{R_i^n}{T_g} \right\rceil C_{INT} \tag{3.21}$$

where sts is the set of sporadic tasks released by interrupts, and C_{INT} is the system interrupt cost (assuming a fixed cost for all interrupts). The other extensions to equation (3.7) would have to incorporate these changes similarly.

3.2.8 Analysis for system transactions

All these methods of analysis allow the worst-case response times for each individual task to be predicted. However, as we noted in the discussion on computational models, the timing requirements usually refer to the end-to-end time for transactions running through an entire system. Although some transactions may be realized by a single task, most are not. The following discussion allows the system-level timing requirements to be verified. This will be done by examining a number of examples. In these illustrations it is assumed that the worst-case response times (R) of the tasks are known.

Case I – a simple control loop

The simplest example is that of a periodic task which reads an input from the environment and produces a control output. The basic requirement for this task is to work at a specified rate (i.e. have a fixed period) and to deliver its output within a known bounded time (this is usually referred to as its deadline, D). With this simple structure, verification is needed to check simply that $R \leqslant D$.

Case II – responding to an event using a sporadic task

A deadline can also be placed on the response time of the system to some external event that manifests itself as an interrupt. Mapping the interrupt onto the release conditions of a sporadic task again requires simple verification that $R \leqslant D$.

Case III – responding to an event using a periodic task

The external event may be the result of polling. In the worst case, the event will occur just after the periodic polling is over and the next check will be in the next period. Hence the required test is $T + R \leqslant D$.

In Cases II and III, improvements can be made by using an internal response time rather than the task's final response time (see Section 3.2.5).

Case IV – precedence chain on the same processor

Figure 3.3 gave an example of a transaction consisting of three tasks, the last two being sporadic tasks released by the completion of a predecessor. One way of structuring this chain on one processor is to assume that all three tasks are released at the same time but run in the correct order because the earlier tasks have higher priorities. The end-to-end response time of the complete transaction is therefore equal to the response time of the final sporadic task, or $R_3 \leqslant D$. Note that this is a different formula to that given in equation (3.5). The value of R_3 is measured relative to the start of the complete transaction and therefore includes R_1 and R_2.

Case V – a distributed precedence chain

In the previous example, assume now that communication between the second and third tasks uses a communication link between independent processors. There still remains an end-to-end transaction deadline but the analysis is now more complicated. When a task releases a local sporadic task for execution, it is appropriate to assume that the response time of the releaser incorporates the time needed to release the sporadic task. But with a remote release this is not the case: the first task constructs the release message but the underlying system software performs the actual transmission across the network (or point-to-point link) and the release of the remote task. Assuming that M_2 is the worst-case communication delay for the the second task to release the third, the verification test is then $R_2 + M_2 + R_3 \leqslant D$. Note that the response time for the third task is calculated according to its priority on its processor, while the first and second tasks are assumed to be on the same processor.

In calculating the response times for the tasks on the second processor it will be necessary to take into account the release jitter of the third task (see Section 3.2.3). If we assume that the third task can be released arbitrarily close to the first, then $J_3 = R_2 + M_2$. This jitter value can be reduced if the minimum execution and communication times are known.

The value of M (the message worst-case communication time) must be obtained from an analysis of the communication medium. Protocols that use priority-based message scheduling are available and with these the analysis presented in this chapter can be used directly.

Case VI – a precedence chain using offsets

Figure 3.3 illustrated another means of implementing precedence relationships. In Section 3.1.1 it was shown that the deadline test was $O_3 + R_3 \leqslant D$. In general where tasks interact asynchronously (i.e. via PSOs) the key question is: how old is the data when the receiving task actually reads it?

As with remote sporadic releases, writing to a remote PSO has a communication cost that must be added to the data's maximum age. It should also be noted that time offsets can only be used to implement precedence relationships if the clocks on the two processors are synchronized. Let Δ be the maximum drift between any two clocks. If, as before, the second and third tasks are on different nodes, then the offset needed (relative to the release of τ_i) is $O_3 \geqslant O_2 + R_2 + M_2 + \Delta$.

3.2.9 Summary

The simple scheduling analysis presented in Chapter 2 has been extended to incorporate the realistic characteristics of a more general computational model. The main new features are listed below:

- the use of ICPI to implement mutual exclusion for PSOs and to provide a deadlock-free efficient means for tasks to share access to PSOs,
- an improved method of analysis to cater for release jitter and arbitrary deadlines,
- analysis to cater for tasks with precedence relations,
- a general priority assignment algorithm,
- analysis to incorporate kernel overheads,
- analysis of system transactions.

Taken together, they allow the timing requirements of realistic applications to be verified.

3.3   Introduction to Ada 95

In order to implement the computational model introduced in Section 3.1 it is necessary to use an implementation language that can support its features, and one such language is Ada.

The Ada programming language has gone through a number of changes since its initial design in the late 1970s. The current version, known as Ada 95, has a number of features that make it suitable as the implementation language for real-time systems. In particular it:

- provides features to implement tasks and PSOs directly,
- supports pre-emptive priority-based scheduling, and
- permits distribution of tasks and PSOs over a system.

Being a general purpose programming language, Ada also has a number of other features but in the following overview we focus mainly on the 'real-time' features.

3.3.1   Tasks and protected objects

Concurrent tasks can be declared statically or dynamically (though static declarations are sufficient for the computational model).

A task type has a *specification* and a *body*. If direct synchronous communication between tasks is required, then the specification must declare *entries* that can be called from other tasks. With asynchronous communication, no entries are necessary. Instead protected objects are used and these are described below. An example of a task type and some task objects follows:

```
task type Controller;
Con1, Con2 : Controller;
task body Controller is
   -- internal declarations
begin
   -- code to be executed by each task
end Controller;
```

This defines two task objects Con1 and Con2. The task body will usually contain a loop that will enable the task to execute repetitive actions.

A protected object type defines data that can be accessed mutually exclusively by tasks. For example, the following simple object allows client tasks to read and write a shared integer data item:

```
protected type Shared is
  procedure Read(D : out Integer);
  procedure Write(D : Integer);
private
  Store : Integer := Some_Initial_Value;
end Shared;
Simple : Shared;
protected body Shared is
  procedure Read(D : out Integer) is
  begin
    D := Store;
  end Read;
  procedure Write(D : Integer) is
  begin
    Store := D;
  end Write;
end Shared;
```

In addition to mutual exclusion, a protected object can also be used for conditional synchronization. A calling task can be suspended until released by the action of some other task, in the following example by a call to Update with a negative value:

```
protected Barrier is
  -- note this defines a single object of an anonymous type
  entry Release(V : out Integer);
  procedure Update(V : Integer);
private
  Store : Integer := 1;
end Barrier;
protected body Barrier is
  entry Release(V : out Integer) when Store < 0 is
  begin
    V := Store;
  end Release;
  procedure Update(V : Integer) is
  begin
    Store := V;
  end Update;
end Barrier;
```

As Release is a conditional routine, it is defined as an entry. To make a call on this protected object a task would execute

```
Barrier.Release(Result);   -- where Result is of type integer
```

To construct a single processor multi-tasking program, all tasks and objects are defined either in library units or at the topmost level of the main procedure. (In Ada, tasks can be arbitrarily nested. However, this is not required for the computational model.)

```
procedure Main is
  -- declaration of protected objects
  -- declaration of tasks
begin
  null;
end Main;
```

All tasks and protected objects can be assigned priorities using the priority pragma. It is also possible to use library units to define units of distribution and to define a task's call on a remote procedure to be asynchronous, but we shall not deal with that here.

3.3.2 Realising the computational model

The computational model requires periodic and sporadic tasks. A periodic task has a fixed period which is controlled by a clock (see the Real-Time Annex of the Ada definition):

```
with Ada.Real_Time; use Ada.Real_Time;
procedure Main is
  pragma Task_Dispatching_Policy(Fifo_Within_Priority);
  task Example_Periodic is  -- example task with priority 10
    pragma Priority(10);     -- and period 25ms
  end Example_Periodic;
  task body Example_Periodic is
    Period : Time_Span := Milliseconds(25);
    Start : Time;
    -- other declarations
  begin
    Start := Clock;
    loop
      -- code of periodic
      Start := Start + Period;
      delay until Start;
    end loop;
  end Example_Periodic;
end Main;
```

Type Time is defined as an abstract data type in a predefined package.

A sporadic task needs a protected object to manage its release conditions and this is enclosed in a package:

```
package Example_Sporadic is
  procedure Release_Sporadic;
end Example_Sporadic;
```

```
package body Example_Sporadic is
   task Sporadic_Thread is
      pragma Priority(15);
   end Sporadic_Thread;
   protected Starter is
      procedure Go;
      entry Wait;
      pragma Priority(15);   -- ceiling priority
   private
      Release_Condition : Boolean := False;
   end Starter;
   procedure Release_Sporadic is
   begin
      Starter.Go;
   end Release_Sporadic;
   task body Sporadic_Thread is
      -- declarations
   begin
      loop
         Starter.Wait;
         -- code of sporadic
      end loop;
   end Sporadic_Thread;
   protected body Starter is
      procedure Go is
      begin
         Release_Condition := True;
      end Go;
      entry Wait when Release_Condition is
      begin
         Release_Condition := False;
      end Wait;
   end Starter;
end Example_Sporadic;
```

The `Wait` entry must reset the release condition so that its next caller will be blocked until `Release_Sporadic` is called again. Variations of this basic structure can deal with bursty releases (with the protected object buffering the releases) and data communication through the protected object from the task that calls `Release_Sporadic` to the sporadic task.

If the sporadic task is to be released by an interrupt then the `Go` procedure is mapped directly onto the interrupt source. An example of this is given in the mine pump example in the next section.

3.4   The mine pump

Chapter 1 introduced the mine pump control problem. In this section we develop a design using the computational model defined earlier. A simple decomposition of the system identifies four major components:

- the pump controller,
- the environmental monitors (for airflow, methane and carbon monoxide),
- the data logging subsystem,
- the operator's subsystem.

The details of the data logging subsystem will be ignored and a protected object will be used as the interface. Calls to the operator will similarly be mapped onto a protected object. The operator can enquire about the status of the pump and attempt to turn the pump on – these operations will be accommodated within the pump controller.

The timing requirements of the environmental monitors have a cyclic behaviour and so these are represented as periodic tasks. The pump itself is a protected resource and is encapsulated within a PSO. Whenever the methane monitor reads a critically high methane level it will call this PSO to turn the pump off.

The high and low water sensors come into the system as interrupts. It is therefore appropriate to define sporadic tasks as the objects that respond to these interrupts and attempt to either turn on or turn off the pump (via calls to the pump PSO).

Although this structure provides an adequate design, one piece of functionality is still missing: after the methane level returns to low how is the pump turned on again? There is also an issue of safety analysis that would normally be applied to this sort of system. With the current design, the methane monitor and the pump controller are safety-critical. It could be argued that the *fail-silent* behaviour of the monitoring subsystem should not lead to failure (i.e. pump working while methane level too high). This leads to two extra elements being added.

- a PSO Methane_Status that holds the current methane level and the time at which the data was read (these values are obtained from the methane monitor),
- a periodic task that reads the Methane_Status PSO and sends control commands to the pump controller.

With this structure the new periodic task has the responsibility for turning the pump on again once the methane level is low enough.

Failure of the methane monitor will lead to a fail-safe state. Of course, this is not a fully reliable situation as the pump would not be able to operate if the mine were flooding and the methane level were low.

Figure 3.11 gives a pictorial representation of the design. Table 3.1 gives the details of the tasks and PSOs (including a key to the labels used in Figure 3.11). Note that both sporadic tasks are released by the same PSO. The design could be implemented on a single processor or a distributed system. Figure 3.12 gives one possible distributed configuration. Note how all the remote actions are legal in the computational model. One advantage of the design of this configuration is that the system fails-silent even when remote communications are unreliable.

Table 3.1 shows, where appropriate, the periods and minimum arrival rates of the tasks. It also includes the deadlines and priorities of the tasks (and hence the PSOs). A single processor implementation is assumed and priorities are in the range 1...10; unlike the analysis in Chapter 2, 1 is the *lowest* and 10 the *highest* priority which is allocated to the

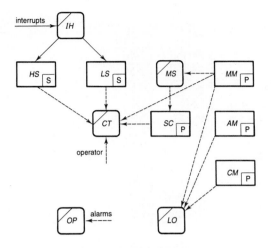

Figure 3.11 Design for the mine pump problem

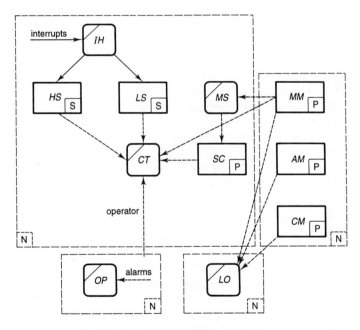

Figure 3.12 Distributed design

interrupt handler. The protected shared objects are given a ceiling priority which is one higher than the maximum priority of the tasks that use them.

Table 3.1 Mine control tasks and protected objects

Name	Class	Label	Symbol	T	D	P
Methane_Monitor	Periodic	MM	τ_M	20	10	8
Air_Monitor	Periodic	AM	τ_A	30	20	7
COo_Monitor	Periodic	CM	τ_C	30	20	6
Operator_Alarm	PSO	OP	PO_a			9
Methane_Status	PSO	MS	PO_m			9
Logger	PSO	LO	PO_l			9
Safety_Checker	Periodic	SC	τ_S	35	30	5
Controller	PSO	CT	PO_c			9
Interrupt_Handler	PSO	IH	PO_i			10
High_Sensor	Sporadic	HS	τ_H	10000	100	3
Low_Sensor	Sporadic	LS	τ_L	10000	75	4

System transactions

The timing requirements of the mine pump system require the following transactions:

1. Emergency shut down following a high methane value reading ($\tau_M \prec PO_c$); this has a bound of 30 milliseconds.
2. Recognition of monitor failure, and pump shut down, ($\tau_S \prec PO_c$); this has a bound of 65 milliseconds.
3. Turning the pump on again when it is safe ($\tau_M \prec PO_m \prec \tau_S \prec PO_c$); the bound is 100 milliseconds.
4. Turning the pump on (if safe) when the water is high ($PO_i \prec \tau_H \prec PO_c$); the bound is 100 milliseconds.
5. Turning the pump off when the low water level has been reached ($PO_i \prec \tau_L \prec PO_c$); the bound is 75 milliseconds.
6. Signalling an alarm if any environmental condition warrants it ($\tau_M \prec PO_a$, $\tau_A \prec PO_a$ and $\tau_C \prec PO_a$); the bound is 50 milliseconds.

Note that the data logging actions do not have explicit timing deadlines. The interrupts for high and low water events cannot occur arbitrarily close to each other. It can be assumed that no two interrupts can occur as close as five seconds or less (and hence no two interrupts from the same source occur within ten seconds).

Given the rates at which the monitoring tasks execute, it is possible to define deadlines for each task such that all transaction deadlines are met. These deadlines then dictate the appropriate priority levels, values of which are included in Table 3.1. For example, τ_M has a period of 20 ms and a deadline of 10 ms; hence in the worst-case PO_c will be called 30ms after the methane level goes high.

The deadlines (and hence the priorities) represented in Table 3.1 are not unique; other allocations are possible. In general, there is a tradeoff between the period and the deadline of a monitoring task.

3.4.1   Ada 95 implementation

The design objects introduced in the previous section can be coded in Ada 95. The following program is for a single processor solution. All the necessary code is included, apart from the instructions that interact with the hardware; these instructions are represented as comments as their actual form would depend upon the particular hardware being used.

Some basic types are first defined in a global package together with constants representing critical input values. For example, if the methane level from the sensor is above 32, then the pump should be disabled. The time-constant `Freshness` indicates the maximum time a data item should reside within PO_m without being overwritten by a more recent reading. Its value is set to $T + D$ for τ_m.

```ada
with Ada.Real_Time; use Ada.Real_Time;
package Data_Defs is
   type Status is (On,Off);
   type Safety_Status is (Stopped, Operational);
   type Alarm_Source is (Methane, Air_Flow, Carbon_Monoxide);
   type Methane_Value is range 0..256;
   type Air_Value is range 0..256;
   type Co_Value is range 0..256;
   Methane_Threshold : constant Methane_Value := 32;
   Air_Threshold : constant Air_Value := 100;
   Co_Threshold : constant Co_Value := 124;
   Freshness : constant Time_Span := Milliseconds(30);
end Data_Defs;
```

There are two main protected objects in the program: one gives the current methane reading, the other controls the pump. First consider the simple `Methane_Status` object:

```ada
protected Methane_Status is
   procedure Read(Ms : out Methane_Value; T : out Time);
   procedure Write(V : Methane_Value; T : Time);
   pragma Priority(9);
private
   Current_Value : Methane_Value := Methane_Value'Last;
   Time_Of_Read : Time := Clock;
end Methane_Status;
protected body Methane_Status is
   procedure Read(Ms : out Methane_Value; T : out Time) is
   begin
      Ms := Current_Value;
      T := Time_Of_Read;
   end Read;
   procedure Write(V : Methane_Value; T : Time) is
   begin
      Current_Value := V;
      Time_Of_Read := T;
   end Write;
end Methane_Status;
```

The pump controller is also a protected object. The sporadic tasks that respond to the high and low water interrupts will call `Turn_On` and `Turn_Off`. The safety controller will call `Stop` and `Start`. Only if the status of the pump is on (following a call of `Turn_On`) and the safety status is operational (i.e. no call of `Stop`) will the pump be actually started (or restarted). The other subprogram defined in this object is called by the operator module:

```
protected Controller is
   procedure Turn_On;
   procedure Turn_Off;
   procedure Stop;
   procedure Start;
   procedure Current_Status(St:out Status;
                                  Safe_St:out Safety_Status);
   pragma Priority(9);
private
   Pump : Status := Off;
   Condition : Safety_Status := Stopped;
end Controller;
protected body Controller is
   procedure Turn_On is
   begin
      Pump := On;
      if Condition = Operational then
         -- turn on pump
      end if;
   end Turn_On;
   procedure Turn_Off is
   begin
      Pump := Off;
      -- turn off pump
   end Turn_Off;
   procedure Stop is
   begin
      -- turn off pump
      Condition := Stopped;
   end Stop;
   procedure Start is
   begin
      Condition := Operational;
      if Pump = On then
         -- turn on pump
      end if;
   end Start;
   procedure Current_Status(St:out Status;
                                  Safe_St:out Safety_Status) is
   begin
      St := Pump;
      Safe_St := Condition;
   end Current_Status;
end Controller;
```

For completeness, the two objects that form the interface between the system and the operator and the data logger are as follows:

```
protected Operator_Alarm is
   procedure Alarm(Al : Alarm_Source);
   pragma Priority(9);
private
   ...
end Operator_Alarm;
protected Logger is
   procedure Methane_Log(V : Methane_Value);
   procedure Air_Log(V : Air_Value);
   procedure Co_Log(V : Co_Value);
   pragma Priority(9);
private
   ...
end Logger;
```

The periodic task that executes the safety check has a simple structure:

```
task Safety_Checker is
   pragma Priority(5);
end;
task body Safety_Checker is
   Reading : Methane_Value;
   Period : Time_Span := Milliseconds(35);
   Next_Start, Last_Time, New_Time : Time;
begin
   Next_Start := Clock;
   Last_Time := Next_Start;
   loop
      Methane_Status.Read(Reading, New_Time);
      if Reading >= Methane_Threshold or
         New_Time - Last_Time > Freshness then
         Controller.Stop;
      else
         Controller.Start;
      end if;
      Next_Start := Next_Start + Period;
      Last_Time := New_Time;
      delay until Next_Start;
   end loop;
end Safety_Checker;
```

The methane monitor is also a simple periodic task:

```
task Methane_Monitor is
   pragma Priority(8);
end;
```

```
task body Methane_Monitor is
  Sensor_Reading : Methane_Value;
  Period : Time_Span := Milliseconds(20);
  Next_Start : Time;
begin
  Next_Start := Clock;
  loop
    -- read hardware register into Sensor_Reading;
    if Sensor_Reading >= Methane_Threshold then
      Controller.Stop;
      Operator_Alarm.Alarm(Methane);
    end if;
    Methane_Status.Write(Sensor_Reading,Next_Start);
    Logger.Methane_Log(Sensor_Reading);
    Next_Start := Next_Start + Period;
    delay until Next_Start;
  end loop;
end Methane_Monitor;
```

To complete the software for the periodic structures, the tasks for air monitoring and carbon monoxide monitoring are as follows:

```
task Air_Monitor is
  pragma Priority(7);
end;
task body Air_Monitor is
  Sensor_Reading : Air_Value;
  Period : Time_Span := Milliseconds(30);
  Next_Start : Time;
begin
  Next_Start := Clock;
  loop
    -- read hardware register into Sensor_Reading;
    if Sensor_Reading <= Air_Threshold then
      Operator_Alarm.Alarm(Air_Flow);
    end if;
    Logger.Air_Log(Sensor_Reading);
    Next_Start := Next_Start + Period;
    delay until Next_Start;
  end loop;
end Air_Monitor;
task Co_Monitor is
  pragma Priority(6);
 end Co_Monitor;
task body Co_Monitor is
  Sensor_Reading : Co_Value;
  Period : Time_Span := Milliseconds(30);
  Next_Start : Time;
```

```
begin
  Next_Start := Clock;
  loop
    -- read hardware register into Sensor_Reading;
    if Sensor_Reading >= Co_Threshold then
      Operator_Alarm.Alarm(Carbon_Monoxide);
    end if;
    Logger.Co_Log(Sensor_Reading);
    Next_Start := Next_Start + Period;
    delay until Next_Start;
  end loop;
end Co_Monitor;
```

The two sporadic tasks are closely related and can therefore be managed by the same protected object:

```
package Flow_Sensors is
  task High_Sensor is
    pragma Priority(4);
  end High_Sensor;
  task Low_Sensor is
    pragma Priority(3);
  end Low_Sensor;
end Flow_Sensors;
package body Flow_Sensors is
  protected Interrupt_Handlers is
    procedure High; pragma Interrupt_Handler(High);
    procedure Low; pragma Interrupt_Handler(Low);
    entry Release_High; entry Release_Low;
    pragma Priority(10);
  private
    High_Interrupt, Low_Interrupt : Boolean := False;
  end Interrupt_Handlers;
  protected body Interrupt_Handlers is
    procedure High is
    begin
      High_Interrupt := True;
    end High;
    procedure Low is
    begin
      Low_Interrupt := True;
    end Low;
    entry Release_High when High_Interrupt is
    begin
      High_Interrupt := False;
    end Release_High;
    entry Release_Low when Low_Interrupt is
    begin
      Low_Interrupt := False;
    end Release_Low;
  end Interrupt_Handlers;
```

Table 3.2 Worst case execution times

Name	Class	Symbol	C
Methane_Monitor	Periodic	τ_M	5.4
Air_Monitor	Periodic	τ_A	3.3
CO_Monitor	Periodic	τ_C	3.3
Safety_Checker	Periodic	τ_S	3.5
Low_Sensor	Sporadic	τ_L	2.9
High_Sensor	Sporadic	τ_H	2.9
Interrupt_Handler	PSO	PO_i	1.2
Controller	PSO	PO_c	1.4
Operator_Alarm	PSO	PO_a	0.1
Methane_Status	PSO	PO_m	1.2
Logger	PSO	PO_l	0.8

```
task body High_Sensor is
begin
   loop
      Interrupt_Handlers.Release_High; Controller.Turn_On;
   end loop;
end High_Sensor;
task body Low_Sensor is
begin
   loop
      Interrupt_Handlers.Release_Low; Controller.Turn_Off;
   end loop;
end Low_Sensor;
end Flow_Sensors;
```

This completes the code for all of the components of the design.

3.4.2   Analysis of the application

Once the code has been developed it must be analyzed to obtain its worst-case execution times. As indicated in Section 3.2.1, these values can be obtained either by direct measurement or by modelling the hardware. None of the code derived is likely to require extensive computations and so it is reasonable to assume that a slow speed processor is adequate. Table 3.2 contains some representative values for the worst-case execution times for each task and PSO in the design. Note that the times for each task include time spent executing within called PSOs. Hence, for example, τ_M will call PO_m and PO_l in each period but will also call PO_c and PO_a when the methane is high. This gives a total of 5.4 milliseconds of execution time.

The execution environment imposes its own set of important parameters – these are

Table 3.3 Overheads

Name	Symbol	C
Context Switch Time	C_{cw}	0.2
Clock Period	T_{CLK}	5
Clock Overhead	C_{CLK}	0.4
Cost of Single Task Move	C_{PER}	0.3
Cost of Interrupt	C_{INT}	0.3
Maximum Kernel Blocking	C_E	1.1

given in Table 3.3. Note that the clock interrupt is of sufficient granularity to ensure no release jitter for the periodic tasks.

Adding the context switch times to the task's own computation times gives an overall computational load of 65.5%. The overheads of delay queue manipulations and the servicing of the timer interrupt add a further load of 12.4%. Hence the total system utilization is 77.9%.

The appropriate equations from Section 3.2 can now be applied to each of the tasks to obtain their worst-case response times. These values are given in Table 3.4. Note that the equations in Section 3.2 must deal with integer values (as they use ceiling functions); hence in Table 3.4 the unit of time is 100 microseconds. The blocking value in this table is 14 time units, on the assumption that whatever operator task calls the controller PSO will have a priority of less than 3. Hence for all tasks the maximum blocking time comes from this task (as the computation time of PO_c is the maximum of all PSOs). Note that the maximum non-pre-emptive section in the kernel is less than 14 (i.e. is 11 – from Table 3.4).

We can look at one task in detail to review how its response time value is obtained. Consider the `Air_Monitor` which has a computation time of 33 units. Context switch costs add a further four units (as there are two context switches per task invocation), which gives a total C value of 37. Blocking B is 14. One task has a higher priority; its total computational time is 58. The interrupt also has a higher priority; this adds three units. The clock has a period of 50 and hence equation (3.20) gives an initial interference of $4 + 3*$(number of periodic tasks), which equates to 16. Taken together, this gives a first value of $37 + 14 + 58 + 3 + 16$, which equals 128. Within this interval the clock will have interrupted two more times but no further periodic tasks will have been released and hence an extra eight units of interference will need to be added. This gives a value of 136, which balances the response time equation. Hence R is 136 (or 13.6 ms).

The final stage of the analysis is to return to the task deadlines. These were given in Table 3.1 and are repeated in Table 3.4. It is clear that all tasks complete before their deadlines and hence all transactions are satisfied.

Table 3.4 Results of schedulability analysis

Name	Class	Symbol	T	D	P	C	R
Methane_Monitor	Periodic	τ_M	200	100	8	58	95
Air_Monitor	Periodic	τ_A	300	200	7	37	136
CO_Monitor	Periodic	τ_C	300	200	6	37	177
Safety_Checker	Periodic	τ_S	350	300	5	39	285
Low_Sensor	Sporadic	τ_L	100000	750	4	33	525
High_Sensor	Sporadic	τ_H	100000	1000	3	33	558

3.5   Historical background

The computational model presented in this chapter is similar to that used in a number of design methods such as Mascot (Bate, 1986) and HRT-HOOD (Burns & Wellings, 1994). A formal representation of the model can be found in the semantic descriptions of the *Temporal Access Method* (TAM) (Scholfield *et al.*, 1994).

Section 3.2 gave an overview of some recent scheduling results; the derivation of these equations is described in Burns (1994), Audsley *et al.* (1993a; 1993b) and Burns *et al.* (1993), and detailed descriptions have been provided by Audsley (1993) and Tindell (1993). Discussion of the inheritance and ceiling protocols can be found in Goodenough and Sha (1988), Sha *et al.* (1990) and Baker (1990; 1991). A detailed case study of the Altitude and Orbital Control System (AOCS) of the Olympus Satellite appears in Burns *et al.* (1993).

Debates over the development of the Ada programming language have raged for a number of years. Readers interested in issues relating to the Ada tasking model will find a discussion in Burns *et al.* (1987). Real-time issues are discussed extensively in the *Proceedings of the International Workshops on Real-Time Ada Issues*.[3]

3.6   Further work

The analysis presented in this chapter covers a level of detail and a range of practical concerns that make it suitable for use on 'real' systems. There is current research in increasing the flexibility of the analysis and further removing restrictions in the computational model. For example, the model can be extended to include invocation interruption (i.e. asynchronously affecting the execution of a periodic task, during execution, to allow it to respond immediately to a mode change), dynamic allocation and re-allocation to cater for processor failure.

There has been much attention recently to the use of on-line techniques because, it is argued, that contemporary systems are too complex for purely off-line analysis. On-line

---

[3]The proceedings of these workshops, which started in 1987, are published annually in *ACM Ada Letters*.

techniques are based on 'best-effort' scheduling to make the most effective use of the system under all possible conditions; they will be described in greater detail in Chapter 4. While priority-based scheduling and best-effort scheduling are often considered to be irreconcilable, there has been work on defining a framework that can accommodate both approaches (Audseley *et al.*, 1993c; 1994; Davis *et al.*, 1993). Within such a framework it would be possible to integrate static analysis, diverse and adaptive software, deadline variations and software fault-tolerance (Bondavalli *et al.*, 1993).

3.7 Exercises

Exercise 3.1   Verify that the system transaction deadlines for the mine control problem are satisfied by the period and deadline definitions in given Table 3.1.

Exercise 3.2   Check the response-time calculations given in Table 3.4. Which value is wrong?

Exercise 3.3   In the analysis of the mine control system, what would be the consequences of running the clock at 10 ms (or 20 ms)?

Exercise 3.4   Do a sensitivity analysis on the mine control task set. Taking each task in turn, consider by how much its computation time must increase before the task set becomes unschedulable. Express this value as a percentage of the original value of the computation time.

Chapter 4

Dynamic Priority Scheduling

Krithi Ramamritham

Introduction

Dynamic scheduling of a real-time program requires a sequence of decisions to be taken during execution on the assignment of system resources to *transactions*. Each decision must be taken without *prior* knowledge of the needs of future tasks. As in the case of fixed priority scheduling, the system resources include processors, memory and shared data structures; but tasks can now have arbitrary attributes: arrival times, resource requirements, computation times, deadlines and importance values.

Dynamic algorithms are needed for applications where the computing requirements may vary widely, making fixed priority scheduling difficult or inefficient. Many real-time applications require support for dynamic scheduling: e.g. in robotics, where the control subsystem must adapt to a dynamic environment. This kind of scheduling also allows more flexibility in dealing with practical issues, such as the need to alter scheduling decisions based on the occurrence of overloads, e.g. when

- the environment changes,
- there is a burst of task arrivals, or
- a part of the system fails.

In a practical system, it can prove costly to assume that overloads and failures will never occur and, at the same time, be inefficient to determine schedulability or *a priori* to construct a fixed schedule for a system with such variable properties.

Dynamic scheduling has three basic steps: feasibility checking, schedule construction and dispatching. Depending on the kind of application for which the system is designed, the programming model adopted and the scheduling algorithm used, all of the steps may not be needed. Often, the boundaries between the steps may also not be clear.

We shall first generalize the definitions of transaction and process used in Chapter 3. A computational transaction will now be assumed to be made up of one or more processes composed in parallel. A process consists of one or more tasks.

66

Feasibility analysis

Feasibility, or schedulability, analysis has been described in Chapters 2 and 3: it is the process of determining whether the timing requirements of a set of tasks can be satisfied, usually under a given set of resource requirements and precedence constraints. With fixed priority scheduling, feasibility analysis is typically done statically, before the program is executed. Dynamic systems perform feasibility checking on-line, as tasks arrive.

There are two approaches to scheduling in dynamic real-time systems:

1. *Dynamic planning-based approaches*: Execution of a task is begun only if it passes a feasibility test, i.e that it will complete execution before its deadline. Often, one of the results of the feasibility analysis is a schedule or plan that is used to decide when a task should begin execution.
2. *Dynamic best-effort approaches*: Here no feasibility checking is done; the system tries to 'do its best' to meet deadlines but, since feasibility is not checked, a task may be aborted during its execution.

In a planning-based approach, the feasibility of a set of tasks is checked in terms of a scheduling policy such as 'earliest-deadline-first' or 'least-laxity-first', before the execution of a set of tasks. By contrast, in a best-effort approach, tasks may be queued according to policies that take account of the time constraints (similar to the kind of scheduling found in a non-real-time operating system). No feasibility checking is done before the tasks are queued.

The relative importance of a task and the value given to its completion are used to take scheduling decisions, whether or not feasibility checking is done. This information is usually given as a time-value function that specifies the contribution of a task to the system upon its successful completion. Figure 4.1 relates value with completion time, for different value functions.

For hard real-time tasks, the value drops immediately after the deadline and dynamic algorithms cannot be used: there should be *a priori* verification that such tasks will meet their deadlines. Dynamic algorithms are suitable for the tasks in the 'firm' and 'soft' categories.

To achieve high system performance, the system must also consider the relative values of tasks, or their *importance*, when determining which tasks to reject and which to execute. Because a dynamic scheduling algorithm takes decisions without prior knowledge of the tasks, the total value is not predictable and the algorithm must attempt to maximize the value accrued from tasks that complete on time. Most dynamic algorithms developed so far assume that a value function assigns a positive value to a task that is successfully completed, and zero to an incomplete task. This corresponds to the curve marked 'firm' in Figure 4.1, where the value for a task remains constant until its deadline and then drops to zero. If all the tasks have the same value, maximizing the accrued value is the same as maximizing the number of completed tasks.

While achieving maximum value, real-time systems must also exhibit a capability for 'graceful degradation'. To achieve this, not only must the fact that a task did not meet its deadline be detected, but the fact that this is going to occur must be detected as soon as

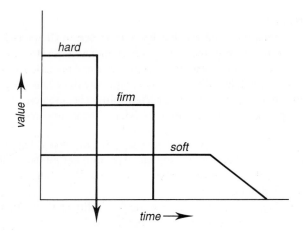

Figure 4.1 Different kinds of value function

possible. An exception must then be signalled to make it possible for the task to be substituted by one or more contingency tasks. Thus on-line schedulability analysis must have an early warning feature which provides sufficient lead time for the timely invocation of contingency tasks, making it possible for the scheduler to take account of a continuously changing environment.

Such schedulability analysis is especially important for transactions for which recovery following an aborted partial execution can be complicated. Error handlers are complex in general and abnormal termination may produce inconsistent system states. This is likely to be the case especially if the transaction involves inter-process interaction. In such situations, it is better to allow a transaction to take place only if it can be *guaranteed* to complete by its deadline. If such a guarantee cannot be provided, then the program can perform an alternative action. And to provide sufficient time for executing the alternative action, a deadline may be imposed on the determination of schedulability. This can be generalized so that there are N versions of the transaction and the algorithm attempts to guarantee the execution of the best possible version. 'Best' refers to the value of the results produced by a particular version; typically, the better the value of the result, the longer the execution time.

Schedule construction

Schedule construction is the process of ordering the tasks to be executed and storing this in a form that can be used by the dispatching step.

Feasibility checking is sometimes performed by checking if there is a schedule or plan in which all the tasks will meet their deadlines. For planning-based approaches, schedule construction is usually a direct consequence of feasibility checking.

In other cases, priorities are assigned to tasks and at run-time the task in execution has the highest priority. This is the case with fixed priority approaches and with some simple dynamic priority approaches, such as earliest-deadline-first or least-laxity-first, where feasibility checking involves ensuring that the total processor utilization is below a bound.

In the remainder of this chapter we will refer to schedule construction simply as *scheduling*. Thus, scheduling involves deciding *when* tasks will execute. The schedule is maintained explicitly in the form of a plan or implicitly as the assignment of priorities to tasks.

Dispatching

Dispatching is the process of deciding which task to execute next. The complexity and requirements for the dispatching step depend on:

1. the scheduling algorithm used in the feasibility checking step,
2. whether a schedule is constructed as part of the schedulability analysis step,
3. the kinds of tasks, e.g. whether they are independent or with precedence constraints, and whether their execution is pre-emptive or non-pre-emptive, and
4. the nature of the execution platform, e.g. whether it has one processor or more and how communication takes place.

For example, with non-pre-emptive scheduling a task is dispatched exactly once; with pre-emptive scheduling, a task will be dispatched once when it first begins execution and again whenever it is resumed.

In the remainder of this chapter, we discuss how the timing requirements of transactions can be specified and how user level transactions can be mapped into tasks with different characteristics including timing constraints, precedence constraints, resource requirements, importance levels and communication characteristics. Issues to be considered for dynamic scheduling are introduced and different ways of assigning priorities to tasks are considered. The two types of dynamic scheduling approach, best-effort scheduling and planning-based scheduling, are discussed in detail and, since the run-time cost of a dynamic approach is an important practical consideration, several techniques are discussed for efficient dynamic scheduling.

4.1   Programming dynamic real-time systems

The requirements for tasks in a real-time system can be quite varied. In this section, we show how they can be specified from within a program. For dynamic real-time applications, it should be possible to specify several important requirements:

- Before initiating a time-constrained transaction, it should be possible for the program to ask for a guarantee from the run-time system that the transaction will be completed within the specified deadline.

A transaction can be guaranteed to complete within its deadline if a schedule can be created for this transaction and the other transactions that have been previously guaranteed to meet their deadlines.

• If the system cannot give a guarantee when it is sought, then it should be possible to choose an alternative activity. When a guarantee is not sought and it is not possible to meet the timing constraint, it should be possible to take alternative action. In either case, the alternative may be a timing-error handler that will allow some corrective action to be taken.

Language constructs to express such constraints are described using a form of pseudocode. In what follows, terminals are shown in `typewriter font`, [ ] encloses optional items and | separates alternatives.

A transaction (shown in *italics*) refers to a statement. A real-time transaction has a time constraint such as a periodicity requirement or a deadline.

4.1.1 Activities with deadlines

Timeouts can be associated with any statement using the `within deadline` statement which has the form

```
within deadline (d) statement₁
[ else  statement₂ ]
```

During execution, if execution of a `within deadline` statement starts at time t and is not completed by $t + d$, then it is terminated and *statement₂*, if provided, is executed. Hence, d is the deadline relative to the current time. The effect of this abnormal termination is local if *statement₁* does not require any inter-process communication; otherwise, the other interacting processes may be affected. We discuss this further in Section 4.1.5.

Example 4.1 *Air traffic control 1.* An air-traffic control system should provide final clearance for a pilot to land within 60 seconds after clearance is requested. Otherwise the pilot will abort the landing procedure:

```
within deadline (60) get clearance
else abort landing
```

4.1.2 Guaranteed transactions

The `guarantee` statement is used to ensure before a transaction is started that it can be completed within the specified time constraint:

```
within deadline (gd ) guarantee
        time_constrained_statement
[else  statement ]
```

where *gd* is the deadline for obtaining the guarantee. If the guarantee is not possible, or if it cannot be given within *gd*, the `else` statement, if provided, is executed. Otherwise, the time-constrained statement is executed.

To provide such a guarantee, the execution time and the resource requirements of the statement must *a priori* be determinable (at least at the time of the guarantee). This makes it important for the execution time to lie within relatively small bounds as resources must be provided for the worst-case needs. In general, the larger the worst-case needs, the less likely it will be to obtain a guarantee; further, even if a guarantee can be given for large bounds, it is likely to affect future guarantees.

Dynamic scheduling makes it possible to use run-time information about tasks, such as execution times and resource constraints. Such information can be derived from formulas provided by the compiler for evaluation at the time of task invocation. For example, the calculation of the execution time can then take into account the specific parameters of the invocation and hence be more accurate (and perhaps less pessimistic) than a statically determined execution time; such calculations can make use of data only available at run-time, such as the number and values of inputs. As for compile-time calculation of worst-case execution times, run-time calculation also requires loop iterations and communication times to be bounded. If synchronous communication statements do not have associated time-constraints, it is necessary to consider the communicating tasks together as a transaction when checking feasibility.

Example 4.2 The following statement tries to guarantee that *statement*$_1$ will be completed within the next *d* seconds:

```
within deadline (gd) guarantee
        within deadline (d) statement₁
        [else ...]
[else  statement₂ ]
```

If execution starts at time *t*, *statement*$_2$ will be executed if it is not possible to obtain the guarantee by $t + gd$. If guaranteed, execution of *statement*$_1$ will start at *st* and end by $t + d$, where *st* lies in the interval $(t, t + gd)$.

Example 4.3 *A simple railway crossing.* The task controlling a railway signal has to determine whether a certain track will be clear by the time a train is expected to reach there. This must be done early enough to give enough time to stop the train if the track is not expected to be clear. Assume that the train will not reach the track before *d* seconds and that it takes at most *s* seconds to stop the train ($s < d$):

```
within deadline (d − s) guarantee
        within deadline (d) clear track
        else ...
else stop train
```

4.1.3   Start-time-constraints

The following statement attaches start time constraints to transactions with deadlines:

    start at (s) within deadline (d) statement₁
    [else statement₂]

If execution of the `within deadline` statement starts at time t, then execution of *statement₁* should start at or after $t + s$ and be completed by $t + d$, where $d > s$. A simple extension gives the guaranteed version of this statement.

The value v of a task is specified by attaching the construct `value v` to the `within deadline` statement.

4.1.4   Flexible time-constraints

The time-constraints described thus far are to ensure that if a transaction is not completed within the specified time, it is terminated and timing-error handling is done. This is appropriate if there is no value in completing the transaction after the specified time.

For many real-time applications, while it may be desirable for all transactions to meet the timing-constraints, it may be better, and sometimes necessary, to complete a transaction even if it is delayed. Such time-constraints will be called *flexible*. Thus a transaction may have a non-zero value up to some point past its deadline; if this point does not lie in a fixed interval, the transaction should be completed regardless of how long it takes.

To express flexible time-constraints, an *overflow* is associated with a time-constraint. If the overflow is positive, a transaction should be terminated only after the end of the interval corresponding to the overflow. This corresponds to a soft deadline.

If the *overflow* has a negative value, it indicates that the transaction must be completed by the specified deadline but, if possible, within *overflow* units before the deadline. (This is like asking the system to 'be nice' to a transaction by trying to complete it before the deadline.)

A deadline-constrained transaction *statement₁* is specified as

    within deadline (d) [overflow] statement₁
    else statement₂

and has the following effect:

- If execution of *statement₁* is not completed by $max(d, d + overflow)$, processing of *statement₁* is terminated and *statement₂*, if provided, is executed.
- If *overflow* is not specified, it is assumed to be zero.
- If a guarantee is requested, it will be first attempted for $min(d, d + overflow)$ and, if this is unsuccessful, for $max(d, d + overflow)$; if the second attempt is also unsuccessful, the `else` clause, if specified, will be executed.
- If a time-constrained component of *statement₁* has an overflow, it can increase the worst-case execution time of *statement₁*.

Example 4.4 *Air traffic control 2.* An air-traffic control system should provide final clearance for a pilot to land within t_1 seconds after the request has been made; if this is not possible, clearance should be given within another t_2 seconds or the pilot will abort the landing procedure:

within deadline $(t_1)(t_2)$ *clear landing*
else *abort landing*

It is easy to see that a large overflow indicates that the transaction has only a *nominal* deadline and should be allowed to complete even if the deadline is past.

4.1.5 Inter-process communication and time-constraints

There are two important considerations when a time-constrained transaction interacts with other transactions. The first is to find the duration of such interactions so that the execution time of the transaction can be determined. The second is the effect on other transactions when a time-constrained transaction is terminated because a specified time-constraint is not met.

The sender of an asynchronous message does not wait (assuming that buffers do not overflow), so the time needed for sending a message is bounded. However, for synchronous communication, the sending task is suspended until the receiver responds and the delay may be unbounded. With timed synchronous communication, the maximum time that a task can wait for a call to complete is bounded.

The execution of a statement with an associated deadline is abandoned when its deadline has expired, and there are a number of consequences when a synchronous send or receive statement is abandoned by the callee:

- A send that is abandoned before the matching receive occurs will clearly not affect the sender. If it is withdrawn during the execution of the receive statement, there is no effect on the receiver. It should be possible for the sender to determine if the message was received or if it was withdrawn while in the process of being received. A special variable t_interrupted can be associated with each task to indicate if the last send was withdrawn during the receive.
- A similar variable t_abandoned can be used to indicate if execution of a receive statement was abandoned by the receiver.

Example 4.5 *Termination during process interaction.* A resource is managed by a Manager task. If a requesting task has not received the resource within *max_wait* time it will take its request to another provider:

within deadline (*max_wait*)
        Manager.get(pid)
else *get resource from another provider*

where `pid` is the id of the calling task.

The `Manager` task may be responding to the `get` request when the specified time limit `max_wait` expires. In this case, although the request is withdrawn, the `Manager` continues with the allocation as if nothing happened and the requester is required to free the resource after examining the value of variable `t_interrupted`:

```
within deadline (max_wait)
        Manager.get(pid)
else if (t_interrupted) then Manager.free(pid);
        get resource from another provider
```

Let us now examine what is involved in guaranteeing whether or not a synchronous `send` can be completed within a deadline:

```
within deadline (d) guarantee
        within deadline (max_wait) Manager.get(pid);
else get resource from another provider;
```

To provide this guarantee, the scheduler must be able to determine when the receiver will actually receive the message. In some special cases, it may be possible to determine this time but, in general, the delay may depend on a number of factors such as the execution times of various code segments within the receiver, when these code segments will be scheduled, etc. Taken together, they make it all but impossible for the sender to determine dynamically when the receiver will receive the message.

However, in the special case of a set of interacting tasks participating in a transaction with a deadline, the transaction can be converted into a set of precedence-related tasks and started only if they are found to be feasible.

A transaction may be suspended at a number of *scheduling points*; these occur at the beginning and end of critical sections, at synchronous communication calls, or where explicit suspend calls appear in the code. A transaction is executed from one scheduling point to the next (a *task*) and it can then be executed without being interrupted for want of resources or for synchronization.

A *task graph* contains tasks related by precedence and communication constraints. Activities without internal scheduling points reduce to a graph with a single task. Activities containing critical sections or other scheduling points will reduce to task graphs with several tasks. During the construction of the task graph, the resources needed for each task can be determined. The description of a transaction is then available for the scheduler as a group of tasks representing the transaction.

Figure 4.2 shows a transaction with two components *A* and *B* which can execute in parallel and communicate synchronously. This transaction is converted into a graph with five tasks. With this, the two components, and hence the transaction, can be executed predictably if the corresponding task graph can be feasibly scheduled.

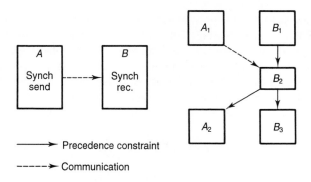

Figure 4.2 Communicating tasks and the corresponding task graph

4.2 Issues in dynamic scheduling

With static priorities, a task's priority is assigned when it arrives and fresh evaluation is not required as time progresses and new tasks arrive. Hence static priorities are well suited for periodic tasks that execute at all times (but, with the extensions shown in Chapter 3, they can be used for aperiodic tasks as well).

In a dynamic system, static feasibility checking is not possible and dynamic decision making algorithms must be used. This has several implications. It is no longer possible to guarantee that all task arrivals *will* be able to meet their deadlines: if the arrival times of tasks are not known, the schedulability of the tasks cannot be guaranteed. However, if the system has only independent, periodic tasks and one processor, static schedulability analysis can be used even if the scheduling policy is dynamic.

For tasks with a more complex structure, other attributes can be used to assign priorities. This gives dynamic algorithms a lot of flexibility and adds to their ability to deal with a wide variety of tasks. But there may be substantial overheads in calculating the priorities of tasks and in selecting the task of highest priority. When dynamic priorities are used, the relative priorities of tasks can change as time progresses, as new tasks arrive or as tasks execute. Whenever one of these events occurs, the priority of all the remaining tasks must be recomputed. This makes the use of dynamic priorities more expensive in terms of run-time overheads, and in practice these overheads must be kept as small as possible.

A shortcoming of static schedulability analysis arises from the assumptions and the restrictions on which off-line guarantees are based. For example, if there is a non-zero probability that these assumptions are unlikely to hold or that restrictions may be violated, a system using a static approach will not perform as designed and tasks may miss their deadlines. And, under some situations, effective control of the system can be lost because of the limited scheduling capability available at run-time. Thus, when constraints assumed by off-line schedulability analysis are likely to be violated, dynamic scheduling approaches provide a solution.

Consider a very simple example. If system overloads are known to be impossible, then the earliest-deadline-first algorithm (EDF) can be used. Since overloads cannot occur, when a task is pre-empted there is an implicit guarantee that the remainder of the task will be completed before its deadline; without overloads, simple algorithms such as EDF and least-laxity-first (LLF) perform very well. But if overloads are possible, in the worst case, EDF and LLF may produce zero value, i.e. none of the tasks that arrive will meet its deadline (even if, under another scheduling discipline, some tasks may meet their deadlines).

An *optimal* dynamic scheduling algorithm always produces a feasible schedule whenever a *clairvoyant* algorithm, i.e. a scheduling algorithm with complete prior knowledge of the tasks, can do so. Unfortunately, it is difficult to construct a good on-line algorithm to compete with a clairvoyant algorithm. *Competitiveness analysis*, involving the comparison of an on-line algorithm with a clairvoyant algorithm, is one way to predict the behaviour of a dynamic algorithm. However, this analysis considers only worst-case behaviours involving all possible task characteristics. For predictability, planning-based scheduling is a viable alternative. Here, given a particular priority assignment policy and the requirements of a task before it begins execution, a check is made to see whether there is a way for the task to meet its deadline. As mentioned earlier, many planning approaches also produce a schedule for task execution as a useful by-product and the added cost of the checking may be well spent.

4.3   Dynamic priority assignment

Construction of a plan in planning-based approaches and determining which task to execute next in best-effort approaches requires assigning priorities to tasks; this raises the question of how priorities are assigned. Further, there is a conflict between priority-based scheduling and the goal of maximizing resource utilization in a real-time system.

4.3.1   Simple priority assignment policies

In a real-time system, priority assignment must be related to the time constraints associated with a task, e.g. according to EDF or LLF ordering. For scheduling independent tasks with deadline constraints on single processors, EDF and LLF are optimal methods, so if any assignment of priorities can feasibly schedule such tasks, then so can EDF and LLF.

For a given task set, if tasks have the same arrival times but different deadlines, EDF generates a non-pre-emptive schedule, while the LLF schedule requires pre-emptions. If both arrival times and deadlines are arbitrary, EDF and LLF schedules may both require pre-emptions. These algorithms use the timing characteristics of tasks and are suitable when the processor is the only resource needed and tasks are independent of each other.

4.3.2 Priority assignment for tasks with complex requirements

Of more practical interest is the scheduling of tasks with timing constraints, precedence constraints, resource constraints and arbitrary values on multi-processors. Unfortunately, most instances of the scheduling problem for real-time systems are computationally intractable. Non-pre-emptive scheduling is desirable as it avoids context switching overheads, but determining such a schedule is an NP-hard problem even on uniprocessors if tasks can have arbitrary ready times. The presence of precedence constraints exacerbates the situation and finding a resource-constrained schedule is an NP-complete problem.

This makes it clear that it serves no effective purpose to try to obtain an optimal schedule, especially when decisions are made dynamically. And, with multi-processors, no dynamic scheduling algorithm is optimal and can guarantee all tasks without prior knowledge of task deadlines, computation times and arrival times. Such knowledge is not available in dynamic systems so it is necessary to resort to approximate algorithms or to use heuristics, as we shall now see.

As in Chapter 3, a task τ is the unit for scheduling; it is characterized by its arrival time AT, its absolute deadline D, its value V, its worst-case computation time C and its resource requirements $\{RR\}$. Tasks are assumed to be independent, non-periodic and non-pre-emptive. A task uses a resource either in shared mode or in exclusive mode and holds a requested resource as long as it executes. EST is the earliest start time at which the task can begin execution (EST is calculated when scheduling decisions are made).

The following condition relates AT, D, C, EST and the current time T :

$$AT \leq EST \leq D - C$$

Let $Pr(\tau)$ be the priority of task τ, and assume that the smaller the value of $Pr(\tau)$, the higher the priority. There are a number of possible priority assignment policies.

1. Smallest arrival time first, or first-come-first served (FCFS): $Pr(\tau) = AT$. FCFS is a fair policy but it does not take any real-time considerations into account. For tasks with the same priority, FCFS may be a suitable policy.
2. Minimum processing time first (Min_C): $Pr(\tau) = C$. In non-real-time environments, the simple heuristic Min_C is often a rule for minimizing average response times but it is not usually adequate for real-time systems.
3. Minimum (or earliest) deadline first (Min_D): $Pr(\tau) = D$. For tasks needing only a processor resource, Min_D can be a suitable policy.
4. Minimum earliest start time first (Min_S): $Pr(\tau) = EST$. This is the first policy to take resource requirements into account through calculation of EST.
5. Minimum laxity first (Min_L): $Pr(\tau) = D - (EST + C)$. Like EDF, (Min_L) is optimal for tasks that have just processing requirements; Min_L takes into account the information used in Min_D and Min_S.
6. Minimum value first (Min_V): $Pr(\tau) = V$. Min_V considers only the value of a task.
7. Minimum value density first (Min_VD): $Pr(\tau) = \frac{T_V}{C}$. Unlike Min_V, which does not take the computation time into account, Min_VD considers the value per unit time when assigning task priorities.

Table 4.1 Task parameters for Example 4.1

Task	τ_1	τ_2	τ_3
computation time	9	10	1
resource request	either copy	either copy	both
deadline	9	74	11

8. Min_D + Min_C: $Pr(\tau) = D + W_1 \times C$, where W_1 is a weighting constant. This policy considers two task parameters, but resource requirements are ignored.

9. Min_D + Min_S: $Pr(\tau) = D + W_1 \times EST$, where W_1 is a weighting constant. For tasks having time- and resource-constraints, this policy has been shown to result in good real-time performance.

10. Min_D + Min_S + Min_VD: $Pr(\tau) = D + W_1 \times EST + W_2 \times \frac{V}{C}$. This considers the value, computation time, deadline and resource requirements of a task.

4.3.3 Priority-based scheduling and resources

There is usually a conflict between keeping resources busy and respecting task priorities: if resources are to be used to the fullest extent possible, there may be task executions that violate task priorities.

Example 4.6 *Greedy scheduling.* Assume that the (Min_D + Min_S) heuristic is used to assign priorities to tasks. Let $W_1 = 6$. Assume there are two processors, three tasks and two copies of a resource, each of which is used only in exclusive mode. The task parameters are listed below in Table 4.1. We first determine the schedule produced by *list scheduling*, a greedy approach. Tasks are ordered on a list by decreasing priority and, when a processor is idle, the list is scanned from the beginning and the first task which does not violate the resource constraints is assigned to the processor.

The task priorities are $Pr(\tau_1) = 9$, $Pr(\tau_2) = 74$ and $Pr(\tau_3) = 11$. So τ_1 has the highest priority and it is scheduled to start at *time*=0. Then, because one processor is still idle, list scheduling is used to find another task that can start at *time*=0. Recomputing the priorities of the remaining tasks gives $Pr(\tau_2) = 74$ and $Pr(\tau_3) = 65$. Although τ_3 has the higher priority, since it requires both resources only τ_2 can start at *time*=0 and so it is chosen. Finally, τ_3 is scheduled to start at *time*=10 when both copies of the resource are available. Thus, tasks are scheduled according to their priority but while the policy is greedy about keeping the resources fully used.

Suppose we used a pure priority-driven approach, one that is not greedy. After τ_1 is scheduled, the remaining task priorities are recomputed and τ_3 will be chosen to be executed next at *time*=9, followed by τ_2 at *time*=10.

Thus with list scheduling, the higher priority task τ_3 will be delayed by one time unit while, without greed, τ_2 will be delayed by ten time units.

The example shows that though list scheduling keeps resources better utilized, it does so by delaying the execution of higher priority tasks. Since the priority of a task reflects its time-constraints and other characteristics of importance, in real-time systems it is usually desirable to take more account of priorities than of the underutilization of resources.

We can attempt to obtain the best of both worlds by adopting pre-emptive priority-driven scheduling. If this is done, then by the time τ_1 completes execution, τ_2 could have been pre-empted by τ_3. Unfortunately, the decision to pre-empt may not be simple:

- There may be tasks which, once pre-empted, will need to be restarted, losing all the computation up to the point of pre-emption. For example, in a communicating task, if a communication is interrupted it may have to be re-started from the beginning: the communication line represents an exclusive resource that is required for the complete duration of the task.
- A task that is pre-empted while *reading* a shared data structure can resume from the point of pre-emption only provided the data structure has not been modified.
- A task that is pre-empted while *modifying* a shared data structure may leave it in an internally inconsistent state; one way to restore consistency is to wait for the pre-empted task to be completed before allowing further use of the resource. An alternative is to rollback the changes made by the pre-empted task but, in general, it is difficult to keep a record of all such changes. A rollback can add considerably to the overhead.

Returning to Example 4.6, τ_2 uses the resource in exclusive mode. So there are two possible ways in which list scheduling can be used, depending on the nature of the resource:

1. If the resource is like the communication line, τ_2 can be pre-empted at *time*=9 and τ_3 can begin using it immediately. This is equivalent to not having started execution of τ_2 at all, and allowing τ_2 to execute ahead of its turn by being greedy has not helped. But, if τ_2's computation time is less than or equal to that of τ_1, greed can be used. In any case, the execution of τ_3 will not be more delayed than it would be for pure priority-driven scheduling.
2. If the resource is a modifiable data structure, τ_3's execution will be delayed, either by the need to rollback τ_2's changes or to wait for τ_2 to complete execution. In either case, τ_3 will complete later than under pure priority-driven scheduling.

This suggests that a limited form of list scheduling can be used in which task computation times and the nature of the resources, as well as their use, is considered when making scheduling decisions. The goal is then to ensure that priorities are not violated when a greedy policy is used. Another alternative is to limit the greed so that the algorithm tries to keep only a specified fraction of each replicated resource busy.

In the examples, we have assumed that the worst-case resource requirements for each task are available. The scheduling algorithm then takes these resource requirements during feasibility checking. Assuming that tasks are non-pre-emptable, the scheduling algorithm will not schedule in parallel two tasks with resource conflicts.

There is another approach to dealing with resource requirements in which the scheduling algorithm does not explicitly consider resource requirements. Instead, the resource requirements of each task are analyzed and also the resource conflicts among the tasks. This allows calculation of the worst-case blocking time for each task due to resource contention, and incorporation of this into the task's worst-case execution time (see Chapter 3). When this is done, the run-time management of the resources must correspond to the assumptions made at analysis time. For example, if the worst-case times are derived assuming that each resource use is guarded by a semaphore, then semaphores must be used at run-time.

4.4 Dynamic best-effort approaches

4.4.1 Best-effort scheduling

In best-effort scheduling, tasks are assigned priorities according to one of the policies of Section 4.3, and task execution occurs in priority order. It is this requirement to always execute the highest priority task that necessitates pre-emption: if a low priority task is in execution and a higher priority task arrives, or becomes eligible to execute, the low priority task is pre-empted and the processor is given to the new arrival.

With priority-driven pre-emptive scheduling using, say, task deadlines to decide on priorities and without any feasibility checking, a task can be pre-empted at any time during its execution. In this case, until the deadline, or until the task finishes, whichever comes first, it is not known whether a timing-constraint will be met.

The overall predictability of best-effort approaches is also difficult to assess. Whereas real-time scheduling algorithms, such as EDF and LLF, have optimal behaviour as long as no overloads occur, extreme performance degradation can occur under overloads and, at times, a system may produce only zero value. This potential for very poor performance under overloads is the major disadvantage of the *dynamic best-effort approaches*. But, since dynamic algorithms must perform well under varying loading conditions, careful choice is needed of the task to execute and of the task to discard when an overload occurs. In practice, this requires confidence to be gained using extensive simulation, re-coding the tasks and adjusting the priorities.

During overloads, tasks with lower values can be shed and there are several ways of accomplishing this. Tasks of lower importance can be removed one at a time and in strict order from low to high importance. This incurs higher overheads than a scheme which chooses any lower valued task, but neither method takes into account the time gained by dropping a task. Shedding tasks in the lowest-value-density-first order does, however, take a task's computation time into consideration.

Let S be an arbitrary task arrival sequence and A an on-line scheduling algorithm that knows about task τ only at its arrival time AT. Let CA be a *clairvoyant* algorithm which gives an ideal, optimal, off-line schedule using information about all the tasks in S. $V_A(S)$ is the total value obtained by A and $V_{CA}(S)$ is the total value obtained by CA.

First overload example: For a single processor system, assume that A uses a simple strategy to take scheduling decisions: it uses EDF when the system is underloaded,

Table 4.2 Task parameters for first overload example

Tasks	AT	C	D	V
τ_1	0	2	2	3
τ_2	1	100	101	100

Table 4.3 Task parameters for second overload example

Tasks	AT	C	D	V	Tasks	AT	C	D	V
τ_1	0	10	10	10	τ_1'	0	9	11	9
τ_2	9	11	20	11	τ_2'	9	10	21	10
τ_3	19	12	31	12	τ_3'	19	11	32	11
τ_4	30	13	43	13	τ_4'	30	12	44	12
τ_5	42	14	56	14	τ_5'	42	13	57	13
τ_6	55	15	70	15	τ_6'	55	14	71	14
τ_7	69	16	85	16	τ_7'	69	15	86	15
τ_8	84	16	100	16					

and it favours the tasks with *larger value density* during overloads. Let the task request sequence be

$$S = \{\tau_1, \tau_2\}$$

with its parameters as specified in Table 4.2.

At *time*=0, τ_1 arrives and gets service. At *time*=1, τ_2 arrives and the system is overloaded. Algorithm A favours the task τ_1 which has the larger value density. Hence, τ_2 is rejected and is lost. The total value obtained by A is 3. On the other hand, the total value obtained by a clairvoyant algorithm can be 100 (v_2). The performance ratio is

$$\frac{V_A(S)}{V_{CA}(S)} = \frac{3}{100}$$

If the computation time, deadline and the value of τ_2 increase at the same rate, the ratio between $V_A(S)$ and $V_{CA}(S)$ goes to zero.

Second overload example: Once again for a single processor system, let A use EDF when the system is underloaded and assume that it favours the task with the *larger value* during overloads. Let the task request sequence be

$$S = \{\tau_1, \tau_1', \tau_2, \tau_2', \tau_3, \tau_3', \tau_4, \tau_4', \tau_5, \tau_5', \tau_6, \tau_6', \tau_7, \tau_7', \tau_8, \}$$

with its parameters as specified in Table 4.3.

Notice that the value density of all the tasks is 1. The CA schedule is

$$(\tau_1', \tau_2', \tau_3', \tau_4', \tau_5', \tau_6', \tau_7', \tau_8)$$

giving a total value of 100. Algorithm A works as follows: τ_1 and τ_1' arrive at *time*=0 and τ_1 is given the processor. τ_1' is discarded because A favours the larger valued task during

overload. (*A* has no information that τ_2 will arrive, otherwise it would have chosen τ'_1.)
At *time*=9, τ_2 and τ'_2 arrive and the system is overloaded again: τ_2 gets the processor
because it is the task with the largest value in the current task set. This pattern continues
until τ_8 arrives at *time*=84. The current running task τ_7 has the same value as τ_8 and
algorithm *A* does not make the switch. The total value obtained by *A* is 16 because only
τ_8 meets its deadline and all other tasks are lost. The performance ratio is

$$\frac{V_A(S)}{V_{CA}(S)} = \frac{16}{100}$$

A task pattern can be constructed in a similar way to give a task arrival sequence for an
arbitrary number of tasks for which the ratio between $V_A(S)$ and $V_{CA}(S)$ goes to zero.

These examples demonstrate a phenomenon that is not uncommon in on-line scheduling: an on-line algorithm will at times unavoidably make the wrong decision because it
lacks future knowledge and, in the worst case, this can reduce the value of the result to
zero.

There is no optimal algorithm for on-line scheduling to maximize the total task value,
so attention has turned to a new, worst-case bound method, competitiveness analysis,
which provides very good insight into the design of best-effort scheduling algorithms.
To evaluate a particular on-line scheduling algorithm, the worst case of a scheduling
algorithm is compared with all possible competing algorithms, including the idealized
clairvoyant algorithm. The results of such analysis can be useful in handling overloads
effectively.

4.4.2   Competitiveness analysis of best-effort approaches

Assume that tasks are aperiodic, independent and pre-emptable without penalty (it helps
to calculate the bound, though this may not be a realistic value). In a multi-processor
system, a pre-empted task can be resumed on any available processor. Assume that the
system has no information about the tasks before they arrive.

The *lower bound*, B_A, of an on-line scheduling *algorithm*, *A*, is defined as

$$\frac{V_A(S)}{V_{CA}(S)} \geq B_A, \quad \text{for all } S$$

where $B_A \in [0, 1]$ because $\forall S \cdot V_A(S) \leq V_{CA}(S)$

The *upper bound*, *B*, is defined as

$$B \geq B_A, \quad \text{for all } A$$

A bound is *tight* if it can be reached.

Suppose a task has a value equal to its execution time when it completes successfully
and no value otherwise. It is known that no dynamic scheduling algorithm can guarantee
a cumulative value greater than 0.25 of the value obtainable by a clairvoyant algorithm.

(In fact, for an algorithm that always sheds the lowest valued task upon an overload, this ratio can be as low as zero.) Thus, in the worst case, an on-line algorithm is only able to complete 0.25 of the work completed by a clairvoyant algorithm and, in fact, such an algorithm can be constructed, showing the bound to be tight.

This result can be extended to cases in which tasks have different value densities. Let γ be the ratio of the highest and lowest value densities of tasks. The upper bound for the on-line scheduling is $1/(\gamma + 1 + 2\sqrt{\gamma})$. As a special case, if γ is 1, the upper bound is 0.25, which is the result mentioned above, and if γ is 2, the upper bound is 1/5.828.

With two processors, the upper bound is 0.5 and is tight when all the tasks have the same value density and zero laxity. Thus, the upper bound doubles and, for the worst case, is twice the value obtained from two separate single processor systems. For a real-time system designer, this can provide an important reason for choosing a two processor system instead of a single processor system.

4.5 Dynamic planning-based approaches

Dynamic planning combines the flexibility of dynamic scheduling with the predictability offered by feasibility checking. When a task arrives, an attempt is made to *guarantee* the task by constructing a plan for task execution by which all previously guaranteed tasks continue to meet their timing constraints. A task is guaranteed subject to a set of assumptions, for example about its worst-case execution time and resource needs, and the nature of the faults in the system. If these assumptions hold, once a task is guaranteed it *will* meet its timing requirements. Thus, predictability is checked with each arrival.

If the attempt to guarantee fails, the task is not feasible and a *timing fault* is forecast. If this is known sufficiently ahead of the deadline, there may be time to take alternative action. For example, it may be possible to trade off quality for timeliness by attempting to schedule an alternative task which has a shorter computation time or fewer resource needs. In a distributed system, it may be possible to transfer the task to a less-loaded node.

If a node with guaranteed tasks fails, the guarantees cease to hold. For a guarantee to hold in spite of node failures, a task must be guaranteed on multiple nodes and we shall discuss this later.

4.5.1 Algorithms for dynamic planning

A dynamic planning algorithm attempts to construct a feasible schedule for a given set of tasks. This can be viewed as a search for a feasible schedule in a tree in which the leaves represent schedules, of which some are feasible. The root is the empty schedule. An internal node is a partial schedule for a task set with one more task than that represented by its parent. Given the NP-completeness of the scheduling problem, it would serve little purpose to search exhaustively for a feasible schedule. So the priority *Pr* of each task is used to direct scheduling choices along the most likely path.

The basic algorithm attempts to schedule a task τ_i non-pre-emptively, given its arrival time AT_i, deadline D_i or period T_i, worst-case computation time C_i and resource requirements $\{RR_i\}$. A task uses a resource R_j either in shared mode or in exclusive mode and holds a requested resource as long as it executes. The algorithm computes the earliest start time, EST_i, at which task τ_i can begin execution after accounting for resource contention among tasks. Given a partial schedule, the earliest time EAT_j at which resource R_j is available can be determined. Then the earliest time that a task τ_i that is yet to be scheduled can begin execution is

$$EST_i = Max(AT_i, EAT_i^u)$$

where u is either s for 'shared' or e for 'exclusive' mode.

The heuristic scheduling algorithm starts at the root of the search tree and repeatedly tries to extend the schedule (with one more task) by moving to one of the vertices at the next level in the search tree until a full feasible schedule is derived. At each level of the search, the priority can be computed for all the tasks that remain to be scheduled. This is a

$$n + (n-1) + \ldots + 2 = O(n^2)$$

search algorithm, where n is the number of tasks in the set. The complexity can be reduced to $O(n)$ if only the k tasks that remain to be scheduled at each level of search are considered. In both cases, the task with the highest priority is selected to extend the current schedule.

While extending the partial schedule at each level of search, the algorithm determines whether the current partial schedule is *strongly feasible* or not. A partial feasible schedule is said to be *strongly feasible* if *all* the schedules obtained by extending this current schedule with any one of the remaining tasks are also feasible. Thus, if a partial feasible schedule is found not to be *strongly feasible* because, say, task τ misses its deadline when the current task set is extended by τ, then it is appropriate to stop the search since none of the future extensions involving task τ will meet its deadline. In this case, a set of tasks cannot be scheduled given the current partial schedule. (In the terminology of branch-and-bound techniques, the search path represented by the current partial schedule is *bounded* since it will not lead to a feasible complete schedule.)

However, it is possible to backtrack to continue the search even after a non-strongly feasible schedule is found. Backtracking is done by discarding the current partial schedule, returning to the previous partial schedule and extending it with a different task, e.g. the task with the *second* highest priority. When backtracking is used, the overheads can be restricted either by restricting the maximum number of possible backtracks or the total number of re-evaluations of priorities.

The algorithm starts with an empty partial schedule and at each step determines whether the current partial schedule is strongly feasible and, if so, extends the current partial schedule by one task. The following variables are used:

- *TR*, the tasks that remain to be scheduled, in order of increasing deadline,

```
TR := task set to be scheduled;
partial schedule := empty; Result := Success;

while TR ≠ empty ∧ Result ≠ Failure loop
if   more than N_TR tasks in TR
 then   TC := first N_TR tasks in TR
else   TC := TR end if
 EST calculation:
  for each task τ_i in TR compute EST_i;
 Priority value generation:
  for each task τ_i in TR compute Pr(τ_i);
 Task selection:
  find task min_τ_i with highest priority in TC;
 Update partial schedule or backtrack:
 if   (partial schedule ⊕min_τ_i) is feasible and strongly feasible
  partial schedule := (partial schedule ⊕min_τ_i);
  TR := TR ⊖ min_T;
 elseif  backtracking is allowed and possible
  backtrack to a previous partial schedule;
 else Result:=Failure;
 endif;
end loop

where ⊕, ⊖ add and remove respectively a task from a schedule
```

Figure 4.3 Basic guarantee algorithm

- $\mathcal{N}(TR)$, the number of tasks in TR,
- $\mathcal{M}(TR)$, the maximum number of tasks considered by each step of scheduling,
- N_{TR}, the actual number of tasks in TR considered at each step of scheduling, where $N_{TR} = \mathcal{M}(TR)$, if $\mathcal{N}(TR) \geq \mathcal{M}(TR)$, $N_{TR} = \mathcal{N}(TR)$, otherwise, and
- TC, the first N_{TR} tasks in TR.

When attempting to extend the partial schedule by one task:

1. strong-feasibility is determined with respect to tasks in TC,
2. if the partial schedule is strongly feasible, then the highest priority task is chosen to extend the current schedule.

After a task τ_i is selected to extend the current partial schedule, its Scheduled Start Time SST_i is equal to EST_i.

Given that only N_{TR} tasks are considered at each step, the complexity is $O(N \times \mathcal{M}(TR))$ for a task set of size N. If $\mathcal{M}(TR)$ is constant (in practice it will be small when compared to N), the complexity is linearly proportional to N.

Figure 4.3 outlines the structure of the basic guarantee algorithm. It can be seen that the algorithm uses only priority-based selection at each step of the search. This means that it may leave some resources idle and, in order to reduce such idle times, while still being driven by task priorities, the algorithm can be extended to select the next task and to keep a specified minimum number of resources busy whenever possible.

We now consider the extensions necessary to deal with periodic tasks, tasks that have fault-tolerance requirements, tasks with different importance levels and tasks with precedence constraints.

Periodic tasks

There are several ways of guaranteeing periodic tasks when they are executed together with non-periodic tasks. Assume that when a periodic task is guaranteed, every release of the task is guaranteed.

Consider a system with only periodic tasks. A schedule can be constructed using the basic planning algorithm; given n periodic tasks with periods $T_1, \ldots, T_n$, the length of the schedule is $LCM(T_1, \ldots, T_n)$. The earliest start time of the jth release of the ith task is $(j-1) \times T_i$ and its deadline is $j \times T_i$. That is, assume that the deadline of a periodic task is the same as its period.

If a periodic task arrives dynamically, an attempt can be made to construct a new schedule. The new task is guaranteed if the attempt succeeds.

Suppose there are periodic *and* non-periodic tasks in the system. If the resources needed by the two sets of tasks are disjoint, then the processors in the system can be partitioned, with one set used for the periodic tasks. The remaining processors are used for non-periodic tasks guaranteed using the dynamic planning algorithm.

If, however, periodic and non-periodic tasks need common resources, a more complicated scheme is needed. If a periodic task arrives in a system consisting of previously guaranteed periodic and non-periodic tasks, an attempt is made to construct a new schedule: if the attempt fails, the new task is not guaranteed and its introduction has to be delayed until either the guaranteed non-periodic tasks complete or its introduction does not affect the remaining guaranteed tasks.

Suppose a new non-periodic task arrives. Given a schedule for periodic tasks, the new task can be guaranteed if there is sufficient time in the idle slots of the schedule. Alternatively, applying the dynamic guarantee scheme, a non-periodic task can be guaranteed if all releases of the periodic tasks and all previously guaranteed non-periodic tasks can also be guaranteed.

Tasks with fault-tolerance requirements

If guarantees are required in spite of the possibility of node failures, they must be provided on multiple nodes. Specifically, if a task is non-periodic and does not share resources with other tasks, or if it is a release of a periodic task and shares resources only with other releases of the same task, then guaranteed execution with respect to t fail-stop node failures can be achieved by guaranteeing the execution of the task at $t+1$ nodes.

When a task does not share resources, the following scheme reduces the overheads of executing its $t+1$ copies: the start times of its copies are staggered such that the ith copy is guaranteed for a start time of

$$s+(i-1)c$$

and a deadline of

$$d - (t + 1 - i)c$$

where s and d are the start time and deadline of the task and c is the communication delay between nodes. As few task copies as possible should be used, so the first copy to complete successfully informs all the others and the resources and time allocated to the other copies can be reclaimed (see Section 4.6). This assumes that all interactions with the environment take place when a copy completes successfully. Obviously, the scheme is applicable only when communication delays and task computation times are small compared to task deadlines.

Tasks with different levels of importance
The deadline and importance of a task are sometimes at conflict: tasks with very short deadlines might be less important than tasks with longer deadlines. For example, reading from a rotating disk may have a relatively short deadline but low importance as a missed disk read can be retried on the next disk revolution. This makes it more difficult to choose the next task to be executed. The question of guarantees may also have to be refined when tasks with differing importance values are present. Suppose a task has been guaranteed and a task of higher importance arrives. It may be that the new task can be guaranteed only if the guarantee of the task of lower importance is withdrawn. Thus the once-guaranteed–always-guaranteed strategy may mean that the new task is not guaranteed even though it has higher importance.

Assume, instead, that tasks are handled using an *acceptance*, rather than the *guarantee* policy. This allows the rejection of previously accepted tasks, while the guarantee policy does not: the acceptance does not imply a guarantee but is conditional upon the non-arrival of tasks of higher importance which conflict with it. In most applications, meeting the deadlines of tasks of higher importance takes precedence over guarantees to tasks of lower importance. It would then be desirable that a task is not guaranteed until it is clear that the guarantee will not be withdrawn.

A compromise approach is to allow an acceptance to be withdrawn until the guarantee deadline but not later. This gives some leeway to the system scheduler and allows a transaction to try alternatives in case one task is not accepted.

There are different ways to choose tasks for rejection so that a new task can be accepted:

1. remove the tasks of lower importance, one at a time and in order from low to high importance, or
2. remove tasks of lower importance, starting with tasks with the largest deadline,

until sufficient resources are released.

Tasks with precedence constraints
Precedence constraints between tasks are used to model end-to-end timing constraints both for a single node and across nodes (see Chapter 3). Let a task group be a collection

of simple tasks with precedence constraints and a single deadline. Each task acquires resources before it begins, and releases them upon completion. Assume that when a task group is invoked, the worst-case computation time and resource requirements of each task can be determined. The first step is to find the set of 'eligible' tasks, i.e those whose ancestors are all in the partial schedule, and then to apply the basic planning algorithm to the set of eligible tasks. Priorities are computed only for tasks whose ancestors have been scheduled.

4.5.2 Timing of the planning

As the number of tasks increases, so does the cost of planning and there is less time available for planning. This is the main reason for the poor performance of planning schemes during overloads. So when a system overload is anticipated, use of a method that controls scheduling overheads is essential. Thus, it is important to address the issue of *when* to plan the execution of a newly arrived task. Two simple approaches are:

1. When a task arrives, attempt to plan its execution along with previously scheduled tasks: this is *scheduling-at-arrival-time* and all tasks that have not yet executed are considered for planning when a new task arrives.
2. Postpone the feasibility check until a task is chosen for execution: this is *scheduling-at-dispatch-time* and can be done very quickly for non-pre-emptive task execution by checking whether the new task will finish by its deadline.

The second approach is less flexible and announces task rejection very late. Consequently, it does not provide sufficient lead time for considering alternative actions when a task cannot meet its timing-constraints. Both avoid resource wastage as a task does not begin execution unless it is known that it will complete before its deadline.

To minimize scheduling overheads while giving enough lead time to choose alternatives, instead of scheduling tasks when they arrive or when they are dispatched, they should be scheduled somewhere in between – at the most opportune time. If they can be scheduled at some *punctual point*, this can limit the number of tasks to be considered for scheduling and avoids unnecessary scheduling (or rescheduling) of tasks that have no effect on the order of tasks early in the schedule.

Choice of the punctual point must take into account the fact that the larger the mean laxity and the higher the load, the more tasks are ready to run. The increasing number of tasks imposes growing scheduling overheads for all except a scheduler with constant overheads. The punctual point is the minimum laxity value, i.e. the value to which a task's laxity must drop before it becomes eligible for scheduling. In other words, the guarantee of a task with laxity larger than the punctual point is postponed *at most* until its laxity reaches the punctual point. Of course, if the system is empty a task becomes eligible for scheduling by default. By postponing scheduling decisions, the number of tasks scheduled at any time is kept under control, reducing the scheduling overheads and potentially improving the overall performance.

The main benefit of scheduling using punctual points is the reduced scheduling over-heads when compared to scheduling at arrival time. This is due to the smaller number of relevant tasks (the tasks with laxities smaller than or equal to the punctual point) that are scheduled at any given time. Clearly, when the computational complexity of a schedul-ing algorithm is higher than the complexity of maintaining the list of relevant tasks, the separation into relevant/irrelevant tasks reduces the overall scheduling cost; that is, the scheduling becomes more efficient.

Scheduling at the opportune time ensures that a scheduling decision is made earlier than when scheduling at dispatch time, but not necessarily as early as when scheduling at arrival time. Consequently, the lead time for alternative actions is adjustable and is based on design and run-time parameters. Scheduling at an opportune time (i.e. at the punctual point) is more flexible, more effective and more tolerant of timing errors than scheduling at dispatch time, primarily due to its early warning characteristics. Hence, ways of finding the punctual point for different system characteristics are required.

Consider the following scheme for tasks with deadlines that are held on a dispatch queue, $Q_1(n)$, maintained in minimum laxity order, and a variant of the *FCFS* queue. When a task arrives, its laxity is compared with that of the n tasks in the queue $Q_1(n)$ and the task with the largest laxity is placed at the end of the *FCFS* queue. When a task in Q_1 is executed, the first task on the *FCFS* queue is transferred to Q_1.

Analysis shows that performance to within 5% of the optimal LLF algorithm is achieved for even small values of n.

A more experimental way to limit the number of scheduled tasks is to have a *Hit* queue and a *Miss* queue: the number of scheduled tasks in the *Hit* queue is continuously ad-justed according to the ratio of tasks that complete on time (the 'hit' ratio). This method is adaptive, handles deadlines and values and is easy to implement. However, it does not define a punctual point.

The weakness of both these approaches is the lack of analytical methods to adjust the number of scheduled tasks. The parameters that control the number of schedulable tasks must be obtained through simulation and a newly arrived task can miss its deadline before it gets considered for execution. By contrast, if the punctual point is derived analytically, it can be ensured that every task that arrives will be considered for execution.

The number of schedulable tasks must be controlled using timing-constraints, rather than by explicitly limiting the number of schedulable tasks; this ensures that every task is considered for scheduling when its laxity reaches the most opportune moment, the punc-tual point. The approach is especially beneficial for systems where tasks have widely differing values, and rejecting a task without considering it for scheduling might result in a large value loss, something that can happen easily when the number of schedulable tasks is fixed.

Finally, the features of a 'well-timed scheduling framework' are summarized below:

- Newly arrived tasks are classified as *relevant* or *irrelevant*, depending on their lax-ity.
- Irrelevant tasks are stored in a *D*-queue (the delay queue), where they are delayed until their laxity becomes equal to the punctual point, at which time they become

relevant.
- Relevant tasks are stored in an *S*-pool (the scheduling pool) as tasks eligible for immediate scheduling.
- When a task is put into the *S*-pool, a feasibility check is performed; if this is satisfied, it is transferred into the current feasible schedule.

It is important to observe that apart from reducing the scheduling cost, the separation of relevant and irrelevant tasks also contributes to reducing the scheduling overheads due to queue handling operations.

4.6   Practical considerations in dynamic scheduling

4.6.1   Implementing best-effort scheduling

The implementation mechanisms needed here are similar to those found in priority-based non-real-time systems, the primary difference being the way in which priorities are assigned.

Ready tasks are maintained in a ready queue according to their priority order. The set of tasks waiting for a resource (other than a processor) are placed in a wait queue. When a task completes execution or when it releases a resource, one or more tasks may move from the wait queue to the ready queue. This, or the arrival of a high priority task, may cause the currently running task to be pre-empted. This is because these events can lead to changes in the relative priorities of tasks and task priorities must be re-evaluated and the ready queue re-ordered according to the new priorities. Dispatching involves pre-emption, context switching and possibly placing the pre-empted task back in the ready queue, according to its priority, for future resumption.

4.6.2   Implementing planning-based scheduling

Here there are two main considerations: feasibility checking and schedule construction. In a multi-processor system, feasibility checking and dispatching can be done independently, allowing these system functions to run in parallel. The dispatcher works with a set of tasks that have been previously guaranteed to meet their deadlines, and feasibility checking is done on the set of currently guaranteed tasks plus any newly invoked tasks.

Feasibility checking and schedule construction
One of the crucial issues in dynamic scheduling is the cost of scheduling: the more time that is spent on scheduling the less there is for task executions.

In a single-processor system, feasibility checking and task executions compete for processing time. If feasibility checking is delayed, there is less benefit from the early warning feature. However, if feasibility checking is performed immediately after a task arrives, this may lead to guaranteed tasks missing their deadlines. Thus, when tasks are guaranteed, some time must be set aside for scheduling-related work and a good balance must be struck depending on task arrival rates and task characteristics such as computation times.

One way is to provide for the periodic execution of the scheduler. Whenever invoked, the scheduler will attempt to guarantee all pending tasks. In addition, if needed, the scheduler could be invoked sporadically whenever these extra invocations will affect neither guaranteed tasks nor the minimum guaranteed periodic rate of other system tasks.

Another alternative, applicable to multi-processor systems, is to designate a 'scheduling' processor whose sole responsibility is to deal with feasibility checking and schedule construction. Guaranteed tasks are executed on the remaining 'application' processors. In this case, feasibility checking can be done concurrently with task execution. Recall that a task is guaranteed as long as it can be executed to meet its deadline and the deadlines of previously guaranteed tasks remain guaranteed. Guaranteeing a new task might require re-scheduling of previously guaranteed tasks and so care must be taken to ensure that currently running tasks will not be re-scheduled.

These considerations suggest that scheduling costs should be computed based on the total number of tasks in the schedule plus the newly arrived tasks, the complexity of the scheduling algorithm and the cost of scheduling one task. Tasks with scheduled start times before the current time plus the scheduling cost are not considered for rescheduling; the remaining tasks are candidates for re-scheduling to accommodate new tasks.

Dispatching

Planning-based schedulers typically use non-pre-emptive schedules. Dispatching depends on whether the tasks are independent and whether there are resource constraints.

If the tasks are independent and have no resource constraints, dispatching can be extremely simple: the task to be executed next is the next task in the schedule, and this task can always be executed immediately even if its scheduled start time has not arrived.

On the other hand, precedence constraints and resource constraints may increase the complexity of dispatching. If tasks have resource or precedence constraints, the dispatching process must take these into account. When the actual computation time of a task differs from its worst-case computation time in a non-pre-emptive multi-processor schedule with resource constraints, run-time anomalies may occur, causing some of the scheduled tasks to miss their deadlines. There are two possible kinds of dispatcher:

1. Dispatch tasks exactly according to the given schedule. In this case, upon the completion of one task, the dispatcher may not be able to dispatch another task immediately because idle time intervals may have been inserted by the scheduler to conform to the precedence constraints or resource constraints. One way to construct a correct dispatcher is to use a hardware (count down) timer in order to enforce the start time constraint.

2. Dispatch tasks taking into consideration the fact that, given the variance in task execution times, some tasks will complete earlier than expected. The dispatcher tries to reclaim the time left by early completion and uses it to execute other tasks.

Clearly, non-real-time tasks can be executed in the idle time slots. More valuable is an approach that improves the guarantees of tasks that have time-constraints. Several issues must be considered to achieve this. Resource reclaiming algorithms used in systems that perform dynamic planning-based scheduling must maintain the feasibility of guaranteed tasks, must have low overheads, as a resource reclaiming algorithm is invoked whenever a task finishes, and must have costs that are independent of the number of tasks in the schedule. They must also be effective in improving the performance of the system.

Complete rescheduling of all remaining tasks is an available option, but, given the complexity of scheduling, it is usually expensive and ineffective.

A feasible multi-processor schedule provides task ordering information that is *sufficient* to guarantee the timing and resource requirements of tasks in the schedule. If two tasks overlap in time on different processors in a schedule, then it can be concluded that no matter which of them is dispatched first at run-time, the deadline of the other will not be affected. On the other hand, if two tasks do not overlap in time, the same conclusion cannot be drawn without re-examining resource constraints or without total re-scheduling.

Assume each task τ_i is assigned a scheduled start time SST_i and a scheduled finish time SFT_i in the given feasible schedule. Resource reclaiming algorithms use this information to perform *local* optimization at run-time, while preserving the correct relative ordering among the scheduled tasks and ensuring the original guarantees. This local optimization is accomplished by reasoning only about the first task scheduled to execute on each of the m processors, and there is no need to examine the availability of the resources needed in order to dispatch a task when reclaiming occurs. Thus, the complexity of the algorithm is independent of the number of tasks in the schedule and depends only on the number of processors.

We now describe the basic reclaiming algorithm:

1. Upon completion of a task, the dispatcher identifies idle intervals on all processors and resources by computing a function

    $$reclaimable\_\delta = min(SST_i) - current\_time$$

    where SST_i is the scheduled start time of the current first task for processor i in the schedule, $1 \leq i \leq m$. The complexity of this is $O(m)$. A positive value of $reclaimable\_\delta$ indicates the length of the idle period. The cumulative value of these idle periods is stored in *total reclaimable time*.

2. Compute

    $$actual\ start\ time = SST_i - total\ reclaimable\ time$$

    for the next task τ_i scheduled for a processor; the task is dispatched if its *actual start time* equals the current time.

Thus the complexity of the basic version is: $O(m) + m \times O(1) = O(m)$.

The Early Start algorithm differs from the basic version by replacing Step 2 with the following:

Compute the Boolean function

$$can\_start\_early = SST_i < SFT_j, 1 \leq j \leq m, i \neq j$$

where SST_i is the scheduled start time of the first task on processor i, SFT_j is the scheduled finish time of the first task on processor j and m is the number of processors.

This function identifies parallelism between the first task on processor i and the first tasks on all other processors. It has a complexity of $O(m)$. If *can_start_early* is true the first task is dispatched and otherwise the *actual start time* is computed as in the basic version.

The second step of the algorithm must be executed for all currently idle processors whenever a positive value of *reclaimable time* is obtained in the first step. Thus, Early Start has a complexity of $O(m) + m \times O(m) = O(m^2)$.

Though Early Start has a higher run-time cost, experimental studies show that it performs much better than the basic version for most parameter settings. Only when the resource conflict probability is very high, or when the system is either extremely overloaded or very lightly loaded, does the basic version demonstrate the same effectiveness.

One of the positive outcomes of reclaiming is that it is possible to be pessimistic about the computation times of tasks. This is because even if the dynamic guarantees are provided with respect to worst-case computation times, since any unused time is reclaimed, the negative effects of pessimism are considerably reduced.

4.7 Historical background

A number of books on scheduling theory (Coffman, 1976; Blazewicz *et al.*, 1986) provide excellent general background. Surveys of work on real-time task scheduling can be found in Stankovic and Ramamritham (1988; 1993).

Liu and Layland (1973) focused on the problem of scheduling periodic tasks on a single processor and proposed two pre-emptive algorithms. In addition to the rate-monotonic algorithm, described in Chapters 2 and 3, they analyzed the earliest-deadline-first dynamic priority assignment algorithm.

Mok and Dertouzos (1978) and Dertouzos and Mok (1989) studied multi-processor on-line scheduling of real-time tasks, noting that in most real-world circumstances, optimal dynamic algorithms do not exist (Hong & Leung, 1988; Chetto & Chetto, 1989; Mok, 1983). Dynamic algorithms that do not *a priori* know the arrival times, deadlines and computation times of tasks cannot guarantee optimal performance (Dertouzos & Mok, 1989).

Different types of heuristic for best-effort algorithms are examined in Locke (1985), including shortest-processing-time-first, earliest-deadline-first, least-laxity-first, first-come-first-served, an algorithm that randomly chooses the next task to execute and one that fixes a task's priority to be its highest possible value. In addition to the standard highest-priority-first scheduling algorithm, an algorithm which discards tasks with low value density when an overload is considered likely is also evaluated. As expected, the new algorithm improves performance under overloads. Dealing with overheads, in general, is a complex problem and solutions are still in their infancy (Baruah *et al.*, 1992; Baruah & Rosier, 1991; Wang, 1993).

With deadline and resource constraints added to tasks, many heuristic approaches have been developed for dynamic planning-based scheduling: see e.g. Ramamritham and Stankovic (1984), Ramamritham *et al.* (1990), Stankovic and Ramamritham (1991), Zhao and Ramamritham (1987), Zhao *et al.* (1987a; 1987b). Extensive simulation studies of the heuristics show that those that combine deadline and resource requirements work well (Zhao & Ramamritham, 1987; Zhao *et al.*, 1987b) according to the performance criterion of maximizing the number of guaranteed tasks. Such an algorithm has been implemented as part of the Spring Kernel (Stankovic & Ramamritham, 1991). Algorithms that attempt to maximize the value of tasks that meet their deadlines can be found in Biyabani *et al.* (1988.), Butazzo and Stankovic (1993), Locke (1985) and Zlokapa (1993).

Well-timed scheduling and the analytical derivation of punctual points applicable to planning-based scheduling for simple task models are discussed in Zlokapa (1993). This tries to optimize the number of tasks considered for scheduling. Approaches using simulation to bound the number of scheduled tasks are presented in Goli *et al.* (1990) and Hong *et al.* (1989); both papers examine the performance of variants of the minimum-laxity-first scheduling policy – the policy that has been shown to be optimal with respect to minimizing the long-term, steady-state percentage of tasks that miss their deadlines, over all work-conserving non-pre-emptive policies (Panwar & Towsley, 1988; Panwar *et al.*, 1988). Details of resource reclaiming algorithms as well as their performance implications are presented in Shen *et al.* (1993).

Several schemes for dynamic distributed scheduling have been reported in the literature (Ramamritham *et al.*, 1989; Blake & Schwan, 1991; Ramamritham & Stankovic, 1984; Stankovic *et al.*, 1985). A detailed discussion of scheduling imprecise computations appears in Liu *et al.* (1991; 1994a); they allow the system to trade quality for the purpose of achieving timeliness.

Though many real-time operating systems assign static priorities to periodic tasks, for the remaining tasks they usually employ best-effort scheduling (Furht *et al.*, 1991; Ready, 1986; Holmes *et al.*, 1987; Jensen, 1992). Experimental operating systems using planning-based scheduling include Spring (Stankovic & Ramamritham, 1991), Maruti (Gudmundsson *et al.*, 1992) and Chaos (Schwan *et al.*, 1990).

4.8   Further work

A comprehensive and integrated set of solutions for the real-time scheduling of complex systems is still being sought. There are some important open research questions:

- What are good sets of integrated scheduling policies that span processor scheduling, input/output scheduling, communication needs and resource allocation?

- Can a single sophisticated scheduling algorithm handle complex task sets cost effectively, or should tasks be partitioned into equivalence classes with algorithms tailored to each class? How would such a set of algorithms interact?
- What type of predictability is possible for distributed real-time computation? Can a comprehensive scheduling approach that supports predictable and analyzable distributed real-time systems be developed?
- How can task importance, computation time, tightness of deadline and fault requirements be traded off to maximize value in the system? What are the roles of the scheduling algorithms in this analysis?
- What is the impact of off-line allocation policies on dynamic on-line scheduling?
- Can worst-case performance bounds be determined for the various algorithms; can these bounds provide insight into practical techniques for avoiding the worst-case performance at run-time?

4.9 Exercises

Exercise 4.1 Why is dynamic scheduling required in many real-time applications?

Exercise 4.2 What are the predictability properties of dynamic priority algorithms *vis-a-vis* static priority algorithms?

Exercise 4.3 Develop algorithms to translate a task group deadline into individual task deadlines.

Exercise 4.4 Develop programming language constructs to support the acceptance policy in place of the guarantee policy.

Exercise 4.5 Develop a guarantee version of the language construct that is used to specify start time constraints.

Exercise 4.6 What characterizes dynamic best-effort scheduling?

Exercise 4.7 What characterizes dynamic planning-based scheduling?

Exercise 4.8 How are task priorities used in (a) dynamic best-effort scheduling? (b) dynamic planning-based scheduling?

Exercise 4.9 Why do dynamic priority approaches incur higher overheads than static priority approaches?

Exercise 4.10 Which incurs higher overheads: dynamic best-effort scheduling or dynamic planning-based scheduling? Why? What are the ways in which these overheads can be reduced?

Exercise 4.11   What is the difference between the interruptions that occur when tasks communicate and when tasks are pre-empted?

Exercise 4.12   Is (Min_L + Min_S) a possible priority assignment policy? Explain the reasons for your answer.

Exercise 4.13   To reduce search time during planning-based scheduling it was suggested that the priority of at most a constant number of tasks be computed at each level of search. What factors influence the choice of this constant?

Exercise 4.14   For greedy scheduling, a limited form of list scheduling was suggested in which task computation times are considered such that priorities are not violated when a greedy policy is used. An alternative is to use a limited form of greed in which the algorithm tries to keep $x\%$ of each replicated resource busy. Develop these ideas into fully fledged scheduling algorithms. Will your algorithms help in keeping a certain number of processors in a multi-processor system busy?

Chapter 5

Assertional Specification and Verification

Jozef Hooman

Introduction

We now introduce a formal framework for the specification and verification of programs for embedded real-time systems. Such programs are often concurrent programs, or distributed programs, and the number of possible executions is so large that exhaustive testing is impossible. However, design faults in the programs can have disastrous consequences and the goal is to devise a formal method whose use will increase confidence in the correctness of the program.

The number of possible states of a complex system is usually exponential in the number of components. To deal with this 'state explosion', we use an *assertional* method of reasoning in which a set of states can be characterized by a single logical formula. Further, to reduce the complexity of the verification task, we use a method which is *compositional*: it allows reasoning about the specifications of components without considering details of their implementation. This makes it possible to consider a part of the system as a black box which is characterized by its specification.

Traditional Hoare logic allows the formulation of convenient and effective compositional rules for sequential composition and iteration in sequential programs. This logic is based on triples of the form $\{p\}$ S $\{q\}$, where p is the precondition, S the program and q the postcondition. We will show how similar triples can be used in a formalism for the specification and verification of distributed, real-time programs. This is achieved by extending the assertion language in which the precondition and the postcondition are expressed and by modifying the interpretation of the triples.

The functional behaviour of a program is expressed in terms of the values of program variables before and after the execution of the program. To express timing, a special variable *now* is added to represent time: placed in the precondition it denotes the starting time of the program; in the postcondition it denotes the termination time. The relation between the starting and completion times can then be used, for example to specify bounds on the execution time of a program. Also, the real-time interface of the program with the environment can be specified using primitives denoting the timing of observable events.

Traditional triples were restricted to expressing partial correctness properties of programs, i.e. properties of terminating computations. Partial correctness is a *safety* property, which means that it can be falsified in finite time. *Liveness* properties are also needed (e.g. to specify the progress of a computation, or its termination) and we shall describe a formalism in which safety and liveness properties can both be described. For example, 'termination within ten time units' and 'communication via channel *c* within 25 time units' are safety properties because they can be falsified after ten and 25 time units, respectively, but they also express the fact that something must happen. Similarly, the real-time safety property 'termination within ten time units' implies the liveness property 'termination'. The interpretation of triples has therefore been adapted to require the post-condition to hold for terminating and non-terminating computations. Combined with the timing primitives, this provides a framework in which liveness properties can be specified.

We shall first formulate a compositional proof system, i.e. a set of rules and axioms which allow a formal derivation of the modified triples. For each compound programming language construct (such as sequential composition and parallel composition) there will be a rule in which the specification of the construct can be deduced from specifications of its constituents (without any further information about the internal structure of these constituents). The proof system can then be used to verify design steps taken in the course of top-down program construction.

In general, the method proceeds according to the following steps.

1. Formulate the top-level requirements specification of the complete system, including the properties of continuous components:

2. Formalize the assumptions about the physical processes in the system.

3. Specify the control requirements in terms of continuous quantities.

4. Verify Step 3, i.e. show that the specifications of Steps 2 and 3 lead to the properties specified in Step 1.

5. Transform the control strategy (of Step 3) into a specification in terms of a discrete interface; this is usually done using formal specifications of sensors and actuators.

6. Implement the discrete specification of Step 5 using a real-time programming language.

5.1   Basic framework

We begin by considering only the parallel composition of processes, without taking account of their implementation (which may be in hardware or in software). We define the semantic model used to describe the behaviour of real-time processes and then present a formalism to specify their properties.

5.1.1 Parallel processes

Assume that a number of processes are composed in parallel using the operator $\|$. Certain objects (e.g. channels, variables, or physical quantities) of a process can be observed by its parallel environment.

Let $obs(P)$ be the set of (representations of) observable objects of process P representing the interface of P. For instance, if P communicates through channels, then $obs(P)$ contains the names of these channels, and if P uses shared variables, then the names of these variables are included in $obs(P)$. Define

$$obs(P_1 \| P_2) = obs(P_1) \cup obs(P_2)$$

The actions of a process that affect its interface are called *observable actions* and the occurrence of an observable action is an *observable event*.

Process P will also have local objects (e.g. local variables) and $loc(P)$ denotes the set of objects of P that are not observable by other parallel processes. For $P_1 \| P_2$ we assume that $loc(P_1) \cap loc(P_2) = \emptyset$. Local variables range over a value domain VAL which is the set of real numbers $\mathbf{R}$.

Reasoning about the real-time behaviour of parallel processes needs information about the progress of actions, i.e. how long the execution of a statement can be postponed. For example, the execution time of the program $x := 0 \| y := 1$ depends on the allocation of processes to processors. Assuming that assignment ':=' takes one time unit, the program $x := 0 \| y := 1$ terminates after one time unit if each process $x := 0$ and $y := 1$ has its own processor and can execute independently. However, if the two processes are executed on a single processor, the program will take at least two time units, since then the processes have to be scheduled in some order. Thus the real-time behaviour of a concurrent program will depend on the number of available processors and the way in which they are allocated to processes. We shall make the *maximal parallelism* assumption that each process has its own processor and local actions are executed as soon as possible.

5.1.2 Semantic model

The timing behaviour of a program is described from the viewpoint of an external observer with a clock. Thus, although components of a system may have local clocks, the observable behaviour of the system is described in terms of a single, conceptual, global clock. This global time is not part of the distributed system and it does not impose any synchronization upon processes. The real-time semantics of programs is defined using a function which assigns a set of records to each point of time to represent the observable events that are taking place at that time.

We use a dense time domain *TIME*: i.e. between any pair of elements of *TIME* there is an intermediate value, also in *TIME*. Such a time domain allows modelling events that are arbitrarily close to each other; dense time is also suitable for the description of *hybrid systems* which interact with an environment that has a time-continuous nature (e.g. the mine pump controller).

Let the non-negative reals be taken as the time domain: $TIME = \{\tau \in \mathbf{R} \mid \tau \geq 0\}$. The real-time behaviour of a process P is described using the following components:

- the initial state (i.e. the values of the local objects at the start of the execution) and the starting time of P,
- the timed occurrence of the observable actions of P, and
- if P terminates, the final state (i.e. the values of the local objects at termination) and the termination time of P (or ∞, if P does not terminate).

The observed real-time behaviour is modelled by a *timed occurrence function*, ρ, which assigns to each point of time a set of records representing the observable events occurring at that time. The starting and termination times of programs are defined using a special variable *now*. Then a *state* σ assigns a value from $TIME \cup \{\infty\}$ to the variable *now* and a value to each local object.

Example 5.1 Consider a system in which we can observe read and write actions on a shared variable x and send and receive actions on two channels c and d. Then part of an occurrence function ρ of this system might be given by

$$\rho(3.14)= \{send(c,0), read(x,5)\}$$
$$\rho(5.1) = \{rec(c,0)\}$$
$$\rho(6) = \emptyset$$
$$\rho(6.3) = \{write(x,7), send(c,2), send(d,3)\}$$
$$\rho(7.4) = \{rec(c,2)\}$$
$$\rho(9) = \{rec(d,3), write(x,9)\}$$

Of course this does not completely describe ρ because $TIME$ is a dense domain, but it shows the events at the moments 3.14, 5.1, 6, etc.

The semantics of a program P starting in a state σ_0 is denoted by $\mathcal{M}(P)(\sigma_0)$; it is a set of pairs of the form (σ, ρ), where σ is a state and ρ a timed occurrence function. $\sigma_0(x)$ gives the value of local object x at the start of the execution and $\sigma_0(now)$ represents the starting time. Consider a pair (σ, ρ) in $\mathcal{M}(P)(\sigma_0)$. If P terminates, σ represents the values of the local objects on termination and $\sigma(now)$ denotes the termination time. When P does not terminate, we define $\sigma(now) = \infty$ and $\sigma(x)$ is an arbitrary value for any $x \not\equiv now$.

Function ρ represents the observable behaviour of P during its execution. Thus, for $\sigma_0(now) \leq \tau < \sigma(now)$, $\rho(\tau)$ represents the observable events of the execution of P at τ. Outside this interval, the occurrence of actions is not restricted by the semantics of P, so arbitrary events may occur.

5.1.3   Specifications

Our specifications are based on traditional triples with some modifications: a slightly different notation is used and the terms 'assumption' and 'commitment' replace 'precondition' and 'postcondition'. Formulas have the structure $\langle\langle A \rangle\rangle \, P \, \langle\langle C \rangle\rangle$, where P is a process and A and C are the *assumption* and the *commitment* respectively.

Assertion A defines the values of local objects *at the start* of P, the *starting time* of P, and the *timed occurrence* of observable events.

Given assumption A, assertion C defines the commitment of P in terms of the values of the local objects *at termination*, if P terminates, the *termination time* (which is taken as ∞ if P does not terminate) and the *timed occurrence* of observable events.

Unlike the postcondition of a traditional triple, the commitment expresses properties of terminating and non-terminating computations. The addition of time makes it possible for the formalism to be used to express partial correctness and liveness properties.

The assertions A and C in a correctness formula $\langle\langle A \rangle\rangle \; P \; \langle\langle C \rangle\rangle$ are expressed in a first-order logic with the following primitives:

- Names denoting local objects, such as $x, y, \ldots$, ranging over *VAL*.
- Logical variables that are not affected by program execution: logical value variables v, v_0, v_1, ... range over *VAL* and logical time variables t, t_0, t_1, ... over $TIME \cup \{\infty\}$.
- A special variable *now*, ranging over $TIME \cup \{\infty\}$, refers to global time; an occurrence of *now* in assumption A represents the starting time of statement P and in commitment C it denotes the termination time (using $now = \infty$ for non-terminating computations).
- For observable action O and expression *exp* which yields a value in *TIME*, the boolean primitive $O@exp$ denotes that O occurs at time *exp*.

Example 5.2 Consider the system described in Example 5.1. We might use $write(x, 7)$ @6.3 to say that value 7 has been assigned to x at time 6.3 and $send(c, 0)@3.14$ to say that value 0 has been sent along channel c at time 3.14.

Let $loc(p)$ be the set of names of the local objects occurring in assertion p. Similarly, let $obs(p)$ denote the set of observables occurring in p. Time intervals will be defined as conventional intervals, for example

$$[t_0, t_1) = \{t \in TIME \mid t_0 \leq t < t_1\}$$

$$(t_0, t_1) = \{t \in TIME \mid t_0 < t < t_1\}$$

Let $\equiv$ denote syntactic equality. Given $P@t$ and a set (usually an interval) $I \subseteq TIME$,

$P \text{ during } I \equiv \forall t \in I : P@t$
$P \text{ in } I \quad \equiv \exists t \in I : P@t$
$(\neg P)@t \quad \equiv \neg(P@t)$, or simply $\neg P@t$ instead of $(\neg P)@t$

Thus, $\neg P \text{ during } I$ is equivalent to $(\neg P) \text{ during } I$ (and also to $\neg(P \text{ in } I)$).

For functions such as $f : TIME \rightarrow VAL$ we will often use these abbreviations for time-dependent predicates of the form $(f > v)@t$, $(f \leq v)@t$, which hold if $f(t) > v$, $f(t) \leq v$ respectively. Thus $(f < 5) \text{ during } [2, 7]$ holds if $f(t) < 5$, for all $t \in [2, 7]$.

The notation $p[exp/var]$ is used to represent the substitution of expression *exp* for each free occurrence of variable *var* in assertion p. We assume the usual properties of ∞. For instance, for all $t \in TIME$, $t < \infty$, $t + \infty = \infty + t = \infty - t = \infty$. Frequently, $\forall t_0, t_1 < \infty$ is used as an abbreviation for $\forall t_0 < \infty, \forall t_1 < \infty$.

Interpretation

Logical variables are interpreted using a logical variable environment γ, which is a mapping which assigns a value from VAL to each logical value variable and a value from $TIME \cup \{\infty\}$ to each logical time variable. The value of expression exp in an environment γ, a state σ and a mapping ρ is denoted by $\mathcal{V}(exp)(\sigma, \rho, \gamma)$. It is defined by induction on the structure of exp. A few illustrative cases are shown below:

$$\mathcal{V}(t)(\sigma, \rho, \gamma) = \gamma(t)$$
$$\mathcal{V}(now)(\sigma, \rho, \gamma) = \sigma(now)$$
$$\mathcal{V}(x)(\sigma, \rho, \gamma) = \sigma(x)$$
$$\mathcal{V}(exp_1 + exp_2)(\sigma, \rho, \gamma) = \mathcal{V}(exp_1)(\sigma, \rho, \gamma) + \mathcal{V}(exp_2)(\sigma, \rho, \gamma)$$

Similarly, we define inductively that an assertion p holds in a triple (σ, ρ, γ), denoted by $(\sigma, \rho, \gamma) \models p$. Two examples illustrate this:

$$(\sigma, \rho, \gamma) \models O@exp \text{ iff } O \in \rho(\mathcal{V}(exp)(\sigma, \rho, \gamma))$$
$$(\sigma, \rho, \gamma) \models p_1 \vee p_2 \text{ iff } (\sigma, \rho, \gamma) \models p_1 \text{ or } (\sigma, \rho, \gamma) \models p_2$$

Example 5.3 Consider the occurrence function ρ from Example 5.1. From this,

$$(\sigma, \rho, \gamma) \models write(x, 7)@6.3$$

$$(\sigma, \rho, \gamma) \models send(c, 0)@3.14$$

and if $\sigma(x) = 2$, then

$$(\sigma, \rho, \gamma) \models send(c, 0)@(x + 1.14)$$

Note that

$$(\sigma, \rho, \gamma) \models \neg(send(c, 2)@7.4)$$

and is also written as

$$(\sigma, \rho, \gamma) \models \neg send(c, 2)@7.4$$

To define the formal interpretation of a correctness formula $\langle\langle A \rangle\rangle \ P \ \langle\langle C \rangle\rangle$, observe that assumption A may refer to points in time after the starting time. Thus A may contain assumptions about the occurrence of actions *during* the execution of P. Therefore, the same occurrence function will interpret A and C. Further, between the start and the termination time of P, this occurrence function should correspond to the execution of P, as represented by the semantics of P.

Definition 5.1 (Validity) For a program P and assertions A and C, a correctness formula $\langle\langle A \rangle\rangle \ P \ \langle\langle C \rangle\rangle$ is *valid*, denoted by $\models \langle\langle A \rangle\rangle \ P \ \langle\langle C \rangle\rangle$, iff for any environment γ, any state $\sigma_0 \in STATE$, and any pair σ, ρ with $(\sigma, \rho) \in \mathcal{M}(P)(\sigma_0)$ we have

$$(\sigma_0, \rho, \gamma) \models A \text{ implies } (\sigma, \rho, \gamma) \models C$$

Examples of specifications

Program F is specified to start at time 6 in a state where local object x has the value 5, assuming that there is some observable action O at 3. The specification expresses the property that F terminates between times 15 and 23 in a state where x has the value $f(5)$. Further, the commitment asserts that O occurs at 3:

$$\langle\langle x = 5 \wedge now = 6 \wedge O@3 \rangle\rangle \ F \ \langle\langle x = f(5) \wedge 15 < now < 23 \wedge O@3 \rangle\rangle$$

Specifications can be generalized using logical variables to represent the starting time and the initial values of program variables. For instance, to specify that a program FUN computes $f(x)$ within certain time bounds and leaves x unchanged, logical variables v and t can be used:

$$\langle\langle x = v \wedge now = t < \infty \rangle\rangle \ FUN \ \langle\langle y = f(v) \wedge x = v \wedge t + 5 < now < t + 13 \rangle\rangle$$

Note that logical variables are implicitly universally quantified.

The real-time communication interface of a non-terminating program can be specified; consider, for instance, process L which sends output periodically:

$$\langle\langle x = 0 \wedge now = 0 \rangle\rangle \ L \ \langle\langle now = \infty \wedge \forall i \in \mathbb{N} : (output, f(i))@T(i) \rangle\rangle$$

Next, consider a program $REACT$ with terminating as well as non-terminating computations; it terminates iff it receives input 0:

$$\langle\langle now = 0 \rangle\rangle$$
$$REACT$$
$$\langle\langle (\forall t < now : (input, v)@t \rightarrow (output, f(v)) \textbf{ in } [t + T_l, t + T_u])$$
$$\wedge (now < \infty \leftrightarrow \exists t_0 < now : (input, 0)@t_0) \rangle\rangle$$

The traditional triple $\{p\} \ P \ \{q\}$ denoting partial correctness (i.e. if p holds initially and if program P terminates, then q holds in the final state) can be expressed as

$$\langle\langle p \wedge now < \infty \rangle\rangle \ P \ \langle\langle now < \infty \rightarrow q \rangle\rangle$$

Total correctness of P with respect to p and q (i.e. if p holds initially, then program P terminates, and q holds in the final state) can be denoted by

$$\langle\langle p \wedge now < \infty \rangle\rangle \ P \ \langle\langle now < \infty \wedge q \rangle\rangle$$

5.1.4 Proof rules

The rule of consequence in the proof system is identical to the original rule for traditional triples and allows assumptions to be strengthened and commitments to be weakened.

Rule 5.1.1 (Consequence)

$$\frac{\langle\langle A_0 \rangle\rangle \ P \ \langle\langle C_0 \rangle\rangle, A \rightarrow A_0, C_0 \rightarrow C}{\langle\langle A \rangle\rangle \ P \ \langle\langle C \rangle\rangle}$$

The proof rule for parallel composition has the following general form, using a combinator *Comb* of assertions which will be defined below.

Rule 5.1.2 (Parallel Composition)

$$\frac{\langle\langle A_1 \rangle\rangle\, P_1\, \langle\langle C_1 \rangle\rangle, \quad \langle\langle A_2 \rangle\rangle\, P_2\, \langle\langle C_2 \rangle\rangle, \quad Comb(C_1, C_2) \to C}{\langle\langle A_1 \wedge A_2 \rangle\rangle\, P_1 \| P_2\, \langle\langle C \rangle\rangle}$$

provided

$$loc(C_1) \cap loc(P_2) = \emptyset \text{ and } loc(C_2) \cap loc(P_1) = \emptyset$$

i.e. the commitment of one process should not refer to local objects of the other, and

$$obs(A_1, C_1) \cap obs(P_2) \subseteq obs(P_1) \text{ and } obs(A_2, C_2) \cap obs(P_1) \subseteq obs(P_2)$$

i.e. if an assertion in the specification of one process refers to the interface of another process, then this is part of a joint interface.

Consider three possibilities for *Comb*:

1. If *now* does not occur in C_1 and C_2 then define

   $$Comb(C_1, C_2) \equiv C_1 \wedge C_2$$

   Without an additional restriction on *now* the rule is not sound. For example,

   $$\langle\langle now = 0 \rangle\rangle\, P_1\, \langle\langle now = 2 \rangle\rangle \text{ and } \langle\langle now = 0 \rangle\rangle\, P_2\, \langle\langle now = 3 \rangle\rangle$$

   would lead to

   $$\langle\langle now = 0 \rangle\rangle\, P_1 \| P_2\, \langle\langle now = 2 \wedge now = 3 \rangle\rangle$$

   and hence by the Consequence rule

   $$\langle\langle now = 0 \rangle\rangle\, P_1 \| P_2 \langle\langle false \rangle\rangle$$

   We shall refer to this version as the Simple Parallel Composition rule.

2. It is not straightforward to use *now* in the commitments because, in general, the termination times of P_1 and P_2 will be different. To obtain a general rule, substitute logical variables t_1 and t_2 for *now* in C_1 and C_2 respectively. Then the termination time of $P_1 \| P_2$, expressed by *now* in its commitment, is the maximum of t_1 and t_2:

   $$Comb(C_1, C_2) \equiv C_1[t_1/now] \wedge C_2[t_2/now] \wedge now = max(t_1, t_2)$$

3. This definition of *Comb* leads to a sound rule but, for completeness, predicates are needed to state that process P_i, $i = 1, 2$, does not perform any action after its termination. Define

   $$\begin{aligned} Comb(C_1, C_2) \equiv\ & C_1[t_1/now] \wedge \bigwedge_{O \in obs(P_1)} \neg O \text{ \textbf{during} } [t_1, now) \\ & \wedge C_2[t_2/now] \wedge \bigwedge_{O \in obs(P_2)} \neg O \text{ \textbf{during} } [t_2, now) \\ & \wedge now = max(t_1, t_2) \end{aligned}$$

This parallel composition rule is compositional, as a specification of the compound construct $P_1 \| P_2$ can be derived using only the specifications of the components P_1 and P_2 and their static interface given by *loc* and *obs*. Basically, compositionality is achieved by requiring that the specification of a process refers only to its interface.

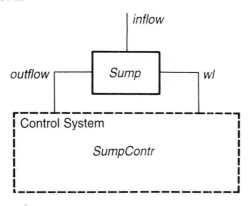

Figure 5.1 The mine pump system

5.2 The mine pump

The function of the mine pump is to prevent flooding in the shaft. But the pump should not be working when the atmosphere contains too much methane as this could lead to an explosion.

Let *wl* be a function from *TIME* to the non-negative reals and let *wl*(*texp*) represent the water level in the sump at time *texp*. Define $obs(wl(texp)) = \{wl\}$. The aim is to keep the water level between certain bounds, say *LWL* and *HWL*, as expressed by the commitment

$$CTL \equiv \forall t < \infty : LWL < wl(t) < HWL$$

Then, the *Mine* can be specified by

$$\langle\langle now = 0 \rangle\rangle \; Mine \; \langle\langle CTL \rangle\rangle$$

with $obs(Mine) = \{wl\}$.

The mine consists of two components: *Sump* and a controller *SumpContr* (see Figure 5.1). *Sump* represents the water level; there is an inflow of water into the sump and the function of *SumpContr* is to remove water (by means of the pump), i.e. control the *outflow* so that the water level stays between the specified bounds. At any time, the water level is the sum of the initial level *wl*(0) at time 0 and the total inflow, minus the total outflow.

Let *inflow*(*texp*) denote the inflow at time *texp*, i.e. the amount of water added per unit of time, and let *outflow*(*texp*) denote the outflow at time *texp*, i.e. the amount of water removed per unit of time. Assume that these two functions are continuous and range over the non-negative reals. Define

$$obs(inflow(texp)) = \{inflow\} \text{ and } obs(outflow(texp)) = \{outflow\}$$

The water level in the sump is determined by the commitment

$$CSump_1 \equiv \forall t < \infty : wl(t) = wl(0) + \int_0^t (inflow(x) - outflow(x))dx$$

By the continuity of *inflow* and *outflow*, *wl* is a continuous function.

Clearly, *CTL* can only be achieved if the water level does not change too fast, i.e. if the inflow is bounded. For some constant $\lambda_{in}^{max} > 0$,

$$CSump_2 \equiv \forall t < \infty : 0 \leq inflow(t) \leq \lambda_{in}^{max}$$

Further, assume that the initial level is between the bounds *LSWL* (Low Water Safety Level) and *HSWL* (High Water Safety Level):

$$CSump_3 \equiv LSWL < wl(0) < HSWL$$

Define $CSump \equiv CSump_1 \wedge CSump_2 \wedge CSump_3$. Then the physical properties of the sump are specified by

$$\langle\langle now = 0 \rangle\rangle \; Sump \; \langle\langle CSump \rangle\rangle$$

with $obs(Sump) = \{wl, inflow, outflow\}$.

The following lemma can be derived by standard mathematical analysis.

Lemma 5.1 $CSump_1$ implies
$$\forall t_0, t_1 < \infty : t_0 \leq t_1 \rightarrow wl(t_1) = wl(t_0) + \int_{t_0}^{t_1} (inflow(x) - outflow(x))dx$$

SumpContr should start to remove water as soon as the water level becomes high. First, we specify that as long as the water level is above *HSWL* there will be an outflow of at least λ_{out}^{min}, allowing a reaction delay of δ_{sc} time units. The constants λ_{out}^{min} and δ_{sc} are non-negative:

$$CSC_1 \equiv \forall t_0, t_1 < \infty : (wl \geq HSWL) \textbf{ during } [t_0, t_1]$$
$$\rightarrow (outflow \geq \lambda_{out}^{min}) \textbf{ during } [t_0 + \delta_{sc}, t_1]$$

Similarly, as soon as the level reaches a minimum level *LSWL* no more water should be removed:

$$CSC_2 \equiv \forall t_0, t_1 < \infty : (wl \leq LSWL) \textbf{ during } [t_0, t_1]$$
$$\rightarrow (outflow = 0) \textbf{ during } [t_0 + \delta_{sc}, t_1]$$

These commitments do not specify the outflow when the water level is between *LSWL* and *HSWL*, or during the reaction periods (of, at most, δ_{sc} time units). Therefore we add a commitment about the maximal outflow, using a non-negative constant λ_{out}^{max}:

$$CSC_3 \equiv \forall t < \infty : 0 \leq outflow(t) < \lambda_{out}^{max}$$

Using $CSC \equiv CSC_1 \wedge CSC_2 \wedge CSC_3$ we have

$$\langle\langle now = 0 \rangle\rangle \; SumpContr \; \langle\langle CSC \rangle\rangle$$

with $obs(SumpContr) \supseteq \{wl, outflow\}$. Note that

$$obs(CSump) \cap obs(SumpContr) \subseteq obs(CSump)$$
$$= \{wl, inflow, outflow\} = obs(Sump)$$

and

$$obs(CSC) \cap obs(Sump) = \{wl, outflow\} \subseteq obs(SumpContr)$$

Since there are no local objects, the specifications of *Sump* and *SumpContr* satisfy the requirements of the Simple Parallel Composition rule and

$$\langle\langle now = 0 \rangle\rangle \; Sump \parallel SumpContr \; \langle\langle CSump \wedge CSC \rangle\rangle$$

Standard mathematical analysis yields the following lemma.

Lemma 5.2 *(Intermediate Value Property)* Consider a continuous function f and two time points t_1 and t_2 with $t_1 < t_2$. Then for any μ with $f(t_1) \leq \mu \leq f(t_2)$ or $f(t_1) \geq \mu \geq f(t_2)$ there exists some $t_3 \in [t_1, t_2]$ such that $f(t_3) = \mu$ and $(\mu \leq f)$ **during** $[t_3, t_2]$ or $(f \leq \mu)$ **during** $[t_3, t_2]$ respectively.

Lemma 5.3 If

$$LSWL \geq LWL + \delta_{sc}\lambda_{out}^{max} \tag{5.1}$$
$$HSWL \leq HWL - \delta_{sc}\lambda_{in}^{max} \tag{5.2}$$
$$\lambda_{in}^{max} < \lambda_{out}^{min} \tag{5.3}$$

then $CSump \wedge CSC \rightarrow CTL$.

Proof: Assume (5.1), (5.2), and (5.3). Suppose $CSump \wedge CSC$. Let $t < \infty$.
First we prove $LWL < wl(t)$ by contradiction. Let

$$wl(t) \leq LWL \tag{5.4}$$

Since the constants are non-negative, (5.1) implies $LWL \leq LSWL$. Thus $wl(t) \leq LSWL$.
By $CSump_3$ we have $LSWL < wl(0)$. Using the continuity of wl, Lemma 5.2 implies that there exists some $t_s \in [0, t]$ such that $wl(t_s) = LSWL$ and $(wl \leq LSWL)$ **during** $[t_s, t]$. Hence, by CSC_2, $(outflow = 0)$ **during** $[t_s + \delta_{sc}, t]$. Using this, $CSump_1$ and Lemma 5.1, and $CSump_2$ and CSC_3, respectively, we obtain

$$
\begin{aligned}
wl(t) &= wl(t_s) + \int_{t_s}^{t}(inflow(x) - outflow(x))dx \\
&= LSWL + \int_{t_s}^{t} inflow(x)dx - \int_{t_s}^{t_s + \delta_{sc}} outflow(x)dx - \int_{t_s + \delta_{sc}}^{t} outflow(x)dx \\
&\geq LSWL - \int_{t_s}^{t_s + \delta_{sc}} outflow(x)dx \\
&> LSWL - \delta_{sc}\lambda_{out}^{max}
\end{aligned}
$$

Hence $wl(t) > LSWL - \delta_{sc}\lambda_{out}^{max}$. Thus, by equation (5.1), $wl(t) > LWL$, which contradicts (5.4).

Similarly, we prove $wl(t) < HWL$ by contradiction. Let

$$wl(t) \geq HWL \tag{5.5}$$

Since all the constants are non-negative, equation (5.2) implies $HWL \geq HSWL$. Thus $wl(t) \geq HSWL$. By $CSump_3$, $wl(0) < HSWL$. Using the continuity of wl, Lemma 5.2 implies that there exists some $t_s \in [0, t]$ such that

$$wl(t_s) = HSWL \text{ and } (wl \geq HSWL) \textbf{ during } [t_s, t]$$

Hence, by CSC_1,

$$(outflow \geq \lambda_{out}^{min}) \textbf{ during } [t_s + \delta_{sc}, t_1]$$

Using this and $CSump_1$ and Lemma 5.1, and $CSump_2$ and CSC_3, respectively, we obtain

$$
\begin{aligned}
wl(t) &= wl(t_s) + \int_{t_s}^{t} (inflow(x) - outflow(x))dx \\
&= HSWL + \int_{t_s}^{t} inflow(x)dx - \int_{t_s}^{t_s + \delta_{sc}} outflow(x)dx - \int_{t_s + \delta_{sc}}^{t} outflow(x)dx \\
&\leq HSWL + (t - t_s)\lambda_{in}^{max} - \int_{t_s + \delta_{sc}}^{t} outflow(x)dx \\
&\leqslant HSWL + (t - t_s)\lambda_{in}^{max} - (t - (t_s + \delta_{sc}))\lambda_{out}^{min} \\
&= HSWL + \delta_{sc}\lambda_{in}^{max} + (t - t_s - \delta_{sc})\lambda_{in}^{max} - (t - (t_s + \delta_{sc}))\lambda_{out}^{min}
\end{aligned}
$$

By (5.3), this gives $wl(t) < HSWL + \delta_{sc}\lambda_{in}^{max}$ and hence, by (5.2), $wl(t) < HWL$, which contradicts (5.5).   □

Thus, by the Consequence rule, we determine that $Sump \parallel SumpContr$ is a correct implementation of $Mine$. It remains to implement $SumpContr$ according to its specification. Now the specification of $SumpContr$ was formulated in terms of the continuous variables wl and $outflow$. Since our implementation by software will be 'discrete', this continuous interface must be 'discretized'. The first step is to refine $SumpContr$ into a component $Pump$ and a pump control component $PumpContr$. But we must recall that a pump can cause an explosion if it operates when the methane concentration in the air is above a critical level CML. We therefore introduce the primitives

$expl@texp$ to denote that an explosion occurs at time $texp$, and
$ml(texp)$ to represent the methane level at time $texp$.

Define $obs(expl@texp) = \{expl\}$, $obs(ml(texp)) = \{ml\}$.

The top-level specification must be altered to express the requirement that no explosion occurs and that if the methane level stays below a safe level SML the water level will stay between the specified bounds. SML, rather than CML, is used to take account of the reaction time needed to switch the pump off:

$$CTL_1 \equiv \forall t < \infty : \neg expl@t$$
$$CTL_2 \equiv \forall t < \infty : (ml < SML) \textbf{ during } [0, t] \rightarrow LWL < wl(t) < HWL$$

Let $CTL \equiv CTL_1 \wedge CTL_2$. Then the specification of $Mine$ is

$$\langle\langle now = 0 \rangle\rangle \; Mine \; \langle\langle CTL \rangle\rangle$$

with $obs(Mine) = \{wl, ml, expl\}$.

The specification of $SumpContr$ must also be changed: CSC_1 is replaced by

$$CSC_1 \equiv \forall t_0, t_1 < \infty :$$
$$(wl \geq HSWL) \text{ during } [t_0, t_1] \wedge (ml < SML) \text{ during } [t_0, t_1]$$
$$\rightarrow (outflow \geq \lambda_{out}^{min}) \text{ during } [t_0 + \delta_{sc}, t_1]$$

To satisfy CTL_1 we simply add $CSC_4 \equiv CTL_1$. Then we have

$$CSC \equiv CSC_1 \wedge CSC_2 \wedge CSC_3 \wedge CSC_4$$

and it is easy to see that Lemma 5.3 is still valid for the modified specifications.

5.3 Communication between parallel components

There are several ways in which parallel processes can communicate, e.g. using shared variables or by passing messages along channels. Formal reasoning about concurrent systems requires a precise axiomatization of communication mechanisms. We shall provide this for three forms of communication: message passing along asynchronous channels, message passing along synchronous channels and communication using physical lines.

5.3.1 Asynchronous channels

Assume that parallel processes communicate by passing messages along unidirectional, point-to-point channels, each connecting two processes. Channels are asynchronous, so a sender does not wait for a receiver, but there is no buffering and a message is lost if there is no waiting receiver. A receiving process waits until a message is available.

Let *CHAN* be a non-empty set of channel names and $c \in CHAN$, and *exp* and *texp* be expressions yielding values in *VAL* and *TIME* respectively:

- *send(c, exp)@texp* denotes a process that starts sending value *exp* along channel *c* at time *texp*.
- *waitrec(c)@texp* states that a process is waiting to receive a message along channel *c* at time *texp*.
- *rec(c, exp)@texp* denotes that a process starts to receive value *exp* along channel *c* at time *texp*.

Define $obs(send(c, exp)@texp) = \{send(c)\}$, $obs(waitrec(c)@exp) = \{waitrec(c)\}$, and $obs(rec(c, exp)@texp) = \{rec(c)\}$.

A process which starts waiting at time t to receive input along c and either receives an input with value v or waits forever, can be specified using the following abbreviation.

$$await\, rec(c, v)@t \equiv waitrec(c) \text{ during } [t, \infty)$$
$$\vee (\exists t_1 \in [t, \infty) : waitrec(c) \text{ during } [t, t_1) \wedge rec(c, v)@t_1)$$

We shall often ignore the value that is transmitted and use the abbreviations

$rec(c)@t \equiv \exists v : rec(c,v)@t,$
$send(c)@t \equiv \exists v : send(c,v)@t,$ and
$await\,rec(c)@t \equiv \exists v : await\,rec(c,v)@t.$

To specify a process which waits for at most Δ time units to receive a message the following abbreviation is introduced:

$$await_{\geq\Delta}rec(c)@t \equiv \quad (\exists t_0 : t \in [t_0, t_0 + \Delta) \wedge waitrec(c) \text{ during } [t_0, t_0 + \Delta))$$
$$\vee (\exists t_1 \in [t, \infty) : waitrec(c) \text{ during } [t, t_1) \wedge rec(c)@t_1)$$

Similar abbreviations can be defined with general expressions instead of v and t and we will sometimes use $(P_1 \wedge P_2)@t$ instead of $P_1@t \wedge P_2@t$, etc.

Communication properties
At any point in time, at most one message is transmitted on an asynchronous channel c:

$$\forall t < \infty \,\forall v_1, v_2 : send(c, v_1)@t \wedge send(c, v_2)@t \rightarrow v_1 = v_2 \qquad \text{(ASYN-1)}$$

Since maximal parallelism is assumed, a process waits only if it has to receive input and no message is available. Assume for simplicity that a message is available to a receiver as soon as the sender starts to send the message. Then a process can receive a message along a channel c only if the message is transmitted simultaneously, i.e.

$$\forall t < \infty \,\forall v : rec(c,v)@t \rightarrow send(c,v)@t \qquad \text{(ASYN-2)}$$

There will be minimal waiting if no process waits to receive along channel c a message that is being transmitted (and hence is available) on c:

$$\forall t < \infty : \neg(send(c)@t \wedge waitrec(c)@t) \qquad \text{(ASYN-3)}$$

It is not difficult to adapt the framework for more realistic assumptions. For instance, suppose that Δ time units pass before a message transmitted by a sender is available for a receiver. Then ASYN-2 becomes

$$\forall t < \infty \,\forall v : rec(c,v)@t \rightarrow (t \geq \Delta \wedge send(c,v)@(t - \Delta))$$

and ASYN-3 changes to

$$\forall t < \infty : \neg(send(c)@t \wedge waitrec(c)@(t + \Delta))$$

Alternatively, an output may be available during a period $[t - \Delta_1, t - \Delta_2]$ and repeated reading during this period will produce the same value (as for a shared variable). Then ASYN-2 and ASYN-3 become

$$\forall t < \infty \,\forall v : rec(c,v)@t$$
$$\rightarrow \exists t_0 \in [t - \Delta_1, t - \Delta_2] : send(c,v)@t_0 \wedge \neg send(c) \text{ during } (t_0, t - \Delta_2]$$

$$\forall t < \infty : \neg(send(c)@t \wedge waitrec(c) \text{ during } [t + \Delta_1, t + \Delta_2])$$

Based on the properties ASYN-1–ASYN-3, we enunciate a few useful lemmas. The first says that if a message is not sent before Δ_1 and appears after a gap of at least Δ_2, and if the receiver is ready to receive before Δ_1 and with a gap of at most Δ_2, then no message gets lost.

Let

$$maxsend(c, \Delta_1, \Delta_2)@t \equiv send(c)@t \rightarrow t \geq \Delta_1 \wedge \neg send(c) \text{ during } (t - \Delta_2, t),$$
$$minwait(c, \Delta_1, \Delta_2)@t \equiv t \geq \Delta_1 \rightarrow await\,rec(c) \text{ in } (t - \Delta_2, t]$$

Lemma 5.4 If $maxsend(c, \Delta_1, \Delta_2)$ **during** $[0, \infty)$ and $minwait(c, \Delta_1, \Delta_2)$ **during** $[0, \infty)$, then $\forall t < \infty : send(c)@t \leftrightarrow rec(c)@t$.

Proof: Consider $t < \infty$. By ASYN-2, we have $rec(c)@t \rightarrow send(c)@t$. Hence it remains to prove $send(c)@t \rightarrow rec(c)@t$. Suppose $send(c)@t$. Assuming $maxsend(c, \Delta_1, \Delta_2)$ **during** $[0, \infty)$ this leads to $t \geq \Delta_1$ and $\neg send(c)$ **during** $(t - \Delta_2, t)$.

Hence, by ASYN-2, $\neg rec(c)$ **during** $(t - \Delta_2, t)$. Since we have derived $t \geq \Delta_1$, the assumption $minwait(c, \Delta_1, \Delta_2)$ **during** $[0, \infty$ leads to $await\,rec(c)$ **in** $(t - \Delta_2, t]$. With $\neg rec(c)$ **during** $(t - \Delta_2, t)$ this implies $await\,rec(c)@t$. By $send(c)@t$ and the minimal waiting property ASYN-3, this leads to $rec(c)@t$. $\quad\square$

By the next lemma, if a message is sent at least once every Δ_s time units, and the receiver is ready to receive a message at least once every Δ_r time units, then there is a communication at least once every $\Delta_s + \Delta_r$ time units.

Lemma 5.5 If $\forall t < \infty : send(c)$ **in** $[t, t + \Delta_s]$ and $\forall t < \infty : await\,rec(c)$ **in** $[t, t + \Delta_r)$, then $\forall t < \infty : rec(c)$ **in** $[t, t + \Delta_s + \Delta_r)$.

Proof: Consider $t < \infty$. By the assumption, we have $await\,rec(c)$ **in** $[t, t + \Delta_r)$.

If $rec(c)$ **in** $[t, t + \Delta_r)$, then $rec(c)$ **in** $[t, t + \Delta_s + \Delta_r)$.

Otherwise, if $\neg(rec(c)$ **in** $[t, t + \Delta_r))$, i.e., $\neg rec(c)$ **during** $[t, t + \Delta_r)$, then $await\,rec(c)$ $@t + \Delta_r$, and assumption $send(c)$ **in** $[t + \Delta_r, t + \Delta_r + \Delta_s)$ leads to $rec(c)$ **in** $[t + \Delta_r, t + \Delta_r + \Delta_s)$. $\quad\square$

A small variation on the previous lemma defines a receiver that has to wait for a message for at least Δ_s time units.

Lemma 5.6 If $\forall t < \infty : send(c)$ **in** $[t, t + \Delta_s)$ and $\forall t < \infty : await_{\geq \Delta_s} rec(c)$ **in** $[t, t + \Delta_r)$, then $\forall t < \infty : rec(c)$ **in** $[t, t + \Delta_s + \Delta_r)$.

Proof: Consider $t < \infty$. By $await_{\geq \Delta_s} rec(c)$ **in** $[t, t + \Delta_r)$, there is a point $t_2 \in [t, t + \Delta_r)$ to which one of the following applies:

1. There is some t_0 such that $t_2 \in [t_0, t_0 + \Delta_s)$ and $waitrec(c)$ **during** $[t_0, t_0 + \Delta_s)$. This leads to a contradiction with the assumption $send(c)$ **in** $[t_0, t_0 + \Delta_s)$ and (ASYN-3).
2. There is some $t_1 \in [t_2, \infty)$ such that $waitrec(c)$ **during** $[t_2, t_1)$ and $rec(c)@t_1$. But $t_1 \geq t_2 + \Delta_s$ implies $waitrec(c)$ **during** $[t_2, t_2 + \Delta_s)$ and hence there is a contradiction, as in the previous case.

Thus we have $t_1 < t_2 + \Delta_s$. Since $t \leq t_2 \leq t_1 < t_2 + \Delta_s < t + \Delta_r + \Delta_s$, then $rec(c)@t_1$ leads to $rec(c)$ **in** $[t, t + \Delta_s + \Delta_r)$. □

Exercise 5.3.1 Prove for an asynchronous channel c,

$$\forall t < \infty : \neg(rec(c)@t \wedge waitrec(c)@t).$$

Exercise 5.3.2 As discussed above, it might be more realistic to assume that for an asynchronous channel c and some Δ, for all $t < \infty$, v, v_1, and v_2:

1. $\neg(send(c)@t \wedge waitrec(c)@(t + \Delta))$
2. $rec(c, v)@t \rightarrow t \geq \Delta \wedge send(c, v)@(t - \Delta)$

Prove the following by means of these properties:

- If $maxsend(c, \Delta_1, \Delta_2)$ **during** $[0, \infty)$ and $minwait(c, \Delta + \Delta_1, \Delta_2)$ **during** $[0, \infty)$, then $\forall t < \infty : rec(c)@t \leftrightarrow t \geq \Delta \wedge send(c)@(t - \Delta)$.
- If $\forall t < \infty : send(c)$ **in** $[t, t + \Delta_s)$ and $\forall t < \infty : await\, rec(c)$ **in** $[t, t + \Delta_r)$, then $\forall t \in [\Delta, \infty) : rec(c)$ **in** $[t, t + \Delta_s + \Delta_r)$.

5.3.2 Synchronous channels

With a synchronous channel, both the sender and the receiver must synchronize to transmit a message: the first must wait until the other is ready to perform the corresponding action.

To characterize this mechanism, we use the primitives *send*, *waitrec* and *rec* of the previous section, together with the primitive *waitsend(c)@texp*, to denote that a process is waiting to send a message on channel c at time *texp*.

We shall use some more abbreviations:

$$await\, send(c, v)@t \equiv waitsend(c) \textbf{ during } [t, \infty)$$
$$\vee (\exists t_1 \in [t, \infty) : waitsend(c) \textbf{ during } [t, t_1) \wedge send(c, v)@t_1)$$
$$await\, send(c)@t \equiv \exists v : await\, send(c, v)@t$$

A synchronous channel c has the following properties:

$$\forall t < \infty \, \forall v_1, v_2 : send(c, v_1)@t \wedge send(c, v_2)@t \rightarrow v_1 = v_2 \qquad \text{(SYN-1)}$$
At any time, at most one message is transmitted on a particular channel.
$$\forall t < \infty \, \forall v : rec(c, v)@t \leftrightarrow send(c, v)@t \qquad \text{(SYN-2)}$$
No message is lost: every message received has been sent and every message sent will be received.
$$\forall t < \infty : \neg(waitsend(c)@t \wedge waitrec(c)@t) \qquad \text{(SYN-3)}$$
Minimal waiting: it is not possible for processes to be simultaneously waiting to send and waiting to receive on a particular channel.

$$\forall t < \infty : \quad \neg(rec(c)@t \wedge waitrec(c)@t)$$
$$\wedge \neg(send(c)@t \wedge waitsend(c)@t) \qquad \text{(SYN-4)}$$

It is not possible for a process to simultaneously be communicating and be waiting to communicate.

With a synchronous channel c, the time at which a communication takes place can be derived from the times at which both partners are ready to communicate.

Lemma 5.7 Assume, for $t_1, t_2 < \infty$, $await\,send(c,v_1)@t_1 \wedge await\,rec(c,v_2)@t_2$:

(a) If $t_1 \leq t_2$ and $\neg rec(c)$ **during** $[t_1, t_2)$, then $rec(c,v_1)@t_2$ and $v_1 = v_2$.
(b) If $t_2 \leq t_1$ and $\neg rec(c)$ **during** $[t_2, t_1)$, then $rec(c,v_1)@t_1$ and $v_1 = v_2$.

Proof:

(a) By assumption SYN-2, $\neg rec(c)$ **during** $[t_1, t_2)$ leads to $\neg send(c)$ **during** $[t_1, t_2)$. Together with $await\,send(c,v_1)@t_1$ this implies $await\,send(c,v_1)@t_2$. Hence this gives $waitsend(c)@t_2 \vee send(c)@t_2$. With ASYN-2, this leads to $waitsend(c)@t_2 \vee rec(c)@t_2$. By SYN-3 and SYN-4 we obtain $\neg waitrec(c)@t_2$. Since $await\,rec(c,v_2)@t_2$, this implies $rec(c,v_2)@t_2$. Hence by ASYN-2, $send(c,v_2)@t_2$ and by SYN-4, $\neg waitsend(c)@t_2$. Hence $await\,send(c,v_1)@t_2$ leads to $send(c,v_1)@t_2$, and thus $rec(c,v_1)@t_2$, using SYN-2. Further, by SYN-1 we obtain $v_1 = v_2$.

(b) The proof is similar. $\qquad\qquad\qquad\qquad\qquad\qquad\qquad\qquad\qquad\qquad\qquad$ □

Exercise 5.3.3 Prove Part (b) of Lemma 5.7.

Exercise 5.3.4 Prove

$$await\,rec(c,v)@t_1 \wedge (\neg rec(c)) \text{ **during** } [t_1, t_2) \wedge t_1 \leq t_2 \to await\,rec(c,v)@t_2$$

5.3.3 Communication using physical lines

Assume that a program component can set a physical line to a value and that other components are able to read the value of this line. For a line l and expressions exp and $texp$ yielding values in *VAL* and *TIME*, respectively, let $l(texp)$ represent the value of line l at time $texp$, and $read(l,exp)@texp$ denote that a process starts reading from line l at time $texp$.

Let $obs(l(texp)) = \{l\}$ and $obs(read(l,exp)@texp) = \{read(l)\}$. Define the following abbreviations:

$(l < v)@t \equiv l(t) < v$, and similarly for other relational operators, and
$read(l)@t \equiv \exists v : read(l,v)@t$

Finally, let the value read from a line be the value of the line:

$$\forall t < \infty \, \forall v : read(l,v)@t \to l(t) = v \qquad \text{(LINE)}$$

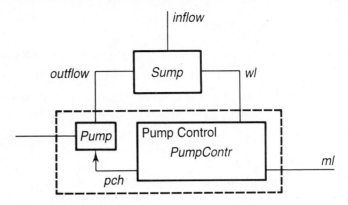

Figure 5.2 Introduction of the mine pump

5.4   Parallel decomposition of the sump control

SumpContr can be decomposed into a number of components executing in parallel.

5.4.1   Introducing a pump

Water is pumped from the sump by a *Pump* which is controlled by *PumpContr*. This control component communicates with the pump by sending messages on the asynchronous channel *pch*. Hence *SumpContr* is refined by *PumpContr* || *Pump* (see Figure 5.2). On channel *pch*, messages of value 1 and 0 are used to switch the pump on and off respectively.

First the pump is specified using the following abbreviations:

$$ON(t_1,t_2) \equiv rec(pch,1)@t_1 \wedge \neg rec(pch,0) \textbf{ during } (t_1,t_2]$$
$$OFF(t_1,t_2) \equiv rec(pch,0)@t_1 \wedge \neg rec(pch,1) \textbf{ during } (t_1,t_2]$$

To specify maximal outflow, let $CPump_1 \equiv CSC_3$.

Assume that after a period *Init* the pump is ready to receive inputs periodically every *Period* units of time, i.e.

$$CPump_2 \equiv minwait(pch, Init, Period) \textbf{ during } [0,\infty)$$

When the pump receives the value 1 along *pch*, it produces an outflow of at least λ_{out}^{min} after a delay of at most δ_p, as long as no value 0 is received (δ_p and λ_{out}^{min} are assumed to be non-negative):

$$CPump_3 \equiv \forall t_1, t_2 < \infty : ON(t_1,t_2) \rightarrow (outflow \geq \lambda_{out}^{min}) \textbf{ during } [t_1 + \delta_p, t_2]$$

The pump will switch off within δ_p if the value 0 is received:

$$CPump_4 \equiv \forall t_1, t_2 < \infty : OFF(t_1, t_2) \rightarrow (outflow = 0) \textbf{ during } [t_1 + \delta_p, t_2]$$

There will be no explosion if the methane level is below a critical level *CML* or if the pump has been switched off:

$$CPump_5 \equiv \forall t < \infty : (ml(t) < CML \vee \exists t_0 \leq t - \delta_p : OFF(t_0, t)) \rightarrow \neg expl@t$$

Let $CPump \equiv CPump_1 \wedge CPump_2 \wedge CPump_3 \wedge CPump_4 \wedge CPump_5$ and assume

$$\langle\!\langle now = 0 \rangle\!\rangle \; Pump \; \langle\!\langle CPump \rangle\!\rangle$$

with $obs(Pump) = \{waitrec(pch), rec(pch), ml, outflow, expl\}$.

PumpContr must contribute towards meeting the commitment of *SumpContr*. First, it must not send messages along *pch* too fast:

$$CPC_1 \equiv maxsend(pch, Init, Period) \textbf{ during } [0, \infty)$$

Then the pump must be switched on (*SETON*) or off (*SETOFF*) if the water level is high or low. Let

$$
\begin{aligned}
SETON(t_1, t_2) &\equiv send(pch, 1)@t_1 \wedge \neg send(pch, 0) \textbf{ during } (t_1, t_2] \\
SETOFF(t_1, t_2) &\equiv send(pch, 0)@t_1 \wedge \neg send(pch, 1) \textbf{ during } (t_1, t_2]
\end{aligned}
$$

But the pump is switched on or kept running only if the methane level is below *SML*:

$$
\begin{aligned}
CPC_2 &\equiv \forall t_0, t_1 < \infty : t_0 + \delta_{pc} \leq t_1 \wedge (wl \geq HSWL) \textbf{ during } [t_0, t_1] \\
&\qquad \wedge (ml < SML) \textbf{ during } [t_0, t_1] \rightarrow \exists t_2 \leq t_0 + \delta_{pc} : SETON(t_2, t_1) \\
CPC_3 &\equiv \forall t_0, t_1 < \infty : t_0 + \delta_{pc} \leq t_1 \wedge (wl \leq LSWL) \textbf{ during } [t_0, t_1] \\
&\qquad \rightarrow \exists t_2 \leq t_0 + \delta_{pc} : SETOFF(t_2, t_1)
\end{aligned}
$$

The methane level cannot be controlled but we make a safety stipulation that if it is above *CML* the pump should have been off for at least δ_p:

$$CPC_4 \equiv \forall t < \infty : ml(t) \geq CML \rightarrow \exists t_0 \leq t - \delta_p : SETOFF(t_0, t)$$

Define $CPC \equiv CPC_1 \wedge CPC_2 \wedge CPC_3 \wedge CPC_4$, and let

$$\langle\!\langle now = 0 \rangle\!\rangle \; PumpContr \; \langle\!\langle CPC \rangle\!\rangle$$

with $obs(PumpContr) \supseteq \{ml\}$.

Now

$$
\begin{aligned}
obs(CPump) \cap obs(PumpContr) &\subseteq obs(CPump) \\
&= \{waitrec(pch), rec(pch), ml, outflow, expl\} \\
&= obs(Pump)
\end{aligned}
$$

Also,

$$obs(CPC) \cap obs(Pump)$$
$$= \{send(pch), wl, ml\} \cap \{waitrec(pch), rec(pch), ml, outflow, expl\}$$
$$= \{ml\} \subseteq obs(PumpContr)$$

So by the Simple Parallel Composition rule

$$\langle\langle now = 0 \rangle\rangle \ Pump \parallel PumpContr \ \langle\langle CPump \wedge CPC \rangle\rangle$$

Lemma 5.8 If

$$\delta_{sc} \geq \delta_{pc} + \delta_p \tag{5.6}$$

then $CPump \wedge CPC \rightarrow CSC$.

Proof: Assume (5.6). Suppose $CPump \wedge CPC$. Since $CPump_2$ and CPC_1, together with Lemma 5.4, show that for all $t < \infty$, $send(pch)@t \leftrightarrow rec(pch)@t$, we have $\neg send(pch, 0)$ **during** $(t_1, t_2]$ is equivalent to $\neg rec(pch, 0)$ **during** $(t_1, t_2]$, and

$$\forall t_1, t_2 < \infty : SETON(t_1, t_2) \leftrightarrow ON(t_1, t_2) \tag{5.7}$$

Similarly,

$$\forall t_1, t_2 < \infty : SETOFF(t_1, t_2) \leftrightarrow OFF(t_1, t_2) \tag{5.8}$$

To prove CSC_1, note that $t_0 + \delta_{sc} > t_1$ implies $[t_0 + \delta_{sc}, t_1] = \emptyset$. Then $(outflow \geq \lambda_{out}^{min})$ **during** $[t_0 + \delta_{sc}, t_1]$ holds. Next assume $t_0 + \delta_{sc} \leq t_1$, $(wl \geq HSWL)$ **during** $[t_0, t_1]$, and $(ml < SML)$ **during** $[t_0, t_1]$. Since the assumption (5.6) implies $t_1 \geq t_0 + \delta_{sc} \geq t_0 + \delta_{pc}$, the commitment CPC_2 shows there exists some $t_2 \leq t_0 + \delta_{pc}$ such that $SETON(t_2, t_1)$. Hence, by (5.7), $ON(t_2, t_1)$. Then $CPump_3$ leads to $(outflow \geq \lambda_{out}^{min})$ **during** $[t_2 + \delta_p, t_1]$. Since $t_2 \leq t_0 + \delta_{pc}$ we obtain $(outflow \geq \lambda_{out}^{min})$ **during** $[t_0 + \delta_{pc} + \delta_p, t_1]$, and this, with (5.6), gives $(outflow \geq \lambda_{out}^{min})$ **during** $[t_0 + \delta_{sc}, t_1]$.

To prove CSC_2, observe that $t_0 + \delta_{sc} > t_1$ implies $[t_0 + \delta_{sc}, t_1] = \emptyset$. Then $(outflow = 0)$ **during** $[t_0 + \delta_{sc}, t_1]$ holds trivially. Assume $t_0 + \delta_{sc} \leq t_1$ and $(wl \leq LSWL)$ **during** $[t_0, t_1]$. Since (5.6) implies $t_1 \geq t_0 + \delta_{sc} \geq t_0 + \delta_{pc}$, CPC_3 shows that there exists some $t_2 \leq t_0 + \delta_{pc}$ such that $SETOFF(t_2, t_1)$. Hence, by (5.8), $OFF(t_2, t_1)$. Then by $CPump_4$ $(outflow = 0)$ **during** $[t_2 + \delta_p, t_1]$. Since $t_2 \leq t_0 + \delta_{pc}$ we obtain $(outflow = 0)$ **during** $[t_0 + \delta_{pc} + \delta_p, t_1]$, and hence by (5.6) $(outflow = 0)$ **during** $[t_0 + \delta_{sc}, t_1]$.

CSC_3 follows from $CPump_1$ by definition.

To prove CSC_4, i.e. $\neg expl@t$, for any $t < \infty$, we use $CPump_5$. We must show that $ml(t) < CML \vee \exists t_0 \leq t - \delta_p : OFF(t_0, t)$. Suppose $ml(t) \geq CML$. Then by CPC_4 there is some $t_0 \leq t - \delta_p$ such that $SETOFF(t_0, t)$. Hence, by (5.8), $OFF(t_0, t)$. □

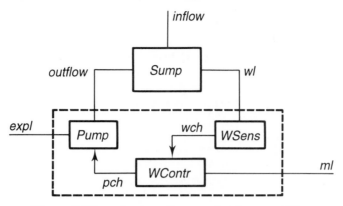

Figure 5.3 Introduction of a water level sensor *WSens*

5.4.2 Introducing sensors

Assume that sensor *WSens* measures the water level and sends the measured values along asynchronous channel *wch* to a control unit *WContr* (see Figure 5.3). *PumpContr* can be then be refined as *WSens* ‖ *WContr*, where sensor *WSens* measures the water level and sends the measured values along asynchronous channel *wch* to a control unit *WContr*.

Assume that a specification of the water level sensor *WSens* is available. We then need to find a specification of the control unit from which we can prove *CPC*.

For the sensor *WSens* assume we are given constants δ_{ws} and ε_{ws}; let the sensor send values along *wch* at least once every δ_{ws} time units:

$$CWSens_1 \equiv \forall t < \infty : send(wch) \textbf{ in } [t, t + \delta_{ws})$$

Further, assume that the value read by the sensor does not differ by more than ε_{ws} from the real water level:

$$CWSens_2 \equiv \forall t < \infty : send(wch, v)@t \rightarrow v - \varepsilon_{ws} \leq wl(t) \leq v + \varepsilon_{ws}$$

Define $CWSens \equiv CWSens_1 \wedge CWSens_2$ and assume *WSens* satisfies

$$\langle\!\langle now = 0 \rangle\!\rangle \; WSens \; \langle\!\langle CWSens \rangle\!\rangle$$

with $obs(WSens) = \{wl, send(wch)\}$.

Next we specify the control component *WContr*. As in CPC_1, there must be a minimal delay between messages sent along *pch*:

$$CWC_1 \equiv CPC_1$$

WContr should be ready to receive input from the sensor along *wch* at least once every δ_{wr} time units:

$$CWC_2 \equiv \forall t < \infty : await_{\geq \delta_{ws}} rec(wch) \textbf{ in } [t, t + \delta_{wr})$$

Define

$$(rec(wch) \geq v_0)@t \equiv \forall v : rec(wch, v)@t \rightarrow v \geq v_0$$

The pump must be switched on if a value above $HSWL - \varepsilon_{ws}$ has been received from the water level sensor; it is not switched off as long as values above $HSWL - \varepsilon_{ws}$ are received.

$$CWC_3 \equiv \forall t_0, t_1 < \infty :$$
$$t_0 + \delta_{wc} \leq t_1 rec(wch, v)@t_0 \wedge v \geq HSWL - \varepsilon_{ws}$$
$$\wedge (rec(wch) \geq HSWL - \varepsilon_{ws}) \textbf{ during } [t_0, t_1]$$
$$\wedge (ml < SML) \textbf{ during } [t_0, t_1] \rightarrow \exists t_2 \leq t_0 + \delta_{wc} : SETON(t_2, t_1)$$

Similarly, let

$$(rec(wch) \leq v_0)@t \equiv \forall v : rec(wch, v)@t \rightarrow v \leq v_0$$

and define

$$CWC_4 \equiv \forall t_0, t_1 < \infty : t_0 + \delta_{wc} \leq t_1 \wedge rec(wch, v)@t_0 \wedge v \leq LSWL + \varepsilon_{ws}$$
$$\wedge (rec(wch) \leq LSWL + \varepsilon_{ws}) \textbf{ during } [t_0, t_1]$$
$$\rightarrow \exists t_2 \leq t_0 + \delta_{wc} : SETOFF(t_2, t_1)$$
$$CWC_5 \equiv CPC_4$$

Let $CWC \equiv CWC_1 \wedge CWC_2 \wedge CWC_3 \wedge CWC_4 \wedge CWC_5$, and

$$\langle\langle now = 0 \rangle\rangle \ WContr \ \langle\langle CWC \rangle\rangle$$

with $obs(WContr) \supseteq \{ml\}$.

This meets the syntactic requirements of the Simple Parallel Composition rule:

$$obs(CWSens) \cap obs(WContr) \subseteq \{wl, send(wch)\} = obs(WSens)$$
$$obs(CWC) \cap obs(WSens)$$
$$= \{send(pch), waitrec(wch), rec(wch), ml\} \cap \{wl, send(wch)\}$$
$$= \emptyset \subseteq obs(WContr)$$

Hence,

$$\langle\langle now = 0 \rangle\rangle \ WSens \parallel WContr \ \langle\langle CWSens \wedge CWC \rangle\rangle$$

Lemma 5.9 If

$$\delta_{pc} \geq \delta_{ws} + \delta_{wr} + \delta_{wc} \tag{5.9}$$

then $CWSens \wedge CWC \rightarrow CPC$.

Proof: Suppose (5.9), *CWSens* and *CWC* hold. Observe that by Lemma 5.6, $CWSens_1$ and CWC_2 imply

$$\forall t < \infty : rec(wch) \textbf{ in } [t, t + \delta_{ws} + \delta_{wr}) \tag{5.10}$$

Also, CPC_1 is equivalent to CWC_1.

To prove CPC_2, assume $t_0 + \delta_{pc} \leq t_1$, $(wl \geq HSWL)$ **during** $[t_0, t_1]$ and $(ml < SML)$ **during** $[t_0, t_1]$. By (5.10) there is a moment $t_3 \in [t_0, t_0 + \delta_{ws} + \delta_{wr})$ and some v such that $rec(wch, v)@t_3$. Using property (ASYN-2) this implies $send(wch, v)@t_3$. By $CWSens_2$ we obtain $v \geq wl(t_3) - \varepsilon_{ws}$. Since, using (5.9), $t_3 < t_0 + \delta_{ws} + \delta_{wr} \leq t_0 + \delta_{pc} \leq t_1$, we have $t_3 \in [t_0, t_1]$ and hence $wl(t_3) \geq HSWL$. Thus $v \geq HSWL - \varepsilon_{ws}$.

To prove $(rec(wch) \geq HSWL - \varepsilon_{ws})$ **during** $[t_3, t_1]$, take $t_4 \in [t_3, t_1]$ with $rec(wch, v_0)@t_4$. Since $t_4 \geq t_3 \geq t_0$, this gives $wl(t_4) \geq HSWL$. Using (ASYN-2), $send(wch, v_0)@t_4$ and, by $CWSens_2$, this leads to $v_0 \geq wl(t_4) - \varepsilon_{ws} \geq HSWL - \varepsilon_{ws}$. Hence $(rec(wch) \geq HSWL - \varepsilon_{ws})$ **during** $[t_3, t_1]$. Note that, using (5.9),

$$t_3 + \delta_{wc} \leq t_0 + \delta_{wc} + \delta_{ws} + \delta_{wr} \leq t_0 + \delta_{pc} \leq t_1$$

Further, $t_0 \leq t_3$, so $(ml < SML)$ **during** $[t_3, t_1]$. Hence from CWC_3 we can conclude that there exists some $t_2 \leq t_3 + \delta_{wc}$ such that $SETON(t_2, t_1)$. Since $t_3 \leq t_0 + \delta_{ws} + \delta_{wr}$ we obtain $t_2 \leq t_0 + \delta_{pc}$ from (5.9).

To prove CPC_3, assume $t_0 + \delta_{pc} \leq t_1$ and $(wl \leq LSWL)$ **during** $[t_0, t_1]$. By (5.10) there is some $t_3 \in [t_0, t_0 + \delta_{ws} + \delta_{wr})$ and some v such that $rec(wch, v)@t_3$. By the communication property (ASYN-2), this implies $send(wch, v)@t_3$. By $CWSens_2$, $v \leq wl(t_3) + \varepsilon_{ws}$. Since, using (5.9), $t_3 < t_0 + \delta_{ws} + \delta_{wr} \leq t_0 + \delta_{pc} \leq t_1$, we have $t_3 \in [t_0, t_1]$ and hence $wl(t_3) \leq LSWL$. Thus by $(wl \leq LSWL)$ **during** $[t_0, t_1]$ we obtain $v \leq LSWL + \varepsilon_{ws}$.

To prove $(rec(wch) \leq LSWL + \varepsilon_{ws})$ **during** $[t_3, t_1]$, take $t_4 \in [t_3, t_1]$ with $rec(wch, v_0)@t_4$. Since $t_4 \geq t_3 \geq t_0$, we have $wl(t_4) \leq LSWL$ and (ASYN-2) gives $send(wch, v_0)@t_4$, and hence, using $CWSens_2$, $v_0 \leq wl(t_4) + \varepsilon_{ws} \leq LSWL + \varepsilon_{ws}$. Thus $(rec(wch) \leq LSWL + \varepsilon_{ws})$ **during** $[t_3, t_1]$. Since, by (5.9),

$$t_3 + \delta_{wc} \leq t_0 + \delta_{wc} + \delta_{ws} + \delta_{wr} \leq t_0 + \delta_{pc} \leq t_1$$

from CWC_4 we conclude that there exists a $t_2 \leq t_3 + \delta_{wc}$ such that $SETOFF(t_2, t_1)$. Since $t_3 \leq t_0 + \delta_{ws} + \delta_{wr}$ we obtain $t_2 \leq t_0 + \delta_{pc}$ from (5.9).

CPC_4 is equivalent to CWC_5. $\qquad\qquad\square$

By Lemma 5.9 and the Consequence rule

$$\langle\langle now = 0 \rangle\rangle \ WSens \parallel WContr \ \langle\langle CWC \rangle\rangle$$

Observe that $obs(WSens \parallel WContr) \supseteq \{ml\}$. Thus $WSens \parallel WContr$ refines *PumpContr*.

To implement *WContr*, introduce a sensor *MSens* to measure the methane level ml and an atmosphere component *Air* to express assumptions about this methane level. The aim is to design a control component *MContr* such that $Air \parallel MSens \parallel MContr$ refines *WContr* (see Figure 5.4).

Assume that the air component *Air* expresses a bound on the initial methane level and a bound on the maximal rise of this level:

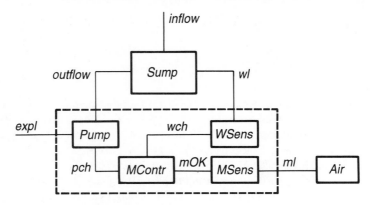

Figure 5.4 Introduction of a methane level sensor *MSens*

$$CAir_1 \equiv ml(0) < SML$$
$$CAir_2 \equiv \forall t_1, t_2 < \infty : t_1 \leq t_2 \rightarrow ml(t_2) - ml(t_1) \leq \lambda_{ml}^{max}(t_2 - t_1)$$

Let $CAir \equiv CAir_1 \wedge CAir_2$ and

$$\langle\langle now = 0 \rangle\rangle \ Air \ \langle\langle CAir \rangle\rangle$$

with $obs(Air) = \{ml\}$.

The methane sensor *MSens* communicates with the control component *MContr* by setting the line *mOK* to 0 or 1 (as in Section 5.3.3). Let the line *mOK* be set to 1 if the methane level is not dangerous, i.e. below the safety level *SML*, and 0 otherwise; let $mOK(t) \in \{0,1\}$, for all $t \in TIME$. Start with the following commitment:

$$CMSens \equiv \forall t < \infty : mOK(t) = 1 \leftrightarrow ml(t) < SML$$

This requires there to be no delay or uncertainty but it is easy to adapt the specification for more realistic assumptions.

Assume that *MSens* satisfies

$$\langle\langle now = 0 \rangle\rangle \ MSens \ \langle\langle CMSens \rangle\rangle$$

with $obs(MSens) = \{ml, mOK\}$.

Component *MContr* reads line *mOK* at least once every Δ_{read} time units:

$$CMC_1 \equiv \forall t < \infty : read(mOK) \ \textbf{in} \ [t, t + \Delta_{read})$$
$$CMC_2 \equiv CWC_1 \ (\text{i.e. } CPC_1)$$

The other commitments of *MContr* are similar to those of *WContr* with the methane level *ml* replaced by reading line *mOK*.

$CMC_3 \equiv CWC_2$

$CMC_4 \equiv \forall t_0, t_1 < \infty : t_0 + \delta_{wc} \leq t_1 \wedge rec(wch, v)@t_0 \wedge v \geq HSWL - \varepsilon_{ws}$
$\qquad \wedge (rec(wch) \geq HSWL - \varepsilon_{ws})$ **during** $[t_0, t_1]$
$\qquad \wedge \neg read(mOK, 0)$ **during** $[t_0, t_1 \rightarrow \exists t_2 \leq t_0 + \delta_{wc} : SETON(t_2, t_1)$

$CMC_5 \equiv CWC_4$

$CMC_6 \equiv \forall t_0, t_1 < \infty : t_0 + \delta_{ml} \leq t_1 \wedge read(mOK, 0)@t_0$
$\qquad \wedge \neg read(mOK, 1)$ **during** $[t_0, t_1] \rightarrow \exists t_2 \leq t_0 + \delta_{ml} : SETOFF(t_2, t_1)$

Define $CMC \equiv CMC_1 \wedge CMC_2 \wedge CMC_3 \wedge CMC_4 \wedge CMC_5 \wedge CMC_6$ and let $MContr$ be specified by

$$\langle\langle now = 0 \rangle\rangle \, MContr \, \langle\langle CMC \rangle\rangle$$

Observe that

$$obs(CAir) \cap obs(MSens) \subseteq obs(CAir) = \{ml\} = obs(Air)$$

and

$$obs(CMSens) \cap obs(Air) = \{ml\} \subseteq obs(MSens)$$

The Simple Parallel Composition rule leads to

$$\langle\langle now = 0 \rangle\rangle \, Air \parallel MSens \, \langle\langle CAir \wedge CMSens \rangle\rangle$$

Similarly, $obs(CAir \wedge CMSens) \cap obs(MContr) \subseteq obs(CAir \wedge CMSens) = \{ml, mOK\}$
$= obs(Air \parallel MSens)$ and that $obs(CMC) \cap obs(Air \parallel MSens) = \{waitrec(wch), rec(wch)$
$, send(pch), read(mOK)\} \cap \{ml, mOK\} = \emptyset \subseteq obs(MContr)$.
Then the Simple Parallel Composition rule gives

$$\langle\langle now = 0 \rangle\rangle \, Air \parallel MSens \parallel MContr \, \langle\langle CAir \wedge CMSens \wedge CMC \rangle\rangle$$

Lemma 5.10 If

$$(\Delta_{read} + \delta_{ml} + \delta_p)\lambda_{ml}^{max} \leq CML - SML \qquad (5.11)$$

then $CAir \wedge CMSens \wedge CMC \rightarrow CWC$.

Proof: Assume (5.11), $CAir$, $CMSens$ and CMC. Note that CWC_1, CWC_2, and CWC_4, are equivalent to CMC_2, CMC_3 and CMC_5 respectively.

To prove CWC_3, assume that

$t_0 + \delta_{wc} \leq t_1$,
$rec(wch, v)@t_0$ and $v \geq HSWL - \varepsilon_{ws}$
$(rec(wch) \geq HSWL - \varepsilon_{ws})$ **during** $[t_0, t_1]$ and
$(ml < SML)$ **during** $[t_0, t_1]$

To apply CMC_4, we first show $\neg read(mOK, 0)$ **during** $[t_0, t_1]$. Consider $t_3 \in [t_0, t_1]$. Since $ml(t_3) < SML$, by $CMSens$ we obtain $mOK(t_3) = 1$. Thus by the communication line property (LINE), $read(mOK, v)@t_3$ implies $v = 1$ and $\neg read(mOK, 0)@t_3$. This gives $\neg read(mOK, 0)$ **during** $[t_0, t_1]$ and so CMC_4 leads to $\exists t_2 \leq t_0 + \delta_{wc} : SETON(t_2, t_1)$.

To prove CWC_5, i.e. CPC_4, assume $ml(t) \geq CML$. Note that (5.11) implies $CML \geq SML$, since all the constants are non-negative. Observe that if $\lambda_{ml}^{max} = 0$, then by $CAir_2$ we have $ml(t) - ml(0) \leq 0$; using $CAir_1$, $CML \leq ml(t) \leq ml(0) < SML$, which is in contradiction with $CML \geq SML$. Hence, $\lambda_{ml}^{max} > 0$. By $CML \geq SML$ and $CAir_1$ we obtain $ml(0) \leq SML \leq ml(t)$. Using Lemma 5.2 (Intermediate Value Property), this implies that there exists a $t_s \in [0, t]$ such that $ml(t_s) = SML$ and $(ml \geq SML)$ **during** $[t_s, t]$. By CMC_1, $read(mOK)$ **in** $[t_s, t_s + \Delta_{read})$. Thus there exists some $t_0 \in [t_s, t_s + \Delta_{read})$ such that $read(mOK)@t_0$. By $CAir_2$ we can derive $ml(t) - ml(t_s) \leq \lambda_{ml}^{max}(t - t_s)$, thus $\lambda_{ml}^{max}(t - t_s) \geq ml(t) - SML \geq CML - SML$. With (5.11), we obtain $\lambda_{ml}^{max}(t - t_s) \geq (\Delta_{read} + \delta_{ml} + \delta_p)\lambda_{ml}^{max}$. Since $\lambda_{ml}^{max} > 0$ and all the constants are non-negative, this implies $t - t_s \geq \Delta_{read}$, and hence $t_s + \Delta_{read} \leq t$. Then $t_0 \in [t_s, t]$ and thus $ml(t_0) \geq SML$. By $CMSens$ this (and the range of mOK) implies $mOK(t_0) = 0$.

By the line property (LINE), $read(mOK, 0)@t_0$. Further, $(ml \geq SML)$ **during** $[t_0, t]$ leads to $(mOK = 0)$ **during** $[t_0, t]$, and by (LINE) we obtain $\neg read(mOK, 1)$ **during** $[t_0, t]$.

Hence, by CMC_6, there exists a $t_2 \leq t_0 + \delta_{ml}$ such that $SETOFF(t_2, t)$. Since $t - t_s \geq \Delta_{read} + \delta_{ml} + \delta_p$, as shown above, we have $t_s + \Delta_{read} + \delta_{ml} \leq t - \delta_p$. Thus $t_2 \leq t_0 + \delta_{ml} < t_s + \Delta_{read} + \delta_{ml} \leq t - \delta_p$, that is, $t_2 \leq t - \delta_p$.   □

Hence, by Lemma 5.10, the Consequence rule leads to

$$\langle\langle now = 0 \rangle\rangle \; Air \parallel MSens \parallel MContr \; \langle\langle CWC \rangle\rangle$$

Note that $obs(Air \parallel MSens \parallel MContr) \subseteq obs(Air) = \{ml\}$. Thus $Air \parallel MSens \parallel MContr$ correctly implements $WContr$.

5.5 Programming language

We shall now describe the main features of a simple language that is sufficiently expressive for the mine pump control program. To show that programs satisfy an assumption/commitment specification we shall then formulate a compositional proof system.

5.5.1 Syntax of the programming language

We choose a simple real-time concurrent programming language with communication along asynchronous channels and physical lines (cf. Section 5.3). Explicit timing is performed using a delay statement which suspends the execution for a specified period.

The statements of the programming language and their informal meanings are listed below, using program variable x, expression e yielding a value in VAL, boolean expression b, asynchronous channel c and line l.

Atomic statements

- **skip** terminates immediately.
- Assignment $x := e$ assigns the value of expression e to the variable x.
- **delay** e suspends execution for e time units; if e is negative then **delay** e is the same as **skip**.
- $c!!e$ sends the value of expression e along channel c without waiting for the receiver.
- $c?x$ assigns to variable x the value received on channel c; an input statement waits until a message is available.
- **read** (l,x) assigns to variable x the value of line l.

Compound statements

- S_1; S_2 is the sequential composition of S_1 and S_2.
- **if** b **then** S_1 **else** S_2 **fi** denotes choice between S_1 and S_2 based on condition b.
- **sel** $c?x$ **then** S_1 **or delay** e **then** S_2 **les** waits to receive a message on channel c; if the message comes within e time units, S_1 is executed otherwise S_2 is executed.
- **while** b **do** S **od** repeatedly tests b and executes S if b is true and terminates if b is false.
- $S_1 \| S_2$ is the parallel composition of *processes* S_1 and S_2 which must not share variables.

if b **then** S **fi** will be used as an abbreviation of **if** b **then** S **else skip fi**.

Example 5.4 The select statement can be used to program a *time-out*. For instance,

> **sel** $in?x$ **then** $out!!f(x)$ **or delay** 8 **then** $alarm!!y$ **les**

With this statement, a process waits to receive a message on channel in for at most eight time units; if a message comes within that time, it executes $out!!f(x)$ and otherwise it executes $alarm!!y$.

Let $loc(S)$ be the set of program variables of S. Then the set of observables of S, $obs(S)$, is defined by induction on the structure of S. For input and output it is defined as

$$obs(c!!e) = \{send(c)\}$$
$$obs(c?x) = \{waitrec(c), rec(c)\} \text{ and}$$
$$obs(\textbf{read}\,(l,x)) = \{read(l)\}$$

The other observables are easily defined:

$$obs(\textbf{skip}) = obs(x := e) = obs(\textbf{delay } e) = \emptyset$$
$$obs(S_1;\ S_2) = obs(S_1 \| S_2) = obs(\textbf{if } b \textbf{ then } S_1 \textbf{ else } S_2 \textbf{ fi})$$
$$= obs(S_1) \cup obs(S_2)$$
$$obs(\textbf{sel } c?x \textbf{ then } S_1 \textbf{ or delay} e \textbf{ then } S_2 \textbf{ les})$$
$$= \{waitrec(c), rec(c)\} \cup obs(S_1) \cup obs(S_2)$$
$$\text{and } obs(\textbf{while } b \textbf{ do } S \textbf{ od}) = obs(S)$$

Observe that processes do not share variables: for $S_1 \| S_2$, $loc(S_1) \cap loc(S_2) = \emptyset$.

5.5.2   Basic timing assumptions

The next step is to make assumptions about the execution time needed for the atomic statements and the relation between the execution time of a compound statement and the timing of its components. Since we assume *maximal progress*, an enabled action will be executed as soon as possible. The execution of a local, non-communication, command or an asynchronous output is never postponed. An input command can cause a process to wait, but only when no message is available.

We assume that an assignment $x := e$ takes the non-negative time T_a. **delay** e waits for exactly e time units if e is positive and 0 otherwise. Each communication takes a non-negative time T_{comm} and $read\,(l,x)$ takes a non-negative T_r time unit.

The evaluation of the boolean b in **if** b **then** S_1 **else** S_2 **fi** or **while** b **do** S **od** takes T_b time units and this has a fixed non-zero lower bound to guarantee finite variability (or 'non-Zeno-ness').

5.5.3   Proof system

The compositional proof system for this logic consists of rules and axioms that apply to any statement and rules and axioms for the atomic and compound programming statements. Fresh logical variables are assumed to be used in the rules.

General rules and axioms

The first axiom says that an assumption which satisfies certain restrictions is not affected by the execution of any program.

Axiom 5.1   *Initial invariance*

$$\langle\!\langle A \rangle\!\rangle \; S \; \langle\!\langle A \rangle\!\rangle$$

provided A does not refer to *now* or the program variables ($loc(A) = \emptyset$).

Similarly, a variable which does not occur in program S is not affected by any terminating computations of S.

Axiom 5.2   *Variable invariance*

$$\langle\!\langle A \rangle\!\rangle \; S \; \langle\!\langle now < \infty \rightarrow A \rangle\!\rangle$$

provided *now* does not occur in A and $loc(A) \cap loc(S) = \emptyset$.

A program S never performs an action which does not syntactically occur in S.

Axiom 5.3 *Observables invariance*

$$\langle\langle now = t_0 \rangle\rangle \; S \; \langle\langle \bigwedge_{O \in oset} \neg O \text{ during } [t_0, now) \rangle\rangle$$

provided *oset* is a finite set of observables with $oset \cap obs(S) = \emptyset$.

Example 5.5 The following examples illustrate the invariance axioms.

(a) By the Initial Invariance axiom, for any program S,

$$\langle\langle rec(c,5)@t \wedge send(d,v)@(t+7) \rangle\rangle \; S \; \langle\langle rec(c,5)@t \wedge send(d,v)@(t+7) \rangle\rangle$$

(b) Applying the Variable Invariance axiom,

$$\langle\langle x = 5 \rangle\rangle \text{ while } y \neq 0 \text{ do } c?y; \; d!!f(y) \text{ od } \langle\langle now < \infty \rightarrow x = 5 \rangle\rangle$$

For non-terminating computations, it is not possible to prove in the commitment that program variables have a particular value.

(c) By the Observables Invariance axiom,

$$\langle\langle now = t_0 \rangle\rangle \; c?x \; \langle\langle(\neg send(c)) \text{ during } [t_0, now)$$
$$\wedge (\neg rec(d)) \text{ during } [t_0, now) \rangle\rangle$$

since $obs(c?x) = \{waitrec(c), rec(c)\}$.

A program which follows a non-terminating computation has no effect.

Axiom 5.4 *Non-termination*

$$\langle\langle A \wedge now = \infty \rangle\rangle \; S \; \langle\langle A \wedge now = \infty \rangle\rangle$$

The substitution rule allows a logical variable in the assumption to be replaced by any expression provided the variable does not occur in the commitment.

Rule 5.5.1 *Substitution*

$$\frac{\langle\langle A \rangle\rangle \; S \; \langle\langle C \rangle\rangle}{\langle\langle A[exp/t] \rangle\rangle \; S \; \langle\langle C \rangle\rangle}$$

provided t does not occur free in C.

The rules for conjunction and disjunction are identical to those used for traditional triples.

Rule 5.5.2 *Conjunction*

$$\frac{\langle\langle A_1 \rangle\rangle \; S \; \langle\langle C_1 \rangle\rangle, \langle\langle A_2 \rangle\rangle \; S \; \langle\langle C_2 \rangle\rangle}{\langle\langle A_1 \wedge A_2 \rangle\rangle \; S \; \langle\langle C_1 \wedge C_2 \rangle\rangle}$$

Rule 5.5.3 *Disjunction*

$$\frac{\langle\langle A_1 \rangle\rangle \; S \; \langle\langle C_1 \rangle\rangle, \langle\langle A_2 \rangle\rangle \; S \; \langle\langle C_2 \rangle\rangle}{\langle\langle A_1 \vee A_2 \rangle\rangle \; S \; \langle\langle C_1 \vee C_2 \rangle\rangle}$$

Axiomatization of the programming constructs

A skip statement terminates immediately and has no effect.

Axiom 5.5   skip

$$\langle\langle A\rangle\rangle \textbf{ skip } \langle\langle A\rangle\rangle$$

The next axiom for an assignment $x := e$ expresses that to obtain commitment C the assumption $C[e/x, now + T_a/now] \wedge now < \infty$ is required (this is the weakest assumption). Note that, in addition to the traditional rule, we also update the time to express that the termination time equals the initial time plus T_a time units.

Axiom 5.6 *Assignment*

$$\langle\langle C[e/x, now + T_a/now] \wedge now < \infty\rangle\rangle \; x := e \; \langle\langle C\rangle\rangle$$

Example 5.6   Show the correctness of the following triple:

$$\langle\langle x = 5 \wedge now = 6 \wedge rec(c,0)@3\rangle\rangle$$
$$x := x + 7$$
$$\langle\langle x = 12 \wedge now = 6 + T_a \wedge rec(c,0)@3\rangle\rangle$$

From the Assignment axiom,

$$\langle\langle x + 7 = 12 \wedge now + T_a = 6 + T_a \wedge rec(c,0)@3 \wedge now < \infty\rangle\rangle$$
$$x := x + 7$$
$$\langle\langle x = 12 \wedge now = 6 + T_a \wedge rec(c,0)@3\rangle\rangle$$

Then the Consequence rule yields the required triple, since $x = 5 \wedge now = 6 \wedge rec(c,0)@3$ implies $x + 7 = 12 \wedge now + T_a = 6 + T_a \wedge rec(c,0)@3 \wedge now < \infty$.

The axiom for the delay statement is similar.

Axiom 5.7   delay

$$\langle\langle C[now + max(0,e)/now] \wedge now < \infty\rangle\rangle \textbf{ delay } e \; \langle\langle C\rangle\rangle$$

In the rule for asynchronous output, $c!!e$, now in Assumption $A \wedge now < \infty$ is replaced by t_0, which is the starting time of the statement, and $send(c,e)@t_0$ denotes that it starts sending at t_0. For completeness, there is a term expressing that no transmission is started after t_0 until it terminates, i.e. $\neg send(c)$ **during** (t_0, now), where now is the termination time, equal to $t_0 + T_{comm}$.

Rule 5.5.4 *Asynchronous output*

$$\frac{(A \wedge now < \infty)[t_0/now] \wedge send(c,e)@t_0 \wedge \neg send(c) \textbf{ during } (t_0, now) \wedge}{now = t_0 + T_{comm} \rightarrow C}$$

$$\langle\langle A \wedge now < \infty\rangle\rangle \; c!!e \; \langle\langle C\rangle\rangle$$

Similarly, in the rule for the input statement $c?x$, *now* in $A \wedge now < \infty$ is replaced by t_0, to represent the starting time. An input statement will need to wait if a message is not available, i.e. the corresponding output statement has not begun sending a value. But to make the proof system compositional, no assumption should be imposed upon the environment. So the rule includes an arbitrary waiting period (including an infinite wait) and, if a communication takes place, any value can be received.

In the rule below, the commitment is split into C_{nt}, representing a non-terminating computation with infinite waiting, i.e. $waitrec(c)$ **during** $[t_0, \infty)$, and a commitment C for the properties of terminating computations; in the latter case there is a point t in time at which a value v is received and until that time the statement waits to receive it (thus also asserting that no message was available earlier). After t, and until the termination time represented by *now*, the statement does not wait or start receiving a message, as expressed by

$$comm(c,v)(t_0,t) \equiv waitrec(c) \text{ \textbf{during} } [t_0,t) \wedge rec(c,v)@t$$
$$\wedge (\neg waitrec(c) \wedge \neg rec(c)) \text{ \textbf{during} } (t,now).$$

The value v is assigned to x at the termination time $t + T_{comm}$.

Rule 5.5.5 *Input*

$$(A \wedge now < \infty)[t_0/now] \wedge waitrec(c) \text{ \textbf{during} } [t_0, \infty) \wedge now = \infty \rightarrow C_{nt}$$
$$(A \wedge now < \infty)[t_0/now] \wedge \exists t \in [t_0, \infty) : comm(c,v)(t_0,t) \wedge now = t + T_{comm}$$
$$\rightarrow C[v/x]$$

$$\langle\langle A \wedge now < \infty \rangle\rangle \; c?x \; \langle\langle C_{nt} \vee C \rangle\rangle$$

provided $loc(C_{nt}) = \emptyset$.

Example 5.7 By the Input rule we can derive

$$\langle\langle now = 5 \rangle\rangle \; c?x \; \langle\langle \; (waitrec(c) \text{ \textbf{during} } [5,\infty) \wedge now = \infty)$$
$$\vee (\exists t \in [5,\infty) : waitrec(c) \text{ \textbf{during} } [5,t) \wedge rec(c,x)@t$$
$$\wedge now = t + T_{comm}) \; \rangle\rangle$$

since

$$t_0 = 5 \wedge waitrec(c) \text{ \textbf{during} } [t_0,\infty) \wedge now = \infty$$
$$\rightarrow waitrec(c) \text{ \textbf{during} } [5,\infty) \wedge now = \infty$$

and

$$t_0 = 5 \wedge \exists t \in [t_0,\infty) : comm(c,v)(t_0,t) \wedge now = t + T_{comm}$$

implies

$$\exists t \in [5,\infty) : waitrec(c) \text{ \textbf{during} } [5,t) \wedge rec(c,v)@t \wedge now = t + T_{comm}$$

i.e.

$$(\exists t \in [5,\infty) : waitrec(c) \text{ \textbf{during} } [5,t) \wedge rec(c,x)@t \wedge now = t + T_{comm})[v/x]$$

The following rule defines the effect of reading a line l.

Rule 5.5.6 *Read*

$$\frac{(A \wedge now < \infty)[t_0/now] \wedge read(l,x)@t_0 \wedge now = t_0 + T_r \rightarrow C}{\langle\langle A \wedge now < \infty\rangle\rangle \; \mathbf{read}\,(l,x) \; \langle\langle C\rangle\rangle}$$

The rule for sequential composition is straightforward.

Rule 5.5.7 *Sequential composition*

$$\frac{\langle\langle A\rangle\rangle \; S_1 \; \langle\langle B\rangle\rangle, \;\; \langle\langle B\rangle\rangle \; S_2 \; \langle\langle C\rangle\rangle}{\langle\langle A\rangle\rangle \; S_1; S_2 \; \langle\langle C\rangle\rangle}$$

Note that assertion B may describe non-terminating executions of S_1. This part of B is not affected by S_2 and can be included in C, as illustrated in the following example.

Example 5.8 Consider a program $c?y; \; y := y + 1$ with

$A \equiv now = 7$ and
$C \equiv (now = \infty \wedge waitrec(c) \; \mathbf{during} \; [7, \infty))$
$\qquad \vee (\exists t \in [7, \infty) : now = t + T_{comm} + T_a \wedge rec(c, y - 1)@t)$

To prove $\langle\langle A\rangle\rangle \; c?y; \; y := y + 1 \; \langle\langle C\rangle\rangle$, define

$B \equiv (now = \infty \wedge waitrec(c) \; \mathbf{during} \; [7, \infty))$
$\qquad \vee (\exists t \in [7, \infty) : now = t + T_{comm} + T_a \wedge rec(c, y)@t)$

Note that we can derive $\langle\langle A\rangle\rangle \; c?y \; \langle\langle B\rangle\rangle$ and, using the Non-termination axiom 5.4 and the Disjunction rule, $\langle\langle B\rangle\rangle \; y := y + 1 \; \langle\langle C\rangle\rangle$. Hence the Sequential Composition rule leads to $\langle\langle A\rangle\rangle \; c?y; \; y := y + 1 \; \langle\langle C\rangle\rangle$.

The rule for the choice statement has a delay of T_b time units added to represent the time taken to evaluate the boolean expression.

Rule 5.5.8 *Choice*

$$\frac{\begin{array}{c}\langle\langle A\rangle\rangle \; \mathbf{delay} \; T_b \; \langle\langle A_0\rangle\rangle \\ \langle\langle A_0 \wedge b\rangle\rangle \; S_1 \; \langle\langle C\rangle\rangle, \;\; \langle\langle A_0 \wedge \neg b\rangle\rangle \; S_2 \; \langle\langle C\rangle\rangle\end{array}}{\langle\langle A\rangle\rangle \; \mathbf{if} \; b \; \mathbf{then} \; S_1 \; \mathbf{else} \; S_2 \; \mathbf{fi} \; \langle\langle C\rangle\rangle}$$

The select statement $\mathbf{sel} \; c?x \; \mathbf{then} \; S_1 \; \mathbf{or} \; \mathbf{delay}\,e \; \mathbf{then} \; S_2 \; \mathbf{les}$ has two possible outcomes. First, a communication on c may occur within e time units after the starting time t_0, leading to assertion A_1, after which S_1 is executed, leading to C_1. Alternatively, there may be a wait in order to communicate on c during e time units (assertion A_2) and S_2 is executed, leading to C_2.

Rule 5.5.9 *Select*

$$(A \wedge now < \infty)[t_0/now] \wedge \exists t \in [t_0, t_0 + e) : comm(c, v)(t_0, t)$$
$$\wedge \, now = t + T_{comm} \rightarrow A_1[v/x]$$
$$(A \wedge now < \infty)[t_0/now] \wedge waitrec(c) \textbf{ during } [t_0, t_0 + e)$$
$$\wedge \, now = t_0 + max(0, e) \rightarrow A_2$$
$$\langle\langle A_1 \rangle\rangle \, S_1 \, \langle\langle C_1 \rangle\rangle, \quad \langle\langle A_2 \rangle\rangle \, S_2 \, \langle\langle C_2 \rangle\rangle$$

$$\overline{\langle\langle A \wedge now < \infty \rangle\rangle \textbf{ sel } c?x \textbf{ then } S_1 \textbf{ or delay } e \textbf{ then } S_2 \textbf{ les } \langle\langle C_1 \vee C_2 \rangle\rangle}$$

The rule for the while statement has clauses to deal with non-terminating computations and a delay statement has been included to model the time T_b taken for the evaluation of the boolean expression.

Rule 5.5.10 *While*

$$\langle\langle I \wedge now < \infty \rangle\rangle \textbf{ delay } T_b \, \langle\langle I_0 \rangle\rangle$$
$$\langle\langle I_0 \wedge b \wedge now < \infty \rangle\rangle \, S \, \langle\langle I \rangle\rangle$$
$$I \rightarrow I_1, \quad loc(I_1) = \emptyset, \quad (\forall t_1 < \infty \, \exists t_2 > t_1 : I_1[t_2/now]) \rightarrow C_{nt}$$

$$\overline{\langle\langle I \rangle\rangle \textbf{ while } b \textbf{ do } S \textbf{ od } \langle\langle (C_{nt} \wedge now = \infty) \vee (I_0 \wedge \neg b) \rangle\rangle}$$

Example 5.9 Consider the program

$$\textbf{while } x \neq 0 \textbf{ do } in?x; \; out!!f(x) \textbf{ od}$$

Clearly this program maintains the relation

$$\forall t < \infty \, \forall v : rec(in, v)@t \rightarrow send(out, f(v))@(t + T_{comm})$$

between input and output. We shall not prove this here (see Section 5.6 for similar proofs) but, rather, will concentrate in this example on the question of termination. The aim is to show

$$\langle\langle now = 0 \wedge x \neq 0 \rangle\rangle$$
$$\textbf{while } x \neq 0 \textbf{ do } in?x; \; out!!f(x) \textbf{ od}$$
$$\langle\langle \quad (now = \infty \wedge \exists t < \infty : waitrec(in) \textbf{ during } [t, \infty))$$
$$\vee \, (now = \infty \wedge \forall t < \infty : \neg rec(in, 0)@t)$$
$$\vee \, (now < \infty \wedge \exists t < \infty : rec(in, 0)@t) \rangle\rangle$$

Thus the program either

- does not terminate because there is a deadlock on input channel *in*, i.e. the program waits forever to receive input along *in* after a certain point in time, or
- does not terminate because it never receives value 0 along *in*, or
- terminates because it receives 0.

The While rule is used to prove this, with

$C_{nt} \equiv (\exists t < \infty : waitrec(in) \textbf{ during } [t, \infty)) \vee (\forall t < \infty : \neg rec(in, 0)@t)$

$I \quad \equiv (now = \infty \wedge \exists t < \infty : waitrec(in) \textbf{ during } [t, \infty))$
$\qquad \vee (now < \infty \wedge \forall t < now, t \neq now - 2T_{comm} : \neg rec(in, 0)@t$
$\qquad\qquad \wedge (x = 0 \leftrightarrow rec(in, 0)@(now - 2T_{comm})))$

$I_0 \quad \equiv now < \infty \wedge \forall t < now, t \neq now - 2T_{comm} - T_b : \neg rec(in, 0)@t$
$\qquad\qquad \wedge (x = 0 \leftrightarrow rec(in, 0)@(now - 2T_{comm} - T_b))$

$I_1 \quad \equiv (\exists t < \infty : waitrec(in) \textbf{ during } [t, \infty)) \vee (\forall t < now - 2T_{comm} : \neg rec(in, 0)@t)$

To apply the While rule, we must prove the following:

- $\langle\langle I \wedge now < \infty \rangle\rangle \textbf{ delay } T_b \langle\langle I_0 \rangle\rangle$
  This formula is easily derived using the proof system.
- $\langle\langle I_0 \wedge x \neq 0 \wedge now < \infty \rangle\rangle \; in?x; \; out!!f(x) \; \langle\langle I \rangle\rangle$
  Note that $I_0 \wedge x \neq 0 \wedge now < \infty$ implies

$$now < \infty \wedge \forall t < now : \neg rec(in, 0)@t$$

Let $B \equiv (now = \infty \wedge \exists t < \infty : waitrec(in) \textbf{ during } [t, \infty))$
$\qquad \vee (now < \infty \wedge \forall t < now, t \neq now - T_{comm} : \neg rec(in, 0)@t$
$\qquad\qquad \wedge (x = 0 \leftrightarrow rec(in, 0)@(now - T_{comm})))$

Then we can easily derive

$\langle\langle now < \infty \wedge \forall t < now : \neg rec(in, 0)@t \rangle\rangle \; in?x \; \langle\langle B \rangle\rangle$
$\langle\langle B \rangle\rangle \; out!!f(x) \; \langle\langle I \rangle\rangle$

which leads to the required formula by the Sequential Composition and Consequence rules:

- $I \rightarrow I_1$, which holds trivially. Further note that $loc(I_1) = \emptyset$.
- $(\forall t_1 < \infty \; \exists t_2 > t_1 : I_1[t_2/now]) \rightarrow C_{nt}$.
  Observe that $\forall t_1 < \infty \; \exists t_2 > t_1 : I_1[t_2/now]$ is equivalent to $\forall t_1 < \infty \; \exists t_2 > t_1 :$

$$(\exists t < \infty : waitrec(in) \textbf{ during } [t, \infty)) \vee (\forall t < t_2 - 2T_{comm} : \neg rec(in, 0)@t)$$

implying

$$(\exists t < \infty : waitrec(in) \textbf{ during } [t, \infty)) \vee (\forall t < \infty : \neg rec(in, 0)@t)$$

i.e., C_{nt}.

Then the While rule leads to

$\langle\langle I \rangle\rangle \textbf{while } x \neq 0 \textbf{ do } in?x; \; out!!f(x) \textbf{ od } \langle\langle (C_{nt} \wedge now = \infty) \vee (I_0 \wedge x = 0) \rangle\rangle$

Note that $now = 0 \wedge x \neq 0 \rightarrow I$. Further, $(C_{nt} \wedge now = \infty) \vee (I_0 \wedge x = 0)$ is equivalent to

$((\exists t < \infty : waitrec(in) \textbf{ during } [t, \infty) \vee \forall t < \infty : \neg rec(in, 0)@t) \wedge now = \infty)$
$\vee (now < \infty \wedge rec(in, 0)@(now - 2T_{comm} - T_b))$

which implies

$(now = \infty \wedge \exists t < \infty : waitrec(in) \textbf{ during } [t, \infty))$
$\vee (now = \infty \wedge \forall t < \infty : \neg rec(in, 0)@t)$
$\vee (now < \infty \wedge \exists t < \infty : rec(in, 0)@t)$

Hence the Consequence rule leads to the triple to be proved.

5.6   The mine pump example: final implementation

We can now implement component *MContr* which was specified in Section 5.4.2:

$$\langle\langle now = 0\rangle\rangle \; MContr \; \langle\langle CMC\rangle\rangle$$

Recall that $CMC \equiv CMC_1 \wedge CMC_2 \wedge CMC_3 \wedge CMC_4 \wedge CMC_5 \wedge CMC_6$, with

$CMC_1 \equiv \forall t < \infty : read(mOK) \textbf{ in } [t, t + \Delta_{read})$

$CMC_2 \equiv \forall t < \infty : send(pch)@t \rightarrow t \geq Init \wedge (\neg send(pch)) \textbf{ during } (t - Period, t)$

$CMC_3 \equiv \forall t < \infty : await_{\geq \delta_{ws}} rec(wch) \textbf{ in } [t, t + \delta_{wr})$

$CMC_4 \equiv \forall t_0, t_1 < \infty : t_0 + \delta_{wc} \leq t_1 \wedge rec(wch, v)@t_0 \wedge v \geq HSWL - \varepsilon_{ws}$
$\qquad\qquad \wedge (rec(wch) \geq HSWL - \varepsilon_{ws}) \textbf{ during } [t_0, t_1]$
$\qquad\qquad \wedge \neg read(mOK, 0) \textbf{ during } [t_0, t_1]$
$\qquad\qquad \rightarrow \exists t_2 \leq t_0 + \delta_{wc} : send(pch, 1)@t_2 \wedge \neg send(pch, 0) \textbf{ during } (t_2, t_1]$

$CMC_5 \equiv \forall t_0, t_1 < \infty : t_0 + \delta_{wc} \leq t_1 \wedge rec(wch, v)@t_0 \wedge v \leq LSWL + \varepsilon_{ws}$
$\qquad\qquad \wedge (rec(wch) \leq LSWL + \varepsilon_{ws}) \textbf{ during } [t_0, t_1]$
$\qquad\qquad \rightarrow \exists t_2 \leq t_0 + \delta_{wc} : send(pch, 0)@t_2 \wedge \neg send(pch, 1) \textbf{ during } (t_2, t_1]$

$CMC_6 \equiv \forall t_0, t_1 < \infty : t_0 + \delta_{ml} \leq t_1 \wedge read(mOK, 0)@t_0$
$\qquad\qquad \wedge \neg read(mOK, 1) \textbf{ during } [t_0, t_1]$
$\qquad\qquad \rightarrow \exists t_2 \leq t_0 + \delta_{ml} : send(pch, 0)@t_2 \wedge \neg send(pch, 1) \textbf{ during } (t_2, t_1]$

To simplify the proof of the implementation, we rewrite the last three, somewhat complicated, commitments as the conjunction of six simpler assertions. That is, we replace *CMC* by

$CC \equiv \forall t < \infty : \bigwedge_{i=1}^{9} CC_i(t)$, where

$CC_1(t) \equiv read(mOK) \textbf{ in } [t, t + \Delta_{read})$

$CC_2(t) \equiv send(pch)@t \rightarrow t \geq Init \wedge (\neg send(pch)) \textbf{ during } (t - Period, t)$

$CC_3(t) \equiv await_{\geq \delta_{ws}} rec(wch) \textbf{ in } [t, t + \delta_{wr})$

$CC_4(t) \equiv rec(wch, v)@t \wedge v \geq HSWL - \varepsilon_{ws}$
$\qquad\qquad \wedge \neg read(mOK, 0) \textbf{ during } [t, t + \delta_{wc}] \rightarrow send(pch, 1) \textbf{ in } [t, t + \delta_{wc}]$

$CC_5(t) \equiv rec(wch, v)@t \wedge v \leq LSWL + \varepsilon_{ws} \rightarrow send(pch, 0) \textbf{ in } [t, t + \delta_{wc}]$

$CC_6(t) \equiv read(mOK, 0)@t \rightarrow send(pch, 0) \textbf{ in } [t, t + \delta_{ml}]$

$CC_7(t) \equiv send(pch, 1)@t \rightarrow \exists t_0 \in [t - \delta_{wc}, t], v :$
$\qquad\qquad rec(wch, v)@t_0 \wedge v \geq HSWL - \varepsilon_{ws} \wedge \neg rec(wch) \textbf{ during } (t_0, t)$

$CC_8(t) \equiv send(pch, 1)@t$
$\qquad\qquad \rightarrow \exists t_0 \in [t - \delta_{ml}, t] : read(mOK, 1)@t_0 \wedge \neg read(mOK) \textbf{ during } (t_0, t)$

$CC_9(t) \equiv send(pch, 0)@t$
$\qquad\qquad \rightarrow [(\exists t_0 \in [t - \delta_{wc}, t], v : rec(wch, v)@t_0 \wedge v \leq LSWL + \varepsilon_{ws}$
$\qquad\qquad \wedge \neg rec(wch) \textbf{ during } (t_0, t))$
$\qquad\qquad \vee (\exists t_0 \in [t - \delta_{ml}, t] : read(mOK, 0)@t_0 \wedge \neg rec(wch) \textbf{ during } (t_0, t))]$

Lemma 5.11   If

$$LSWL - \varepsilon_{ws} < HSWL + \varepsilon_{ws} \tag{5.12}$$

then $CC \rightarrow CMC$

Proof: Since, for $i = 1, 2, 3, \forall t < \infty : CC_i(t) \leftrightarrow CMC_i$ it remains to prove CMC_4, CMC_5, and CMC_6.

To prove CMC_4, assume it is given that

$$t_0 + \delta_{wc} \leq t_1, rec(wch, v)@t_0$$
$$v \geq HSWL - \varepsilon_{ws}, (rec(wch) \geq HSWL - \varepsilon_{ws}) \textbf{ during } [t_0, t_1] \text{ and}$$
$$\neg read(mOK, 0) \textbf{ during } [t_0, t_1]$$

As $t_0 + \delta_{wc} \leq t_1$, we obtain $\neg read(mOK, 0) \textbf{ during } [t_0, t_0 + \delta_{wc}]$. Hence $CC_4(t_0)$ implies $send(pch, 1) \textbf{ in } [t_0, t_0 + \delta_{wc}]$, i.e. there is a $t_2 \in [t_0, t_0 + \delta_{wc}]$ such that $send(pch, 1)@t_2$. It remains to show $\neg send(pch, 0) \textbf{ during } (t_2, t_1]$. Suppose $send(pch, 0)@t_3$, for some $t_3 \in (t_2, t_1]$. Then by $CC_9(t_3)$ there are two possibilities:

- There exist $t_4 \in [t_3 - \delta_{wc}, t_3]$ and v_0 with $rec(wch, v_0)@t_4$, $v_0 \leq LSWL + \varepsilon_{ws}$ and $\neg rec(wch) \textbf{ during } (t_4, t_3)$.
  Since $rec(wch)@t_0$ and $t_3 > t_2 \geq t_0$, this implies that $t_4 \geq t_0$. Further, $t_4 \leq t_3 \leq t_1$, thus $t_4 \in [t_0, t_1]$. By $(rec(wch) \geq HSWL - \varepsilon_{ws}) \textbf{ during } [t_0, t_1]$ we obtain $v_0 \geq HSWL - \varepsilon_{ws}$. Using (5.12), this leads to a contradiction with $v_0 \leq LSWL + \varepsilon_{ws}$.
- There is some $t_4 \in [t_3 - \delta_{ml}, t_3]$ such that $read(mOK, 0)@t_4$ and $\neg rec(wch) \textbf{ during } (t_4, t_3)$. Then, as above, we can show $t_4 \in [t_0, t_1]$, which leads to a contradiction with $\neg read(mOK, 0) \textbf{ during } [t_0, t_1]$.

To prove CMC_5, let $t_0 + \delta_{wc} \leq t_1$, $rec(wch, v)@t_0$, $v \leq LSWL + \varepsilon_{ws}$, and $(rec(wch) \leq LSWL + \varepsilon_{ws}) \textbf{ during } [t_0, t_1]$. By $CC_5(t_0)$, $send(pch, 0) \textbf{ in } [t_0, t_0 + \delta_{wc}]$, i.e., there is a $t_2 \in [t_0, t_0 + \delta_{wc}]$ such that $send(pch, 0)@t_2$. It remains to prove $\neg send(pch, 1) \textbf{ during } (t_2, t_1]$. Suppose $send(pch, 1)@t_3$, for some $t_3 \in (t_2, t_1]$. Then by $CC_7(t_3)$ there exist $t_4 \in [t_3 - \delta_{wc}, t_3]$ and v_0 such that $rec(wch, v_0)@t_4$, $v_0 \geq HSWL - \varepsilon_{ws}$, and $\neg rec(wch) \textbf{ during } (t_4, t_3)$. As above, we can prove $t_4 \in [t_0, t_1]$. Then it is easy to see that $(rec(wch) \leq LSWL + \varepsilon_{ws}) \textbf{ during } [t_0, t_1]$ and (5.12) lead to a contradiction with $v_0 \geq HSWL - \varepsilon_{ws}$.

To prove CMC_6, assume

$$t_0 + \delta_{ml} \leq t_1, read(mOK, 0)@t_0, \text{ and } \neg read(mOK, 1) \textbf{ during } [t_0, t_1]$$

By $CC_6(t_0)$ we obtain $send(pch, 0) \textbf{ in } [t_0, t_0 + \delta_{ml}]$; i.e. there exists a $t_2 \in [t_0, t_0 + \delta_{ml}]$ with $send(pch, 0)@t_2$. It remains to prove $\neg send(pch, 1) \textbf{ during } (t_2, t_1]$. Let $send(pch, 1)@t_3$, for $t_3 \in (t_2, t_1]$. By $CC_8(t_3)$ there exists

$$t_4 \in [t_3 - \delta_{ml}, t_3] \text{ such that } read(mOK, 1)@t_4 \text{ and } \neg read(mOK) \textbf{ during } (t_4, t_3)$$

Since $read(mOK)@t_0$ and $t_3 > t_2 \geq t_0$, this implies that $t_4 \geq t_0$. Further, $t_4 \leq t_3 \leq t_1$. Thus $t_4 \in [t_0, t_1]$ and $read(mOK, 1)@t_4$ which contradicts $\neg read(mOK, 1) \textbf{ during } [t_0, t_1]$. □

By Lemma 5.11 it remains to implement *MContr* according to the specification

$$\langle\langle now = 0 \rangle\rangle \; MContr \; \langle\langle CC \rangle\rangle$$

We show that component *MContr* can be implemented by the program:

> **while** *true* **do**
> > **sel** *wch*?*x* **then skip or delay** δ_{ws} **then** $x := timeoutval$ **les**;
> > **read** $(mOK, mOKvar)$;
> > **if** $mOKvar = 1 \wedge x \geq HSWL - \varepsilon_{ws}$ **then** *pch*!!1
> > **else if** $mOKvar = 0 \vee x \leq LSWL + \varepsilon_{ws}$ **then** *pch*!!0 **fi fi**
> **od**

Let S be the body of the **while** construct above, i.e. $MContr \equiv$ **while** *true* **do** S **od**.

The program has a select statement which sets an upper bound of δ_{ws} on the waiting period for a message along *wch* (conform CC_3). This allows us to prove CC_1, which specifies a maximum delay between read actions on mOK. An alternative is to obtain this bound from commitment $CWSens_1$ of the water level sensor, but then this information would need to have been incorporated in the specification of $MContr$ (e.g. in the assumption).

To prove $\langle\langle now = 0 \rangle\rangle$ **while** *true* **do** S **od** $\langle\langle CC \rangle\rangle$ we use the While rule with

$$I \equiv \bigwedge_{i=1}^{9} I_i$$

where

$$I_1 \equiv \forall t \leq now - T_r - 2T_b - T_{comm} : CC_1(t)$$
$$I_2 \equiv maxsend(pch, Init, Period) \textbf{ during } [0, now - T_{comm}]$$
$$\wedge (\neg send(pch)) \textbf{ during } (now - T_{comm}, now)$$
$$I_3 \equiv \forall t \leq now - max(T_{comm}, T_a) - T_r - 2T_b - T_{comm} : CC_3(t)$$

and

$$I_i \equiv \forall t < now : CC_i(t), \ i = 4, \ldots, 9$$

Let $I_0 \equiv \bigwedge_{i=1}^{9} I_{0i}$, where

$$I_{01} \equiv \forall t \leq now - T_r - 3T_b - T_{comm} : CC_1(t)$$
$$I_{02} \equiv maxsend(pch, Init, Period) \textbf{ during } [0, now - T_{comm} - T_b)$$
$$\wedge (\neg send(pch)) \textbf{ during } (now - T_{comm} - T_b, now) \wedge now \geq T_b$$
$$I_{03} \equiv \forall t \leq now - max(T_{comm}, T_a) - T_r - 3T_b - T_{comm} : CC_3(t)$$
$$I_{0i} \equiv I_i, \text{ for } i = 4, \ldots, 9$$

Then it is easy to derive

$$\langle\langle I \rangle\rangle \textbf{ delay } T_b \langle\langle I_0 \rangle\rangle$$

Let $\hat{I}_1 \equiv I$. Then $I \rightarrow \hat{I}_1$ and $loc(\hat{I}_1) = \emptyset$. Further, $\forall t_1 < \infty \ \exists t_2 > t_1 : \hat{I}_1[t_2/now] \rightarrow CC$ can be proved rather easily. For instance,

$$\forall t_1 < \infty \ \exists t_2 > t_1 : I_1[t_2/now]$$
$$\equiv \forall t_1 < \infty \ \exists t_2 > t_1 : (\forall t \leq t_2 - T_r - 2T_b - T_{comm} : read(mOK) \textbf{ in } [t, t + \Delta_{read}))$$

which implies

$$\forall t < \infty : read(mOK) \text{ in } [t, t + \Delta_{read}), \text{ i.e. } \forall t < \infty : CC_1$$

Then, assuming $\langle\langle I_0 \wedge now < \infty \rangle\rangle \, S \, \langle\langle I \rangle\rangle$, the While rule leads to

$$\langle\langle I \rangle\rangle \text{ while } true \text{ do } S \text{ od } \langle\langle CC \wedge now = \infty \rangle\rangle$$

Since $now = 0 \rightarrow I$ (recall that $T_{comm} > 0$), the Consequence rule leads to

$$\langle\langle now = 0 \rangle\rangle \text{ while } true \text{ do } S \text{ od } \langle\langle CC \rangle\rangle$$

Hence it remains to prove $\langle\langle I_0 \wedge now < \infty \rangle\rangle \, S \, \langle\langle I \rangle\rangle$. By the conjunction rule, this can be divided into the proofs of

$$\langle\langle I_{0i} \wedge now < \infty \rangle\rangle \, S \, \langle\langle I_i \rangle\rangle, \text{ for } i = 1, \ldots, 9$$

Proof of I_i requires the intermediate assertions A_i, B_i, C_i, and D_i where

$$\langle\langle I_{0i} \wedge now < \infty \rangle\rangle$$

$$\textbf{sel } wch?x \textbf{ then skip or delay } \delta_{ws} \textbf{ then } x := timeoutval \textbf{ les } \langle\langle A_i \rangle\rangle \tag{1i}$$

$$\langle\langle A_i \wedge now < \infty \rangle\rangle \textbf{ read }(mOK, mOKvar) \langle\langle B_i \rangle\rangle \tag{2i}$$

$$\langle\langle B_i \wedge now < \infty \rangle\rangle \textbf{ delay } T_b \langle\langle C_i \rangle\rangle \tag{3i}$$

$$\langle\langle C_i \wedge mOKvar = 1 \wedge x \geq HSWL - \varepsilon_{ws} \wedge now < \infty \rangle\rangle \, pch!!1 \, \langle\langle I_i \rangle\rangle \tag{4i}$$

$$\langle\langle C_i \wedge (\neg(mOK = 1) \vee x < HSWL - \varepsilon_{ws}) \wedge now < \infty \rangle\rangle \textbf{ delay } T_b \langle\langle D_i \rangle\rangle \tag{5i}$$

$$\langle\langle D_i \wedge (mOKvar = 0 \vee x \leq LSWL + \varepsilon_{ws}) \wedge now < \infty \rangle\rangle \, pch!!0 \, \langle\langle I_i \rangle\rangle \tag{6i}$$

The proofs of these invariants have a similar structure and we shall illustrate the basic idea by giving the proof of I_{05}, i.e. $\forall t < now : CC_5(t)$. Define

$$A_5 \equiv I_{05} \vee (\forall t < now, t \neq now - T_{comm} : CC_5(t) \wedge rec(wch, x)@(now - T_{comm}))$$
$$B_5 \equiv I_{05} \vee (\forall t < now, t \neq now - T_{comm} - T_r : CC_5(t)$$
$$\wedge rec(wch, x)@(now - T_{comm} - T_r - T_b))$$
$$C_5 \equiv I_{05} \vee (\forall t < now, t \neq now - T_{comm} - T_r - T_b : CC_5(t)$$
$$\wedge rec(wch, x)@(now - T_{comm} - T_r - T_b))$$
$$D_5 \equiv I_{05} \vee (\forall t < now, t \neq now - T_{comm} - T_r - 2T_b : CC_5(t)$$
$$\wedge rec(wch, x)@(now - T_{comm} - T_r - 2T_b))$$

Finally, recall that $I_5 \equiv \forall t < now : CC_5(t)$. Then using $i = 5$, properties (15) to (65) can be derived provided, for (65),

$$\delta_{wc} \geq T_{comm} + T_r + 2T_b$$

The following constraints are required to prove the other invariants:

I_{01}: $\Delta_{read} = T_r + 3T_b + T_{comm} + \delta_{ws} + T_a$

I_{02}: $Init = 3T_b + T_{comm} + T_r$ and $Period = 3T_b + 2T_{comm} + T_r$

I_{03}: $\delta_{wr} = max(T_{comm}, T_a) + T_r + 3T_b + T_{comm}$

I_{04}: $\delta_{wc} \geq T_{comm} + T_r + T_b$

I_{06}: $\delta_{ml} \geq T_r + 2T_b$

I_{07}: $\delta_{wc} \geq T_{comm} + T_r + T_b$ and $timeoutval < HSWL - \varepsilon_{ws}$

I_{08}: $\delta_{wc} \geq T_r + T_b$

I_{09}: $\delta_{wc} \geq T_{comm} + T_r + 2T_b$, $\delta_{ml} \geq T_r + 2T_b$, $timeoutval > LSWL + \varepsilon_{ws}$

5.6.1 Conclusion: mine pump example

Finally, we can combine the design steps of the mine pump system and derive the constraints that are needed to ensure correctness. The previous section showed a program which correctly implements *MContr* with

$$
\begin{aligned}
\Delta_{read} &= T_r + 3T_b + T_{comm} + \delta_{ws} + T_a \\
Init &= 3T_b + T_{comm} + T_r \\
Period &= 3T_b + 2T_{comm} + T_r \\
\delta_{wr} &= max(T_{comm}, T_a) + T_r + 3T_b + T_{comm} \\
\delta_{wc} &= T_{comm} + T_r + 2T_b \\
\delta_{ml} &= T_r + 2T_b
\end{aligned}
$$

and provided

$$
LSWL + \varepsilon_{ws} < timeoutval < HSWL - \varepsilon_{ws}
$$

The design steps of preceding sections were proved to be correct, provided the following held:

- For Lemma 5.3, $LSWL \geq LWL + \delta_{sc}\lambda_{out}^{max}$, $HSWL \leq HWL - \delta_{sc}\lambda_{in}^{max}$ and $\lambda_{in}^{max} < \lambda_{out}^{min}$.
- For Lemma 5.8, $\delta_{sc} \geq \delta_{pc} + \delta_p$.
- For Lemma 5.9, $\delta_{pc} \geq \delta_{ws} + \delta_{wr} + \delta_{wc}$.
- For Lemma 5.10, $(\Delta_{read} + \delta_{ml} + \delta_p)\lambda_{ml}^{max} \leq CML - SML$.
- For Lemma 5.11, $LSWL - \varepsilon_{ws} < HSWL + \varepsilon_{ws}$.

These can be combined into the following list of constraints:

$$
\begin{aligned}
LSWL + 2\varepsilon_{ws} &< HSWL \\
LSWL &\geq LWL + (\delta_{ws} + \delta_{wr} + \delta_{wc} + \delta_p)\lambda_{out}^{max} \\
HSWL &\leq HWL - (\delta_{ws} + \delta_{wr} + \delta_{wc} + \delta_p)\lambda_{in}^{max} \\
\lambda_{in}^{max} &< \lambda_{out}^{min} \\
(\Delta_{read} + \delta_{ml} + \delta_p)\lambda_{ml}^{max} &\leq CML - SML
\end{aligned}
$$

To represent the reaction time we define an auxiliary parameter

$$
\begin{aligned}
\Delta_{react} &= \delta_{ws} + \delta_{wr} + \delta_{wc} + \delta_p \\
&= \delta_{ws} + \delta_p + max(T_{comm}, T_a) + 2T_r + 5T_b + 2T_{comm}.
\end{aligned}
$$

To satisfy these requirements, define

$$
\begin{aligned}
LSWL &= LWL + \Delta_{react}\lambda_{out}^{max} & (5.13) \\
HSWL &= HWL - \Delta_{react}\lambda_{in}^{max} & (5.14) \\
SML &= CML - (\Delta_{read} + \delta_{ml} + \delta_p)\lambda_{ml}^{max} & (5.15) \\
&= CML - (2T_r + 5T_b + T_{comm} + T_a\delta_{ws} + \delta_p)\lambda_{ml}^{max} & (5.16)
\end{aligned}
$$

Note that the constraint $LSWL + 2\varepsilon_{ws} < HSWL$ then corresponds to

$$LWL + \Delta_{react}\lambda_{out}^{max} + 2\varepsilon_{ws} < HWL - \Delta_{react}\lambda_{in}^{max}$$

Combining the constraints leads to the correctness of

$$\langle\langle now = 0 \rangle\rangle \; Sump \parallel Pump \parallel WSens \parallel Air \parallel MSens \parallel MContr \; \langle\langle CTL \rangle\rangle$$

provided

$$\lambda_{in}^{max} < \lambda_{out}^{min}$$
$$LWL + \Delta_{react}(\lambda_{out}^{max} + \lambda_{in}^{max}) + 2\varepsilon_{ws} < HWL$$

where $MContr$ is the program given at the start of this section, with *timeoutval* such that $LSWL + \varepsilon_{ws} < timeoutval < HSWL - \varepsilon_{ws}$ (note that by (5.13) such a value exists) and given the specifications of:

- *Sump* with *LSWL* and *HSWL* and a given maximum inflow λ_{in}^{max},
- *Pump* with $Init = 3T_b + T_{comm} + T_r$, $Period = 3T_b + 2T_{comm} + T_r$ and given values of δ_p and minimal outflow λ_{out}^{min},
- *WSens* for given values of δ_{ws} and ε_{ws},
- *Air* for a given value of λ_{ml}^{max} and with *SML* as defined above,
- *MSens* with *SML* as defined above.

5.7 Further work

The proof system described in this chapter can be extended and used in different ways. We shall consider briefly a few of these: scheduling, protocol verification and mechanical verification.

5.7.1 Scheduling

With maximal parallelism, each process has its own processor. This model can be generalized to multi-programming where several processes share a one processor and scheduling is based on priorities. Execution on a single processor is modelled as an interleaving of the atomic actions of the processes assigned to it. This interleaving can be restricted by the programmer by assigning priorities to statements. Then a processor only starts the execution of a statement when no other statement with a higher priority is ready to execute. In this extended formalism, the correctness of a program is based on a fixed (priority-based) scheduling algorithm (Hooman, 1991).

It might, however, be more convenient to have an intermediate level between scheduling theory and formal top-down system design in which the scheduling strategy is not yet fixed but requirements on the scheduler are specified. For instance, the implementation of the mine pump control system can be split into two parts. First we derive a set of tasks with periods and deadlines of the form

> **schedule** (*wch?x*) **with period** $\in [0, \delta_{ws}]$
> **schedule** (**read**$(mOK, mOKvar)$) **with period** $\in [0, \Delta_{read}]$
> **schedule** (*T*) **with period** $\in [\Delta_1, \Delta_2]$ **deadline** $\in [0, \Delta_3]$
> where $T \equiv$ **if** $mOKvar = 1 \wedge x \geq HSWL - \varepsilon_{ws}$ **then** *pch*!!1
> **else if** $mOKvar = 0 \vee x \leq LSWL + \varepsilon_{ws}$ **then** *pch*!!0 **fi fi**

Scheduling theory (see Chapters 3 and 4) can then be used to construct a feasible schedule for these tasks.

Alternatively, timing requirements can be specified explicitly by annotating programs with timing expressions (as was done in the Dedos project (Hammer *et al.*, 1994)). No assumptions are made about the execution time of statements but with the timing annotations requirements can be expressed for the execution time of statements. It is then left to a scheduler to guarantee that these timing requirements are satisfied. The formalization of this approach is a topic of current research.

5.7.2   Protocol verification

In Hooman (1993; 1994a), a distributed real-time arbitration protocol based on an algorithm of the IEEE 896 Futurebus specification (IEEE, 1988) for networks of processes $P_1 \| \cdots \| P_n$ using a general strategy:

1. Formulate a top-level specification for the network $P_1 \| \cdots \| P_n$, say
   $$\langle\langle A \rangle\rangle \; P_1 \| \cdots \| P_n \; \langle\langle C \rangle\rangle$$
2. Axiomatize the communication mechanism between the processes $P_1, \ldots, P_n$ by an axiom *COMAX*.
3. Find a suitable specification for each process P_i, for $i = 1, \ldots, n$,
   $$\langle\langle A_i \rangle\rangle \; P_i \; \langle\langle C_i \rangle\rangle$$
   in terms of the external communication interface of P_i only.
4. Prove $A \to A_1 \wedge \ldots \wedge A_n$ and $Comb(C_1, \ldots, C_n) \wedge COMAX \to C$.
5. Derive a correct implementation of process P_i, for $i = 1, \ldots, n$, using the proof method extended with rules for domain specific programming constructs.

This allows the development of a distributed program which satisfies the top-level specification. In Step 4, the protocol is verified at an abstract level using the compositionality of the parallel composition rule. Similar verification could be performed in another logic, e.g. a real-time version of temporal logic (Abadi & Lamport, 1994) or the duration calculus (Zhou *et al.*, 1991a) (see Chapter 7). The triples find use in Step 5, where their structure is very convenient for the formal derivation of programs.

Step 2 requires the communication mechanism to be axiomatized. For this, the assertion language is extended with suitable primitives (e.g. to denote send and receive actions) and the proof system is given axioms for these primitives (such as the relation between send and receive actions) and rules to relate communication statements of the programming language to the corresponding primitives of the assertion language.

Zhou and Hooman (1995) apply the first four steps of the method mentioned above to an atomic broadcast protocol (Cristian *et al.*, 1989) which requires timing correctness and fault-tolerance. The reliability of real-time systems requires the use of techniques that ensure the correct functioning of the system despite failures in some components. But providing such fault-tolerance usually influences the timing behaviour of a system. Given this strong relation between real-time and fault-tolerance, it would be desirable to extend our real-time framework to deal with fault-tolerance (see Chapter 8).

5.7.3 Mechanized support

Most of the work mentioned here has been based on manual, deductive verification but it is obvious that for a system of reasonable size some mechanized tool support is essential. This would allow proofs to be constructed interactively and checked mechanically so that simple verification conditions can be discharged automatically.

The Prototype Verification System PVS (Owre *et al.*, 1992) has been used to verify design steps during top-down design in the assumption–commitment framework presented in this chapter. The PVS specification language is a strongly typed higher-order logic. Specifications are structured into a hierarchy of parameterized 'theories' and some theories are built-in (e.g., reals, lists, sets, ordering relations, etc.). There is a mechanism to automatically generate theories for abstract data types. The PVS system has an interactive proof checker with induction rules, automatic rewriting and decision procedures for arithmetic. PVS proof steps can be composed into proof strategies.

To use the PVS specification language, a slight reformulation (Hooman, 1994b) was made in the framework to obtain a mixed formalism in which programs and specifications are unified (similar to, e.g. the mixed terms of Olderog (1985) and Zwiers (Zwiers, 1989)). In such a framework, assertional specifications can be freely mixed with constructs from the programming language. This makes it possible to formalize the process of program design and to describe the intermediate stages.

Use of this tool was demonstrated for the top-down derivation of a distributed real-time control system (a chemical batch processing system). Simple details are proved automatically using the PVS decision procedures. This improves the speed of the design and the verification and allows the user to concentrate on the essential structure of proofs. Further, the possibility of building hierarchies of parameterized theories is also very useful.

5.8 Historical background

5.8.1 Semantics

The programming language of this chapter and its semantics are to a large extent influenced by the work of Koymans *et al.* (1988) who defined a denotational real-time semantics for the maximal parallelism model. In Huizing *et al.* (1987), a fully abstract version of this semantics was developed. These semantic models are based on the linear history semantics of Francez *et al.* (1984).

The approach was extended to communicating shared resources by Gerber and Lee (1989; 1990). To obtain a calculus for shared resources a priority-based process algebra was presented. The computation model was defined by an operational semantics in which priorities are not taken into account but were incorporated later using an equivalence. Global, discrete time is obtained by assuming that all actions take one time unit.

An alternative, topological, approach can be found in Reed and Roscoe (1986), where the real-time behaviour of CSP programs is defined by means of complete metric spaces (see Chapter 6).

5.8.2   Hoare logic

Our formalism is based on classical Hoare triples (Hoare, 1969). These correctness formulae have been used for the specification and verification of many non-real-time programming languages. A good survey was given by Apt (1981; 1984) and an extensive formal treatment can be found in de Bakker (1980).

Usually, verification methods such as that by Manna and Pnueli (1982) for temporal logic and others by Owicki and Gries (1976), Apt *et al.* (1980) and Levin and Gries (1981) for the verification of parallel programs using Hoare triples, require the complete program text to be available. In contrast with these methods, we have formulated compositional proof systems which allow reasoning with the specifications of components without knowing their implementation. Compositionality can be considered to be a prerequisite for hierarchical, structured program derivation. A separation of concerns is then possible between the use of (and the reasoning about) a module and its implementation (Dijkstra, 1976; Lamport, 1983). With a compositional proof system, design steps can be verified during the process of top-down program construction. An overview of the transition from non-compositional proof methods towards compositional proof systems can be found de Roever (1985) and Hooman and de Roever (1986; 1990). The compositional proof system for our modified Hoare triples was inspired by the work of Zwiers (1989) and preliminary accounts can be found in Hooman (1987; 1990; 1991).

Related work was done by Haase (1981) who introduced real-time as a variable in the data space of the program and derived assertions using Dijkstra's weakest precondition calculus (Dijkstra, 1976). Bernstein (1987) discusses several ways of modelling message passing with time-out in the non-compositional framework of Levin and Gries (1981). A non-compositional approach can be found in Schneider *et al.* (1992), where a logic of proof outlines with control predicates is extended to concurrent real-time programs by adding a primitive to express the time at which a control predicate last became true. A similar extension of Hoare Logic was given by Shankar (1993) using a more general primitive to express the time that has elapsed since an assertion last held.

PVS (Owre *et al.*, 1992) and its predecessor, EHDM, have been used for a number of applications. EHDM was used to model digital flight-control systems (Rushby, 1993), for proof of an interactive convergence clock synchronization algorithm (Rushby & von

Henke, 1993) and Byzantine fault-tolerant clock synchronization (Shankar, 1993). An application of PVS was described by Lincoln and Rushby (1993), where an algorithm for interactive consistency has been verified.

5.8.3   Related work

Traditional linear time temporal logic (Pnueli, 1977; Manna & Pnueli, 1982; Owicki & Lamport, 1982) has been shown to be valuable in the specification and verification of the non-real-time behaviour of programs. It allows the expression of safety and liveness properties by using a qualitative notion of time. For instance, for an assertion φ, this logic can express the safety property 'henceforth φ will hold' ($\Box \varphi$) and the liveness property 'eventually φ will hold' ($\Diamond \varphi$). To specify real-time constraints, a quantitative notion of time has to be introduced. As already observed (Pnueli & Harel, 1988; Harel *et al.*, 1990), there are two main approaches to defining real-time versions of temporal logic. In the first, this logic is extended with a special variable which explicitly refers to the value of a global clock, the so-called Explicit Clock Temporal Logic. Descriptions of non-compositional proof methods using Explicit Clock Temporal Logic based on Manna and Pnueli (1982), can be found in Harel (1988) and Ostroff (1989), where decision procedures for this logic are given. A compositional proof method using Explicit Clock Temporal Logic was formulated by Hooman *et al.* (1991).

An alternative approach uses an extension proposed by Koymans *et al.* (1983) and Koymans and de Roever (1985), in which the scope of temporal operators is restricted by using time-bounds. Then we can express, for instance, 'during the next seven time units φ will hold' ($\Box_{<7} \varphi$) and 'eventually within five time units φ will hold' ($\Diamond_{<5} \varphi$). This logic is called Metric Temporal Logic (MTL), since in general it extends temporal logic by a metric point structure with a distance function to measure time; Koymans (1990; 1992) has a detailed discussion on MTL and several examples to illustrate its application to the specification of real-time systems. An early use of temporal operators with time-bounds can be found in Bernstein and Harter (1981), where a quantitative 'leads to' operator was introduced to verify real-time applications. In Koymans *et al.* (1983) a version of MTL was applied to the specification of real-time communication properties of a transmission medium. A temporal logic with statements about time intervals has been used by Shasha *et al.* (1984) to prove the correctness of local area network protocols. Hooman (1991) formulated a compositional proof system for formulae of the form S **sat** φ, where S is a program and φ a (real-time) property expressed in MTL. This proof system is based on compositional proof methods for classical temporal logic (Barringer *et al.*, 1984; Nguyen *et al.*, 1986) and a preliminary version, for a simplified language, appeared in Hooman and Widom (1989).

Logics for reasoning about real-time systems were classified by Alur and Henzinger (1990) according to their complexity and expressiveness. A tableau-based decision procedure is given for a version of metric temporal logic. For decidability, a discrete time domain is used. In a decidable version of the explicit clock approach (called TPTL), special variables represent values of a global clock and a 'freezing' quantification binds a variable to the value of the clock in a certain state. In Harel *et al.* (1990) a decision procedure and a model checking algorithm are given for a suitably restricted version of Explicit Clock Temporal Logic. The expressibility of this logic is shown to be incomparable with TPTL. Similar to the extension of linear time temporal logic to MTL, branching time temporal logic, also called Computation Tree Logic (CTL), can be extended to real-time by adding time-bounds to the modal operators. For instance, in Emerson *et al.* (1989), algorithms for model checking and satisfiability analysis are presented for a logic with discrete time. It is shown in Alur *et al.* (1990) that model checking results can be extended to CTL over a dense time domain. Finally, the logic defined by Hansson and Jonsson (1989) extends CTL with discrete time and probabilities.

Lamport's temporal logic of actions (TLA) is a formal specification language and a refinement method to support the top-down design of systems (Lamport, 1994). It has been extended to real-time by adding a special variable *now* to represent time (Abadi & Lamport, 1994). The extended notation was applied to a hybrid system – the gas burner – and to a solution of the Byzantine generals problem (Lamport, 1993; Lamport & Merz, 1994).

Zwarico and Lee (1985) adapted Hoare's trace model to real-time. Jahanian and Mok (1986) defined a real-time logic to analyze safety properties based on a function which assigns a time-value to each occurrence of an event. Real-time properties of sliding window protocols were verified by Shankar and Lam (1987) using special state variables, called timers, to measure the passage of time.

5.9 Exercises

Exercise 5.1 Consider, for asynchronous channels *in*, *c*, and *out*, the processes

$S_1 \equiv in?x;\ x := x + 1;\ c!!x,$
$S_2 \equiv$ **while** *true* **do sel** $c?y$ **then** $y := y + 2;\ out!!y$
  or delay 5 **then** *alarm*!!1 **les od**

and the specification

$$\langle\langle now = 0 \rangle\rangle\ S_1 \| S_2\ \langle\langle rec(in, 4)@0 \rightarrow send(out, 7) \in [\delta_1, \delta_2] \rangle\rangle$$

Give constraints on the parameters and determine δ_1 and δ_2 such that this triple can be derived. Give the main steps of this derivation.

Exercise 5.2 Consider a real-time system M which reacts on input v along asynchronous channel *in* by sending the value $f_2(f_1(v))$ via asynchronous channel *out* in less than Δ time units. With the parameters Δ_1, Δ_2, Δ_3, and Δ_4 we have $\{waitrec(in), rec(in), send(out)\} \subseteq obs(M)$ and the specification

$$\langle\langle now = 0 \rangle\rangle\ M\ \langle\langle q_0 \wedge q_1 \wedge q_2 \rangle\rangle$$

where

$q_0 \quad \equiv \quad maxsend(out, \Delta_1, \Delta_2)$ **during** $[0, \infty)$

$q_1 \quad \equiv \quad minwait(in, \Delta_3, \Delta_4)$ **during** $[0, \infty)$

$q_2 \quad \equiv \quad \forall t < \infty : rec(in, v)@t \rightarrow send(out, f_2(f_1(v)))$ **in** $[t, t + \Delta)$

(a) Suppose we have an environment E with

$$\{send(in), waitrec(out), rec(out)\} \subseteq obs(E)$$

satisfying

$$\langle\!\langle\, now = 0 \,\rangle\!\rangle \; E \; \langle\!\langle\, r_1 \wedge r_2 \,\rangle\!\rangle$$

where

$r_1 \quad \equiv \quad maxsend(in, \Delta_3, \Delta_4)$ **during** $[0, \infty)$

$r_2 \quad \equiv \quad minwait(out, \Delta_1, \Delta_2)$ **during** $[0, \infty)$.

Prove

$$\langle\!\langle\, now = 0 \,\rangle\!\rangle \; M\|E \; \langle\!\langle\, q \,\rangle\!\rangle$$

with $q \equiv \forall t < \infty : send(in, v)@t \rightarrow rec(out, f_2(f_1(v)))$ **in** $[t, t + \Delta)$.

(b) Implement M by two parallel components M_1 and M_2 which compute f_1 and f_2, respectively, and communicate internally via the asynchronous channel mid. Component M_1 is given by $\{waitrec(in), rec(in), send(mid)\} \subseteq obs(M_1)$ and

$$\langle\!\langle\, now = 0 \,\rangle\!\rangle \; M_1 \; \langle\!\langle\, q_1 \wedge q_3 \,\rangle\!\rangle$$

where $q_3 \equiv \forall t < \infty : rec(in, v)@t \rightarrow send(mid, f_1(v))@(t + \delta_1)$. M_2 is specified as $\{waitrec(mid), rec(mid), send(out)\} \subseteq obs(M_2)$ and

$$\langle\!\langle\, now = 0 \,\rangle\!\rangle \; M_2 \; \langle\!\langle\, q_0 \wedge q_4 \wedge q_5 \,\rangle\!\rangle$$

where

$q_4 \quad \equiv \quad \forall t < \infty : await\, rec(mid)$ **in** $[t, t + \delta_2)$

$q_5 \quad \equiv \quad \forall t < \infty : (mid, v_0)@t \rightarrow send(out, f_2(v_0))$ **in** $[t, t + \delta_3)$

Prove, under certain requirements on the parameters δ_1, δ_2, δ_3 and Δ, that

$$\langle\!\langle\, now = 0 \,\rangle\!\rangle \; M_1\|M_2 \; \langle\!\langle\, q_0 \wedge q_1 \wedge q_2 \,\rangle\!\rangle$$

(c) Construct programs that satisfy the specifications of M_1 and M_2 and formulate the required constraints on the parameters.

Exercise 5.3 Consider an asynchronous channel c and a parameter $T \in TIME$. Prove the following implication:

$(\exists t_0 : waitrec(c) \textbf{ during } [0,t_0) \land (rec(c)@t_0 \lor t_0 = T))$
$\land (\exists t_1 < T : \neg send(c) \textbf{ during } [0,t_1) \land send(c,v)@t_1) \rightarrow rec(c,v) \textbf{ in } [0,T)$

(Informally this says that if a process waits to receive input on c until either a message has been received or time T has been reached, and if another process sends v along c before T, then v is received along c in less than T time units.)

Exercise 5.4 Consider the program $S_1 \| S_2$ with asynchronous channels *in*, *mid*, *out* and *alarm*. For S_1 we have $obs(S_1) = \{waitrec(in), rec(in), send(mid)\}$ and

$$\langle\langle now = 0 \rangle\rangle \, S_1 \, \langle\langle q_1 \rangle\rangle$$

with

$$q_1 \equiv \forall t < \infty : rec(in,v)@t \rightarrow \exists t_1 < 10 : \neg send(mid) \textbf{ during } [0,t_1)$$
$$\land \, send(mid, v+1)@t_1$$

S_2 is specified by $obs(S_2) = \{waitrec(mid), rec(mid), send(out), send(alarm)\}$ and

$$\langle\langle now = 0 \rangle\rangle \, S_2 \, \langle\langle q_2 \land q_3 \land q_4 \rangle\rangle$$

with

$q_2 \;\equiv\; \forall t < \infty : rec(mid,v)@t \rightarrow send(out, v+2) \textbf{ in } [t, t+25)$
$q_3 \;\equiv\; \exists t_0 : waitrec(mid) \textbf{ during } [0,t_0) \land (rec(mid)@t_0 \lor t_0 = 10)$ and
$q_4 \;\equiv\; waitrec(mid) \textbf{ during } [0, 0+10) \rightarrow send(alarm)@10$

(a) Prove that, under a certain condition on the parameter Δ,

$$\langle\langle now = 0 \rangle\rangle \, S_1 \| S_2 \, \langle\langle r \rangle\rangle$$

with $r \equiv rec(in,v)@0 \rightarrow send(out, v+3) \textbf{ in } [0,\Delta)$. Hint: use Exercise 5.3.
(b) Derive programs that satisfy the specifications of S_1 and S_2, given certain conditions on the parameters T_a, T_{comm}, etc.

Exercise 5.5 Process P, specified below, used the asynchronous channels *in*, *out* and *alarm*:

$\{waitrec(in), rec(in), send(out), send(alarm)\} \subseteq obs(P)$
$\langle\langle now = 0 \rangle\rangle \, P \, \langle\langle q_1 \land q_2 \land q_3 \rangle\rangle$

with

$q_1 \equiv \forall t < \infty : rec(in,v)@t \rightarrow send(out, f(v)) \textbf{ in } [t, t+2)$
$q_2 \equiv \forall t < \infty : await\, rec(in) \textbf{ in } [t, t+3)$ and
$q_3 \equiv \forall t < \infty : waitrec(in) \textbf{ during } [t, t+10) \rightarrow send(alarm) \textbf{ in } [0, t+11)$

Consider the following two possible specifications of the environment E of P:

(a) Suppose E satisfies the following specification:

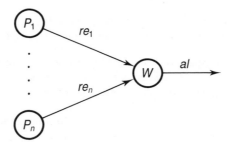

Figure 5.5 Watchdog timer network

$$\{send(in), waitrec(out), rec(out), waitrec(alarm), rec(alarm)\} \subseteq obs(E)$$
$$\langle\!\langle now = 0 \rangle\!\rangle \ E \ \langle\!\langle r_1 \rangle\!\rangle$$

with $r_1 \equiv \forall t < \infty : send(in)@t \to t \geq 3 \wedge (\neg send(in))$ **during** $[t-3, t)$. Prove

$$\langle\!\langle now = 0 \rangle\!\rangle \ P\|E \ \langle\!\langle q_4 \rangle\!\rangle$$

with $q_4 \equiv \forall t < \infty : send(in, v)@t \to send(out, f(v))$ **in** $[t, t+2)$.

(b) Now suppose E satisfies

$$\{send(in), waitrec(out), rec(out), waitrec(alarm), rec(alarm)\} \subseteq obs(E)$$
$$\langle\!\langle now = 0 \rangle\!\rangle \ E \ \langle\!\langle r_2 \rangle\!\rangle$$

where $r_2 \equiv (\neg send(in))$ **during** $[4, 17)$. Then prove

$$\langle\!\langle now = 0 \rangle\!\rangle \ P\|E \ \langle\!\langle q_5 \rangle\!\rangle$$

where $q_5 \equiv send(alarm)$ **in** $[0, 18)$.

(c) Derive a program satisfying the specification of P, given certain conditions on the parameters T_a, T_g, T_{comm}, etc.

Exercise 5.6 Design a 'watchdog' process W whose job is to check whether the processes $P_1, \ldots, P_n$ are functioning properly. The network is shown in Figure 5.5, where $re_1, \ldots, re_n$, and al are asynchronous channels.

Ignore the actual task to be performed by each P_i but assume that it is functioning correctly iff it sends a reset signal to W on channel re_i at least once every ten time units. As long as all processes P_i send a reset signal in time, the watchdog timer W does not communicate on the alarm channel al. But if W has to wait for a reset signal on a particular re_i for ten time units or more, it will send an alarm message on channel al within K time units. Ignore the behaviour of W after a communication on al. W can therefore be specified by

$$\langle\!\langle now = 0 \rangle\!\rangle \ W \ \langle\!\langle C_w \rangle\!\rangle$$

where

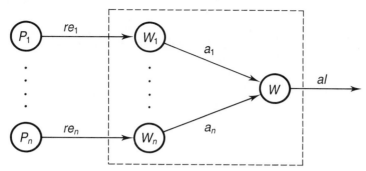

Figure 5.6 Refinement of the watchdog timer network

$$C_w \equiv \forall t < \infty : ((\exists i : waitrec(re_i) \textbf{ during } [t, t+10))$$
$$\rightarrow \exists t_0 < t + 10 + K : send(al)@t_0)$$
$$\wedge (send(al)@t$$
$$\rightarrow \exists i \in \{1, \dots, n\} \, \exists t_1 < \infty : waitrec(re_i) \textbf{ during } [t_1, t_1 + 10))$$

(a) Prove that if each P_i sends a signal on channel re_i at least once every ten time units then no signal is sent on al. To specify that the P_i are functioning properly, assume

$$\langle\!\langle now = 0 \rangle\!\rangle \; P_i \; \langle\!\langle \forall t < \infty : send(re_i) \textbf{ in } [t, t+10) \rangle\!\rangle$$

Then prove that an alarm message never occurs in the network, i.e.

$$\langle\!\langle now = 0 \rangle\!\rangle \; P_1 \| \cdots \| P_n \| W \; \langle\!\langle \neg send(al) \textbf{ during } [0, \infty) \rangle\!\rangle$$

(By compositionality, the properties of the network $P_1 \| \cdots \| P_n \| W$ can be verified using the specifications of the components, without knowing their implementations.)

(b) Design a program to implement the watchdog process W and satisfy the commitment C_w. Since the reset signals of any of the processes $P_1, \dots, P_n$ may arrive at the same time, implement W as a parallel composition $W \equiv W_1 \| \cdots \| W_n \| A$ (in Figure 5.6 the $a_1, \dots, a_n$ are synchronous channels). Process W_i is the watchdog for P_i and signals process A via channel a_i as soon as there is no communication on re_i for at least ten time units; process A waits for a signal on any of the a_is; after receipt of a signal it sends a message on al.

Since the exact timing requirements for W_i and A may not be clear at this level, use parameters K_i and K_a in their specifications. This leads to

$$\langle\!\langle now = 0 \rangle\!\rangle \; W_i \; \langle\!\langle C_{w_i} \rangle\!\rangle$$

where

$$C_{w_i} \equiv \forall t < \infty : (waitrec(re_i) \textbf{ during } [t, t+10)$$
$$\rightarrow (waitsend(a_i) \vee send(a_i)) \textbf{ in } [t+10, t+10+K_i))$$
$$\wedge ((waitsend(a_i) \vee send(a_i))@t$$
$$\rightarrow \exists t_2 < \infty : waitrec(re_i) \textbf{ during } [t_2, t_2+10))$$

Process A is specified by

$$\langle\langle now = 0 \rangle\rangle \ A \ \langle\langle C_a \rangle\rangle$$

where

$$C_a \equiv (\bigwedge_{j=1}^{n} waitrec(a_j) \textbf{ during } [0, \infty) \wedge (\neg send(al)) \textbf{ during } [0, \infty))$$
$$\vee (\exists i \in \{1, \ldots, n\} \ \exists t_3 < \infty : \bigwedge_{j=1}^{n} waitrec(a_j) \textbf{ during } [0, t_3)$$
$$\wedge rec(a_i)@t_3 \wedge send(al) \textbf{ in } [t_3, t_3 + K_a))$$

Prove

$$\langle\langle now = 0 \rangle\rangle \ W_1 \| \cdots \| W_n \| A \ \langle\langle C_w \rangle\rangle$$

provided certain constraints on K, K_i and K_a hold.

Chapter 6

Specification and Verification in Timed CSP

Steve Schneider

Introduction

Communicating sequential processes (CSP) is a language designed to describe formally the patterns of communication behaviour of system components or processes and how these components may be combined. The theory of CSP enables the formal description of system specifications and supports their analysis, judging them against the requirements. A theory of refinement allows CSP descriptions at a high level of abstraction to be refined to a level of description more appropriate for implementation. This allows abstract CSP processes to act as specifications, describing the behaviour expected of any implementation.

Timed CSP is a direct extension of the original CSP, and includes explicit timing constructs enabling the description of quantitative timing behaviour. A theory of *timewise refinement* allows mappings between untimed and timed processes. We will use the abbreviation CSP to refer to the timed extension of the language.[1]

6.1 The language of real-time CSP

The CSP language describes processes in terms of their communication behaviour, removing internal state information that does not affect the communication behaviour. This abstraction is appropriate for real-time systems since they are reactive and interact continually with their environment. The requirements of such systems are concerned primarily with the interactions between a component and its environment.

---

[1]The reader should be aware that this is not the usual practice: the timed language is more commonly called real-time CSP.

147

6.1.1 Events and processes

A process is modelled in terms of the possible interactions it can have with its environment, which may be thought of as another process or set of processes, the 'outside world', or a combination of these. The first step in the description of a process is to decide on the ways in which interactions can take place.

Interactions are described in terms of instantaneous atomic synchronizations, or *events*. This kind of synchronization is sufficiently simple to model asynchronous and shared memory communication. A process cooperating with its environment for some length of time is described in terms of a single event occurring at the point at which they agree to cooperate. A process can be considered as a 'black box' with an interface containing a number of events through which it interacts with other processes. The set of all events in the interface of a process is called its alphabet. In this set, interface events are treated as synchronizations between the participating processes and not as autonomous actions under the control of a single process. A process containing an event in its interface is required to participate in the occurrence of that event. The refusal of a single participant to cooperate will block its occurrence.

6.1.2 Computational model

Before we formally describe the language of CSP and how it is to be understood, we must make explicit a number of assumptions concerning the underlying model of computation and the nature of time:

- *Maximal progress:* A synchronization event occurs as soon as all participants are ready to perform it.
- *Maximal parallelism:* Every process has a dedicated processor; processes do not compete for processor time.
- *Finite variability:* No process may perform infinitely many events, or undergo infinitely many state changes, in a finite interval of time.
- *Real-time:* The time domain is taken to be the non-negative real numbers. Thus it is possible for events to occur at any non-negative real time. Since the reals are dense, our maximal parallelism assumption above means that there is no positive lower bound on the time difference between two independent events occurring at different times.
- *Newtonian time:* Time progresses in all processes at the same rate, and all with respect to the same unique global time frame.

The assumption of maximal progress has close connections with the treatment of processes and the events that they may perform. In addition to the events in the interface of a process (external events), a process description may also include internal events. The interface of a process P will not contain its internal events as they will be performed by P

without the participation of its environment. In practice, an internal event usually corresponds to a synchronization between parallel components of P. Maximal progress means that an internal event occurs as soon as P is ready to perform it, and this will be as soon as all the participating components of P are ready.

External events, on the other hand, require the participation of the environment of P. An external event a can occur only when all processes which contain a in their interface agree to perform it. If P is one of a number of such processes which are components of a composite process R, and the event a is external for R, then the occurrence of a will be influenced by R's environment. If a is internal to R, then by maximal progress it will occur as soon as all the participants, one of which is P, are able to perform it.

6.1.3   The operators of CSP

The language of CSP is defined by the following pseudo Backus–Naur form definitions:

$$P \quad ::= \quad STOP \mid SKIP \mid P; P \mid a \rightarrow P \mid \qquad \text{sequential}$$

$$P \,\square\, P \mid P \sqcap P \mid P \overset{t}{\triangleright} P \mid \qquad \text{choice}$$

$$P \,\|[A\,|\,A]\|\, P \mid P \,\|\|\, P \mid \qquad \text{parallel}$$

$$P \setminus A \mid f(P) \mid f^{-1}(P) \mid \qquad \text{abstraction}$$

$$X \mid \mu X \bullet P \qquad \text{recursion}$$

Σ is the set of all possible events, a is in Σ, A in $\mathcal{P}(\Sigma)$, t in $[0, \infty)$, f is a function $\Sigma \rightarrow \Sigma$ and X is a process variable. CSP *processes* are terms with no free process variables (i.e. every process variable is bound by some μ expression). In a CSP process, every recursive expression is time-guarded to ensure finite variability (i.e. there is some $t > 0$ for which any execution must take at least t to reach a recursive invocation). Since the only operator that introduces a delay is the timeout operator $\overset{t}{\triangleright}$, every occurrence of a process variable must be guarded by a non-zero timeout.

We shall use the convention that events are written in lower case, and processes are written in upper case.

Sequential
The process $STOP$ is the deadlocked process, unable to engage in any events or make any progress (this might adequately describe a surly waiter in a restaurant who refuses to serve any customer). It might be used to describe a system which has crashed, or which has deadlocked: no further events are possible.

The process $SKIP$ is the immediately terminating process. This might describe the waiter whose shift ends as soon as it starts. No events are performed, but in contrast to $STOP$ it can signal to its environment that it has terminated, and an appropriate environment would be able to pass control to another process.

The sequential composition $P; Q$ behaves as P until P terminates, and then behaves as Q. Thus $WAITER_1; WAITER_2$ initially behaves as $WAITER_1$ until the shift finishes; the subsequent behaviour is that of $WAITER_2$.

As we might expect, $SKIP$; $P = P$ for any P, and $STOP$; $P = STOP$; indeed the semantic model supports these equations. The first equation states that since $SKIP$ does nothing except immediately pass control to P, the resulting behaviour is indistinguishable from that of P. In the second equation, the deadlocked process $STOP$ does not indicate termination so P will never be reached and the result is equivalent to $STOP$.

The prefix process $a \rightarrow P$ is ready to engage in event a (and in no other event). It will continue to wait until its environment is also ready to perform a, at which point synchronization on this event will occur. Once the event is performed, the subsequent behaviour of $a \rightarrow P$ will be that of process P. By default, there is no delay between the occurrence of a and the beginning of P. A waiter who is prepared to take a customer's coat before serving may be described by the process $coat \rightarrow SERVE$, where the event $coat$ models the synchronization between customer and waiter achieved by the removal of the coat.

We later define a form of prefix which explicitly introduces a delay: $a \xrightarrow{t} P$ is also ready initially to engage in a; but once that event is performed, there is a delay of t before it behaves as P. The waiter who takes ten minutes between removing the coat and serving would be described by $coat \xrightarrow{10} SERVE$.

The behaviour of a waiter to a single customer may be described by the following process:

$$WAITER = table \xrightarrow{2} coat \xrightarrow{5} order \xrightarrow{20} serve \xrightarrow{30}$$
$$pay \xrightarrow{0.01} tip \xrightarrow{3} coat \rightarrow SKIP$$

The waiter is prepared to show a customer to a table, then, after a short delay, to remove a coat, then take an order, serve, accept payment, accept a tip and finally return the coat. Observe that each of these events indicates a readiness to interact: if the customer is not ready to order until ten minutes after the coat is taken, the waiter will wait; if the customer is ready after only three minutes, the waiter will not yet be ready to interact.

Choice

An *external* choice $P \square Q$ is initially ready to engage in events that either P or Q is ready to engage in. The first event performed resolves the choice in favour of the component that was able to perform it, and the subsequent behaviour is given by this component.

A choice offered to the customer between two items on the menu could be modelled using this choice:

$$duck \xrightarrow{20} SERVE_d \square grouse \xrightarrow{20} SERVE_g$$

Here, a choice of two processes, $duck \xrightarrow{20} SERVE_d$ and $grouse \xrightarrow{20} SERVE_g$, is offered to the customer. Both initial events are available, and the choice is resolved at the point the customer performs one of these events.

An *internal* choice $P \sqcap Q$ behaves either as P or as Q but, unlike the external choice, the environment cannot influence the way the choice is resolved. The choice

$$duck \xrightarrow{20} SERVE_d \sqcap grouse \xrightarrow{20} SERVE_g$$

is not made by the customer, but is made instead by the system (the restaurant in this case), and the customer has no influence over which way it is resolved. It may be resolved by always choosing *duck*, by tossing a coin, by alternating between *duck* and *grouse* or by choosing whichever is cheaper. Any of these approaches will be acceptable to a customer who does not mind which of the items is eventually served, as long as at least one of *duck* or *grouse* is offered.

The timeout choice $P \overset{t}{\triangleright} Q$ initially behaves as process P. If an event is performed before time t, then the choice is resolved in favour of P, which continues to execute, and Q is discarded. If no such event is performed, then the timeout occurs at time t, and the subsequent behaviour is that of Q. An impatient customer may wait five minutes for a table, but will leave the restaurant if no table becomes available in that time. This may be described by the process $CUST = (table \rightarrow MEAL) \overset{5}{\triangleright} LEAVE$. If the event *table* is not performed within five units of time (minutes in this case), then the timeout will occur, since the first process will not have performed any events, and the customer will behave as the exception process.

Timeout may be used to handle exceptions in a number of ways. It may provide opportunities for disagreement. The following fragment from the wedding service provides an illustration:

$$(speak\_now \rightarrow DISRUPTION) \overset{10}{\triangleright} FOREVER\_HOLD\_PEACE$$

The expectation is that the timeout should occur (i.e. that the event *speak_now* does not occur), but an opportunity should be provided to prevent it if necessary.

More often, timeout is used to detect errors: if an expected response is not received within a certain time, some corrective action should be taken.

Parallel

The parallel combination $P \,\|[A\,|\,B]\|\, Q$ allows P to engage in events from the set A (only), and Q to engage in events from the set B (only). The processes P and Q must synchronize on all events in the intersection $A \cap B$ of these two interfaces, but other events are performed independently.

The customer $CUST$ may have a set of possible interactions:

$$A_C = \{table, order, serve, eat, pay, tip, coat\}$$

Although any real customer will have other actions of interest, we are interested in modelling interactions with the restaurant, and so we have abstracted all activity irrelevant to the situation we are modelling.

Events of interest in the restaurant might be described by the set

$$A_R = \{table, order, pay, tip, coat, serve, cook\}$$

A waiter who has a table ready will be able to interact with the customer:

$$CUST \,\|[A_C\,|\,A_R]\|\, WAITER$$

But, a waiter who has a cigarette before showing a customer to a table may lose the customer:

$$CUST \; |[A_C \,|\, A_R]| \; CIGARETTE; \; WAITER$$

If *CIGARETTE* takes too long to terminate, the customer may no longer wish to be shown to a table but if it terminates sufficiently quickly, the waiter will be ready before the customer walks out. The event *table* can occur only at times when both participants are prepared to engage in it.

If the process *MEAL* is $eat \xrightarrow{15} coat \rightarrow SKIP$, then the customer *CUST* (defined in terms of *MEAL*) is not prepared to offer a tip and requires the return of his coat after eating. Since the waiter is not prepared to return the coat until a tip has been received, the parallel combination of *CUST* with *WAITER* will deadlock: although each participant is able to continue on some event, there is no event on which they can they can agree.

The asynchronous parallel combination $P \;|||\; Q$ represents the independent concurrent execution of P and Q, with no synchronization between them on any events. A number of separate waiters might be described using this construct:

$$WAITERS = WAITER \;|||\; WAITER \;|||\; \ldots \;|||\; WAITER$$

None of the waiters interacts with any other, though they may all interact with a customer. In the combination

$$CUST \; |[A_C \,|\, A_R]| \; WAITERS$$

the customer can cooperate with any waiter; the choice between waiters is nondeterministic: any that is prepared to perform *table* when the customer performs it may be chosen.

Abstraction

The *hiding* operator $P \setminus A$ makes the events in the set A internal to the process, thus removing them from the control of the environment. The only participants will then be the components of P. From the maximal progress assumption, the internal events will occur as soon as P is ready to perform them. In general, internal events occur as soon as they are ready, unless they are pre-empted because of conflict, such as when there is a choice between events.

A print spooler *SPOOL* and *PRINTER* communicate via channel *print*:

$$SPOOL \;\; = \;\; in \xrightarrow{2} print \xrightarrow{3} SPOOL$$

$$PRINTER \;\; = \;\; print \xrightarrow{30} out \rightarrow PRINTER$$

The parallel combination $SPOOL \;|[in, print \,|\, print, out]|\; PRINTER$ has *print* as a visible channel and further processes may participate in it. Since only *SPOOL* and *PRINTER* should participate in that synchronization, we make *print* internal:

$$(SPOOL \;|[in, print \,|\, print, out]|\; PRINTER) \setminus print$$

and the event *print* will occur as soon as both processes are ready to perform it.

The *renaming* operators $f(P)$ and $f^{-1}(P)$ change the names of events through the alphabet mapping function f. This allows a generic pattern of communication to be defined for use with different events. For example, a waiter responsible for table i might be described by a generic *WAITER* process and a renaming f_i which maps any event a to a_i. Thus $f_1(WAITER)$ is prepared to show a customer to table 1, but to no other table.

Renaming using the inverse function f^{-1} allows a number of events to trigger a particular communication. If function g has $g(credit\_card) = pay$ and $g(cash) = pay$, then the process $g^{-1}(WAITER)$ is prepared to engage in a *credit_card* event or a *cash* event whenever *WAITER* is prepared to accept a *pay* event. The function h satisfying $h(table_i) = table$ allows $h^{-1}(WAITER)$ to show a customer to any table:

$$g^{-1}(WAITER) = table \xrightarrow{2} coat \xrightarrow{5} order \xrightarrow{20} serve \xrightarrow{30}$$
$$(credit\_card \xrightarrow{0.01} tip \xrightarrow{3} coat \to SKIP$$
$$\Box \; cash \xrightarrow{0.01} tip \xrightarrow{3} coat \to SKIP)$$

$$h^{-1}(WAITER) = (table_1 \xrightarrow{2} coat \xrightarrow{5} order \xrightarrow{20} serve \xrightarrow{30}$$
$$credit\_card \xrightarrow{0.01} tip \xrightarrow{3} coat \to SKIP)$$
$$\Box \; (table_2 \xrightarrow{2} coat \xrightarrow{5} order \xrightarrow{20} serve \xrightarrow{30}$$
$$credit\_card \xrightarrow{0.01} tip \xrightarrow{3} coat \to SKIP)$$
$$\vdots$$
$$\Box \; (table_n \xrightarrow{2} coat \xrightarrow{5} order \xrightarrow{20} serve \xrightarrow{30}$$
$$credit\_card \xrightarrow{0.01} tip \xrightarrow{3} coat \to SKIP)$$

Recursion

A recursive term $\mu X \bullet P$ behaves as P, with every occurrence of X in P representing an immediate recursive invocation. Thus we will have the usual law

$$\mu X \bullet P = P[\mu X \bullet P / X]$$

Every recursive term of the form $\mu X \bullet P$ that has P must be t-guarded for X for some $t > 0$ — so that every occurrence of X in P requires the passage of at least t units of time before it can be reached.

A waiter who deals with customers repeatedly may be described by the recursive process $\mu X \bullet WAITER; X$, or alternatively by a recursive definition.

$$RWAITER = table \xrightarrow{2} coat \xrightarrow{5} order \xrightarrow{20} serve \xrightarrow{30}$$
$$pay \xrightarrow{0.01} tip \xrightarrow{3} coat \to RWAITER$$

6.1.4   Generalized operators

The delay process *Wait t* is a timed form of *SKIP* which does nothing for *t* units of time and then terminates successfully:

$$Wait\ t\ =\ STOP \overset{t}{\triangleright} SKIP$$

The timeout choice will wait for *t* units of time, but the process *STOP* cannot perform any event and at time *t* control is passed to *SKIP*, which then terminates immediately.
   A delayed form of prefixing can be defined as

$$a \overset{t}{\to} P\ =\ a \to (Wait\ t;\ P)$$

After the event *a*, there is a delay of *t* before control reaches *P*.
   Generalizing choice to allow infinite choices is often useful. The prefix choice

$$a : A \to P_a$$

remains willing to perform any event from set *A* until one is chosen. Its subsequent behaviour, given by P_a, is dependent on that event. Thus a construct can be defined to allow the input on channel *in* of any item *x* in a set *M*, and the value *x* determines the subsequent behaviour:

$$in?x : M \to Q(x)\ =\ a : in.M \to P_a$$

where the set $in.M = \{in.m \mid m \in M\}$ and $P_{in.m} = Q(m)$ for every $m \in M$. The atomic synchronization events here are of the form *in.m*. The complement is the output prefix which has the form $out!x \to P$ and this is simply shorthand for $out.x \to P$.
   Thus a one-place delaying buffer might be described by the recursive process

$$DBUFFER = in?x \overset{1}{\to} out!x \to DBUFFER$$

There is a one-second delay between *in?* and *out!*, but no delay is enforced between *out!* output and the subsequent *in?*.
   Infinite nondeterministic choice may also be defined. The process $\bigsqcap_{j \in J} P_j$ for some indexing set *J* may behave as any of its arguments P_j. Thus, for example, a nondeterministic delay over some interval *I* may be defined:

$$Wait\ I\ =\ \bigsqcap_{t \in I} Wait\ t$$

The delay may be for any time in the interval *I*. If each P_i is *t*-guarded for *X*, then so is their infinite choice and if *P* is *t*-guarded for X, then *Wait I*; *P* is $(t + \inf I)$-guarded for X.
   Alphabet parallel composition generalizes as expected. The process $\big\|_{A_i} P_i$ gives interface A_i to each process P_i. To perform an event *a*, all processes with *a* in their interface must participate.

A form of parallel composition which allows synchronization on some events and interleaving on others may be defined by the use of event renaming. Define

$$
\begin{aligned}
f_A(x) &= a.x \quad \text{if } x \notin A \\
& \; x \quad\;\; \text{otherwise} \\
g_A(x) &= b.x \quad \text{if } x \notin A \\
& \; x \quad\;\; \text{otherwise} \\
h(y) &= x \quad\;\; \text{if } y = a.x \text{ or } y = b.x \\
& \; y \quad\;\; \text{otherwise}
\end{aligned}
$$

The process $P\|[A]\|Q$ synchronizes on events in A, and interleaves on all other events.

$$
P\|[A]\|Q \;=\; h(f_A(P) \, \|[A \cup a.\Sigma \,|\, A \cup b.\Sigma]\| \, g_A(P))
$$

If two runners are defined as

$$
\begin{aligned}
RUNNER1 &= start \xrightarrow{t_1} finish \rightarrow STOP \\
RUNNER2 &= start \xrightarrow{t_2} finish \rightarrow STOP
\end{aligned}
$$

then a race between the two runners may be modelled as

$$
RUNNER1 \,\|[start]\| \, RUNNER2
$$

They must both start at the same time (so they synchronize on *start*) but they may finish at different times.

Exercise 6.1.1 Write CSP processes which describe the following situations. Decide first which events are to be used (the alphabet of the process), and then provide a CSP description:

1. A vending machine which is initially ready to accept a coin, and is then always ready to accept a coin within two seconds of the last item being dispensed; and it offers the customer the choice of a biscuit or a chocolate five seconds after insertion of a coin.
   Its interface will be the set of events $\{coin, bisc, choc\}$.
2. A transmitter which sends a message every five seconds until an acknowledgement is received.
3. An oven with a timer set to T which rings after T minutes of being switched on, if not switched off beforehand.
4. A baby who wakes up nondeterministically between one and eight hours after going to sleep.
5. A baby who needs to be rocked for five minutes to get to sleep. If rocking stops before then, she cries; otherwise she sleeps.
6. A baby who starts to cry if not fed within two minutes of waking.
7. A baby who has all of the above characteristics. (Hint: use a parallel combination of the CSP processes you have already defined.)

6.2   Observations and processes

The language of CSP has a formal meaning and the behaviour of a CSP process is precisely defined. This makes it possible to judge CSP descriptions against specifications which characterize desired behaviour. Such specifications may be written in a language oriented towards expression of properties (such as temporal logic), or even as a CSP process which describes the desired behaviour.

6.2.1   Notation

Let Σ be the set of events, variables t and t' represent times and range over $\mathbf{R}^+$ and variable s range over *Traces*, the finite and infinite sequences of timed events (t, a). We use $\aleph$ to range over sets of timed events in *IRSET*, the set of refusals, defined below.

The following operations will be used on sequences of events: $\#s$ is the length of the sequence s; $s_1 \frown s_2$ denotes the concatenation of s_1 and s_2. The beginning and end of a sequence is defined as follows: $begin(\langle (t, a) \rangle \frown s) = t, end(s \frown \langle (t, a) \rangle) = t, first(\langle (t, a) \rangle \frown s) = a, last(s \frown \langle (t, a) \rangle) = a$. The notation $s_1 \preccurlyeq s_2$ means that s_1 is a subsequence of s_2 and $s_1 \leqslant s_2$ means that s_1 is a prefix of s_2. The following projections on sequences are defined by list comprehension, where

$$\langle f(x) \mid x \leftarrow s, P(x) \rangle$$

is the maximal subsequence of s whose elements all satisfy P, with f applied to each term:

$$
\begin{aligned}
s \triangleleft t &= \langle (t', a) \mid (t', a) \leftarrow s, t' \leqslant t \rangle \\
s \uparrow I &= \langle (t', a) \mid (t', a) \leftarrow s, t' \in I \rangle \\
s \downarrow A &= \langle (t', a) \mid (t', a) \leftarrow s, a \in A \rangle \\
s - t &= \langle (t' - t, a) \mid (t', a) \leftarrow s, t' \geqslant t \rangle
\end{aligned}
$$

The set of events occurring in a trace is extracted by a set comprehension:

$$\sigma(s) = \{ a \mid s \downarrow \{a\} \neq \langle \rangle \}$$

$s \triangleleft t$ is that part of the trace that occurs no later than time t and $s \uparrow I$ is the part that occurs during interval I. $s \downarrow A$ is the subsequence of the trace whose events occur in the set A. In $s - t$, the trace s is moved backward through t units of time (and truncated so no event occurs before time 0), and $\sigma(s)$ is the set of events which occur in s.

There are similar projections on refusal sets:

$$
\begin{aligned}
\aleph \triangleleft t &= \{ (u, a) \mid (u, a) \in \aleph, u < t \} \\
\aleph \downarrow A &= \{ (u, a) \mid (u, a) \in \aleph, a \in A \} \\
\aleph - t &= \{ (u - t, a) \mid (u, a) \in \aleph, u \geqslant t \} \\
\sigma(\aleph) &= \{ a \mid (u, a) \in \aleph \}
\end{aligned}
$$

$\aleph \lhd t$ is the set of events in $\aleph$ occurring strictly before time t. $\aleph \downarrow A$ is that part of $\aleph$ containing events from the set A and $\aleph - t$ is the set $\aleph$ moved backward through t units of time. $\sigma(\aleph)$ is the set of events occurring at some time in $\aleph$.

6.2.2 Observations

The formal semantics of CSP is defined in terms of *timed failures*. Each timed failure corresponds to a record of an execution of the system and consists of a *timed trace* and a *timed refusal*.

Any observation of an execution of a process must include a record of the events that were performed and the times at which they occurred. A *timed trace* is a finite sequence of timed events from the set $[0, \infty) \times \Sigma$ such that the times associated with events appear in non-decreasing order.

$$
\begin{array}{|l}
Traces : \mathbb{P}(\mathrm{seq}^{\omega}(\mathbf{R}^+ \times \Sigma)) \\
\hline
s \in Traces \Leftrightarrow \\
\quad \langle (t_1, a_1), (t_2, a_2) \rangle \preccurlyeq s \Rightarrow t_1 \leqslant t_2 \\
\quad \wedge \\
\quad \#s = \infty \Rightarrow \sup\{t \mid \langle (t, a) \rangle \preccurlyeq s\} = \infty
\end{array}
$$

Real-time systems are reactive and it is important to know when a process is willing to interact with its environment and when this is not possible. For deterministic systems, this information can be obtained from the trace but for nondeterministic systems the trace information is not sufficient. For example, the traces of

$$a \to STOP \quad \text{and} \quad STOP \sqcap a \to STOP$$

are the same but the first must *always* respond in an environment in which a is ready, whereas the second may refuse to respond.

We will therefore also record *timed refusal* information. A timed refusal contains the events (with times) which the process refused to engage in during an execution. From the assumption of finite variability, only finitely many state changes are possible in a finite time. Since a process will continue to refuse an event while it remains in the same state, a timed refusal can be considered as a step function from times to sets of events. The set *IRSET* is the set of all such refusals. It is defined in terms of *RSET*, those sets which record refusal information only for some finite time:

$$
\begin{array}{|l}
RSET : \mathbb{P}(\mathbf{R}^+ \times \Sigma) \\
IRSET : \mathbb{P}(\mathbf{R}^+ \times \Sigma) \\
\hline
\aleph \in RSET \Leftrightarrow \\
\quad \exists b_1 \ldots b_n, e_1 \ldots e_n : \mathbf{R}^+; A_1 \ldots A_n : \mathbb{P}(\Sigma) \bullet \\
\qquad \aleph = \bigcup_1^n([b_i, e_i) \times A_i) \\
\aleph \in IRSET \Leftrightarrow \forall t \bullet \aleph \cap [0, t) \times \Sigma \in RSET
\end{array}
$$

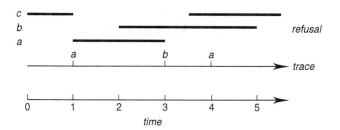

Figure 6.1 A timed observation

Refusal information at any particular time is considered to be subsequent to the events recorded in the trace at that time. For example, in the process

$$a \rightarrow STOP \ \Box \ b \rightarrow STOP$$

the event b cannot be refused before any events have occurred. But when a occurs, the possibility of b is withdrawn and so it may thereafter be refused. Thus the step function may be considered to be closed at the lower end of a step, and open at the upper end. Further, once a has occurred, it, too, may be refused from that instant onwards since no further copies of a are possible for the process. Thus a timed event may occur in both a timed trace and in a corresponding timed refusal.

A single observation will consist of a *CSP!timed failure*, made up of a trace $s \in Traces$, and a refusal set $\aleph \in IRSET$ from the same execution. The trace and refusal are considered to be a record of the behaviour of the process over all time, even if s and $\aleph$ both end at some finite time. If $(s, \aleph)$ is an observation of P, then P has some execution during which the events in s were performed and the events in $\aleph$ were refused. In contrast to the untimed failures model for CSP, this refusal contains information concerning events that were refused both during and after the performance of s, whereas an untimed refusal set contains only information after the end of the trace.

Figure 6.1 shows the first 5.5 seconds of one possible observation of the recursive process:

$$P \ = \ a \rightarrow (\ Wait \ 2; \ b \rightarrow P$$
$$\Box$$
$$c \rightarrow STOP)$$

Initially, event c is refused over the interval $[0, 1)$. At time 1, event a occurs and further copies of it are refused over the interval $[1, 3)$. Event b is refused over the interval $[2, 3)$, occurs at time 3 and then further occurrences are refused until time 5. b's refusals up to that time therefore consist of the interval $[2, 5)$, indicating that the occurrence of b at time 3 must have been at the instant it was made available. c is refused over the interval $[3.5, 5.5)$. During this refusal, another occurrence of a is observed, at time 4. The diagram corresponds to the timed failure

$$(\langle (1,a),(3,b),(4,a)\rangle, \; [1,3) \times \{a\}$$
$$\cup [2,5) \times \{b\}$$
$$\cup [0,1) \times \{c\} \cup [3.5,5.5) \times \{c\})$$

The refusal set could also be written in the form of a step function:

$$(\langle (1,a),(3,b),(4,a)\rangle, \; [0,1) \times \{c\}$$
$$\cup [1,2) \times \{a\}$$
$$\cup [2,3) \times \{a,b\}$$
$$\cup [3,3.5) \times \{b\}$$
$$\cup [3.5,5) \times \{b,c\}$$
$$\cup [5,5.5) \times \{c\})$$

The refusal information is not a complete record of everything the process could have refused – for example, it could have also refused b over the interval $[0,2)$ – but it may be considered as a record of what the process refused in an environment which made particular offers.

The set of all possible observations is given by

$$OBS \;=\; TT \times IRSET$$

Any pair $(s, \aleph)$ is a possible observation of some execution, so OBS consists of all pairs. Processes are associated with subsets of OBS. The notation $\mathcal{M}_{TI}$ denotes the space of all such subsets of OBS

6.2.3 The semantic function

The semantic function

$$\mathcal{F}_{TI} : CSP \to \mathcal{M}_{TI}$$

is defined by giving an equation for each of the operators of the language:

$$\mathcal{F}_{TI}\llbracket STOP \rrbracket \;\widehat{=}\; \{(\langle\rangle, \aleph) \mid \aleph \in IRSET\}$$

No event may ever be performed by the process $STOP$ and any set of events may be refused at any time:

$$\mathcal{F}_{TI}\llbracket SKIP \rrbracket \;\widehat{=}\; \{(\langle\rangle, \aleph) \mid \checkmark \notin \sigma(\aleph)\}$$
$$\cup$$
$$\{(\langle (u,\checkmark)\rangle, \aleph) \mid \checkmark \notin \sigma(\aleph \lhd u)\}$$

The special event $\checkmark$ denotes termination in the semantics of processes but it is not an event in syntactic CSP expressions. There are two possibilities for $SKIP$: either it has not yet terminated, in which case it cannot refuse to do so (though anything else may be refused), or it has terminated at time u, in which case it may refuse anything after termination but could not have refused $\checkmark$ before u:

$$\mathcal{F}_{TI}[\![P;\ Q]\!] \triangleq \{(s, \aleph)\ |\ \checkmark \notin \sigma(s)$$
$$\wedge\ (s, \aleph \cup ([0,\infty) \times \{\checkmark\})) \in \mathcal{F}_{TI}[\![P]\!]$$
$$\vee$$
$$s = s_P \frown s_Q \wedge \checkmark \notin \sigma(s_P)$$
$$\wedge\ (s_Q, \aleph) - u \in \mathcal{F}_{TI}[\![Q]\!] \wedge begin(s_Q) \geqslant u$$
$$\wedge\ (s_P \frown \langle(u,\checkmark)\rangle, \aleph \triangleleft u \cup ([0,u) \times \{\checkmark\})) \in \mathcal{F}_{TI}[\![P]\!]\}$$

There are two possibilities for an execution of a sequential composition $P;\ Q$: either it is an execution of P, in which case it must have refused to terminate throughout the execution, or it is some terminating execution of P followed by an execution of Q; again P must have refused to terminate throughout its execution until it actually did so:

$$\mathcal{F}_{TI}[\![a \to P]\!] \ \triangleq\ \{(\langle\rangle, \aleph)\ |\ a \notin \sigma(\aleph)\}$$
$$\cup$$
$$\{(\langle(u,a)\rangle \frown s, \aleph)\ |\ a \notin \sigma(\aleph \triangleleft u)$$
$$\wedge\ (s, \aleph) - u \in \mathcal{F}_{TI}[\![P]\!]\}$$

The prefix process $a \to P$ is unable initially to refuse a, which is the first event it must perform. Either a does not occur, in which case anything except a may be refused, or a occurs at some time u, having previously not been refused, and the subsequent behaviour is that of P starting at time u rather than at time 0:

$$\mathcal{F}_{TI}[\![P \,\square\, Q]\!] \ \triangleq\ \{(\langle\rangle, \aleph)\ |\ (\langle\rangle, \aleph) \in \mathcal{F}_{TI}[\![P]\!] \cap \mathcal{F}_{TI}[\![Q]\!]\}$$
$$\cup$$
$$\{(s, \aleph)\ |\ s \neq \langle\rangle \wedge (s, \aleph) \in \mathcal{F}_{TI}[\![P]\!] \cup \mathcal{F}_{TI}[\![Q]\!]$$
$$\wedge$$
$$(\langle\rangle, \aleph \triangleleft begin(s)) \in \mathcal{F}_{TI}[\![P]\!] \cap \mathcal{F}_{TI}[\![Q]\!]\}$$

In an external choice $P \,\square\, Q$, initial events are available from either process; events can be refused only if both processes are able to refuse them. Once the choice has been resolved (at the time of the first event) in favour of one of the processes, the subsequent behaviour is given by that process:

$$\mathcal{F}_{TI}[\![P \,\sqcap\, Q]\!] \ \triangleq\ \mathcal{F}_{TI}[\![P]\!] \cup \mathcal{F}_{TI}[\![Q]\!]$$

An execution of an internal choice is an execution of one of the component processes:

$$\mathcal{F}_{TI}[\![P \overset{u}{\triangleright} Q]\!] \ \triangleq\ \{(s, \aleph)\ |\ begin(s) \leqslant u \wedge (s, \aleph) \in \mathcal{F}_{TI}[\![P]\!]\}$$
$$\cup$$
$$\{(s, \aleph)\ |\ begin(s) \geqslant u \wedge (\langle\rangle, \aleph \triangleleft u) \in \mathcal{F}_{TI}[\![P]\!]$$
$$\wedge$$
$$(s, \aleph) - u \in \mathcal{F}_{TI}[\![Q]\!]\}$$

In an execution of a timeout process $P \overset{u}{\triangleright} Q$, either P performs its first event before time u, in which case the execution is simply one of P, or no event occurs before time u, and the timeout passes control to Q. In the second case, the refusal up to time u is governed by P, and the behaviour after u is that of Q translated to start at time u instead of at time 0:

$$\mathcal{F}_{TI}[\![P \, |[A|B]| \, Q]\!] \; \widehat{=} \; \{(s, \aleph) \mid \exists \, \aleph_P, \aleph_Q \bullet$$
$$\aleph \downarrow (A \cup B) = (\aleph_P \downarrow A) \cup (\aleph_Q \downarrow B)$$
$$\wedge \, s = s \downarrow (A \cup B)$$
$$\wedge \, (s \downarrow A, \aleph_P) \in \mathcal{F}_{TI}[\![P]\!]$$
$$\wedge \, (s \downarrow B, \aleph_Q) \in \mathcal{F}_{TI}[\![Q]\!] \, \}$$

In the parallel combination $P \, |[A|B]| \, Q$, the execution projected onto the set A is due to P, and that onto the set B is due to Q. Where A and B intersect, both P and Q must agree on events in the trace, but if any of them refuses an event the combination will refuse it:

$$\mathcal{F}_{TI}[\![P \, ||| \, Q]\!] \; \widehat{=} \; \{(s, \aleph) \mid \exists s_P, s_Q \bullet \; s \in s_P \, ||| \, s_Q$$
$$\wedge \, (s_P, \aleph) \in \mathcal{F}_{TI}[\![P]\!]$$
$$\wedge \, (s_Q, \aleph) \in \mathcal{F}_{TI}[\![Q]\!]\}$$

where $s_P \, ||| \, s_Q$ is the set of timed traces consisting of an interleaving of s_P and s_Q: in an interleaved combination, each event requires the participation of precisely one component so both processes must refuse an event for the combination to refuse it.

$$\mathcal{F}_{TI}[\![P \setminus A]\!] \; \widehat{=} \; \{(s \setminus A, \aleph) \mid (s, \aleph \cup ([0, \infty) \times A)) \in \mathcal{F}_{TI}[\![P]\!]\}$$

In an encapsulated process $P \setminus A$, the events in A are made internal to the process (they do not appear in the trace) and no longer require the participation of the environment: they are autonomous events under the control of P. By the maximal progress assumption, this means they should occur as soon as they are enabled. This corresponds to the condition that A should be refusible for P over the entire execution: if this were not the case, then there would be some period during which an event from A was enabled but had not occurred, violating maximal progress:

$$\mathcal{F}_{TI}[\![f(P)]\!] \; \widehat{=} \; \{(f(s), \aleph) \mid (s, f^{-1}(\aleph)) \in \mathcal{F}_{TI}[\![P]\!]\}$$
$$\mathcal{F}_{TI}[\![f^{-1}(P)]\!] \; = \; \{(s, \aleph) \mid (f(s), f(\aleph)) \in \mathcal{F}_{TI}[\![P]\!]\}$$

Processes whose alphabets are renamed have similar behaviour, but the names of the events are transformed by the renaming function f:

$$\mathcal{F}_{TI}[\![\sqcap_{i \in I} P_i]\!] \; \widehat{=} \; \bigcup_{i \in I} \mathcal{F}_{TI}[\![P_i]\!]$$

The possible executions of a general choice are those of its components:

$$\mathcal{F}_{TI}[\![a : A \to P_a]\!] \; = \; \{(\langle\rangle, \aleph) \mid A \cap \sigma(\aleph) = \emptyset\}$$
$$\cup \{(\langle(u, a)\rangle \frown s, \aleph) \mid$$
$$a \in A \wedge A \cap \sigma(\aleph \vartriangleleft u) = \emptyset$$
$$\wedge \, (s, \aleph) - t \in \mathcal{F}_{TI}[\![P(a)]\!]\}$$

An execution of a prefix choice $a : A \rightarrow P_a$ takes one of two forms: either no event occurs, in which case nothing in A may be refused, or some event $a \in A$ is chosen at some time u, in which case no event in A may be refused before u, and the subsequent behaviour is that of the chosen process P_a, translated through u time units.

The recursive process $\mu X \bullet P$ is a solution of the equation $X = P$; this is the fixed point of the semantic mapping corresponding to P with the most timed failures. The fixed point will exist for time-guarded recursive equations. Recursive equations may be process definitions: the equation $P = F(P)$ defines P to be the process $\mu X \bullet F(X)$.

Exercise 6.2.1 Consider the process $P = (a \xrightarrow{4} b \rightarrow STOP) \square c \rightarrow STOP$. Which of the following are failures of P?

1. $(\langle (1, a) \rangle, \emptyset)$ 2. $(\langle (3, b), (1, a) \rangle, \emptyset)$
3. $(\langle (6, b), (1, a) \rangle, \emptyset)$ 4. $(\langle (1, a), (3, b) \rangle, \emptyset)$
5. $(\langle (1, a), (5, b) \rangle, \emptyset)$ 6. $(\langle (1, a), (5, b), (6, c) \rangle, \emptyset)$
7. $(\langle (6, c) \rangle, \emptyset)$ 8. $(\langle \rangle, \emptyset)$
9. $(\langle \rangle, [0, 1) \times \{b\})$ 10. $(\langle (1, a) \rangle, [0, 1) \times \{b\})$
11. $(\langle (1, a) \rangle, (0, 1) \times \{b\})$ 12. $(\langle (1, a) \rangle, [0, 1) \times \{a\})$
13. $(\langle (1, a), (5, b) \rangle, [0, 10) \times \{c\})$ 14. $(\langle (1, a), (5, b) \rangle, [1, 10) \times \{c\})$
15. $(\langle (1, a), (5, b) \rangle, [1, 2) \times \{a\})$ 16. $(\langle (6, c) \rangle, [0, 4) \times \{b\})$

Exercise 6.2.2 Give a single process which has all of the following behaviours:

$(\langle \rangle, [0, 2) \times \{a\} \cup [5, 8) \times \{a\})$
$(\langle (3, a) \rangle, [0, 2) \times \{a\})$
$(\langle (1, b) \rangle, [0, 2) \times \{a\})$

Give a process which has both of the following behaviours:

$(\langle \rangle, [0, \infty) \times \{a\})$
$(\langle (1, a) \rangle, \emptyset)$

6.3 Specification

A specification is a predicate S on timed failures. It describes the behaviour required of the system. Process P meets specification S (written P **sat** S) if S holds for every timed failure in the semantics of P:

$$P \text{ sat } S(s, \aleph) \quad \Leftrightarrow \quad \forall (s, \aleph) \in \mathcal{F}_{TI} [\![P]\!] \bullet S(s, \aleph) \qquad (6.1)$$

For example, the following specification requires the first event observed to be *start*:

$$S(s, \aleph) = (s = \langle \rangle \vee first(s) = start)$$

In any execution, either no event is observed (the trace will be empty) or the first event is *start*.

The requirement that P performs *on*s and *off*s alternately is represented by the specification

$$S(s, \aleph) = \forall u \leqslant s \bullet 0 \leqslant \#(s \downarrow on) - \#(s \downarrow off) \leqslant 1$$

In every prefix of the trace s, the number of *on* events is equal to or one more than the number of *off* events. The specification says nothing about the presence or absence of other events.

If *on* should be available initially,

$$S(s, \aleph) = (s \downarrow \{on, off\} = \langle \rangle \Rightarrow on \notin \sigma(\aleph))$$

When neither *on* nor *off* have yet been performed, P cannot refuse to perform *on*.

Writing specifications directly as predicates upon traces s and refusals $\aleph$ can become cumbersome. Also, there are many similar specification patterns for safety, liveness and commonly occurring assumptions about the environment of the process. It is convenient to define a number of specification macros or idioms as a shorthand for these patterns and for use with proof rules to reason about specifications at a higher level of abstraction:

$$a \text{ at } t (s, \aleph) \quad \widehat{=} \quad \langle (t,a) \rangle \preccurlyeq s \tag{6.2}$$

$$a \text{ live } t (s, \aleph) \quad \widehat{=} \quad a \text{ at } t \vee (t,a) \notin \aleph \tag{6.3}$$

$$a \text{ live from } t \text{ until } A (s, \aleph) \quad \widehat{=} \quad [t, begin(s \uparrow [t, \infty) \downarrow A)) \times \{a\} \cap \aleph = \emptyset \tag{6.4}$$

$$a \text{ open } t (s, \aleph) \quad \widehat{=} \quad a \text{ at } t \vee (t,a) \in \aleph \tag{6.5}$$

$$a \text{ closed } t (s, \aleph) \quad \widehat{=} \quad \neg a \text{ at } t \tag{6.6}$$

$$a \text{ at } I (s, \aleph) \quad \widehat{=} \quad \exists t \in I \bullet a \text{ at } t \tag{6.7}$$

$$a \text{ open } I (s, \aleph) \quad \widehat{=} \quad \forall t \in I \bullet a \text{ open } t \tag{6.8}$$

$$a \text{ closed } I (s, \aleph) \quad \widehat{=} \quad \neg a \text{ at } I \tag{6.9}$$

The first is straightforward: a **at** t for a particular execution whenever the timed event (t,a) appears in the trace. In a **live** t, the process is prepared to perform a at time t and in a **live from** t **until** A will remain so until disabled by some event from the set A. Generally, the event a is in the set A: if it is not, then no CSP process could meet the specification.

a **open** t states that the event a is open to the process at time t, i.e. the environment of the process is ready to see a performed. If a is not actually performed at that time, the process must have been unwilling to perform it because of the maximal progress assumption (so the event appears in the refusal set). In a **closed** t, the environment was not ready to perform the event a at time t. The last three definitions are generalizations for intervals.

For example, if a is initially available, then

a **live from** 0 **until** Σ

a process which will perform event a whenever it is offered, is specified by

$$\forall t \bullet a \ \textbf{open} \ t \Rightarrow a \ \textbf{at} \ t$$

No CSP process could meet such a specification, as the implementation must be finitely variable. A process which performs a when offered if it has not performed one within the last time unit is specified by

$$\forall t \bullet \neg(a \ \textbf{at} \ [t-1,t)) \wedge a \ \textbf{open} \ t \Rightarrow a \ \textbf{at} \ t$$

A specification that requires output to be offered from one time unit after input, until it occurs, might be expressed as

$$\forall t \bullet in \ \textbf{at} \ t \Rightarrow out \ \textbf{live from} \ t+1 \ \textbf{until} \ out$$

For a process to meet such a specification, *all* observations of the process must satisfy the predicate.

Exercise 6.3.1 Formalize the following requirements, using the specification macro language where appropriate.

1. *out* can only occur exactly five units after *in*.
2. *out* cannot occur exactly five units after *in*.
3. *choc* is available until *choc* or *bisc* occurs.
4. *fire* never occurs.
5. *on* occurs at time 5.
6. If the environment offers *on* at time 5, then it will occur.
7. If *in* occurs, then *out* is enabled five seconds later.
8. Between any *up* and *down* there must be a *mid*.
9. Deadlock-freedom.
10. *in* is always available.

Which of these specifications cannot be satisfied by any CSP process?

6.4 Verification

It is possible to prove that a CSP implementation meets a specification by checking that every timed failure meets the specifying predicate. But it is usually more convenient to use a more structured approach to verification.

6.4.1 Proof rules for processes

The semantic equations allow the definition of a set of proof rules using a satisfaction relation. The equations for a composite process built using an operator can be deduced from the specifications of the components.

The rule for delayed prefix has the following form:

Rule 1

$$P \text{ sat } S(s, \aleph)$$

$$a \xrightarrow{d} P \text{ sat } s = \langle\rangle \wedge \forall t \bullet a \text{ live } t$$
$$\vee$$
$$s = \langle(t,a)\rangle ^\frown s' \wedge begin(s') \geqslant t + d$$
$$\wedge \ \forall t' \in [0,t) \bullet a \text{ live } t' \wedge S(s' - (t+d), \aleph - (t+d))$$

If P sat S, then for any behaviour of the process $a \xrightarrow{d} P$, either no event has yet occurred (it is live on a) or a occurred at time t (it is live on a up to t) and the behaviour after time $t + d$ meets predicate S, since it came from P. No event occurs between t and $t + d$ and there is no constraint on the refusal over that interval (so anything could be refused).

A delayed process has a simpler rule:

Rule 2

$$P \text{ sat } S(s, \aleph)$$

$$Wait \ d; \ P \text{ sat } begin(s) \geqslant d \wedge S(s - d, \aleph - d)$$

No event can occur before d; and the behaviour after d is produced by P, so it must meet S, but it is shifted by d units of time because P began execution at time d.

The rule for external choice again directly reflects the semantic equation for that operator.

Rule 3

$$P \text{ sat } S(s, \aleph)$$
$$Q \text{ sat } T(s, \aleph)$$

$$P \ \square \ Q \text{ sat } (S(s, \aleph) \vee T(s, \aleph))$$
$$\wedge \ s \lhd t = \langle\rangle \Rightarrow S(s \lhd t, \aleph \lhd t) \wedge T(s \lhd t, \aleph \lhd t)$$

Any behaviour of $P \ \square \ Q$ is a behaviour of P or Q and before the first event is performed, it must be a behaviour of both, since both processes are available.

If P and Q are defined recursively by the functions F and G, a recursion induction rule can be used.

Rule 4

$$\forall X, Y \bullet \quad \left. \begin{array}{c} X \text{ sat } S \\ \wedge\ Y \text{ sat } T \end{array} \right\} \Rightarrow \begin{array}{c} F(X, Y) \text{ sat } S \\ \wedge\ G(X, Y) \text{ sat } T \end{array}$$

$$\frac{\left[\begin{array}{c} P = F(P, Q) \\ Q = G(P, Q) \\ S, T \text{ admissible} \end{array} \right] \quad P \text{ sat } S}{Q \text{ sat } T}$$

If F and G satisfy the specifications S and T, respectively, the mutual fixed points of F and G meet those specifications.

A specification is admissible, continuous, or closed if $\forall t \bullet S(s \lhd t, \aleph \lhd t) \Rightarrow S(s, \aleph)$: S holds for an infinite behaviour if it holds for the finite approximations to that behaviour. For example, the predicate specifying a's availability from time 0 is admissible, whereas a predicate specifying that there are an infinite number of events in the trace is not.

6.4.2   Proof rules for macros

The preceding proof rules simply expand the semantic definitions so on their own they do not offer any advantage over using the semantic equations directly. But use of the **sat** operator can reduce the complexity of each stage of verification by breaking a large verification into smaller units whose results can be combined using logical operators.

Rule 5

$$\frac{\begin{array}{c} P \text{ sat } S \\ P \text{ sat } T \end{array}}{P \text{ sat } S \wedge T}$$

Rule 6

$$\frac{\begin{array}{c} P \text{ sat } S \\ S \Rightarrow T \end{array}}{P \text{ sat } T}$$

Rule 5 uses logical conjunction to combine two smaller verifications. Rule 6 allows a specification to be weakened, so that unnecessary information about a process can be removed.

Use of Rule 6 requires showing that $S \Rightarrow T$. Since S and T are written using the specification macros, rules are provided for reasoning at this level. The soundness of the rules follows from the definitions in terms of traces and refusals. An advantage of this approach taken here is that new macros, and new rules, can be defined to suit particular applications, and consistency is guaranteed by the underlying model. Some sample rules follow and they will be used later in the chapter.

Rule 7

$$a \ \textbf{live} \ t \ (s, \aleph)$$
$$a \ \textbf{open} \ t \ (s, \aleph)$$
$$\overline{a \ \textbf{at} \ t \ (s, \aleph)}$$

If both the process and its environment are willing to perform an event at a particular time, then it will occur.

The next two rules follow directly from the definitions.

Rule 8

$$a \ \textbf{live from} \ t \ \textbf{until} \ a$$
$$a \ \textbf{open} \ t + t_0$$
$$\overline{a \ \textbf{at} \ [t, t + t_0]}$$

Rule 9

$$a \ \textbf{live from} \ t \ \textbf{until} \ \{a, b\}$$
$$b \ \textbf{at} \ t' \Rightarrow a \ \textbf{live from} \ t' \ \textbf{until} \ \{a, b\}$$
$$\overline{a \ \textbf{live from} \ t \ \textbf{until} \ a}$$

6.4.3 Proof rules for compound behaviours

The rules in this section have specific application for the verification of the mine pump controller specification and use the parallel operator.

The proof rule for the parallel operator $P\|[A]\|Q$ relates behaviours of the combined process with behaviours of P and Q.

Rule 10

$$P \ \textbf{sat} \ S(s, \aleph)$$
$$Q \ \textbf{sat} \ T(s, \aleph)$$
$$\overline{\begin{aligned} P\|[A]\|Q \ \textbf{sat} \ \exists s_P, s_Q, \aleph_P, \aleph_Q \bullet \\ S(s_P, \aleph_P) \wedge T(s_Q, \aleph_Q) \\ \wedge (s, \aleph) \in (s_P, \aleph_P)\|[A]\|(s_Q, \aleph_Q) \end{aligned}}$$

$(s_P, \aleph_P)\|[A]\|(s_Q, \aleph_Q)$ is the set of all compound behaviours of $P\|[A]\|Q$ that can arise from those concurrent behaviours of P and Q.

The following rules deduce information about s and $\aleph$ from the component specifications.

Rule 11

$$\frac{\begin{array}{c} a \text{ live } t\,(s_P, \aleph_P) \\ (s, \aleph) \in (s_P, \aleph_P)\,|[A]|\,(s_Q, \aleph_Q) \end{array}}{a \text{ live } t\,(s, \aleph)} \quad [\,a \notin A\,]$$

If the processes do not synchronize on event a and one of them is live on a, then so is the combination.

Rule 12

$$\frac{\begin{array}{c} a \text{ live } t\,(s_P, \aleph_P) \\ a \text{ live } t\,(s_Q, \aleph_Q) \\ (s, \aleph) \in (s_P, \aleph_P)\,|[A]|\,(s_Q, \aleph_Q) \end{array}}{a \text{ live } t\,(s, \aleph)} \quad [\,a \in A\,]$$

If they do synchronize on a, then the parallel combination will be ready to participate on a when both components are.

Rule 13

$$\frac{\begin{array}{c} a \text{ open } t\,(s, \aleph) \\ (s, \aleph) \in (s_P, \aleph_P)\,|[A]|\,(s_Q, \aleph_Q) \end{array}}{a \text{ open } t\,(s_P, \aleph_P)} \quad [\,a \notin A, a \notin \sigma(s_Q)\,]$$

If Q does not perform event a, and the processes do not need to synchronize on a, then if the environment offers a to the whole process it is offered to P.

Rule 14

$$\frac{\begin{array}{c} a \text{ closed } t\,(s, \aleph) \\ (s, \aleph) \in (s_P, \aleph_P)\,|[A]|\,(s_Q, \aleph_Q) \end{array}}{a \text{ closed } t\,(s_P, \aleph_P)}$$

If a is not offered to the combined process, it is not offered to either component.

Rule 15

$$\frac{\begin{array}{c} \neg a \text{ at } t\,(s, \aleph) \\ (s, \aleph) \in (s_P, \aleph_P)\,|[A]|\,(s_Q, \aleph_Q) \end{array}}{\neg a \text{ at } t\,(s_P, \aleph_P)}$$

If a does not occur in the combined process, it does not occur in either component.

Other rules allow projections of events from the combined process to the components.

Rule 16

$$\frac{(s, \aleph) \in (s_P, \aleph_P) \, |[A]| \, (s_Q, \aleph_Q)}{\begin{array}{l} s \downarrow B = \langle\rangle \Rightarrow s_P \downarrow B = \langle\rangle \wedge s_Q \downarrow B = \langle\rangle \\ last(s \downarrow B) = b \Rightarrow last(s_P \downarrow B) = b \vee last(s_Q \downarrow B) = b \end{array}}$$

If no events from B have been performed, then they have not been performed by either component; if b is the last event that was performed, then it must be the last event performed by one of the components.

Finally, if the set B is completely independent of anything Q has performed, and P and Q do not interact on any events from B, and the specification S depends only on events from B, then it will be true if and only if it is true for P's contribution.

Rule 17

$$\frac{\begin{array}{l}(s, \aleph) \in (s_P, \aleph_P) \, |[A]| \, (s_Q, \aleph_Q) \\ S(s, \aleph) \Leftrightarrow S(s \downarrow B, \aleph \downarrow B)\end{array}}{S(s, \aleph) \Leftrightarrow S(s_P, \aleph_P)} \quad [\, B \cap (A \cup \sigma(s_Q) \cup \sigma(\aleph_Q)) = \emptyset \,]$$

6.5 Case study: the mine pump

Using the specifications in Chapter 1 to describe the problem, we verify the CSP description of the pump used to keep water levels safe in a mine.

- The pump is used to remove accumulated water in the mine.
- The pump can be used only when the methane level is not dangerous.
- At most one shift in 1000 should be lost due to dangerous water levels.

The problem is to produce a control system for the *Pump Motor* which meets this requirement.

6.5.1 A CSP pump controller

PumpControl describes relationships between states. In designing a control system to meet these relationships, it is necessary to decide how and when the *changes* between states will occur.

The state-based definitions of Chapter 1 must be converted to event-based (or state-transition-based) definitions in order to consider an implementation which performs state transitions at different points of time. For the system to be in one state at time t_1 and another at time t_2, the implementation must change the state at some time between t_1 and t_2.

In the following CSP implementation, there is a component to monitor the behaviour of the water and another the behaviour of the methane:

$$WATER_{low} \quad = \quad water.high \xrightarrow{d} WATER_{high} \tag{6.10}$$
$$\square$$
$$Wait \; \varepsilon; \; pump.off \rightarrow WATER_{low}$$

$$WATER_{high} \quad = \quad water.low \xrightarrow{d'} WATER_{low} \tag{6.11}$$
$$\square$$
$$Wait \; \varepsilon; \; pump.on \rightarrow WATER_{high}$$

$$METHANE_{safe} \quad = \quad methane.danger \xrightarrow{d''} METHANE_{danger} \tag{6.12}$$
$$\square$$
$$Wait \; \varepsilon; \; pump.on \rightarrow METHANE_{safe}$$

$$METHANE_{danger} \quad = \quad methane.safe \xrightarrow{d'''} METHANE_{safe} \tag{6.13}$$
$$\square$$
$$Wait \; \varepsilon; \; pump.off \rightarrow METHANE_{danger}$$

These components must agree on when the pump is to be switched on, but either of them can switch it off, independently of the state of the other:

$$CONTROL \quad = \quad (WATER_{low} \, \| [pump.on] \| \, METHANE_{safe}) \tag{6.14}$$

The delays ε and ds will be constrained as we proceed through the verification.

To verify that this CSP implementation meets the specification, it is required that

$$CONTROL \quad \textbf{sat} \quad Ass \Rightarrow PumpControl \tag{6.15}$$

where

$$Ass \quad = \quad HW1 \wedge HW2 \wedge HW3 \wedge DM1 \wedge DM2 \wedge DM3 \tag{6.16}$$
$$\wedge \, PU1 \wedge PU2 \wedge PU3 \wedge PU4 \tag{6.17}$$

We prove this by contradiction: assume that there is some behaviour $(s, \aleph)$ of *CONTROL* for which *Ass* holds but not *PumpControl*. Let *HW* and *LM* be abbreviations for *HighWater* and *LowMethane* respectively.

If *PumpControl* does not hold, then either

1. $\exists \Delta : cov(HW \cap LM) \bullet \neg(Pumping \; \textbf{on} \; (inf\Delta + React, sup\Delta)) \tag{6.18}$

or

2. $\exists \Delta : cov(HM) \bullet \neg((\neg Pumping) \; \textbf{on} \; (inf\Delta + React, sup\Delta)) \tag{6.19}$

To establish that case (1) leads to a contradiction, we will need some preliminary results. The following specification of *CONTROL*, that the pump remains on for at least ε, will be useful:

$$CONTROL \quad \textbf{sat} \quad SPEC_{pumping} \tag{6.20}$$

where

$$SPEC_{pumping} \quad = \quad pump.on \textbf{ at } t \Rightarrow \neg pump.off \textbf{ at } [t, t+\varepsilon] \tag{6.21}$$

This follows from the fact that *WATER* and *METHANE* must both participate in the event *pump.on*; since both processes satisfy $SPEC_{pumping}$, neither can perform *pump.off* over the interval $[t, t+\varepsilon]$.

The process *WATER* must meet the specification $SPEC_{water}$:

$$\left. \begin{array}{l} water.high \textbf{ open } [T - React, T](s, \aleph) \\ water.low \textbf{ closed } [T - React, T](s, \aleph) \\ \neg pump.on \textbf{ at } [T - \varepsilon, T](s, \aleph) \end{array} \right\} \Rightarrow pump.on \textbf{ live } T(s, \aleph) \tag{6.22}$$

Verification of *WATER* **sat** $SPEC_{water}$ follows in Section 6.5.2.

Let Δ be an interval whose existence is asserted by statement (6.18). Then

$$\exists t \in (inf\Delta + React, sup\Delta), \delta > 0 \bullet \tag{6.23}$$

$$(t - \delta, t + \delta) \subseteq (inf\Delta + React, sup\Delta) \wedge \neg Pumping(t) \tag{6.24}$$

Now

$$\neg Pumping(t) \quad \Rightarrow \quad \neg SysPumping(s, t) \tag{6.25}$$

There is some T with $t < T < t + \delta$ for which $s \uparrow (t, T] = \langle \rangle$. Thus, $\neg SysPumping(s, T)$, since the system state remains constant over this interval. Further, $H_2O(t') > HighH_2O$ and $CH_4(t') < DangerCH_4$ for all $t' \in [T - React, T]$. Then from *HW2* and *DM3*, respectively,

$$water.high \textbf{ open } [T - React, T](s, \aleph) \tag{6.26}$$

$$\wedge \; water.low \textbf{ closed } [T - React, T](s, \aleph) \tag{6.27}$$

and

$$methane.safe \textbf{ open } [T - React, T](s, \aleph) \tag{6.28}$$

$$\wedge \; methane.danger \textbf{ closed } [T - React, T](s, \aleph) \tag{6.29}$$

Now

$$(s, \aleph) \in (s_W, \aleph_W) | [pump.on] | (s_M, \aleph_M) \tag{6.30}$$

for behaviours $(s_W, \aleph_W)$ of *WATER* and $(s_M, \aleph_M)$ of *METHANE*. $H_2O(T) > HighH_2O$, from (6.26) and so using proof rules 13 and 14:

$$water.high \textbf{ open } [T - React, T](s_W, \aleph_W) \tag{6.31}$$

$$water.low \textbf{ closed } [T - React, T](s_W, \aleph_W) \tag{6.32}$$

From $\neg SysPumping(s, T)$ and 6.21, $\neg pump.on \textbf{ at } [T - \varepsilon, T](s, \aleph)$, and so, from proof rule 15, $\neg pump.on \textbf{ at } [T - \varepsilon, T](s_P, \aleph_P)$. In conjunction with (6.31) and (6.32) this is the antecedent to $SPEC_{water}$. It follows that

$$pump.on \textbf{ live } T(s_W, \aleph_W) \tag{6.33}$$

Similar reasoning is used for the specification $SPEC_{methane}$ for $METHANE$:

$$
\left.
\begin{array}{l}
methane.safe \ \textbf{open} \ [T - React, T](s, \aleph) \\
methane.danger \ \textbf{closed} \ [T - React, T](s, \aleph) \\
\neg pump.on \ \textbf{at} \ [T - \varepsilon, T](s, \aleph)
\end{array}
\right\} \Rightarrow pump.on \ \textbf{live} \ T(s, \aleph)
\tag{6.34}
$$

to obtain

$$
pump.on \ \textbf{live} \ T(s_M, \aleph_M)
\tag{6.35}
$$

$pump.on$ **live** $T(s, \aleph)$ holds by application of Rule 12.

But from $PU1$ we have $pump.on$ **open** $T(s, \aleph)$, so from Rule 7 $pump.on$ **at** $T(s, \aleph)$. This is a contradiction, since $s \uparrow (t, T] = \langle \rangle$. So case (1) is not possible.

Case (2) may be similarly shown to yield a contradiction.

Hence $PumpControl$ holds for all executions of $CONTROL$ where the sensors operate correctly:

$$
CONTROL \quad \textbf{sat} \quad Ass \Rightarrow PumpControl
\tag{6.36}
$$

6.5.2   CSP verification

Since $WATER$ is defined to be $WATER_{low}$, we need to establish that

$$
WATER_{low} \quad \textbf{sat} \quad SPEC_{water}
\tag{6.37}
$$

This is achieved by establishing three specifications that more closely follow the structure of the recursive definition and can be done directly from the proof rules for processes given in Section 6.4.1. Lemma 6.1 is proved in Section 6.5.3.

Lemma 6.1 $WATER$ **sat** $WL1$, where

$$
WL1 \ \widehat{=} \ water.low \ \textbf{at} \ t \Rightarrow water.high \ \textbf{live from} \ t + d \ \textbf{until} \ water.high
\tag{6.38}
$$

$$
s \downarrow water.low = \langle \rangle \Rightarrow water.high \ \textbf{live from} \ 0 \ \textbf{until} \ water.high
\tag{6.39}
$$

Lemma 6.2 $WATER$ **sat** $WL2$, where

$$
WL2 \ \widehat{=} \ water.high \ \textbf{at} \ t \wedge \neg water.low \ \textbf{at} \ [t, t + d' + \varepsilon]
\tag{6.40}
$$

$$
\Rightarrow pump.on \ \textbf{live from} \ t + d' + \varepsilon \ \textbf{until} \ \{water.low, pump.on\}
$$

Lemma 6.3 $WATER$ **sat** $WL3$, where

$$
WL3 \ \widehat{=} \ pump.on \ \textbf{at} \ t \wedge \neg water.low \ \textbf{at} \ [t, t + \varepsilon]
\tag{6.41}
$$

$$
\Rightarrow pump.on \ \textbf{live from} \ t + \varepsilon \ \textbf{until} \ \{water.low, pump.on\}
$$

These three lemmas are sufficient to establish that *WATER* **sat** $SPEC_{water}$.

First, assume the antecedents of $SPEC_{water}$:

$$water.high \textbf{ open } [T - React, T](s, \aleph) \tag{6.42}$$

$$water.low \textbf{ closed } [T - React, T](s, \aleph) \tag{6.43}$$

$$\neg pump.on \textbf{ at } (T - \varepsilon, T] \tag{6.44}$$

Now consider $s_l = s \uparrow [0, T] \downarrow water.low$.

If $s_l = \langle \rangle$ then *water.high* **live from** $t_l + d$ **until** *water.high* (from *WL1*) (where we say $t_l = -d$).

If $s_l \neq \langle \rangle$, then $end(s_l) = (t_l, water.low)$ for some $t_l < T - React$, as *water.low* **closed** $[T - React, T]$. So *water.high* **live from** $t_l + d$ **until** *water.high* (from *WL1*). In either case, from the antecedent *water.high* **open** $[T - React, T]$, if $d \leqslant React$ we may deduce that *water.high* **open** $T - React + d$. So Rule 8 yields *water.high* **at** $[t_l + d, T - React + d]$. Thus there is some $t_h \in [t_l + d, T - React + d]$ for which *water.high* **at** t_h.

This provides a constraint on the relationship between the delay d and the reaction time *React*.

Then *WL2* and the second antecedent of $SPEC_{water}$ yield

$$pump.on \textbf{ live from } t_h + d' + \varepsilon \textbf{ until } \{water.low, pump.on\}$$

Now consider $s_p = s \uparrow [t_h + d' + \varepsilon, T] \downarrow pump.on$.

If $s_p = \langle \rangle$ then *pump.on* **live from** $t_h + d' + \varepsilon$ **until** $\{water.low, pump.on\}$ implies *pump.on* **live** T. To make this final step we require that $t_h + d' + \varepsilon \leqslant T$, i.e. $d + d' + \varepsilon \leqslant React$.

This provides a stronger constraint on the relative values of some of the delays with respect to *React*. (The constraint $d'' + d''' + \varepsilon \leqslant React$ is obtained by the corresponding verification for *METHANE*.)

If $s_p \neq \langle \rangle$, then $end(s_p) = (t_p, pump.on)$ for some $t_p \leqslant T - \varepsilon$ (by the third antecedent). But then *pump.on* **live from** $t_p + \varepsilon$ **until** $\{water.low, pump.on\}$ follows from *WL3*. So the second antecedent and the definition of t_p yield *pump.on* **live** T.

The conclusion follows in each case.

6.5.3 Verifying mutually recursive processes

To prove a specification W of the process *WATER*, we require two satisfiable specifications, *WL* and *WH*. If from the assumptions X **sat** *WL* and Y **sat** *WH* we can prove $F(X, Y)$ **sat** *WL* and $G(X, Y)$ **sat** *WH* (where F and G are the defining equations for the two processes respectively), then from Rule 4 for mutual recursion $WATER_{low}$ **sat** *WL* and $WATER_{high}$ **sat** *WH*. Since *WATER* is defined to be $WATER_{low}$, we require finally that $WL \Rightarrow W$.

Assume the two following satisfiable specifications:

$$X \quad \textbf{sat} \quad WL \tag{6.45}$$

$$Y \quad \textbf{sat} \quad WH \tag{6.46}$$

Two functions are used in the defining equations of these two processes:

$$F(X,Y) \quad = \quad (water.high \xrightarrow{d} Y) \,\square\, (Wait\ \varepsilon;\ pump.off \to X) \qquad (6.47)$$

$$G(X,Y) \quad = \quad (water.low \xrightarrow{d'} X) \,\square\, (Wait\ \varepsilon;\ pump.on \to Y) \qquad (6.48)$$

Then if we can show that

$$F(X,Y) \quad \textbf{sat} \quad WL \qquad (6.49)$$

and

$$G(X,Y) \quad \textbf{sat} \quad WH \qquad (6.50)$$

from the two assumptions (6.45) and (6.46), then by recursion induction we may conclude $WATER_{low}$ **sat** $WL \wedge WATER_{high}$ **sat** WH.

Without knowing anything further about WL and WH, we may still derive the proof obligations for $F(X,Y)$ and $G(X,Y)$.

Using rule 1 for the event prefix we obtain

$$water.high \xrightarrow{d} Y \quad \textbf{sat} \quad s = \langle\rangle \wedge \forall t \bullet water.high \ \textbf{live}\ t \qquad (6.51)$$
$$\vee$$
$$s = \langle(t, water.high)\rangle \frown s' \wedge begin(s') \geqslant t + d$$
$$\wedge\, \forall t' \in [0, t) \bullet water.high \ \textbf{live}\ t'$$
$$\wedge\, WH(s' - (t+d), \aleph - (t+d))$$

Using Rule 1 for event prefix (with delay 0) we obtain

$$pump.off \to X \quad \textbf{sat} \quad s = \langle\rangle \wedge \forall t \bullet pump.off\ \textbf{live}\ t \qquad (6.52)$$
$$\vee$$
$$s = \langle(t, pump.off)\rangle \frown s' \wedge begin(s') \geqslant t$$
$$\wedge\, \forall t' \in [0, t) \bullet pump.off\ \textbf{live}\ t' \wedge WL(s' - t, \aleph - t)$$

Now apply Rule 2 for delay to (6.52):

$$Wait\ \varepsilon;\ pump.off \to X\ \textbf{sat} \qquad (6.53)$$
$$s - \varepsilon = \langle\rangle \wedge \forall t_0 \bullet pump.off\ \textbf{live}\ t_0(s - \varepsilon, \aleph - \varepsilon) \qquad (6.54)$$
$$\vee$$
$$begin(s) \geqslant \varepsilon$$
$$\wedge\, s - \varepsilon = \langle(t_0, pump.off)\rangle \frown s' \wedge begin(s') \geqslant t_0$$
$$\wedge\, \forall t' < t_0 \bullet pump.off\ \textbf{live}\ t'(s - \varepsilon, \aleph - \varepsilon)$$
$$\wedge\, WL(s' - t_0, \aleph - t_0)$$

This may be recast in a more usable form using $t = t_0 - \varepsilon$:

$$Wait\ \varepsilon;\ pump.off \to X \quad \textbf{sat} \quad s = \langle\rangle \wedge \forall t \geqslant \varepsilon \bullet pump.off\ \textbf{live}\ t \qquad (6.55)$$
$$\vee$$
$$s = \langle(t, pump.off)\rangle \frown s' \wedge begin(s') \geqslant t \geqslant \varepsilon$$
$$\wedge\, \forall t' \in [\varepsilon, t) \bullet pump.off\ \textbf{live}\ t'$$
$$\wedge\, WL(s' - t, \aleph - t)$$

Combining (6.51) and (6.55) using Rule 3 we have finally shown that

$$water.high \xrightarrow{d} Y$$
$$\square$$
$$Wait\ \varepsilon;\ pump.off \to X$$

meets the specification

$$
\begin{aligned}
WL' \quad\widehat{=}\quad & s = \langle\rangle \wedge \forall t \geqslant 0 \bullet water.high\ \mathbf{live}\ t \wedge \forall t \geqslant \varepsilon \bullet pump.off\ \mathbf{live}\ t \qquad (6.56)\\
& \vee\\
& s = \langle(t, water.high)\rangle \frown s' \wedge \forall t' \in [0, t) \bullet water.high\ \mathbf{live}\ t'\\
& \qquad\qquad\qquad\qquad\quad \wedge \forall t' \in [\varepsilon, t) \bullet pump.off\ \mathbf{live}\ t'\\
& \qquad\qquad\qquad\qquad\quad \wedge begin(s') \geqslant t + d\\
& \qquad\qquad\qquad\qquad\quad \wedge WH(s' - (t+d), \aleph - (t+d))\\
& \vee\\
& s = \langle(t, pump.off)\rangle \frown s' \wedge \forall t' \in [\varepsilon, t) \bullet pump.off\ \mathbf{live}\ t'\\
& \qquad\qquad\qquad\qquad\quad \wedge \forall t' \in [0, t) \bullet water.high\ \mathbf{live}\ t'\\
& \qquad\qquad\qquad\qquad\quad \wedge begin(s') \geqslant t\\
& \qquad\qquad\qquad\qquad\quad \wedge WL(s' - t, \aleph - t)
\end{aligned}
$$

Using entirely similar reasoning, it may also be derived that

$$water.low \xrightarrow{d'} WATER_{low}$$
$$\square$$
$$Wait\ \varepsilon;\ pump.on \to WATER_{high}$$

meets the specification

$$
\begin{aligned}
WH' \quad\widehat{=}\quad & s = \langle\rangle \wedge \forall t \bullet water.low\ \mathbf{live}\ t \wedge \forall t \geqslant \varepsilon \bullet pump.on\ \mathbf{live}\ t \qquad (6.57)\\
& \vee\\
& s = \langle(t, water.low)\rangle \frown s' \wedge \forall t' \in [0, t) \bullet water.low\ \mathbf{live}\ t'\\
& \qquad\qquad\qquad\qquad\quad \wedge \forall t' \in [\varepsilon, t) \bullet pump.on\ \mathbf{live}\ t'\\
& \qquad\qquad\qquad\qquad\quad \wedge begin(s') \geqslant t + d'\\
& \qquad\qquad\qquad\qquad\quad \wedge WL(s' - (t+d'), \aleph - (t+d'))\\
& \vee\\
& s = \langle(t, pump.on)\rangle \frown s' \wedge \forall t' \in [\varepsilon, t) \bullet pump.on\ \mathbf{live}\ t'\\
& \qquad\qquad\qquad\qquad\quad \wedge \forall t' \in [0, t) \bullet water.low\ \mathbf{live}\ t'\\
& \qquad\qquad\qquad\qquad\quad \wedge begin(s') \geqslant t\\
& \qquad\qquad\qquad\qquad\quad \wedge WH(s' - t, \aleph - t)
\end{aligned}
$$

Up to this point, we have needed to know nothing about the specifications WL and WH! However, we now need to prove that $WL' \Rightarrow WL$, and that $WH' \Rightarrow WH$. Our choice of WL and WH should also be strong enough to entail the required specification: in this case, we want $WL \Rightarrow W$.

To prove Lemma 6.1, we choose *WL* and *WH* as follows:

$$WL \quad = \quad water.low \text{ at } t \tag{6.58}$$
$$\Rightarrow water.high \text{ live from } t + d \text{ until } \{water.high, pump.off\}$$
$$s \downarrow water.low = \langle \rangle \tag{6.59}$$
$$\Rightarrow water.high \text{ live from } 0 \text{ until } \{water.high, pump.off\}$$
$$pump.off \text{ at } t \tag{6.60}$$
$$\Rightarrow water.high \text{ live from } t \text{ until } \{water.high, pump.off\}$$

$$WH \quad = \quad water.low \text{ at } t \tag{6.61}$$
$$\Rightarrow water.high \text{ live from } t + d \text{ until } \{water.high, pump.off\}$$
$$pump.off \text{ at } t \tag{6.62}$$
$$\Rightarrow water.high \text{ live from } t \text{ until } \{water.high, pump.off\}$$

Then $WL' \Rightarrow WL$ by straightforward case analysis on the three component clauses of WL'; each possibility yields *WL*. We obtain $WH' \Rightarrow WH$ in a similar way.

Finally, we show $WL \Rightarrow WL1$. Using Rule 9 with (6.59) and (6.61) we obtain (6.38); and using that rule with (6.60) and (6.61) we obtain (6.39). Thus both clauses of *WL*1 are obtained from the three clauses of *WL*.

Lemmas 6.2 and 6.3 are established in a similar way. To prove Lemma 6.2 choose *WL* and *WH* as follows:

$$WL \quad = \quad WL2 \tag{6.63}$$

$$WH \quad = \quad WL2 \tag{6.64}$$
$$\wedge s \downarrow water.high = \langle \rangle \wedge \neg water.low \text{ at } [0, \varepsilon] \tag{6.65}$$
$$\Rightarrow \quad pump.on \text{ live from } \varepsilon \text{ until } \{water.low, pump.on\} \tag{6.66}$$

To prove Lemma 6.3, use the following definitions:

$$WL \quad = \quad WL3 \tag{6.67}$$

$$WH \quad = \quad WL3 \tag{6.68}$$
$$\wedge s \downarrow pump.on = \langle \rangle \wedge \neg(water.low \text{ at } [0, \varepsilon]) \tag{6.69}$$
$$\Rightarrow \quad pump.on \text{ live from } \varepsilon \text{ until } \{water.low, pump.on\} \tag{6.70}$$

To show how a CSP description of the control system for a mine pump can be verified with respect to the specification in Chapter 1, states of the system were related to corresponding sequences of events that might be observed until some particular time. The CSP description produces possible traces which correspond to system states that can be checked against the description in Chapter 1. The interaction between the quantities being measured and the internal states of the system is obtained from the specifications of the sensors.

The proofs presented in this example have been more detailed than would generally be desirable in a verification of such a system, but they illustrate the foundations of this method of verification. It would be desirable for much of the routine work to be auto-mated, so that the insight that $SPEC_{water}$ is the property required of $WATER$ in this par-ticular case could be checked with machine assistance, as could the claim that $WATER$ **sat** $SPEC_{water}$.

This example confirms that one of the most difficult refinement steps in moving from specification to implementation of real-time systems is the transition from a state-based to an event-based description. This is a part of the development process that cannot be avoided, but it can be cumbersome when done rigorously.

The CSP description is an abstract implementation of the process $CONTROL$, but the choice of the CSP description was not entirely constrained by the specification in Chap-ter 1. For example, there is flexibility in when the pump should be switched off when the water is low and the methane is safe. We chose to switch it off as soon as possible (an energy-efficient solution!) but we could have chosen to allow the pump to run for a while longer, or even to leave it running until the methane became dangerous. These possibilities are represented in an alternative description of $WATER_{low}$:

$$WATER_{low} = water.high \xrightarrow{d} WATER_{high} \qquad (6.71)$$
$$\square$$
$$\sqcap_{t \in [\varepsilon, \infty]} Wait\ t;\ pump.off \rightarrow WATER_{low}$$

where any delay (and we treat $Wait\ \infty$ as $STOP$) may be chosen before the pump is to be turned off. An implementation need not contain this degree of nondeterminism but the implementor is free to resolve the nondeterminism at a later point in the development process.

This chapter has illustrated how complementary approaches to specification can be for-mally integrated. Decisions concerning the required maximum power of the pump should be made by reasoning at the level of the abstract description. The minimum delay $React$ is determined by the minimum values of delays such as ε and d physically allowed in this CSP implementation. (If a smaller reaction time is required, then perhaps a differ-ent implementation should be developed.) The water level $HighH_2O$ should then be low enough that the constraint on $React$ can be met; the calculations required to achieve this are again performed at the most abstract level. A formal approach is required to support the interplay between information obtained by calculations at different levels of abstrac-tion.

6.6 Historical background

The seminal paper on communicating sequential processes (Hoare, 1978) defined a lan-guage for describing systems as high-level parallel combinations of low-level communi-cating sequential components. Subsequently, an abstract process algebra version of the language was produced, which gave rise to the failures model (Brookes *et al.*, 1984) and the failures/divergences model (Brookes & Roscoe, 1985) for CSP processes. This is the language presented in the book by Hoare (1985).

Reed (1988) and Reed and Roscoe (1986; 1987; 1990; 1991) developed a hierarchy of timed and untimed models for CSP. This mathematical hierarchy supports a uniform treatment of concurrent processes at different levels of abstraction: in reasoning about complex systems, we may use the simplest semantic model that is sufficient to express the current requirement, safe in the knowledge that the argument remains valid in the other models of the hierarchy. The proof system for the timed failures model was presented in Davis and Schneider (1990), Schneider (1990b) and Davies (1993). It gives a complete set of rules for verifying process descriptions compositionally, in the style of the rules given here. A more detailed study of single and mutual recursion is presented in Davis and Schneider (1993), where the metric space approach to the fixed point theory is reviewed, and a number of proof techniques for verifying recursively defined processes are given.

Work on providing the specification macro language for timed CSP began with the presentation of the specification macros in Davies (1993). Concurrently, the use of temporal logic as a specification language was investigated by Jackson (1990; 1992), where a complete proof system for such specifications was developed consistent with the existing timed semantics. The atomic statements are $\mathbf{O}_a$ ('*a* is offered') and $\mathbf{P}_a$ ('*a* is performed'). These may then be used with standard logic and real-time temporal logic connectives to write real-time specifications. For example, the specification $\Box(\Box_{\leq 5}\neg\mathbf{P}_a \Rightarrow \Diamond_{=5}\mathbf{O}_a)$ states that whenever five units of time pass without *a* being performed it will be offered at the end of that five unit period.

A theory of timewise refinement was presented in Schneider (1990b; 1994). It provides a way of exploiting the links between various models in the hierarchy, notably between untimed and timed models, to allow results established in untimed models (such as deadlock-freedom) to be retained provided timing information is added to a process description in a suitable way.

An operational semantics has been given for the language of timed CSP (Schneider, 1995), describing processes in terms of how they are to be executed, rather than in terms of the more abstract timed failures that they might exhibit; these two views are consistent. The operational semantics was used to underpin the fixed point theory for a model of processes in terms of potentially infinite executions (Schneider, 1991; Mislove *et al.*, 1995) which are more appropriate for specification. This is the model presented here; its projection to finite executions yields the original timed failures model, but it also enables analysis of infinite non-terminating executions.

The theory of timed CSP has also been extended in other directions. A timed probabilistic model for CSP developed by Lowe (1993) allows descriptions and analysis of probabilistic aspects of a system's behaviour and extensions include an element of broadcast concurrency (Davies, 1993; Davies *et al.*, 1992).

CSP has been successfully applied to many examples: the alternating bit protocol, a sliding window protocol (Schneider, 1990b), Fischer's protocol (Schneider, 1993), a watchdog timer and a railroad crossing (Davies & Schneider, 1995). It has also been used for other case studies such as the design of control software for aircraft engines (Jackson, 1989), real-time robotics (Scattergood, 1990; Stamper, 1990; Wallace, 1991), the specification of a realistic telephone switching network (Kay & Reed, 1990; Superville,

1991), the verification of a local area network protocol (Davies, 1993), the specification of asynchronous neural nets (Gibbins *et al.*, 1993) and the verification of the Futurebus+ distributed arbitration protocol (Howles, 1993).

Research continues both into broadening the theoretical foundations of timed CSP, and into its application. One area of current research involves the development of a normal form, which will underpin a complete set of algebraic laws for processes. This in turn will enable the transformation of complex processes into other descriptions that may be easier to reason about, or whose validity with respect to a given specification is clear. Another use concerns new operators such as those included in the language of timed CSP when case studies demonstrate their utility; a normal form would make it possible to define these operators algebraically, without the need to give a new semantic equation. It further allows a translation from an appropriate subset of timed CSP into occam (Scott, 1994), another form of refinement in which properties proved about the timed CSP descriptions remain valid in the occam programs.

Another area of current research involves extending the language to allow unguarded recursion. Although no such recursion could ever be implemented, it would allow timed CSP to be used more cleanly as a specification language, since the need to include an artificial non-zero time-guard is often distracting when expressing requirements. For example, the constraint that the only possible events a and b alternate is naturally expressed as $C = \mu X \bullet a \to b \to X$. To constrain a process P to this alternation it is sufficient to place it in parallel: $P |[a, b]| C$. The requirement that there should be some non-zero delay round the loop is distracting and obscures the intention of the constraint. However, the semantic model required to handle such instant recursions will be significantly more complicated than any of the models in the existing hierarchy.

The applicability of the theory to the emerging timed LOTOS standard is under investigation, with encouraging results. It appears that much of the theory developed within the context of timed CSP is applicable to many of the features suggested for inclusion within a timed version of LOTOS, and that it may be considered to provide a semantic theory for timed LOTOS.

In the longer term, it seems clear that performing large scale verifications will require some form of machine assistance, perhaps in the form of model-checking (which has proved extremely successful in untimed CSP (Roscoe, 1994)), or else in the use of a proof assistant. The theory is now sufficiently mature to support investigation into this promising area for future research.

6.7 Exercises

Exercise 6.1 Write CSP processes which describe the following situations. Decide first which events are to be used (the interface of the process), and then provide a CSP description:

1. A watchdog timer, which will accept up to one reset per second, and raises the alarm if there is a ten second period in which it is not reset.

2. A talk described by process *TALK* which will be stopped in 30 minutes if it has not already finished.

3. A single place lossy channel, which is ready to accept input when empty, and is prepared to output its contents when non-empty. However, it will erase its contents and revert to being empty precisely two seconds after input, if the message has not already been output.

4. A buffer which inputs messages initially at a maximum rate of one every two seconds; but if no input arrives over a period of 20 seconds then its maximum input rate reduces to one message every six seconds. It returns to its initial input rate either when empty, or when the user resets it. The maximum output rate remains constant at one message per second.

Exercise 6.2 Consider the processes

$$P = a \rightarrow STOP \,\Box\, b \rightarrow STOP$$
$$Q = a \rightarrow STOP \stackrel{2}{\triangleright} b \rightarrow STOP$$

Show that P and Q are different by giving a behaviour of P that is not a behaviour of Q. Show also that neither refines the other by giving a behaviour of Q that is not a behaviour of P. Is $a \rightarrow STOP$ the same as $a \stackrel{2}{\rightarrow} STOP$? Is $a \rightarrow SKIP$ the same as $a \stackrel{2}{\rightarrow} SKIP$?

Exercise 6.3 Given the definitions

$$P = a \stackrel{2}{\rightarrow} b \rightarrow STOP$$
$$Q = b \stackrel{3}{\rightarrow} c \rightarrow STOP$$
$$R = a \rightarrow STOP \stackrel{5}{\triangleright} b \rightarrow STOP$$

Rewrite the following processes so that they contain no parallel operator:

1. $P \| [b] \| Q$
2. $P \| [a,b,c] \| Q$
3. $Q \| [b] \| R$
4. $Q \| [a,b] \| R$

Rewrite $P \| [b] \| Q \setminus b$ so that it contains no parallelism or hiding.

Exercise 6.4 A component of the system not presented in this chapter is an alarm, which should sound when danger is present:

. Specify formally when the alarm should sound.
. Provide a CSP implementation *ALARM* which meets this specification.
. Use the proof rules to establish that *ALARM* meets the specification.

Exercise 6.5 It is observed that if the water level oscillates around the high water mark, then the pump may switch on and off repeatedly. It is decided to introduce a sensor to detect when the water reaches a lower level, and to leave the pump on until the water recedes below this point:

- Specify the new sensor: give the assumptions the controller can make about readings from it.
- Modify the CSP description of the pump controller to reflect the new intention.
- Does your new pump controller meet the original specification?
- Does it refine the old pump controller?

Chapter 7

Specification and Verification in the Duration Calculus

Zhiming Liu

Introduction

The duration calculus is an interval temporal logic which allows formal description of the dynamic properties of a system. It is well suited for the specification of the requirements of embedded systems. A distinctive feature of the logic is that, without explicit mention of absolute time, it permits reasoning about the durations of different states in a given time interval.

This chapter introduces the duration calculus and demonstrates how the behaviour of a system is defined in terms of its states. To implement a requirement, assumptions must be made about the environment of the system and the physical components used in the implementation. We also illustrate how the specification and the design of the system can be described in the same notation, and how to reason about the validity of a design in relation to the requirement.

The basic duration calculus is described in terms of its syntax and an informal but rigorous semantic explanation; the axioms and rules are described and their use is illustrated for proving some theorems. We show how the logic can be used for specification and refinement, using the mine pump example, and for the specification of real-time scheduling of shared processors. Finally, the duration logic is extended into a probabilistic logic to allow formalization and reasoning about the reliability requirements of a system.

7.1 Modelling real-time systems

The first step in formalizing the requirements of a system is to agree on a system model. The duration calculus uses a *time-domain model* in which a system is described by a collection of *states* which are functions of time. Time is represented by the non-negative real numbers. A state variable is a function from time to the real numbers; a boolean state variable takes the values 1 (for *true*) and 0 (for *false*) and can therefore be used in integrals over time.

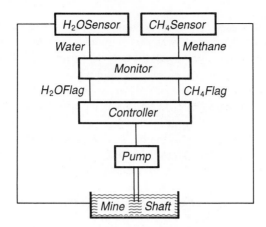

Figure 7.1 Physical components of the mine pump

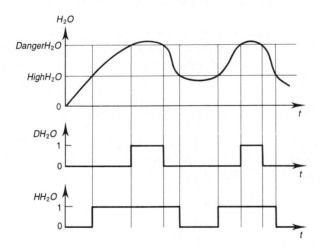

Figure 7.2 Sample timing diagram for water levels

Consider the diagram in Figure 7.1, showing the components connected to the mine pump controller. The arcs denote possible interaction between components and labels denote the information being exchanged: e.g. *Water* and *Methane* represent the water and methane levels in the mine shaft. H_2OFlag and CH_4Flag are boolean state variables.

The water level inside the mine shaft is measured using the sensor $H_2OSensor$. The pump controller is required to keep the water level below a critical level denoted by the real *constant DangerH₂O*. Let the boolean state variable DH_2O be set to 1 if the water level is higher than $DangerH_2O$ (Figure 7.2).

In order to work towards an implementation, a water level $HighH_2O$ slightly lower than the danger level is used to give the control system time to react. Let the boolean variable HH_2O be set to 1 when the water level exceeds $HighH_2O$; when this occurs for at least a period δ of time, the monitor sets the boolean variable H_2OFlag (see Figure 7.2).

A high level of methane can make use of the pump hazardous and the control process must then turn off the pump. The sensor $CH_4Sensor$ measures the methane level and the boolean valued state variable DCH_4 is set to 1 if the methane level is higher than the critical level $DangerCH_4$.

As in the case of water levels, let the boolean variable HCH_4 be set to 1 when the methane level reaches a high level $HighCH_4$ which is slightly lower than the critical level $DangerCH_4$. The monitor sets the boolean variable CH_4Flag when the methane level exceeds $HighCH_4$ for at least a period δ of time.

An alarm *Alarm* is set when either the water level or the methane level stays above its critical level for a period δ of time.

The pump controller uses the values of H_2OFlag and CH_4Flag to decide when to turn the pump on or off. When the system has been *stable* for δ time units in a state in which $H_2OFlag \wedge \neg CH_4Flag$ holds, i.e. H_2Oflag is up and CH_4Flag is down, the pump must be turned on. We denote this state by *SafePump*. When the system has been stable for δ time units in a state in which *SafePump* does not hold, the pump should be turned off.

Note that when the condition *SafePump* is changing, nothing is specified about the pump and it could even be in the process of being switched on or off for up to δ time units.

PumpOn denotes that the pump is on and water is being pumped out, reducing the water level in the mine shaft.

The states H_2OFlag, CH_4Flag, *Alarm*, *PumpOn* DH_2O, HH_2O, DCH_4 and HCH_4 are treated as *basic state variables*, while *SafePump* is a *composite state* defined in terms of the basic state variables H_2OFlag and CH_4Flag.

Behaviour

A *behaviour* or trajectory of a system is given by an assignment, called an *interpretation*, of state functions to the basic state variables.

Observation of a behaviour for a bounded interval is illustrated by the timing diagram in Figure 7.3 where boolean values are represented by 0 and 1.

7.2 Requirements

A *requirement* is a property expected of the system. A *property* is expressed as a constraint over the system behaviours, i.e. the states of the system over time. For the mine pump system, the following properties must hold for the water level controller and the monitor.

Safe water: In any period of up to 1000 shifts, the total time when the water level is dangerous must not exceed one shift.

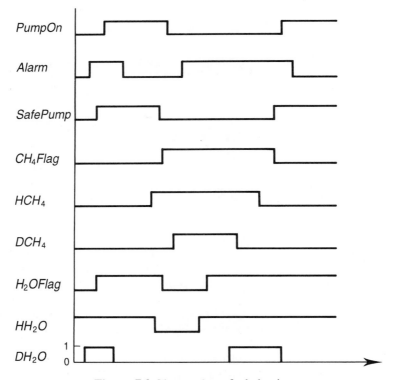

Figure 7.3 Observation of a behaviour

Set flags: The flags H_2OFlag and CH_4Flag, respectively, must be set (or 1) when the water or methane levels have been high for at least a period δ of time.

Reset flags: The flags H_2OFlag and CH_4Flag, respectively, must be cleared (or 0) when the water or methane levels have not been high for at least a period δ of time.

Safe water

For an observation of the mine pump system behaviour in a bounded interval $[b,e]$ of time, the *duration* of DH_2O is measured by the integral $\int_b^e DH_2O(t)dt$, shown shaded in the timing diagram in Figure 7.4.

This duration is the total time for which the water level is dangerous. Thus the property **Safe water** for an interval $[b,e]$ is

$$(e-b) \le 1000 \Rightarrow \int_b^e DH_2O(t)dt \le 1$$

To simplify reasoning, it is always desirable to avoid explicit reference to time in formulas; thus, the use of t and the bounding points b and e together with universal quantification over the interval should be avoided. Let the symbol $\int DH_2O$ denote the duration of

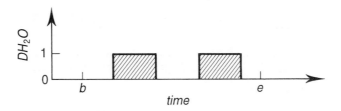

Figure 7.4 A duration of DH_2O

DH_2O. Let ℓ be the length of the interval. Then the property **Safe water** can be expressed without explicit mention of time as

$$\ell \leq 1000 \Rightarrow \int DH_2O \leq 1$$

For a given behaviour of the mine pump and a given bounded interval (an observation), this formula is either *true* or *false*. A formula *holds for a behaviour* if it is true for any prefix interval $[0,t]$, $t \geq 0$, of the behaviour. Thus, the formula tells us that a behaviour of the mine pump is safe if for any prefix interval $[0,t]$, $t \leq 1000$, the duration of DH_2O in that interval is not more than 1. But **Safe water** does not require the system to be safe for only the first 1000 shifts. So we need to express this property over *any* observation interval $[b,e]$, $b \geq 0$.

The modal operator $\square$ is used to denote that a formula holds for any subinterval of a given observation. The property *Safe* states that for any subinterval of a given observation, the duration of DH_2O is at most 1.

$$Safe \stackrel{\Delta}{=} \square(\ell \leq 1000 \Rightarrow \int DH_2O \leq 1)$$

The property holds for a behaviour when the constraint on DH_2O holds for any subinterval of any prefix interval, i.e. any bounded interval.

Set flags
The requirement for the water level flag is that for an observation interval longer than δ, H_2OFlag must be set to 1 when the water level has been high for at least a period δ of time. So the constraint is that HH_2O is true for a period δ of time, or more.

To express such properties, we need some notation to describe when a state P has been true in a *non-point* interval. The operator $\lceil \cdot \rceil$ *lifts* a state to a predicate (or a property). For state P, the property $\lceil P \rceil$ holds for an interval $[b,e]$ iff $b < e$ and there are only finite many t in this interval such that $P(t) = 0$. The formula $\lceil P \rceil$ can be read as 'P is true almost everywhere in the non-point interval'. The value of P is ignored at possible points of discontinuity and these will be a finite set for any finite observation. In particular, we avoid discussion of the values at end points, making it irrelevant whether we choose closed, open, or half-open intervals as the durations remain the same. Taking closed intervals may be intuitively a little bit clearer, because a point is an interval.

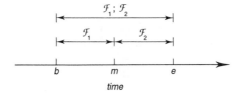

Figure 7.5 The *chop* operator

Exercise 7.2.1 Define $\lceil P \rceil$ in terms of $\int P$ and ℓ.

The property that HH_2O holds for a period δ of time can now be written as

$$\lceil HH_2O \rceil \wedge (\ell = \delta)$$

Similarly, if H_2OFlag is 0 in an interval we have $\lceil \neg H_2OFlag \rceil$. These two formulas can be combined to express the property **Set flags** using the binary modal operator *chop*. The formula $(\mathcal{F}_1 \; ; \; \mathcal{F}_2)$ is read as '$\mathcal{F}_1$ chop $\mathcal{F}_2$': it holds in an interval $[b, e]$ iff this interval can be divided into an initial subinterval $[b, m]$ in which $\mathcal{F}_1$ holds, and a final subinterval $[m, e]$ in which $\mathcal{F}_2$ holds, $b \leq m \leq e$. This is illustrated by the timing diagram in Figure 7.5.

The property **Set flags** is defined using the chop operator as:

$$\neg ((\lceil HH_2O \rceil \wedge \ell = \delta); \lceil \neg H_2OFlag \rceil)$$

which states that it is not the case that the observation starts with DH_2O holding for δ units of time followed by the alarm being off for a non-point subinterval.

The property should hold for all observations, so to complete the specification we have

$$\Box \neg (\lceil HH_2O \rceil \wedge \ell = \delta); \lceil \neg HH_2OFlag \rceil)$$

The formula can be rewritten using an abbreviation: for a formula $\mathcal{F}$ and a state P,

$$\mathcal{F} \xrightarrow{t} \lceil P \rceil \triangleq \Box \neg (\mathcal{F} \wedge (\ell = t); \lceil \neg P \rceil)$$

which is read as '$\mathcal{F}$ for time t leads to state P'; it is defined by stating that it is never the case that $\mathcal{F}$ holds for time t and P does not then hold. A similar abbreviation reads '$\mathcal{F}$ for up to time t leads to state P' and is defined below:

$$\mathcal{F} \xrightarrow{\leq t} \lceil P \rceil \triangleq \Box \neg (\mathcal{F} \wedge (\ell \leq t); \lceil \neg P \rceil)$$

Thus F can go to state P only after it has held for up to t time units.

The setting of the flag to indicate a high water level is then specified as

$$SetWaterFlag \triangleq \lceil HH_2O \rceil \xrightarrow{\delta} \lceil H_2OFlag \rceil$$

Down flags

This property is analogous to **Set flags**. For the water flag, it states that if the observation interval is longer than δ, the flag H_2OFlag must be 0 if HH_2O has been 0 for δ:

$$ResetWaterFlag \overset{\Delta}{=} \lceil \neg HH_2O \rceil \xrightarrow{\delta} \lceil \neg H_2OFlag \rceil$$

We can similarly obtain formulas for *SetMethaneFlag, ResetMethaneFlag, SetAlarm* and *ResetAlarm* and complete the specification of the mine pump monitor.

Exercise 7.2.2   Write formulas for the following requirements:

SetMethaneFlag: the flag CH_4Flag must be set when the methane level has been high for a period δ of time.

ResetMethaneFlag: the flag CH_4Flag must be cleared when the methane level has been not high for a period δ of time.

SetAlarm: the alarm must be raised when the water level has been dangerous for a period δ of time.

ResetAlarm: the alarm must be turned off when the water level has been below the critical level for a period δ of time.

7.3   Assumptions

For a design to implement a requirement, it is necessary to make assumptions about both the environment in which the system will operate and the physical properties of the implementation. The assumptions may be made initially, or as the design develops.

For the mine pump, assume that each component takes some time to react: e.g. for simplicity we assume that the monitor takes δ time units from the onset of a high water level to set H_2OFlag, the controller also takes δ time units to turn on the pump and, assuming that there is limited inflow of water, the pump takes some time, say ε time units, to bring the water level down. Therefore, to meet the safety requirement *Safe*, the high water level $HighH_2O$ should be set low enough to allow for these reaction times before water reaches the critical level $DangerH_2O$:

$$As_1 \overset{\Delta}{=} \Box(\lceil DH_2O \rceil \Rightarrow \lceil HH_2O \rceil)$$

This states that in any non-point interval, if the water level is dangerous it is high. Further, after the water level becomes high, it will not reach the critical level for $w \leq 1$ units of time:

$$As_2 \overset{\Delta}{=} ((\lceil \neg HH_2O \rceil \ ; \ \lceil HH_2O \rceil) \xrightarrow{\leq w} \lceil \neg DH_2O \rceil) \wedge (w \leq 1)$$

w depends on the reaction times of the monitor and the controller, and on the capacity of the pump. This assumption is valid only if the rate at which water flows into the mine shaft is bounded.

7.4 Design

Design involves making choices and taking decisions about how requirements are to be met. For example, to meet the safety requirement *Safe* according to the assumptions As_1 and As_2, it is necessary to bring a high water level down within w time units, i.e. before it reaches the critical level:

$$\Box(\lceil HH_2O \rceil \Rightarrow \ell \leq w) \text{ or, equivalently, } \lceil HH_2O \rceil \xrightarrow{\ w\ } \lceil \neg HH_2O \rceil$$

But this may not always be possible as a high methane level may make it unsafe for the controller to turn on the pump. The property *Safe* allows limited occurrences of dangerous water levels provided they do not last too long or occur too often. Let

$$Failure \overset{\Delta}{=} \lceil HH_2O \rceil \wedge \ell > w$$

Since each occurrence of *Failure* takes at least time w and at most time 1, the following two design decisions can be made:

- A *Failure* can only occur in an interval not longer than one time unit.
- Any two occurrences of *Failure* must be separated by at least 1001 time units; in other words, *Failure* occurs at most once in any interval that is not longer than 1000.

The first decision can be formalized easily as

$$Des_{11} \overset{\Delta}{=} \Box(Failure \Rightarrow \ell \leq 1)$$

which is equivalent to $\Box(\lceil HH_2O \rceil \Rightarrow \ell \leq 1)$ when $w \leq 1$.

The second decision says that if an observation interval can be divided into three adjacent subintervals such that *Failure* holds in the first and last subintervals, and somewhere in the middle subinterval *Failure* does not hold, then the observation interval must be at least 1001 time units long.

This needs some notation to describe a property that holds somewhere in an interval, and the conventional modal operator $\Diamond$ (read as 'somewhere') serves the need. For a formula $\mathcal{F}$, $\Diamond \mathcal{F}$ holds in an interval $[b, e]$ iff there is a subinterval $[b', e']$, $b \leq b'$ and $e' \leq e$, such that $\mathcal{F}$ holds in $[b', e']$. This is illustrated by the following diagram:

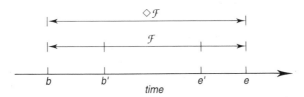

The second design decision then becomes

$$Des_{12} \overset{\Delta}{=} \Box((Failure \ ; \ \Diamond\neg Failure \ ; \ Failure) \Rightarrow \ell \geq 1001)$$

At all times, if *Failure* is followed at some time by ¬*Failure* and then by *Failure*, the length l of the observation interval must be at least 1001.

Let $Des_1 \triangleq Des_{11} \wedge Des_{12}$. To verify that Des_1 guarantees the safety requirement we must prove the implication

$$Des_1 \Rightarrow Safe$$

But the implication does not hold without the assumptions As_1 and As_2 about the high water level. So what we must prove is that the implication does hold under these assumptions:

$$As_1 \wedge As_2 \wedge Des_1 \Rightarrow Safe$$

Exercise 7.4.1 Give arguments for the validity of this implication in the context of the mine pump.

In general, proving that the conjunction of assumptions and design decisions implies a requirement is called the verification of the *correctness of the design with respect to the requirement*. Such an implication has the form

$$\mathcal{A} \wedge \mathcal{D} \Rightarrow C$$

where $\mathcal{A}$ is the specification of the assumption, $\mathcal{D}$ is the specification of the design, and C is the specification of the requirement (i.e. *commitment*).

Note that $\mathcal{A} \wedge \mathcal{D} \Rightarrow C$ is equivalent to $\mathcal{D} \Rightarrow (\mathcal{A} \Rightarrow C)$. Thus, $\mathcal{A} \Rightarrow C$ is sometimes called the requirement, i.e. 'the requirement is a commitment under the assumption'.

A design decision can be refined into lower level design decisions. For example, Des_1 can be refined into the following control plans:

1. The pump must be on when the water level has been high and the methane level has been low for δ time units:

$$StartPump \triangleq \lceil SafePump \rceil \xrightarrow{\delta} \lceil PumpOn \rceil$$

2. The pump must be off when the water level has been low or the methane level has been high for δ time units:

$$StopPump \triangleq \lceil \neg SafePump \rceil \xrightarrow{\delta} \lceil \neg PumpOn \rceil$$

Let $Des_2 \triangleq StartPump \wedge StopPump$. To prove the correctness of this refined design with respect to Des_1, we need the following assumptions (these will be formalized in Section 7.6):

As_3: assumption about the capacity of the pump.
As_4: assumption about the duration of a high methane level.
Monitor: the full specification of the monitor as an assumption.
As_5: assumption about the choice of the constants w and δ.

Then, the goal is to prove

$$As_3 \wedge As_4 \wedge As_5 \wedge Monitor \wedge Des_2 \Rightarrow Des_1$$

This kind of refinement procedure can be repeated until an implementation of the system is obtained. The correctness of the implementation is guaranteed by the transitivity of the logical implication. For example, the two implications above guarantee the implication

$$As \wedge Des_2 \Rightarrow Safe$$

where

$$As \triangleq As_1 \wedge As_2 \wedge As_3 \wedge As_4 \wedge As_5 \wedge Monitor$$

The informal introduction in this section has provided a notation for the specification of requirements, assumptions and designs of real-time embedded systems. The mine pump example has been used to illustrate the steps in the formal development of such a system. But for formal verification of properties and the correctness of a design, we need a set of axioms and rules.

7.5   The basic duration calculus (DC)

The simplicity of temporal logic comes from the removal of explicit time. In Interval Temporal Logic (ITL), the variables b and e, denoting the end points of an arbitrary observation interval $[b, e]$, are removed from expressions such as *Safe* and *SetWaterFlag* (Section 7.2). A variable v is interpreted as a function from intervals to values. A formula in ITL, such as $v_1 \leq v_2$, holds for an interval $[b, e]$ under a given interpretation I of v_1 and v_2; i.e. if $I(v_1)([b, e]) \leq I(v_2)([b, e])$ holds in the value domain. ITL uses the modal operator *chop* to define the usual modalities $\Diamond$ and $\Box$.

DC develops on ITL by introducing integrals (i.e. durations) of states over intervals as variables in the interval temporal logic. Thus, DC adopts primitives such as the *chop* operator of ITL. We shall be concerned mainly about the axioms and rules dealing with integrals of states. But we shall also consider some ITL axioms for the *chop* operator; although they will not be called axioms or theorems, they will be used to prove properties of durations.

7.5.1   Time

DC uses continuous time, *Time*, represented by the set of non-negative real numbers. t, t_1, etc. are assumed to range over the real numbers. A *time interval* is a closed interval $[b, e]$ of the real numbers, i.e. $b, e \in Time$ and $b \leq e$ and $[b, e]$ is the set of time points from b to e.

7.5.2 States

A *basic state* is a state variable. An interpretation I assigns a basic state P to a function $I(P)$ from *Time* to the set $\{0, 1\}$ of boolean values. $I(P)(t) = 1$ means that state P is 'on' at time t, and $I(P)(t) = 0$ that it is 'off' at time t, under the interpretation I. In the mine pump example, DH_2O, DCH_4, HH_2O and HCH_4 are basic states. An observation of a behaviour of this system, such as the one illustrated by the diagram in Figure 7.3, gives an interpretation for these states over the observation interval.

States will be ranged over by P, Q, P_1, Q_1, etc., and will consist of expressions formed by the following rules:

- Each basic state P is a state.
- If P and Q are states, then so are $\neg P$, $(P \wedge Q)$.

A *composite state* is interpreted as a function from *Time* to the set $\{0, 1\}$ which is defined by the interpretation for the basic states and the boolean operators. For example,

$$SafePump \stackrel{\Delta}{=} HH_2O \wedge \neg HCH_4$$

is a composite state. For an interpretation I and some $t \in Time$,

$$I(SafePump)(t) = I(HH_2O)(t) \wedge \neg I(HCH_4)(t)$$

The timing diagram in Figure 7.3 gives an illustration of an interpretation for *SafePump*. The conventional boolean operators $\vee$, $\Rightarrow$ and $\Leftrightarrow$ can be defined from $\neg$ and $\wedge$ in the usual way. Specifically, the constant state 0 and 1 can be defined as $P \wedge \neg P$ and $\neg 0$ respectively.

7.5.3 Duration terms

The *duration* of a state P is denoted by $\int P$. Given an interpretation I of states, the duration $\int P$ is interpreted over time intervals and denotes the accumulated time when P is 'on' within the time interval. So, for an arbitrary interval $[b, e]$, the interpretation $I(\int P)([b, e])$ is defined as the integral of the function $I(P)$ over the interval $[b, e]$, i.e.

$$I(\int P)([b, e]) \stackrel{\Delta}{=} \int_b^e I(P)(t)dt$$

which is a real number. An interpretation for the duration $\int DH_2O$ was illustrated by the timing diagram in Figure 7.4.

Let $\mathbf{R}$ denote the set of real numbers and be ranged over by *logical variables x, y, z*, with or without subscripts. The set of *basic duration terms* consists of variables and constants over the real numbers $\mathbf{R}$, such as x and 5, and durations of states, such as $\int P$. A *duration term* is either a basic duration term or an expression formed from duration terms using the usual operators on real numbers, such as $+$ (addition) and $*$ (multiplication). For example,

$$\int SafePump \text{ and } 5 * (\int HCH_4) * (\int SafePump)$$

are duration terms.

7.5.4 Duration formulas

A *basic duration formula* is an expression formed from duration terms using the usual relational operators on real numbers, such as = (equality) and < (inequality), with their standard meanings. The set of *duration formulas*, ranged over by $\mathcal{F}$, $\mathcal{G}$, etc., consists of expressions formed by the following rules:

- Each basic duration formula is a duration formula.
- If $\mathcal{F}$ and $\mathcal{G}$ are duration formulas, so are $\neg\,\mathcal{F}$, $\mathcal{F}\wedge\mathcal{G}$.
- If $\mathcal{F}$ is a duration formula and x is a logical variable over the real numbers, then $\exists x.\,\mathcal{F}$ is a duration formula.
- If $\mathcal{F}$ and $\mathcal{G}$ are duration formulas, so is $(\mathcal{F}\,;\,\mathcal{G})$.

As before, the first-order logic operators $\vee$, $\Rightarrow$ and $\Leftrightarrow$ can be defined in terms of the given operators $\neg$ and $\wedge$; the universal quantifier $\forall$ can be defined in terms of the given quantifier $\exists$ and the operator $\neg$ in the usual way.

In these definitions, we use the conventional rules of precedence for each first-order operator; e.g. $\neg$ has the highest precedence and the precedence of conjunction $\wedge$ is higher than that of disjunction $\vee$. In addition, the precedence of the *chop* operator is higher than that of implication and lower than that of disjunction.

A duration formula $\mathcal{F}$ is *satisfied* by an interpretation I over an interval $[b,e]$ when it evaluates to *true*. This satisfaction relation is written as

$$I,[b,e]\models\mathcal{F}$$

For example, if I_1 assigns HH_2O to 1 over $[0,2]$, and assigns HCH_4 to 0 over $[0,1)$ and to 1 over $(1,2]$, we have

$$I_1,[0,2]\models(2*\textstyle\int SafePump)=\int HH_2O \quad I_1,[0,1]\ \models\int SafePump=1$$
$$I_1,[1,2]\models\textstyle\int SafePump=0 \qquad\qquad I_1,[0.5,1]\models\int HH_2O=\int SafePump$$

Exercise 7.5.1 For the interpretation I_1 for HH_2O and HCH_4, find two subintervals of $[0,2]$ such that $3*\int SafePump<\int HH_2O$ holds in one subinterval but not in the other.

The 'chopped' formula $(\mathcal{F}\,;\,\mathcal{G})$ is true for an interpretation I within interval $[b,e]$ if there exists m such that $b\leq m\leq e$ and $\mathcal{F}$ and $\mathcal{G}$ are true for I with $[b,m]$ and $[m,e]$ respectively; i.e.

$$I,[b,m]\models\mathcal{F}\quad\text{and}\quad I,[m,e]\models\mathcal{G}$$

The timing diagram in Figure 7.5 illustrates the semantics of the *chop* operator. As an example, considering again interpretation I_1 for HH_2O and HCH_4 over $[0,2]$, we have

$$I_1,[0,2]\models(\textstyle\int SafePump=1)\,;\,(\int SafePump=0)$$

Exercise 7.5.2   Under the interpretation I_1, find a subinterval of $[0, 2]$ for which

$$true ; \ (\int SafePump = \int 1); \ true$$

holds but the following formula does not hold:

$$\neg(true ; \ \neg(\int SafePump = \int 1); \ true)$$

Give an informal meaning to these two formulas.

A duration formula is *valid* if it is true for any interpretation over any bounded time interval. For example,

$$\int P + \int \neg P = \int 1$$

is valid. More obviously, $\int P \leq \int 1$ is valid.

7.5.5   Axioms and rules

We are now in a position to define the axioms and rules with which to calculate the durations of states.

We begin by listing some simple theorems of analysis which are sufficiently useful to be taken as axioms in the calculus.

Axiom 7.1 $\int 0 = 0$.

Axiom 7.2   For an arbitrary state P, $\int P \geq 0$.

Axiom 7.3   For arbitrary states P and Q, $\int P + \int Q = \int(P \vee Q) + \int(P \wedge Q)$.

Using these axioms, we can readily prove properties such as the following theorem.

Theorem 7.1   For an arbitrary state P

(a) $\int P + \int \neg P = \int 1$ (b) $\int P \leq \int 1$

Proof: (a):

$$
\begin{aligned}
\int P + \int \neg P &= \int(P \vee \neg P) + \int(P \wedge \neg P) && \text{Axiom 3} \\
&= \int 1 + \int 0 && \text{boolean operations} \\
&= \int 1 && \text{Axiom 1}
\end{aligned}
$$

Proof of (b) follows from (a) and **Axiom 2**.

□

Abbreviations

For any observation interval $[b,e]$, the integral $\int 1$ is the length $e - b$ of the interval.

Definition 7.1 $\ell \overset{\Delta}{=} \int 1$

Notice that a state P holds almost everywhere in a non-point interval $[b,e]$ iff the integral of P over this interval equals the integral of 1 over the same interval. Thus the lifting operator $\lceil \cdot \rceil$ can be defined in the following way.

Definition 7.2 For an arbitrary state P, $\lceil P \rceil \overset{\Delta}{=} (\int P = \ell) \wedge (\ell > 0)$.

We use $\lceil \; \rceil$ to denote formulas that are true only for point intervals.

Definition 7.3 $\lceil \; \rceil \overset{\Delta}{=} (\ell = 0)$

It is easy then to prove that an observation interval is either a proper interval or a point interval.

Theorem 7.2 $\lceil 1 \rceil \vee \lceil \; \rceil$

This says that the length of any interval is greater than or equals 0. The proof is very simple but shows how the definitions can be used.

Theorem 7.3 For any state P

$\quad$ (a) $\lceil P \rceil \Rightarrow (\int \neg P = 0)$ $\quad$ (b) $\lceil \; \rceil \Rightarrow (\int P = 0)$

Exercise 7.5.3 Prove Theorem 7.3.

The following theorem expresses the monotonicity of $\int$.

Theorem 7.4 For any states P and Q, $\lceil P \Rightarrow Q \rceil \Rightarrow (\int P \leq \int Q)$.

To prove this theorem (and some others), we shall use the following ITL axiom:

$$\exists x.(v = x)$$

for any interval variable v. Thus, in DC we can use $\exists x.(\int P = x)$ as an axiom for an arbitrary state P. We shall refer to this axiom as Ax.$\exists$ in the following proofs.

Proof:

$$
\begin{array}{lll}
\lceil P \Rightarrow Q \rceil & \Rightarrow \int (P \Rightarrow Q) = \int 1 & \text{Def. 2} \\
& \Rightarrow \int (\neg P \vee Q) = \int 1 & \text{Def. of } \Rightarrow \\
& \Rightarrow \int \neg P + \int Q - \int (\neg P \wedge Q) = \int 1 & \text{Axiom 3} \\
& \Rightarrow \int Q - \int (\neg P \wedge Q) = \int 1 - \int \neg P & \text{AX.}\exists \\
& \Rightarrow \int Q - \int (\neg P \wedge Q) = \int P & \text{Th.1(a)} \\
& \Rightarrow \int P \leq \int Q & \text{Axiom 2}
\end{array}
$$

$\hfill \square$

The conventional modal operators $\Diamond$ and $\square$ can be defined in terms of the *chop* operator,

Definition 7.4 For a duration formula $\mathcal{F}$

$\quad \Diamond \mathcal{F} \overset{\Delta}{=} true \; ; \; \mathcal{F} \; ; \; true$ $\quad$ and $\quad \square \mathcal{F} \overset{\Delta}{=} \neg \Diamond \neg \mathcal{F}$

Properties of the *chop* **operator**

We now present some basic properties of the ITL *chop* operator which we shall use as axioms.

The first property, referred to as the *chop-unit*, is that the *chop* operator has $\lceil \rceil$ as unit. Formally, for an arbitrary duration formula $\mathcal{F}$:

$$\text{(a)}\quad \lceil \rceil; \ \mathcal{F} \Leftrightarrow \mathcal{F} \qquad \text{(b)}\quad \mathcal{F}; \ \lceil \rceil \Leftrightarrow \mathcal{F}$$

The *chop* operator has *false* as *zero*. That is, for an arbitrary duration formula $\mathcal{F}$:

$$\text{(a)}\quad \textit{false}; \ \mathcal{F} \Leftrightarrow \textit{false} \qquad \text{(b)}\quad \mathcal{F}; \ \textit{false} \Leftrightarrow \textit{false}$$

We shall call this property *chop-zero*. It means that no interval can be split into two subintervals such that *false* holds for the first or the last subinterval, since *false* does not hold for any interval.

The *chop* operator is associative, denoted as *chop-associative*; i.e. for any duration formulas $\mathcal{F}_1$, $\mathcal{F}_2$ and $\mathcal{F}_3$

$$(\mathcal{F}_1; \ \mathcal{F}_2); \ \mathcal{F}_3 \Leftrightarrow \mathcal{F}_1; \ (\mathcal{F}_2; \ \mathcal{F}_3)$$

and both sides of this formula can be written as $\mathcal{F}_1; \ \mathcal{F}_2; \ \mathcal{F}_3$.

The *chop* operator is distributive through disjunction; i.e. for any duration formulas $\mathcal{F}_1$, $\mathcal{F}_2$ and $\mathcal{F}_3$

$$\mathcal{F}_1; \ \mathcal{F}_2 \vee \mathcal{F}_3 \Leftrightarrow (\mathcal{F}_1; \ \mathcal{F}_2) \vee (\mathcal{F}_1; \ \mathcal{F}_3)$$

This property is called *chop-distributive*.

Exercise 7.5.4 Find a counterexample to show that the *chop* operator does not distribute through conjunction.

The *chop* operator is monotonic, referred to as *chop-monotonic*; i.e. for any duration formulas $\mathcal{F}_1$, $\mathcal{F}_2$ and $\mathcal{F}_3$

$$\Box(\mathcal{F}_1 \Rightarrow \mathcal{F}_2) \Rightarrow \Box((\mathcal{F}_1; \ \mathcal{F}_3 \Rightarrow \mathcal{F}_2; \ \mathcal{F}_3) \wedge (\mathcal{F}_3; \ \mathcal{F}_1 \Rightarrow \mathcal{F}_3; \ \mathcal{F}_2))$$

The basic axiom relating the *chop* operator and the integral operator states that the duration of a state in an interval is the sum of its durations in each partition of the interval into subintervals.

Axiom 7.4 Let P be a state and r, s be non-negative real-numbers:

$$(\textstyle\int P = r + s) \Leftrightarrow (\textstyle\int P = r); \ (\textstyle\int P = s)$$

With these axioms, we can prove properties such as the following theorem.

Theorem 7.5 For a state P and non-negative real numbers r, s, t and u

$$(r \leq \textstyle\int P \leq s); \ (t \leq \textstyle\int P \leq u) \Rightarrow (r + t \leq \textstyle\int P \leq s + u)$$

Proof:

$$r \leq \int P ; \ t \leq \int P \ \Leftrightarrow \ \exists x. \exists y. ((\int P = x; \ \int P = y) \land (r \leq x \land t \leq y)) \quad \text{Ax.}\exists$$
$$\Leftrightarrow \ \exists x. \exists y. ((\int P = x + y) \land (r \leq x \land t \leq y)) \quad \text{Ax.4}$$
$$\Rightarrow \ \exists x. \exists y. ((\int P = x + y) \land (r + t \leq x + y))$$
$$\Leftrightarrow \ r + t \leq \int P \quad \text{Ax.}\exists$$

Proof of $\int P \leq s ; \ \int P \leq u$ is similar (and is left as an exercise).

$\square$

The next theorem is about the arbitrary divisibility of intervals, i.e. the density of time.

Theorem 7.6 For a state P

$$\lceil P \rceil; \ \lceil P \rceil \Leftrightarrow \lceil P \rceil$$

Exercise 7.5.5 Prove Theorem 7.6.

It is useful to have an induction rule which extends a hypothesis over adjacent subintervals. Such a rule relies on the finite variability of states and the finiteness of intervals, so that any interval can be split into a *finite* alternation of state P and state $\neg P$.

Induction rule: For a formula variable X occurring in the duration formula $R(X)$, and state P:

1. If $R(\lceil \ \rceil)$ holds, and $R(X \lor (X ; \ \lceil P \rceil) \lor (X ; \ \lceil \neg P \rceil))$ is provable from $R(X)$, then $R(true)$ holds.
2. If $R(\lceil \ \rceil)$ holds, and $R(X \lor (\lceil P \rceil ; \ X) \lor (\lceil \neg P \rceil ; \ X))$ is provable from $R(X)$, then $R(true)$ holds.

The following theorem illustrates the use of the induction rules.

Theorem 7.7 For state P:

1. $(true ; \ \lceil P \rceil) \lor (true ; \ \lceil \neg P \rceil) \lor \lceil \ \rceil$
2. $(\lceil P \rceil ; \ true) \lor (\lceil \neg P \rceil ; \ true) \lor \lceil \ \rceil$

Proof:

(1) As the induction hypothesis, let

$$R(X) \overset{\Delta}{=} X \Rightarrow ((true ; \ \lceil P \rceil) \lor (true ; \ \lceil \neg P \rceil) \lor \lceil \ \rceil)$$

Then for $X = \lceil \ \rceil$

$$R(\lceil \ \rceil) \overset{\Delta}{=} \lceil \ \rceil \Rightarrow ((true ; \ \lceil P \rceil) \lor (true ; \ \lceil \neg P \rceil) \lor \lceil \ \rceil)$$

must hold. Now $R(X \lor (X ; \ \lceil P \rceil) \lor (X ; \ \lceil \neg P \rceil))$ is

$$X \lor (X ; \ \lceil P \rceil) \lor (X ; \ \lceil \neg P \rceil) \Rightarrow ((true ; \ \lceil P \rceil) \lor (true ; \ \lceil \neg P \rceil) \lor \lceil \ \rceil)$$

Assuming that $R(X)$ holds, the following formulas hold since $X \Rightarrow \textit{true}$ holds and the *chop* operator is monotonic:

$$X \Rightarrow ((\textit{true} ; \lceil P \rceil) \vee (\textit{true} ; \lceil \neg P \rceil) \vee \lceil \rceil)$$

$$X ; \lceil P \rceil \Rightarrow \textit{true} ; \lceil P \rceil \text{ and } X ; \lceil \neg P \rceil \Rightarrow \textit{true} ; \lceil \neg P \rceil$$

So it must be that $R(X \vee (X ; \lceil P \rceil) \vee (X ; \lceil \neg P \rceil))$. Hence, by the induction rule, we have $R(\textit{true})$ holds which, by definition, is

$$\textit{true} \Rightarrow ((\textit{true} ; \lceil P \rceil) \vee (\textit{true} ; \lceil \neg P \rceil) \vee \lceil \rceil)$$

This is obviously equivalent to (1).

(2) can be proved symmetrically using the second induction rule.

□

The four axioms and the induction rules can be shown to constitute a sound formal proof system of durations which is relatively complete with respect to the interval temporal logic.

7.6 The mine pump

We are now ready to formally verify the correctness of the design of the mine pump system. We first summarize the specifications given in Sections 7.1–7.4.

Specification of the safety requirement

For the mine pump system, in any observation interval that is not longer than 1000 time units the accumulated time when the water level is dangerous is not more than one time unit. This safety requirement is specified as

$$\textit{Safe} \stackrel{\Delta}{=} \Box(\ell \leq 1000 \Rightarrow \int DH_2O \leq 1)$$

Specification of the monitor

The monitor is required to behave in the following way:

1. The water flag H_2OFlag must be set when the water level has been high for δ time units and cleared when it has not been high for that time; likewise for the methane flag CH_4Flag.

2. The alarm must be set when either the water level or the methane level has been dangerous for δ time units and cleared when they have both been below the danger level for δ time units.

The monitor is specified by the following formulas:

$$SetWaterFlag \triangleq \lceil HH_2O \rceil \xrightarrow{\delta} \lceil H_2OFlag \rceil$$

$$ResetWaterFlag \triangleq \lceil \neg HH_2O \rceil \xrightarrow{\delta} \lceil \neg H_2OFlag \rceil$$

$$SetMethaneFlag \triangleq \lceil HCH_4 \rceil \xrightarrow{\delta} \lceil CH_4Flag \rceil$$

$$ResetMethaneFlag \triangleq \lceil \neg HCH_4 \rceil \xrightarrow{\delta} \lceil \neg CH_4Flag \rceil$$

$$SetAlarm \triangleq \lceil DH_2O \rceil \xrightarrow{\delta} \lceil Alarm \rceil$$
$$\wedge \lceil DCH_4 \rceil \xrightarrow{\delta} \lceil Alarm \rceil$$

$$ResetAlarm \triangleq \lceil \neg DH_2O \wedge \neg DCH_4 \rceil \xrightarrow{\delta} \lceil \neg Alarm \rceil$$

$$Monitor \triangleq SetWaterFlag \wedge ResetWaterFlag$$
$$\wedge SetMethaneFlag \wedge ResetMethaneFlag$$
$$\wedge SetAlarm \wedge ResetAlarm$$

Specification of assumptions
The high water level is lower than the dangerous water level; in other words, if the water level is dangerous, it must also be high:

$$As_1 \triangleq \Box(\lceil DH_2O \rceil \Rightarrow \lceil HH_2O \rceil)$$

The high water level is chosen such that, after it has been reached, the water will not reach the critical level within w units of time, $w \leq 1$:

$$As_2 \triangleq ((\lceil \neg HH_2O \rceil ; \lceil HH_2O \rceil) \xrightarrow{\leq w} \lceil \neg DH_2O \rceil) \wedge (w \leq 1)$$

The capacity of the pump is sufficient to bring the water level down to a level lower than the high level in ε units of time:

$$As_3 \triangleq \lceil PumpOn \rceil \xrightarrow{\varepsilon} \lceil \neg HH_2O \rceil$$

If the methane level is stable at a low level for long enough, and the methane level is high for a sufficiently short time, it should always be possible to turn on the pump and reduce the water level before it reaches the dangerous level. This stability and boundedness can be specified, respectively, as

$$StableCH_4 \triangleq (\lceil HCH_4 \rceil ; \lceil \neg HCH_4 \rceil ; \lceil \neg HCH_4 \rceil) \Rightarrow \ell \geq \xi$$

$$BoundCH_4 \triangleq \lceil HCH_4 \rceil \Rightarrow \ell \leq w - 2\xi$$

Recall that *Safe* allows limited occurrences of dangerous water levels. This means that it allows limited failure in reducing the high water levels. So we do not have to assume that *StableCH_4* and *BoundCH_4 always* hold, i.e. bad methane levels are sometimes allowed. Let

$$BadCH_4 \triangleq \neg(StableCH_4 \wedge BoundCH_4)$$

To constrain bad methane levels, we assume that they will occur only in an interval not longer than one time unit; any two occurrences of bad methane levels must be separated by at least 1001 time units. The conjunction of these two constraints is specified as

$$As_4 \ \stackrel{\Delta}{=} \qquad \Box(BadCH_4 \Rightarrow \ell \leq 1)$$
$$\wedge \quad \Box((BadCH_4 \ ; \ \Diamond\neg BadCH_4 \ ; \ BadCH_4) \Rightarrow \ell \geq 1001)$$

Finally, the constants must be chosen in the following way:

$$As_5 \stackrel{\Delta}{=} (\xi \geq 2\delta + \varepsilon) \wedge (w \geq 2\xi)$$

Specification of the design

Refinements to the safety requirements were made in two steps in Section 7.4: the first step was to make the design decision that in any interval not longer than 1000 time units, the high water level must almost always be reduced within w time units, i.e. before it reaches the dangerous level:

$$Des_1 \ \stackrel{\Delta}{=} \qquad \Box(Failure \Rightarrow \ell \leq 1)$$
$$\wedge \quad \Box((Failure \ ; \ \Diamond\neg Failure \ ; \ Failure) \Rightarrow \ell \geq 1001)$$

where $Failure \stackrel{\Delta}{=} \lceil HH_2O \rceil \wedge \ell > w$.
   The second step was to decide the control strategies of the pump:

$$Des_2 \stackrel{\Delta}{=} StartPump \wedge StopPump$$

where

$$StartPump \ \stackrel{\Delta}{=} \quad \lceil SafePump \rceil \ \stackrel{\delta}{\longrightarrow} \ \lceil PumpOn \rceil$$
$$StopPump \ \stackrel{\Delta}{=} \quad \lceil \neg SafePump \rceil \ \stackrel{\delta}{\longrightarrow} \ \lceil \neg PumpOn \rceil$$

Recall that $SafePump \stackrel{\Delta}{=} HH_2O \wedge \neg HCH_4$.

Proving correctness

We shall state correctness results as theorems and then provide proofs.

Theorem 7.8 $As_1 \wedge As_2 \wedge Des_1 \Rightarrow Safe$

This theorem is derived from the following lemma:

Lemma 7.1

1. $(\ell \leq 1000) \wedge Des_1 \Rightarrow \qquad \Box Failure \wedge \ell \leq 1$
   $$\vee \quad Failure \wedge \ell \leq 1 \ ; \ \Box\neg Failure$$
   $$\vee \quad \Box\neg Failure \ ; \ Failure \wedge \ell \leq 1 \ ; \ \Box\neg Failure$$
2. $Ass_1 \wedge Ass_2 \wedge \Box\neg Failure \wedge (\lceil\neg HH_2O\rceil \ ; \ true) \Rightarrow \int DH_2O = 0$

Proof: We prove case (2) of the lemma. Recall that

$$\neg Failure = \lceil HH_2O \rceil \Rightarrow \ell \leq w$$

Therefore, we have to prove that

$$As_1 \wedge As_2 \wedge \square(\lceil HH_2O \rceil \Rightarrow \ell \leq w) \wedge (\lceil \neg HH_2O \rceil \; ; \; true) \Rightarrow \int DH_2O = 0$$

Let $\mathcal{A} \triangleq As_1 \wedge As_2 \wedge \square(\lceil HH_2O \rceil \Rightarrow \ell \leq w)$. Use the second induction rule with $R(X)$ defined as

$$R(X) \triangleq \quad \mathcal{A} \wedge (\lceil \neg HH_2O \rceil \; ; \; X) \Rightarrow (\int DH_2O = 0)$$
$$\wedge \quad \mathcal{A} \wedge (\lceil \neg HH_2O \rceil \; ; \; \lceil HH_2O \rceil \; ; \; X) \Rightarrow (\int DH_2O = 0)$$

$R(\lceil \; \rceil)$ holds since $\mathcal{A} \wedge \lceil \neg HH_2O \rceil \Rightarrow \lceil \neg DH_2O \rceil$ because of As_1. And, by As_2,

$$\mathcal{A} \wedge (\lceil \neg HH_2O \rceil \; ; \; \lceil HH_2O \rceil \wedge \ell \leq w) \Rightarrow \lceil \neg DH_2O \rceil$$

Using the chop-distributive property and Theorem 7.6:

$$R(X \vee (\lceil HH_2O \rceil \; ; \; X) \vee (\lceil \neg HH_2O \rceil \; ; \; X))$$
$$\Leftrightarrow \mathcal{A} \wedge ((\lceil \neg HH_2O \rceil \; ; \; X) \vee (\lceil \neg HH_2O \rceil \; ; \; \lceil HH_2O \rceil \; ; \; X)) \Rightarrow (\int DH_2O = 0)$$
$$\wedge \quad \mathcal{A} \wedge (\lceil \neg HH_2O \rceil \; ; \; \lceil HH_2O \rceil \; ; \; \lceil \neg HH_2O \rceil) \Rightarrow (\int DH_2O = 0)$$

We next prove that this formula holds assuming that $R(X)$ holds. The first conjunct comes directly from $R(X)$. For the second conjunct:

$$\mathcal{A} \wedge (\lceil \neg HH_2O \rceil \; ; \; \lceil HH_2O \rceil \; ; \; \lceil \neg HH_2O \rceil \; ; \; X)$$
$$\Rightarrow \quad \lceil \neg HH_2O \rceil \; ; \; \lceil HH_2O \rceil \wedge (\ell \leq w) \; ; \; \lceil \neg HH_2O \rceil \; ; \; X \quad (\square \neg Failure)$$
$$\Rightarrow \quad \lceil \neg DH_2O \rceil \; ; \; \lceil \neg HH_2O \rceil \; ; \; X \quad (As_1 \wedge As_2)$$
$$\Rightarrow \quad \int DH_2O = 0 \; ; \; \int DH_2O = 0 \quad (R(X))$$
$$\Rightarrow \quad \int DH_2O = 0 \quad (Axiom4)$$

Hence case 2 of the lemma is implied by $R(true)$.

$\square$

Exercise 7.6.1 Complete the proof of the lemma, and then prove Theorem 7.8.

Theorem 7.9 $As_3 \wedge As_4 \wedge As_5 \wedge Monitor \wedge Des_2 \Rightarrow Des_1$

This theorem can be proved using the following lemma.

Lemma 7.2 $As_3 \wedge As_4 \wedge \square \neg BadCH_4 \wedge Monitor \Rightarrow \square \neg Failure$

Proof: Assume that *Failure* holds, i.e. $\lceil HH_2O \rceil \wedge \ell > w$ holds. By *Monitor* we have

$$\lceil HH_2O \rceil \wedge \ell > w \Rightarrow \lceil HH_2O \rceil \wedge (\ell \leq \delta) \,;\, \lceil H_2OFlag \rceil \wedge (\ell > w - \delta)$$

Let the consequent (right-hand side) of this implication be *RH*, and let $\alpha \stackrel{\Delta}{=} 2\delta + \varepsilon$. Then from As_5 we have $w \geq 2\xi \geq 2\alpha$ and, since $\square \neg BadCH_4$,

$$(\ell > w) \Rightarrow$$

$$\begin{aligned}
& \lceil \neg HCH_4 \rceil \wedge (\ell \geq \alpha) \,;\, true && (D_1) \\
\vee \;\; & \lceil \neg HCH_4 \rceil \wedge (\ell < \alpha) \,;\, \lceil HCH_4 \rceil \wedge (\ell \leq w - 2\alpha) \,;\, \\
& \lceil \neg HCH_4 \rceil \wedge (\ell \geq \alpha) \,;\, true && (D_2) \\
\vee \;\; & \lceil HCH_4 \rceil \wedge (\ell \leq w - 2\alpha) \,;\, \lceil \neg HCH_4 \rceil \wedge (\ell \geq \alpha) \,;\, true && (D_3)
\end{aligned}$$

By *Monitor*, As_3 and Des_2 we have

$$\begin{aligned}
(D_1) \wedge RH \;\; \Rightarrow \;\; & \lceil HH_2O \rceil \wedge (\ell \leq \delta) \,;\, \lceil SafePump \rceil \wedge (\ell \geq \delta + \varepsilon) \,;\, true \\
\Rightarrow \;\; & (\ell \leq 2\delta) \,;\, \lceil PumpOn \rceil \wedge (\ell \geq \varepsilon) \,;\, true \\
\Rightarrow \;\; & (\ell \leq 2\delta + \varepsilon) \,;\, \lceil \neg HH_2O \rceil \,;\, true \\
\Rightarrow \;\; & \Diamond \lceil \neg HH_2O \rceil
\end{aligned}$$

Similarly, it can be proved that $D_i \wedge RH \Rightarrow \Diamond \lceil \neg HH_2O \rceil$ for $i = 2, 3$. This gives the obvious contradiction

$$\lceil HH_2O \rceil \wedge (\ell > w) \Rightarrow \Diamond \lceil \neg HH_2O \rceil$$

and so $\square(\lceil HH_2O \rceil \Rightarrow \ell \leq w)$ holds. $\qquad\qquad\qquad\qquad\qquad\qquad\qquad\quad\;\;\square$

Exercise 7.6.2 Complete the proof of the lemma and then prove Theorem 7.9.

Theorem 7.8 and Theorem 7.9 have the following corollary which states the correctness of the final design.

Corollary 1 $Ass \wedge Des_2 \Rightarrow Safe$, where

$$Ass \stackrel{\Delta}{=} As_1 \wedge As_2 \wedge As_3 \wedge As_4 \wedge As_5 \wedge Monitor$$

7.6.1   Specification of scheduling policies

As we have seen in Chapters 2 and 3, real-time programs are often executed on systems with limited resources (e.g. processors) that must be shared through the actions of a scheduler. Let a real-time program P with a set of processes be specified by a duration formula $C(P)$ and let the scheduling *policy* (which is a property of the scheduler) be specified by the duration formula S (which is a constraint on the execution of the program). Given a real-time property specified by a duration formula $\mathcal{F}$, we say that execution of program P under the scheduler S is *feasible* with respect to the real-time property $\mathcal{F}$ if it can be proved that the following implication holds:

$$C(P) \wedge S \Rightarrow \mathcal{F}$$

This means that the time-constraint defined by $\mathcal{F}$ is satisfied.

We shall now show how different real-time scheduling policies can be specified in DC.

Processes and processors

For simplicity, assume that a set of processes is allocated statically to $n > 0$ processors. Such an allocation defines a partition of the processes into n classes $\{PS_1, \ldots, PS_n\}$. Let $PS = \{p_1, \ldots, p_m\}$ be an arbitrary class of this partition containing $m > 0$ processes sharing one processor. For each process $p \in PS$:

- $p.rdy$: is 1 when process p is ready to run on a processor, otherwise it is 0.
- $p.run$: is 1 when process p is running on a processor, otherwise it is 0.

We assume that when a process is running it is ready, i.e. $p.run \Rightarrow p.rdy$ is always 1. This assumption is illustrated in the following timing diagram.

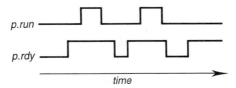

Specification

There is a physical *no conflict* requirement that at most one process is running on a processor at any time:

$$\Box \bigwedge_{k \neq j} (\lceil p_j.run \rceil \Rightarrow \lceil \neg p_k.run \rceil)$$

or, equivalently,

$$\Box \bigwedge_{k \neq j} (\smallint (P_j.run \wedge p_k.run) = 0)$$

Assume that if a process is ready, there must be a running process:

$$\Box (\lceil \bigvee_j p_j.rdy \rceil \Rightarrow \lceil \bigvee_j p_j.run \rceil)$$

This means that the scheduler has *no overhead*, i.e. takes no time to initiate execution of a process on a processor.

A scheduler is said to make progress if

$$\Box ((\sum_i \smallint p_i.rdy > \delta) \Rightarrow (\sum_i \smallint p_i.run > \delta'))$$

where δ and δ' are constants such that $0 \leq \delta' \leq \delta$. This says that at all times if the sum of the ready time of the processes is greater than δ, the sum of their running times must be greater than δ'. Thus, progress will always be made in the execution of the processes in terms.

An extremely fair scheduling policy is one where each process has *equal rights* and the processes share the available processor equally; it is unlikely that a scheduler can implement such a policy strictly:

$$\bigwedge_j ((\int p_j.run * \sum_i \int p_i.rdy) = (\sum_i \int p_j.run) * \int p_j.rdy)$$

For non-zero running time and ready time, the ratio between p_j's total running time and the total running time of all processes is at all times the same as that between p_j's total ready time and the total ready time of all processes.

A *first-come-first-served* (or first-ready-first-run) policy is often used in operating systems. It is specified as:

$$\Box \bigwedge_{j \neq i} \neg(\lceil p_j.rdy \wedge \neg p_i.run \rceil \wedge (\lceil \neg p_i.rdy \rceil \; ; \; \Diamond \lceil p_i.run \rceil))$$

This means that when p_i becomes ready and eventually runs there is no other process p_j that is ready and not running.

Scheduling often makes use of the priorities of processes. Assume that p_j has higher priority than p_i if $j > i$. A priority-based scheduling policy may then enforce the condition

$$\Box \bigwedge_{i < j} (\lceil p_j.rdy \rceil \Rightarrow \lceil \neg p_i.run \rceil)$$

Note that this may require the use of pre-emption (and perhaps a protocol making use of priority ceilings – see Chapter 3).

Exercise 7.6.3 Specify a priority-based, non-pre-emptive scheduling policy.

Finally we specify a Δ-*fair* policy, where $\Delta > 0$:

$$\bigwedge_i \left(\begin{array}{l} (\lceil p_i.run \rceil \; ; \; \lceil p_i.rdy \wedge \neg p_i.run \rceil \Rightarrow \ell \geq \Delta \\ \wedge \;\; \Box((\lceil \neg p_i.run \rceil \; ; \; \lceil p_i.run \rceil \; ; \; \lceil p_i.rdy \wedge \neg p_i.run \rceil) \Rightarrow \ell \geq \Delta) \\ \wedge \;\; \Box((\lceil p_i.rdy \rceil \wedge \ell \geq 2m\Delta) \Rightarrow \Diamond \lceil p_i.run \rceil) \end{array} \right)$$

In a Δ-*fair* policy, a process is guaranteed an execution 'slice' of at least Δ when it is running; when it is ready and not running, it will wait for at most $2m\Delta$ before running (m is the number of processes).

We have seen that both programs and scheduling policies can be specified in DC and the properties of programs and schedulers can be kept separate. This allows a division of concerns when a program executed under a particular scheduler has to be shown to meet hard real-time constraints. The advantage of this approach is that the schedulability of a program can be considered at the specification level without going into implementation level details of either the program or the scheduler.

7.7 Probabilistic duration calculus (PDC)

The requirements for an embedded, real-time system include functional and safety properties. For the mine pump, we proved that the design decisions Des_1 and Des_2 guarantee the requirement *Safe*. But, in practice, we cannot expect an actual implementation to satisfy this requirement at all times. For example, any physical component such as a sensor, the monitor, or the pump may fail to react in time.

Within any given period, an actual implementation can only satisfy the design decisions with a certain probability. How then can we model the physical limitations of an implementation? How can we define and reason about the probability of satisfaction of a duration formula? The solution here, as in other fields, is to analyze the probability of failure using probability theory.

Assume that we consider not only the correct system behaviours $\mathcal{B}_C = \{b_1, \dots\}$ but also some incorrect, but plausible, failure behaviours $\mathcal{B}_F = \{f_1, \dots\}$. The model for an implementation is then $\mathcal{B} = \mathcal{B}_C \cup \mathcal{B}_F$ and probabilities can be assigned to subsets of $\mathcal{B}$. In this section, we consider how to calculate the probability of a subset specified by some duration formula D for some finite initial segment $[0, t]$ of the behaviours. This probabilistic extension of DC makes it possible for designers of real-time systems to reason about and calculate the probability that safety and functionality requirements are satisfied in practical implementations.

In the probabilistic duration calculus (PDC), it is assumed that requirements are expressed as formulas in DC, and that imperfect (i.e. failure-prone) designs can be modelled using probabilistic automata with fixed transition probabilities. Then discrete Markov chains can provide the basis for PDC.

The calculus provides a notation and a set of rules for determining the probability that a given duration formula D holds for a given probabilistic automaton over a specified time interval $[0, t]$. This probability, called the satisfaction probability $\mu(D)[t]$, is defined as the sum of the probabilities of all behaviours of the automaton which satisfy D over the time interval.

DC uses continuous time represented by non-negative real-numbers. In order to have a simple, well-understood probabilistic model (see Section 7.7.1), discrete time is used in PDC; thus, *Time* is the set of all non-negative integers. For this discrete time domain, axiom 4 of Section 7.5 must be modified.

For a state P and non-negative integers r, s, t and u:

$$(r \le \int P \le s) \, ; \, (t \le \int P \le u) \Rightarrow (r + t \le \int P \le s + u)$$

Accordingly, Theorem 7.6.6 is also modified; for any state P:

$$\ell \ge 2 \Rightarrow (\lceil P \rceil \Leftrightarrow \lceil P \rceil \, ; \, \lceil P \rceil)$$

No other axioms or rules of DC need to be changed.

In this section, we define the reliability of two simplified versions of the mine pump. In both cases, we ignore the methane levels. The satisfaction probability $\mu(D)[t]$ is then defined as the sum of probabilities of all behaviours that satisfy D in the time interval

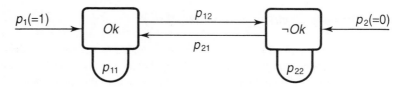

Figure 7.6 Failure-prone mine pump with unreliable detector

$[0, t]$. When the basic rules of the probabilistic calculus are applied directly, the result can be a recursive, rather problem-dependent solution. A more systematic solution technique is to develop and apply high-level theorems to express the satisfaction probability of specific important duration formulas in terms of probability matrix products.

7.7.1   Imperfect systems and probabilistic automata

Consider a *finite probabilistic automaton* as a mathematical model of the behaviour of an imperfect system in a discrete time domain. Such an automaton is well described by its transition graph.

Mine pump with failing pump and unreliable detector

For a simple mine pump system, assume that HH_2O (i.e. the water level is high) and activation of the pump are 'on' at $t = 0$ and that the HH_2O remains 'on'. The activation is assumed to be instantaneous, i.e. the pump is 'on' at $t = 0$ or whenever activation is re-applied. When the pump is 'on', it may fail (i.e. go 'off') at any time. Detection of a pump failure may be delayed by any number of time units, but, once detected, re-activation takes place immediately.

For this mine pump system, let *PumpOn* be the only basic state. This leads to a two-state model with states *PumpOn* and $\neg PumpOn$. However, since the pump is assumed to have failed when it is off, $Ok\ (= PumpOn)$ could also be taken as the basic state and the system states can then be called Ok and $\neg Ok$ (see the transition graph in Figure 7.6).

The probabilities of starting in the states Ok and $\neg Ok$ are p_1 and p_2 respectively; according to the assumptions, $p_1 = 1$ and $p_2 = 0$. The probability that the pump remains 'on' for one time unit is p_{11} and that it fails within one time unit is p_{12}. The probability that the pump failure remains undetected for one time unit is p_{22} and the probability that the failure is detected within one time unit is p_{21}. These probabilities are all non-negative and are governed by the equations: $p_1 + p_2 = 1$, $p_{11} + p_{12} = 1$, $p_{21} + p_{22} = 1$. Assume, as for Markov chains, that the transition probabilities are independent of the transition history.

Mine pump with unreliable activation, unreliable detector and failing pump

Assume now that when the water level is high (i.e. HH_2O is 'on'), the pump is activated for a very short period. Detection of pump failure may then be delayed for any number of time units. When HH_2O is 'on', the pump may be off on account of activation failure or pump failure. Assume that when HH_2O is 'off', the pump is also off.

The transition graph for this system is shown in Figure 7.7 There are two basic states: HH_2O (water level is high) and *PumpOn* (pump is on).

At any time, the system is in one of the following mutually exclusive states:

$$V = \{\neg HH_2O \wedge \neg PumpOn, \, HH_2O \wedge PumpOn, \, HH_2O \wedge \neg PumpOn\}$$

i.e. we assume that

$$\neg HH_2O \wedge PumpOn = 0$$

and

$$\neg HH_2O \wedge \neg PumpOn \vee HH_2O \wedge PumpOn \vee HH_2O \wedge \neg PumpOn = 1$$

The system probabilities are defined below:

- The system starts in the idle state $\neg HH_2O \wedge \neg PumpOn$: $p_1 = 1, p_2 = p_3 = 0$.
- It remains idle with probability p_{11} for one time unit.
- HH_2O becomes 'on' (water level becomes high) in one time unit with probability $(p_{12}+p_{13})$ and the pump is activated. p_{12} is the probability that activation succeeds and p_{13} that it fails.
- HH_2O becomes 'off' within one time unit with probability p_{21}.
- The pump remains on for one time unit with probability p_{22}.
- The pump fails within one time unit with probability p_{23}.
- Pump failure is detected in one time unit with probability p_{32}.
- Pump failure remains undetected for one time unit with probability p_{33}.

Notice that p_{31} is assumed to be zero. This means that when the pump fails, the water level cannot be reduced.

These probabilities are non-negative and are related by the following equations: $p_1 + p_2 + p_3 = 1$ and $p_{i1} + p_{i2} + p_{i3} = 1$, $(i = 1, 2, 3)$. *Ok* is now a composite state: $Ok \stackrel{\Delta}{=} \neg HH_2O \vee PumpOn$.

Probabilistic automaton

We end with a general definition of a probabilistic automaton (PA). First define a *minterm* of a set A of basic states as a conjunction of the states in A which contains every state in A or its negation, but not both.

Definition 7.5 A PA is a tuple $G = (A, V, \tau_0, \tau)$ where the following hold:

- A is a finite, non-empty set of basic states.
- $V = \{v_1, \ldots, v_m\}$ is a non-empty set of states; each v_i in V is a minterm of A and V is ranged over by v, v', v_i, etc.

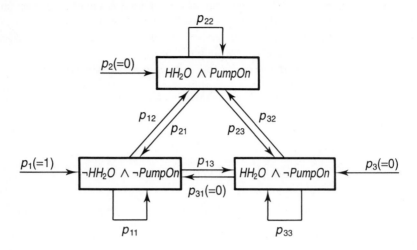

Figure 7.7 Mine pump with unreliable activation, unreliable detector and failing pump

- $\tau_0 : V \to [0, 1]$ is called the initial probability mass function and it satisfies

$$\sum_{v \in V} \tau_0(v) = 1$$

where $\tau_0(v)$ is the probability that the system starts in state v.

- $\tau : V \times V \to [0, 1]$ is called the single-step probability transition function: for every $v \in V$ it satisfies

$$\sum_{v' \in V} \tau(v, v') = 1$$

For example, in Figure 7.6, $A = \{Ok\}$, $V = \{\neg Ok, Ok\}$. The initial probability mass function is $\tau_0(Ok) = p_1 = 1$, $\tau_0(\neg Ok) = p_2 = 0$, and the transition probability function is

$$\tau(Ok, Ok) = p_{11} \qquad \tau(Ok, \neg Ok) = p_{12}$$
$$\tau(\neg Ok, Ok) = p_{21} \qquad \tau(\neg Ok, \neg PumpOk) = p_{22}$$

7.7.2 Satisfaction probability

For a given automaton $G = (A, V, \tau_0, \tau)$, we now define *behaviour*, *satisfaction* and *satisfaction probability*.

Behaviour

Given a non-negative integer t, the sequence of states in V,

$$\sigma^{[t]} : v_1, \ldots, v_t$$

defines a possible *behaviour* of G for its first t units of operation. Thus the system performs $t - 1$ state transitions such that it is in state v_i at time $i - 1$, $(i = 1, \ldots, t)$.

For a specified sequence of states, $v_1, \ldots, v_t$ the probability that the system enters state v_1 at time 0 is $\tau_0(v_1)$, and, given that it is in state v_i at time $i - 1$, the probability that it is in state v_{i+1} at time i is $\tau(v_i, v_{i+1})$. Therefore, τ_0 and τ together determine the probability of the behaviour $\sigma^{[t]}$ for the first t time units.

For example, $\sigma^{[1]} = \neg Ok$ is a behaviour of length 1 of the PA of Figure 7.6. According to this, the system starts with $\neg Ok$. But $\tau_0(\neg Ok) = p_2 = 0$, so the system cannot start with $\neg Ok$. So the probability of $\sigma^{[1]}$ is zero. Let $\mu(\sigma^{[1]})$ denote the probability of $\sigma^{[1]}$ with respect to the given PA; then $\mu(\sigma^{[1]}) = 0$.

$$\sigma^{[5]} : Ok, Ok, \neg Ok, \neg Ok, Ok$$

is another behaviour of this PA, with length 5. For this behaviour,

$$\mu(\sigma^{[5]}) = p_1 * p_{11} * p_{12} * p_{22} * p_{21}$$

In general, if $\sigma^{[t]} = v_1, \ldots, v_t$,

$$\mu(\sigma^{[t]}) \triangleq \tau_0(v_1) * \prod_{i=1}^{t-1} \tau(v_i, v_{i+1})$$

where $\mu(\sigma^{[t]}) = 1$ when $t = 0$ and $\mu(\sigma^{[t]}) = \tau_0(v_1)$ when $t = 1$. Let V^t be the set of all state sequences of V with length t. Then, V^t defines all the possible behaviours of G with length t. From the definitions of τ_0 and τ, it is easy to prove the following theorems.

Theorem 7.10 For any non-negative integer t and any behaviour $\sigma^{[t]} \in V^t$ of length t,

$$0 \leq \mu(\sigma^{[t]}) \leq 1$$

Theorem 7.11 For any non-negative integer t, $\sum_{\sigma^{[t]} \in V^t} \mu(\sigma^{[t]}) = 1$.

Thus, for every non-negative integer t there is a *probability space* $\langle V^t, \mu \rangle$ with V^t, the set of behaviours of length t, as the set of samples.

Satisfaction

A behaviour $\sigma^{[t]}$ of G determines the presence and absence of the basic states in V at each of the first t time units, and thus defines an interpretation $I_{\sigma^{[t]}}$ of duration formulas with A as the basic states for the first t time units. This interpretation is defined by:

$$I_{\sigma^{[t]}}(P)(j) \triangleq \begin{cases} 1 & \text{if } \sigma(j) \Rightarrow P \\ 0 & \text{if } \sigma(j) \Rightarrow \neg P \end{cases}$$

where $0 \leq j \leq t$.

Recalling Section 7.2, the satisfaction of a duration formula D (with A as basic states) can be defined by a behaviour $\sigma^{[t]}$ of G.

D is *satisfied* by $\sigma^{[t]}$, denoted by $\sigma^{[t]} \models D$, if and only if there is an interpretation I which is an *extension* of $I_{\sigma^{[t]}}$ over $[0,t]$, such that $I, [0,t] \models D$. An interpretation I_2 over *Time* is an *extension* of I_1 over the interval $[t_1, t_2]$ if for every basic state P and any time point $t \in [t_1, t_2]$, $I_1(P) = I_2(P)$.

For the PA of Figure 7.6, let $\sigma^{[5]} \triangleq Ok, Ok, \neg Ok, \neg Ok, Ok$. Then,

$$\sigma^{[5]} \models \ell = 5, \quad \sigma^{[5]} \models \int Ok = 3, \quad \sigma^{[5]} \models \Box(\lceil \neg Ok \rceil \Rightarrow \ell \leq 2)$$

$$\sigma^{[5]} \not\models \ell \leq 3, \quad \sigma^{[5]} \not\models \Box(\lceil \neg Ok \rceil \Rightarrow \ell \leq 1)$$

where $\not\models$ stands for 'not satisfied'.

Satisfaction probability

The probability that a PA satisfies a duration formula over the time interval $[0,t]$ is the sum over all behaviours of the probability that a behaviour satisfies the formula over that time interval. Let D be a duration formula, and let $V^t(D)$ be a subset of V^t (the set of behaviours of length t) such that each behaviour in that subset satisfies D in $[0,t]$. Then the *satisfaction probability* of D by G within the time interval $[0,t]$, denoted by $\mu(D)[t]$, is defined by

$$\mu(D)[t] \triangleq \sum_{\sigma^{[t]} \in V^t(D)} \mu(\sigma^{[t]})$$

By Theorems 7.10 and 7.11, this definition guarantees that $\mu(D)[t]$ is a probability. For example, for the PA of Figure 7.6, let $D \triangleq \Box(\lceil \neg Ok \rceil \Rightarrow \ell \leq 1)$. Then the behaviours of length 2 satisfying D are

$$V^2(D) = \{(Ok, Ok), (Ok, \neg Ok), (\neg Ok, Ok)\}$$

Thus $\mu(D)[2] = p_1 * p_{11} + p_1 * p_{12} + p_2 * p_{21} = p_{11} + p_{12} = 1$, since $p_1 = 1$ and $p_2 = 0$.

7.7.3   The probabilistic calculus

The probabilistic duration logic is an extension of first-order real arithmetic with the $\mu(D)$s as the only additional functions. For an arbitrary duration formula D, $\mu(D)$ belongs to $N \rightarrow [0,1]$ and assigns to each time point t the satisfaction probability $\mu(D)[t]$. In this logic, a *basic probabilistic term* is $\mu(D)[t]$ or a variable x ranging over the real numbers. A *probabilistic term* is a basic probabilistic term, or an expression built from probabilistic terms using operators on real numbers, such as addition $+$ and multiplication $*$, with their standard meanings. A *basic probabilistic formula* is an expression built from probabilistic terms using relational operators, such as equality $=$ and less than $<$, with their standard meanings. A *probabilistic formula* is a basic probabilistic formula or an expression built from probabilistic formulas using the operators of first-order logic and quantifiers over variables (including t in the term $\mu(D)[t]$). The standard interpretations are assumed for the operators and quantifiers.

In this logic, we can write down and reason about probabilistic formulas such as

$$\forall t : \mu(\neg Safe)[t] \leq \mu(\neg As_1)[t] + \mu(\neg Des_1)[t]$$

which asserts that the probability of violating the safety requirement *Safe* will not be greater than the sum of the probabilities of violating the assumption and the design decision. This formula tells the designer that there is a 'trade off' between the design decisions with respect to the probabilities of their violation. It also permits these probabilities to be analyzed separately. Satisfaction probabilities can also be calculated by reasoning about formulas such as $\mu(D)[t] = p$.

PDC includes the axioms and rules of real arithmetic. In the following, we present the additional rules for the satisfaction probabilities ($\mu(D)$s) and show how to use the combined axioms and rules to prove simple theorems. We use the abbreviation $R(f,g)$ to stand for $\forall t : R(f[t], g[t])$, where R is a relation between functions f and g over *Time*.

The duration formula *true* defines the set of all behaviours of G for any interval:

AR 1 $\mu(true) = 1$

For any given interval, the set of behaviours defined by D and $\neg D$ forms a partition of all the behaviours and therefore the sum of their probabilities is 1.

AR 2   For an arbitrary duration formula D, $\mu(D) + \mu(\neg D) = 1$.

The following axiom formalizes the additivity rule in probability theory.

AR 3   For arbitrary duration formulas D_1 and D_2

$$\mu(D_1 \vee D_2) + \mu(D_1 \wedge D_2) = \mu(D_1) + \mu(D_2)$$

The satisfaction probability is monotonic:

AR 4   If $D_1 \Rightarrow D_2$ holds in DC, then $\mu(D_1) \leq \mu(D_2)$ holds in PDC.

Therefore, if $D_1 \Rightarrow D_2$, then no more behaviours satisfy D_1 than satisfy D_2.

These four axioms and rules follow directly from probability theory. The following theorem can easily be proved from them.

Theorem 7.12 For arbitrary duration formulas D, D_1, D_2 and D_3:

1. $\mu(\textit{false}) = 0$.
2. $0 \leq \mu(D) \leq 1$.
3. If $D_1 \Leftrightarrow D_2$ holds in DC, then $\mu(D_1) = \mu(D_2)$ holds in PDC.
4. If $D_1 \wedge D_2 \Rightarrow D_3$ holds in DC, then $(\mu(D_1) = 1) \Rightarrow (\mu(D_2) \leq \mu(D_3))$ holds in PDC.

Proof: Proofs of $(1) - (3)$ are trivial. (4) is proved as follows:

$$
\begin{aligned}
\mu(D_1) = 1 \ &\Rightarrow \ \mu(D_1 \vee D_2) = 1 && (TH.7.3(2), AR3, AR4) \\
&\Rightarrow \ \mu(D_1 \vee D_2) = \mu(D_2) && (AR3) \\
&\Rightarrow \ \mu(D_1 \wedge D_2) \leq \mu(D_3) && (AR4, D_1 \wedge D_2 \Rightarrow D_3) \\
&\Rightarrow \ \mu(D_2) \leq \mu(D_3)
\end{aligned}
$$

$\square$

Duration formulas D and $D \wedge (\ell = t)$ are satisfied by the same behaviours of length t.

AR 5 For an arbitrary duration formula D, $\mu(D)[t] = \mu(D \wedge (\ell = t))[t]$.

Theorem 7.13 $(\mu(\ell = t)[t] = 1) \wedge (\mu(\ell \neq t)[t] = 0)$

A behaviour of length t, $\sigma^{[t]}$, satisfies a duration formula D if and only if each extension of $\sigma^{[t]}$ to a behaviour of length $t + t'$ satisfies the duration formula $(D ; \ell = t')$.

AR 6 For an arbitrary duration formula D, $\mu(D; \ell = t')[t + t'] = \mu(D)[t]$.

Axioms AR3, AR4, AR5, AR6 and Theorem 7.12 can be used to prove the following theorem.

Theorem 7.14 For arbitrary duration formulas D_1 and D_2, if $\mu(D_1) = 0$, then

$$\mu(D_1; D_2) = 0$$

Exercise 7.7.1 Prove Theorem 7.14.

The axioms and rules described so far are independent of the Markov properties of the PA defined by the probability space $\langle V^t, \mu \rangle$. We shall consider here only PAs which are Markov chains; for these, the following additional axioms and theorems apply.

The initial probability mass function τ_0 is governed by the next axiom, where we use the convention $\lceil v \rceil^1 \stackrel{\Delta}{=} \lceil v \rceil \wedge (\ell = 1)$.

AR 7 For an arbitrary state $v \in V$, $\mu(\lceil v \rceil^1)[1] = \tau_0(v)$.

The transition probability function τ is governed by the next axiom.

AR 8 For an arbitrary duration formula D and states $v_i, v_j \in V$,

$$\mu((D \wedge (true; \lceil v_i \rceil^1)); \lceil v_j \rceil^1)[t+1] = \tau(v_i, v_j) * \mu(D \wedge (true; \lceil v_i \rceil^1))[t]$$

From AR8 and the equivalence:

$$(D; \lceil v_i \rceil^1; \lceil v_j \rceil^1) \Leftrightarrow ((D; \lceil v_i \rceil^1) \wedge (true; \lceil v_i \rceil^1); \lceil v_j \rceil^1)$$

we obtain the following theorem.

Theorem 7.15 For an arbitrary duration formula D and states $v_i, v_j \in V$:

$$\mu(D; \lceil v_i \rceil^1; \lceil v_j \rceil^1)[t+1] = \tau(v_i, v_j) * \mu(D; \lceil v_i \rceil^1)[t]$$

This provides a way of calculating the probability of behaviours by chopping them into unit intervals. The following axiom gives a way of calculating the probability from the middle of a behaviour.

Exercise 7.7.2 Prove Theorem 7.15.

AR 9 For arbitrary duration formulas D_1 and D_2, and $v_i, v_j, v_k \in V$:

$$\tau(v_i, v_j) * \tau(v_j, v_k) * \mu(D_1 \wedge (\ell = r); \lceil v_i \rceil^1; \lceil v_k \rceil^1; D_2)[t]$$

$$= \tau(v_i, v_k) * \mu(D_1 \wedge (\ell = r); \lceil v_i \rceil^1; \lceil v_j \rceil^1; \lceil v_k \rceil^1; D_2)[t+1]$$

Finally, it is possible to prove the following theorem using axioms AR4, AR7 and AR8 and Theorems 7.13 and 7.14.

Theorem 7.16 For arbitrary duration formulas D, D_1 and D_2, and $v, v' \in V$:

1. $(\tau_0(v) = 0) \Rightarrow (\mu(\lceil v \rceil; D) = 0)$.
2. $(\tau(v, v') = 0) \Rightarrow (\mu(D_1; \lceil v \rceil; \lceil v' \rceil; D_2) = 0)$.

Exercise 7.7.3 Prove theorem 7.16.

7.7.4   Example

We can now apply PDC to the simple mine pump with an unreliable detector and failing pump (Section 7.7.1). We show how to estimate the satisfaction probability of requirement MP which states that the pump must not fail for more than four minutes in any period of 30 minutes. Assuming time units of minutes, this safety requirement is specified in DC as

$$MP \stackrel{\Delta}{=} \Box(l \leq 30 \Rightarrow \int \neg Ok \leq 4)$$

or, equivalently, as

$$(\int \neg Ok \geq 4) \stackrel{\leq 30}{\Longrightarrow} \lceil Ok \rceil$$

Assuming that detection of failures and subsequent recovery works perfectly, the following design decisions can be taken:

MP_1: Failure should be detected and stopped within one minute:

$$MP_1 \stackrel{\Delta}{=} \lceil \neg Ok \rceil \stackrel{1}{\longrightarrow} \lceil Ok \rceil$$

MP_2: Any two occurrences of failure must be separated by at least 30 minutes:

$$MP_2 \stackrel{\Delta}{=} (\lceil \neg Ok \rceil \; ; \; \lceil Ok \rceil) \stackrel{\leq 31}{\Longrightarrow} \lceil Ok \rceil$$

From Exercise 7.3(4), we have

$$MP_1 \wedge MP_2 \Rightarrow MP \text{ (i.e. } \neg MP \Rightarrow (\neg MP_1 \vee \neg MP_2))$$

From axioms AR3 and AR4, we then have

$$\mu(\neg MP) \leq \mu(\neg MP_1 \vee \neg MP_2) \leq \mu(\neg MP_1) + \mu(\neg MP_2)$$

where, from DC,

$$\mu(\neg MP_1) = \mu(true; \; (\lceil \neg Ok \rceil \wedge (\ell > 1)); \; true)$$

$$\mu(\neg MP_2) = \mu(true; \; ((\lceil \neg Ok \rceil; \; \lceil \neg Ok \rceil; \; \lceil \neg Ok \rceil) \wedge (\ell < 32)); \; true)$$

In what follows, we calculate $\mu(\neg MP_1)[t]$ recursively. From DC,

$$\neg MP_1 \wedge (\ell \leq 1) \Leftrightarrow false$$

Therefore, by Theorem 7.12.1 and Theorem 7.12.3,

$$t \leq 1 \Rightarrow \mu(\neg MP_1)[t] = 0$$

Also,

$$(\neg MP_1 \wedge \ell = 2) \Leftrightarrow \lceil \neg Ok \rceil^1; \; \lceil \neg Ok \rceil^1$$

but $\tau_0(\neg Ok) = 0$. Thus $\mu(\neg MP_1)[2] = 0$, by Theorem 7.12 and axioms AR7 and AR8. For any $t > 1$, MP_1 is violated in the first $t + 1$ minutes, if and only if MP_1 has already been violated in the first t minutes, or MP_1 holds for the first t minutes but is violated during the $(t+1)$th minute. This is written as

$$(\neg MP_1 \wedge \ell = t+1) \quad \Leftrightarrow \quad ((\neg MP_1 \wedge \ell = t); \ell = 1)$$
$$\vee((MP_1; \ell = 1) \wedge \neg MP_1 \wedge \ell = t+1)$$

where the two terms in the disjunction on the right are mutually exclusive. For $t \geq 2$ and from MP_1, the second term on the right-hand side is equivalent to

$$(MP_1; \lceil Ok \rceil^1; \lceil \neg Ok \rceil^1; \lceil \neg Ok \rceil^1) \wedge (\ell = t+1)$$

From Theorem 7.12, axioms AR3, AR5 and AR6 and Theorem 7.15 it then follows that

$$\mu(\neg MP_1)[t+1] \quad = \quad \mu(\neg MP_1)[t] + p_{12}*p_{22}*\mu(MP_1; \lceil Ok \rceil^1)[t-1]$$

where $t \geq 2$. To solve this recursive equation, we need an auxiliary recursive equation for the second μ-expression on the right-hand side. This is established next.

For $t \geq 2$ and MP_1 we have

$$((MP_1; \lceil Ok \rceil^1) \wedge \ell = t+1)$$

$$\Leftrightarrow \quad ((MP_1; \lceil Ok \rceil^1; \lceil Ok \rceil^1) \wedge \ell = t+1)$$
$$\vee((MP_1; \lceil \neg Ok \rceil^1; \lceil Ok \rceil^1) \wedge \ell = t+1)$$

$$\Leftrightarrow \quad ((MP_1; \lceil Ok \rceil^1; \lceil Ok \rceil^1) \wedge \ell = t+1)$$
$$\vee((MP_1; \lceil Ok \rceil^1; \lceil \neg Ok \rceil^1; \lceil Ok \rceil^1) \wedge \ell = t+1)$$

Again, the two terms on the right hand side are mutually exclusive. From Theorem 7.12, axioms AR3 and AR5 and Theorem 7.15 it then follows that

$$\mu(MP_1; \lceil Ok \rceil^1)[t+1] \quad = \quad p_{11}*\mu(MP_1; \lceil Ok \rceil^1)[t]$$
$$+ \quad p_{12}*p_{21}*\mu(MP_1; \lceil Ok \rceil^1)[t-1]$$
$$\text{where } t \geq 2$$

It is easy to show that $\mu(MP_1; \lceil Ok \rceil^1)[1]$ and $\mu(MP_2; \lceil Ok \rceil^1)[2]$ are both 1. These are the initial values for the recursion.

In summary, if we introduce the functions $\mathcal{P}(t)$ and $Q(t)$ by

$$\begin{cases} \mathcal{P}(t) \overset{\Delta}{=} \mu(\neg MP_1)[t] \\ Q(t) \overset{\Delta}{=} \mu(MP_1; \lceil \neg Ok \rceil)[t] \end{cases}$$

the probability $\mathcal{P}(t+1)$ that design decision 1 is violated in the observation interval $[0, t+1]$, $t \geq 2$, can be calculated by the solution of the mutually recursive equations

$$\begin{cases} \mathcal{P}(t+1) = \mathcal{P}(t) + p_{12}*p_{22}*Q(t-1) \\ Q(t+1) = p_{11}*Q(t) + p_{12}*p_{21}*Q(t-1) \\ \text{where } t \geq 2; \; \mathcal{P}(2) = 0, Q(1) = 1 \text{ and } Q(2) = 1 \end{cases}$$

The calculation of $\mu(\neg MP_2)[t]$ is done similarly. From axiom AR2,

$$\mu(\neg MP_2) = 1 - \mu(MP_2)$$

and, in DC,

$$MP_2 \wedge \ell > 0 \Leftrightarrow (MP_2 \wedge (true; \lceil \neg Ok \rceil^1)) \vee (MP_2 \wedge (true; \lceil Ok \rceil^1))$$

So by axiom AR3 and Theorem 7.12, we have

$$\mu(MP_2) = \mu(MP_2 \wedge (true; \lceil \neg Ok \rceil^1)) + \mu(MP_2 \wedge (true; \lceil Ok \rceil^1))$$

Let $\mathcal{U}(t)$ and $\mathcal{V}(t)$ be functions defined as

$$\left\{ \begin{array}{l} \mathcal{U}(t) \overset{\Delta}{=} \mu(MP_2 \wedge (true; \lceil \neg Ok \rceil^1))[t] \\ \mathcal{V}(t) \overset{\Delta}{=} \mu(MP_2 \wedge (true; \lceil Ok \rceil^1))[t] \end{array} \right.$$

Then, recalling that $p_1 (= \tau_0(Ok)) = 1$ and $p_2 (= \tau_0(\neg Ok)) = 0$, we can derive the following recursive equations for $\mathcal{U}(t)$ and $\mathcal{V}(t)$ in the calculus:

$$\left\{ \begin{array}{l} \mathcal{U}(t+1) = p_{22} * \mathcal{U}(t) + \left\{ \begin{array}{ll} (p_{11})^{28} * p_{12} * \mathcal{V}(t-29) & \text{if } t > 29 \\ (p_{11})^{t-1} * p_{12} & \text{if } 1 \le t \le 29 \\ 0 & \text{if } t < 1 \end{array} \right. \\ \\ \mathcal{V}(t+1) = \left\{ \begin{array}{ll} p_{21} * \mathcal{U}(t) + p_{11} * \mathcal{V}(t) & \text{if } t \ge 1 \\ 1 & \text{if } t < 1 \end{array} \right. \\ \\ \text{where } t \ge 0 \text{ and } \mathcal{U}(0) = \mathcal{V}(0) = 0 \end{array} \right.$$

Using these mutually recursive equations, we can calculate $\mu(MP_2)$ and then $\mu(\neg MP_2)$. Another way of calculating $\mu(MP_1)$ and $\mu(MP_2)$ is described in the following section.

7.7.5   Matrix-based, calculation-oriented theorems

The simple mine pump example shows that the direct use of PDC rules in probabilistic analysis can be rather *ad-hoc*. This indicates the need for high-level theorems leading to a more systematic analysis. We now extend PDC with matrices of real numbers and introduce the *single-step transition probability matrix* **P** and the *initial state probability vector* **p** in order to prove some auxiliary theorems using PDC. This will enable us to state and prove some useful calculation-oriented theorems.

Introducing matrices

An $m \times n$ *matrix* $\mathbf{M}_{m \times n}$ of real numbers is a function

$$\mathbf{M}_{m \times n}: \{1, \ldots, m\} \times \{1, \ldots, n\} \longrightarrow \mathbf{R}$$

where m and n range over the positive integers and $\mathbf{R}$ is the set of real numbers.

$\mathbf{M}_{m \times n}$ is therefore totally determined by assigning a real number m_{ij} to $\mathbf{M}_{m \times n}(i,j)$ for $(i,j) \in \{1,\ldots,m\} \times \{1,\ldots,n\}$. Such a matrix is also written as

$$\mathbf{M}_{m \times n} \stackrel{\Delta}{=} \begin{pmatrix} m_{11} & \cdots & m_{1n} \\ \vdots & & \vdots \\ m_{m1} & \cdots & m_{mn} \end{pmatrix}$$

where m_{ij} is called the (i,j)th *element* of $\mathbf{M}_{m \times n}$. When there is no confusion, $\mathbf{M}_{m \times n}$ will simply be written as $\mathbf{M}$.

Let $\mathcal{M}_{m \times n}$ denote the set of all $m \times n$ matrices and $\mathcal{M}$ the set of all matrices of real numbers. Operations on matrices are defined in terms of their elements. For example, the operation of addition '+' on matrices is defined on $\mathcal{M}_{m \times n} \times \mathcal{M}_{m \times n}$ by

$$(\mathbf{M} + \mathbf{M}')(i,j) \stackrel{\Delta}{=} \mathbf{M}(i,j) + \mathbf{M}'(i,j)$$

where $(i,j) \in \{1,\ldots,m\} \times \{1,\ldots,n\}$.

Similarly, multiplication '$\cdot$' is defined on $\mathcal{M}_{m \times n} \times \mathcal{M}_{n \times m'}$ by

$$(\mathbf{M}_{m \times n} \cdot \mathbf{M}'_{n \times m'})_{m \times m'}(i,j) \stackrel{\Delta}{=} \sum_{k=1}^{n} \mathbf{M}(i,k) * \mathbf{M}'(k,j)$$

where $(i,j) \in \{1,\ldots,m\} \times \{1,\ldots,m'\}$.

Predicates of matrices are defined in terms of predicates of their elements. For example, equality '=' between two matrices is defined by

$$\mathbf{M}_{m \times n} = \mathbf{M}'_{m' \times n'} \stackrel{\Delta}{=} (m = m') \wedge (n = n') \wedge (\bigwedge_{(i,j)=(1,1)}^{(m,n)} (\mathbf{M}(i,j) = \mathbf{M}'(i,j)))$$

These definitions show that the arithmetic of matrices of real numbers is in first-order real arithmetic, which is the basis of the probabilistic calculus.

Auxiliary notation

Definition 7.6 The following notation is needed:

$\mathbf{E}$ is the $m \times m$ identity matrix ($\mathbf{E}(i,j) = 1$ for $i = j$ and $\mathbf{E}(i,j) = 0$ for $i \neq j$).

$\mathbf{1}_c$ is the $m \times 1$ matrix (column vector) in which all elements are 1.

$\mathbf{z}_i$ is the $1 \times m$ matrix (row vector) of zeros with the ith element changed from 0 to 1.

$\mathbf{h}_i$ is the $m \times 1$ matrix (column vector) of zeros with the 1 in the ith element.

$\mathbf{I}$ is the index set $\{1,\ldots,m\}$

$\mathbf{I}_i$ denotes the subset $\mathbf{I} \setminus \{i\}$ of $\mathbf{I}$ where $i \in \mathbf{I}$.

Probability matrices and some basic theorems

Definition 7.7 With $V = \{v_1, \ldots, v_m\}$ (Definition 7.5), the single-step transition probability matrix $\mathbf{P}$ is a real $m \times m$ matrix defined by

$$\mathbf{P} \stackrel{\Delta}{=} \begin{pmatrix} p_{11} & \cdots & p_{1m} \\ \vdots & & \vdots \\ p_{m1} & \cdots & p_{mm} \end{pmatrix} \quad \text{where} \quad \begin{cases} p_{ij} \stackrel{\Delta}{=} \tau(v_i, v_j) \quad (0 \le p_{ij} \le 1) \\ \sum_{j \in \mathbf{I}} p_{ij} = 1 \end{cases}$$

and the initial state occupation probability vector $\mathbf{p}$ is a real $1 \times m$ row vector defined by

$$\mathbf{p} \stackrel{\Delta}{=} (p_1, \ldots, p_m) \quad \text{where:} \quad \begin{cases} p_i \stackrel{\Delta}{=} \tau_0(v_i) \quad (0 \le p_i \le 1) \\ \sum_{i \in \mathbf{I}} p_i = 1 \end{cases}$$

The first theorem is well known from the theory of Markov chains.

Theorem 7.17 For $t \ge 0$ and with $\mathbf{P}^0$ defined to be the identity matrix $\mathbf{E}$:

$$\mathbf{P}^t \cdot \mathbf{1}_c = \mathbf{1}_c$$

The theorem states that the sum of each row in the tth power of the single-step transition probability matrix is 1.

Exercise 7.7.4 Prove Theorem 7.17.

Definition 7.8 Let $\mathbf{p}^{(t)}$ ($t \ge 0$) denote the row vector $(p_1^{(t)}, \ldots, p_m^{(t)})$ defined by $\mathbf{p}^{(t)} \stackrel{\Delta}{=} \mathbf{p} \cdot \mathbf{P}^t$

The following theorem states that $p_i^{(t)}$ is the (unconditional) probability, that the system occupies state v_i after the tth transition. This is also well known from the theory of Markov chains, but it is expressed and proved here in terms of PDC.

Theorem 7.18 For $t \ge 0$,

$$(\mu(true;\ \lceil v_1 \rceil^1)[t+1], \ldots, \mu(true;\ \lceil v_m \rceil^1)[t+1]) = \mathbf{p}^{(t)}$$

Proof: We use induction on t:

For $t = 0$, the result follows from axiom AR7 and the fact that

$$\mathbf{p} = (\tau_0(v_1), \ldots, \tau_0(v_m))$$

Assume that the result holds for $t = k$; then from Theorem 7.15 and the definition of p_{ji},

$$\begin{aligned} \mu(true;\ \lceil v_i \rceil^1)[k+2] &= \sum_{j \in \mathbf{I}} \mu(true;\ \lceil v_j \rceil^1;\ \lceil v_i \rceil^1)[k+2] \\ &= \sum_{j \in \mathbf{I}} \mu(true;\ \lceil v_j \rceil^1)[k+1] * \tau(v_j, v_i) \\ &= \sum_{j \in \mathbf{I}} \mu(true;\ \lceil v_j \rceil^1)[k+1] * p_{ji} \end{aligned}$$

By the induction assumption,

$$\mu(\text{true};\ \lceil v_j\rceil^1)[k+1] = p_j^{(k)}$$

Therefore, for $i \in \mathbf{I}$,

$$\mu(\text{true};\ \lceil v_i\rceil^1)[k+2] = \sum_{j\in\mathbf{I}} p_j^{(k)} * p_{ji}$$

By the rules given in Section 7.7.5, this leads to

$$(\mu(\text{true};\ \lceil v_1\rceil^1)[k+2],\ldots,\mu(\text{true};\ \lceil v_m\rceil^1)[k+2]) = \mathbf{p}^{(k)}\cdot\mathbf{P}$$

But, by Definition 7.8,

$$\mathbf{p}^{(k)}\cdot\mathbf{P} = (\mathbf{p}\cdot\mathbf{P}^k)\cdot\mathbf{P} = \mathbf{p}\cdot\mathbf{P}^{k+1} = \mathbf{p}^{(k+1)}$$

This proves the theorem.

□

Theorems 7.17 and 7.18 imply that the initial probability vector $\mathbf{p}$ and the single-step transition probability matrix $\mathbf{P}$ are sufficient to determine the distribution $\mathbf{p}^{(t)}$. Taken together, the theorems characterize $\mathbf{P}^t$ as the *t-step transition probability matrix*. In the theory of stochastic processes the elements of $\mathbf{P}^t$, denoted by $p_{ij}^{(t)}$, are defined by

$$p_{ij}^{(t)} \overset{\Delta}{=} \mathcal{P}[v = v_j \text{ at time } n+t\mid v = v_i \text{ at time } n]\quad (t \geq 0)$$

The last theorem in this subsection expresses $\mu(\text{true})[t+1]$ (known to be 1) explicitly in terms of $\mathbf{p}$, $\mathbf{P}$ and t. The theorem is not very useful for computation, but it provides a semantic background for the subsequent computation-oriented theorems.

Theorem 7.19 For a non-negative integer t,

$$\mu(\text{true})[t+1] = \mathbf{p}\cdot\mathbf{P}^t\cdot\mathbf{1}_c = 1$$

Exercise 7.7.5 Prove Theorem 7.19.

Example
For a two-state system such as the simple mine pump and for a time interval of length 3

$$
\begin{aligned}
\mu(\text{true})[3] &= (p_1,p_2)\cdot\begin{pmatrix} p_{11} & p_{12} \\ p_{21} & p_{22} \end{pmatrix}^2\cdot\begin{pmatrix} 1 \\ 1 \end{pmatrix} \\
&= p_1p_{11}p_{11} + p_1p_{11}p_{12} + p_1p_{12}p_{21} + p_1p_{12}p_{22} \\
&+ p_2p_{21}p_{11} + p_2p_{21}p_{12} + p_2p_{22}p_{21} + p_2p_{22}p_{22} = 1
\end{aligned}
$$

This shows that the matrix expression for $\mu(\text{true})[t+1]$ can be expanded into a sum of symbolic products where each product defines the probability of a unique behaviour of length $t+1$ and all such products are represented.

Clearly, the effect of replacing the duration formula *true* by a more restrictive formula D must be to eliminate all products in the sum except those representing behaviours which satisfy D. For a simple class of D formulas, this elimination is obtained by replacing certain elements in $\mathbf{P}$ or $\mathbf{p}$ in the matrix expressions by zeros. This is used in the following theorems.

Computation-oriented theorems

The first theorem is useful for computation of the probability that a transition to a catastrophic state does not occur (Case a) or does occur (Case b) within the the first $t+1$ time units.

Theorem 7.20 Let $\mathbf{p}_{\overline{p}_i}$ denote $\mathbf{p}$ with element p_i replaced by zero and let $\mathbf{P}_{\overline{c}_i}$ denote $\mathbf{P}$ with all elements in column i replaced by zeros; then for a state v_i and a non-negative integer t:

(a) $\mu(\Box\neg\lceil v_i\rceil)[t+1] = \mathbf{p}_{\overline{p}_i} \cdot (\mathbf{P}_{\overline{c}_i})^t \cdot \mathbf{1}_c$

(b) $\mu(\Diamond\lceil v_i\rceil)[t+1] = 1 - \mathbf{p}_{\overline{p}_i} \cdot (\mathbf{P}_{\overline{c}_i})^t \cdot \mathbf{1}_c$

To prove this theorem we need the following lemma.

Lemma 7.3 For a state v_i and a non-negative integer t:

$$(\mu(D_1)[t+1],\ldots,\mu(D_m)[t+1]) = \mathbf{p}_{\overline{p}_i} \cdot (\mathbf{P}_{\overline{c}_i})^t$$

where: for $k \in \mathbf{I}$, $D_k \overset{\Delta}{=} (\Box\neg\lceil v_i\rceil) \wedge (true; \lceil v_k\rceil)$.

According to this lemma, the kth element of the row vector $\mathbf{p}_{\overline{p}_i} \cdot (\mathbf{P}_{\overline{c}_i})^t$ is the probability that the system occupies state v_k after the tth transition and that state v_i does not occur during the first $t+1$ time units.

Proof: We use induction on t. For $t=0$ we have $\mathbf{p}_{\overline{p}_i} \cdot (\mathbf{P}_{\overline{c}_i})^t = \mathbf{p}_{\overline{p}_i} \cdot \mathbf{E} = \mathbf{p}_{\overline{p}_i}$. The result then follows from AR7 and the fact that

$$\mathbf{p}_{\overline{p}_i} = (\tau_0(v_1),\ldots,\tau_0(v_{i-1}),0,\tau_0(v_{i+1}),\ldots,\tau_0(v_m))$$

For $t \geq 0$, assume that the result holds for $t=n$. Then for $t=n+1$ and for the kth element of the vector:

$$\mu((\Box\neg\lceil v_i\rceil) \wedge (true; \lceil v_k\rceil))[n+2] = \mu((\Box\neg\lceil v_i\rceil) \wedge (true; \lceil v_k\rceil^1))[n+2]$$
$$= \sum_{j\in\mathbf{I}} \mu((\Box\neg\lceil v_i\rceil) \wedge (true; \lceil v_j\rceil^1; \lceil v_k\rceil^1))[n+2]$$

For $k=i$ this sum is zero by Theorem 7.12 ($\mu(false) = 0$). For $k \neq i$ we can rewrite the sum, denoted *Sum*, as follows (notice the parentheses!):

$$Sum = \sum_{j\in\mathbf{I}} \mu(((\Box\neg\lceil v_i\rceil) \wedge (true; \lceil v_j\rceil^1)); \lceil v_k\rceil^1)[n+2]$$

By axiom AR8 we then obtain

$$Sum = \sum_{j\in\mathbf{I}} \mu((\Box\neg\lceil v_i\rceil) \wedge (true; \lceil v_j\rceil^1))[n+1] * \tau(v_j,v_k)$$

Replacing $\tau(v_j,v_k)$ by p_{jk} and returning to the vector form, this implies:

$$(\mu(D_1)[n+2],\ldots,\mu(D_m)[n+2]) = (\mu(D_1)[n+1],\ldots,\mu(D_m)[n+1]) \cdot \mathbf{P}_{\overline{c}_i}$$

By the induction assumption, the last expression is equal to

$$\mathbf{p}_{\overline{p}_i} \cdot (\mathbf{P}_{\overline{c}_i})^n \cdot \mathbf{P}_{\overline{c}_i} = \mathbf{p}_{\overline{p}_i} \cdot (\mathbf{P}_{\overline{c}_i})^{n+1}$$

This proves the lemma.

□

Exercise 7.7.6 Prove Theorem 7.20.

Notice, that if state v_i is absorbing ($p_{ii} = 1$), then Theorem 7.20 gives the probability that absorption in this state has occurred (b) or has not occurred (a) within the first $t + 1$ time units.

The next theorem is useful for computation of the probability that a transition from a hazardous state v_i to a catastrophic state v_j does not occur (case a) or occurs (case b) within the first $t + 1$ time units.

Theorem 7.21 Let $\mathbf{P}_{\bar{p}_{ij}}$ denote $\mathbf{P}$ with element p_{ij} replaced by a zero. Then for states v_i, v_j and a non-negative integer t:

(a) $\quad \mu(\square\neg(\lceil v_i \rceil; \lceil v_j \rceil))[t + 1] = \mathbf{p} \cdot (\mathbf{P}_{\bar{p}_{ij}})^t \cdot \mathbf{1}_c$

(b) $\quad \mu(\lozenge(\lceil v_i \rceil; \lceil v_j \rceil))[t + 1] = 1 - \mathbf{p} \cdot (\mathbf{P}_{\bar{p}_{ij}})^t \cdot \mathbf{1}_c$

The proof of this theorem follows exactly the same pattern as the proof of Theorem 7.20, and is omitted. The required lemma, which resembles Lemma 7.3, is as follows.

Lemma 7.4 For states v_i and v_j and a non-negative integer t:

$$(\mu(D_1)[t + 1], \ldots, \mu(D_m)[t + 1]) = \mathbf{p} \cdot (\mathbf{P}_{\bar{p}_{ij}})^t$$

where: for $k \in \mathbf{I}$, $D_k \triangleq (\square\neg(\lceil v_i \rceil; \lceil v_j \rceil)) \wedge (\textit{true}; \lceil v_k \rceil)$.

This lemma states that the kth element of the row vector $\mathbf{p} \cdot (\mathbf{P}_{\bar{p}_{ij}})^t$ is the probability that the system occupies state v_k after the tth transition and no transition from state v_i to state v_j occurs during the first $t + 1$ time units.

Theorem 7.21 has the following immediate corollary.

Corollary 2 For a state v_i and a non-negative integer t:

(a) $\quad \mu(\square(\lceil v_i \rceil \Rightarrow \ell \leq 1))[t + 1] = \mathbf{p} \cdot (\mathbf{P}_{\bar{p}_{ii}})^t \cdot \mathbf{1}$

(b) $\quad \mu(\lozenge(\lceil v_i \rceil \wedge \ell > 1))[t + 1] = 1 - \mathbf{p} \cdot (\mathbf{P}_{\bar{p}_{ij}})^t \cdot \mathbf{1}$

The next theorem deals with certain chopped formulas, which generalize and unite axioms AR2 and AR8. However, before we can state the theorem a definition is needed.

Definition 7.9 For each subset J of the index set $\mathbf{I} = \{1, \ldots, m\}$, $J \subseteq \mathbf{I}$, we define:

1. an auxiliary matrix $\mathbf{P}_J$ from the single step transition probability matrix $\mathbf{P}$ as follows:

$$\mathbf{P}_J \triangleq \begin{pmatrix} p'_{11} & \cdot & \cdot & p'_{1m} \\ \cdot & & & \cdot \\ \cdot & & & \cdot \\ p'_{m1} & \cdot & \cdot & p'_{mm} \end{pmatrix} \quad \text{where} \quad p'_{ij} = \begin{cases} p_{ij} & \text{if } j \in J \\ 0 & \text{if } j \in \bar{J} \end{cases}$$

and $\bar{J}$ denotes the complement $\mathbf{I} \setminus J$ of J.

2. a composite state V_J as follows:

$$v_J \overset{\Delta}{=} \bigvee_{j \in J} v_j$$

Notice that, according to the definition of v_J, $(\lceil v_J \rceil \wedge \ell = t)$ represents any sequence

$$(\lceil v_{j_1} \rceil^1; \lceil v_{j_2} \rceil^1; \ldots \lceil v_{j_t} \rceil^1)$$

of elementary states of duration 1 such that $j_i \in J$ for $i \in \{1, \ldots, t\}$.

The theorem makes use of the auxiliary row vector $\mathbf{z}_i$ and column vector $\mathbf{1}_c$ from Definition 7.7.5.

Theorem 7.22 For an arbitrary index set $J \subseteq \mathbf{I}$, an arbitrary duration formula D and an arbitrary state $v_i \in V$

(a) $\mu(D \wedge (true; \lceil v_i \rceil) \wedge (\ell = k); \lceil v_J \rceil)[t+k+1]$
$= \mu(D \wedge (true; \lceil v_i \rceil)[k] \cdot \mathbf{z}_i \cdot (\mathbf{P}_J)^{t+1} \cdot \mathbf{1}_\mathbf{c})$

(b) $\mu(D \wedge (true; \lceil v_i \rceil) \wedge (\ell = k); \Diamond \lceil v_J \rceil)[t+k+1]$
$= \mu(D \wedge (true; \lceil v_i \rceil)[k] \cdot (1 - \mathbf{z}_i \cdot (\mathbf{P}_{\bar{J}})^{t+1} \cdot \mathbf{1}_\mathbf{c})$

To prove this theorem, the following notation and lemma are useful:

$$q \overset{\Delta}{=} \mu(D \wedge (true; \lceil v_i \rceil))[k]$$

and for $j \in \mathbf{I}$

$$q_j[t] \overset{\Delta}{=} \begin{cases} \mu((D \wedge (true; \lceil v_i \rceil) \wedge (\ell = k); \lceil v_J \rceil) \wedge (true; \lceil v_j \rceil))[t+k+1] & \text{if } j \in J \\ 0 & \text{if } j \in \bar{J} \end{cases}$$

We first present the lemma below.

Lemma 7.5 For q and $q_j[t]$ as defined above,

$$(q_1[t], \ldots, q_m[t]) = q \cdot \mathbf{z}_i \cdot (\mathbf{P}_J)^{t+1}$$

Exercise 7.7.7 Prove Lemma 7.5 and Theorem 7.22(a).

Proof: (Proof of Theorem 7.22(b)) Case (b) is proved from case (a):

$$q \cdot (1 - \mathbf{1_i} \cdot (\mathbf{P_{\bar{j}}})^{t+1} \cdot \mathbf{1_c} = q - q \cdot \mathbf{1_i} \cdot (\mathbf{P_{\bar{j}}})^{t+1} \cdot \mathbf{1_c}$$

$$= \quad q - \mu(D \wedge (true; \lceil v_i \rceil) \wedge (\ell = k); \lceil v_{\bar{j}} \rceil)[t + k + 1] \qquad \text{(Th.17(a))}$$

$$= \quad \mu(D \wedge (true; \lceil v_i \rceil) \wedge (\ell = k); (\ell = t + 1))[t + k + 1] \qquad \text{(AR6)}$$

$$\quad - \mu(D \wedge (true; \lceil v_i \rceil) \wedge (\ell = k); \lceil v_{\bar{j}} \rceil)[t + k + 1]$$

$$= \quad \mu(D \wedge (true; \lceil v_i \rceil) \wedge (\ell = k); \lceil v_{\bar{j}} \rceil \vee \Diamond \lceil v_J \rceil)[t + k + 1] \qquad \text{(Th.6(3))}$$

$$\quad - \mu(D \wedge (true; \lceil v_i \rceil) \wedge (\ell = k); \lceil v_{\bar{j}} \rceil)[t + k + 1]$$

$$= \quad \mu(D \wedge (true; \lceil v_i \rceil) \wedge (\ell = k); \lceil v_{\bar{j}} \rceil)[t + k + 1]$$

$$\quad + \mu(D \wedge (true; \lceil v_i \rceil) \wedge (\ell = k); \Diamond \lceil v_J \rceil)[t + k + 1] \qquad \text{(AR3)}$$

$$\quad - \mu(D \wedge (true; \lceil v_i \rceil) \wedge (\ell = k); \lceil v_{\bar{j}} \rceil)[t + k + 1]$$

$$= \quad \mu(D \wedge (true; \lceil v_i \rceil) \wedge (\ell = k); \Diamond \lceil v_J \rceil)[t + k + 1]$$

□

Application to the mine pump example

Consider the simple mine pump of Section 7.7.1 which was analyzed in Section 7.7.4. Let

$$V \triangleq \{v_1, v_2\} \text{ where: } v_i \triangleq \begin{cases} Ok & \text{if } i = 1 \\ \neg Ok & \text{if } i = 2 \end{cases}$$

$$\mathbf{p} \triangleq (p_1, p_2) \text{ (where } p_1 = 1 \text{ and } p_2 = 0)$$

$$\mathbf{P} \triangleq \begin{pmatrix} p_{11} & p_{12} \\ p_{21} & p_{22} \end{pmatrix}$$

A simple explicit expression for $\mu(\neg MP_1)[t + 1]$ follows directly from Corollary 2(b) of Theorem 7.21:

$$\mu(\neg MP_1)[t + 1] = 1 - \mathbf{p} \cdot (\mathbf{P_{\bar{p}_{22}}})^t \cdot \mathbf{1_c} = 1 - (p_1, p_2) \cdot \begin{pmatrix} p_{11} & p_{12} \\ p_{21} & 0 \end{pmatrix}^t \cdot \begin{pmatrix} 1 \\ 1 \end{pmatrix}$$

It is more difficult to express $\mu(\neg MP_2)[t + 1]$ explicitly by means of the present collection of theorems. In DC, we can rewrite $\neg MP_2$ as follows:

$$\neg MP_2 \quad \Leftrightarrow \quad \Diamond((\lceil \neg Ok \rceil; \rceil Ok\lceil; \lceil \neg Ok \rceil) \wedge (\ell \leq 31))$$
$$\Leftrightarrow \quad \exists k : ((true; \lceil \neg Ok \rceil) \wedge (\ell = k); \lceil Ok \rceil \wedge (\ell \leq 29); \lceil \neg Ok \rceil^1; true)$$

For a given t, $\mu(\neg MP_2)[t]$ is non-zero only if $t \geq k + h + 1$, where $k \geq 1$ and $1 \leq h \leq 29$. Introducing

$$h_{max} = min((t - k - 1), 29)$$

we can express $\mu(MP_2)[t]$ by a double summation over all possible ks and hs (this is because we can treat the existential quantification as a disjunction over all possible ks and hs in which the disjuncts are mutually exclusive):

$$\mu(\neg MP_2)[t]$$

$$\text{(by AR6)}$$

$$= \sum_{k=1}^{t-2} \sum_{h=1}^{h_{max}} \mu(true; \lceil \neg Ok \rceil) \wedge (\ell = k); \lceil Ok \rceil \wedge (\ell = h); \lceil \neg Ok \rceil^1 [k+h+1]$$

$$\text{(by Theorem 7.22 and Definition 7.7.5)}$$

$$= \sum_{k=1}^{t-2} \sum_{h=1}^{h_{max}} \mu(true; \lceil \neg Ok \rceil) \wedge (\ell = k); \lceil Ok \rceil \wedge (\ell = h))[k+h] \cdot (\mathbf{z}_1 \cdot \mathbf{P}_{\{2\}} \cdot \mathbf{1_c})$$

$$\text{(by Theorem 7.22 again)}$$

$$= \sum_{k=1}^{t-2} \sum_{h=1}^{h_{max}} \mu(true; \lceil \neg Ok \rceil)[k] \cdot (\mathbf{z}_2 \cdot \mathbf{P}_{\{1\}}^h \cdot \mathbf{1_c}) \cdot (\mathbf{z}_1 \cdot \mathbf{P}_{\{2\}} \cdot \mathbf{1_c})$$

$$\text{(by Theorem 7.18, Definition 7.7.5 and Definition 7.7.5)}$$

$$= \sum_{k=1}^{t-2} \sum_{h=1}^{h_{max}} (\mathbf{p} \cdot \mathbf{P}^{k-1} \cdot \mathbf{h}_2) \cdot (\mathbf{z}_2 \cdot \mathbf{P}_{\{1\}}^h \cdot \mathbf{1_c}) \cdot (\mathbf{z}_1 \cdot \mathbf{P}_{\{2\}} \cdot \mathbf{1_c})$$

7.8 Historical background

The motivation for DC originally came from the gas burner problem which was chosen as the main case study of the ProCoS project (Bjørner *et al.*, 1993; He *et al.*, 1994). It was then realized that control engineers use the properties of integrals and differentials of functions widely in the description of requirements and for reasoning about the designs of embedded systems. For example, the case study was required to formulate the safety requirement of the gas burner in terms of variables denoting undesirable but unavoidable states such as *Leak*, which represents the flow of unlit gas from the nozzle: '*The proportion of time when gas leaks is not more than one twentieth of the elapsed time, if the system is observed for more than one minute*'.

A direct formulation of this requirement can be obtained using mathematical analysis; for any interval $[b, e]$ of the real-numbers:

$$(e - b) \geq 60 \Rightarrow 20 \int_b^e Leak(t)dt \leq (e - b)$$

where *Leak* is a boolean valued step-function from the real-numbers (representing *time*). But at the time of the start of the ProCoS project no calculus, apart from set theory, was available to express and reason about the properties of integrals or differentials of functions. Set theory is far too rich and thus difficult to use for system designs.

Working on the formalization of integrals of boolean-valued functions, Zhou *et al.* (1991a) developed the duration calculus. Integrals were considered as *curried* functions from state functions and intervals to real numbers:

$$\int : \quad \mathbf{S} \to (\mathbf{I} \to \mathbf{R})$$

where $\mathbf{S}$ denotes the set of states (i.e. boolean-valued step-functions) and $\mathbf{I}$ the set of bounded intervals of real numbers. Moszkowski's ITL (1985), which uses a discrete time domain and was developed for reasoning about hardware was extended with continuous time and then adopted as the base logic for DC. Interval functions such as $\int P$ and $\int Q$ then become interval variables of ITL.

As we have seen in this chapter, DC is a logic for formalizing and reasoning about a system's functional and safety properties. It does not provide the means for specifying and reasoning about the reliability properties of an implementation in which imperfect components are used. Since perfect components are not used in practice, and there is no perfect implementation, there is a need for an extension to deal with probabilities. Liu *et al.* (1993c) described a probabilistic duration calculus which is a modal logic about prefix time intervals; this did not need reference to the time variable t in a probabilistic term $\mu(D)$. The same authors developed a first-order logic (Liu *et al.*, 1994b) for the calculation of $\mu(D)[t]$ and this is the version presented in Section 7.7.

Liu *et al.* (1993c; 1994b) assume discrete time and model an imperfect implementation as a finite automaton with fixed history, independent of the transition probabilities. This makes discrete Markov processes appropriate as the basis for the calculus. In comparison with Liu *et al.* (1993c), the first-order logic in Liu *et al.* (1994b) is easier to understand and can be used without loss of expressiveness; the latter also gives more details and adds computation-oriented theorems to the theory, making the calculus more mechanizable and also more accessible to reliability engineers.

7.9 Further work

After its initial development, there has been considerable further research on DC: theoretical developments of the calculus, extensions and application-related work.

7.9.1 Theoretical work

Assuming *finite variability* of states, a formal semantics of DC was given in Hansen and Zhou (1992). Based on this semantics, they also proved that the axioms and rules presented here in Section 7.5 constitute a relatively *complete* calculus for DC. Results on decidability and undecidability of DC have appeared in Zhou *et al.* (1993a) and a prototype mechanized proof assistant has been implemented by coding the semantics of DC in the logic of PVS (Skakkebæk & Shankar, 1994). An efficient model checking algorithm for *linear duration invariants* has been given in Zhou *et al.* (1994). An overview on DC and its extensions can be found in Zhou (1993).

For PDC, parallel composition of (open) probabilistic automata is defined in Liu *et al.* (1993a; 1993b). There, refinement of a probabilistic automata into another through parallel composition (or decomposition) is formalized, and some compositional proof rules in terms of PDC are investigated. PDC has been extended by Dang and Zhou (1994) for continuous time.

7.9.2 Extensions

The basic DC has several extensions, among which are the probabilistic calculi of Liu *et al.* (1993c; 1994b). Another extension, called the Extended Duration Calculus (Zhou *et al.*, 1993b), was designed for the specification and verification of *hybrid systems* which include continuous and discrete states. Here, the arguments of the lifting operator $\lceil \cdot \rceil$ are generalized to allow not only boolean-valued functions but also properties like equality and inequality (we have already seen these used in the mine pump example), continuity, etc. For example, with formulas like $\lceil Continuous(v) \rceil$ it is possible to assert that function v is continuous in an interval and with $\lceil \dot{v} = 0 \rceil$ to assert that v is stable (or constant) in an interval.

Ravn (1994) uses DC and its extensions to investigate both fundamental and practical issues involved in the formal development of embedded real-time systems, including hybrid systems. The paper links DC to the mathematical analysis of continuous functions by allowing the initial and final values, $\mathbf{b}.f$ and $\mathbf{e}.f$, of a function f to be defined, as well as its duration $\int f$ over an interval. The basic DC has also been extended to the Mean Value Calculus (Zhou & Xiaoshan, 1994) by replacing integrals of boolean-valued functions with their mean values. In this extended calculus, both durations of states and point values of states can be expressed, and the latter become significant when a state-based system requirement is to be refined into a communication-based set of components, because communications are instant actions.

The basic DC and these extensions are restricted to *finite* intervals and use the *chop* operator as the only means of contracting subintervals to a given interval. The restriction prevents the use of DC for specifying *unbounded* liveness and fairness properties, such as two users who are served so fairly that they have exactly equal service durations. To accommodate unbounded liveness and fairness, several extensions to DC have been proposed. The first approach to extending DC for specifying unbounded liveness and fairness was to introduce *expanding* modalities in DC, while keeping the restriction of finite intervals. Pandya (1994) defined two *weakest inverses* of the *chop* operator. Engel and Rischel (1994) generalized the *chop* operator by introducing *backward* intervals. Based on Venema's (1991) interval temporal logic Skakkebæk (1994) added two expanding modalities into DC, which are symmetric and designated as ▷ and ◁. An interval satisfies $D_1 \triangleright D_2$ iff there exists c such that $c \geq b$, $[a,c]$ satisfies D_1 and $[b,c]$ satisfies D_2.

Although these extensions can express liveness and fairness properties, they are still unable to differentiate *syntactically* between a finite and an infinite system behaviour. An infinite behaviour determines a system eternally, while a finite behaviour determines system states up to some moment in time, possibly allowing arbitrary continuation. It is still difficult to define sequential composition using these finite interval based extensions of DC. Zhou *et al.* (1995) addresses this problem by introducing new states, rather than new modalities, to indicate *termination, refusals* or *ready* syntactically. This resembles the method used for extending the *finite trace* based version of CSP (see Chapter 6).

Zhou *et al.* (1995) mainly investigates a third way of extending DC for liveness and fairness properties by introducing infinite intervals into the calculus. The extended calculus, called a *Duration Calculus with Infinite Intervals* (DC^i), is a first-order logic of finite and infinite satisfactions of DC. The basic formulas of DC^i are D^f and D^i, where D is a formula of DC. D^f may hold only for finite intervals, and D^i may hold only for infinite intervals . A finite interval satisfies D^f iff the interval satisfies D in terms of the semantics of DC. An infinite interval satisfies D^i iff all its *finite* prefixes satisfy D in terms of the semantics of DC. It was shown that DC^i could conveniently specify unbounded liveness and fairness properties, and define sequential composition in a programming language in a much simpler way.

7.9.3 Application work

DC has been used to define and refine requirements and designs for a number of examples including a gas burner (Ravn *et al.*, 1993), a railway crossing (Skakkebæk *et al.*, 1992), a water level controller (Engel *et al.*, 1993) and an auto pilot (Ravn & Rischel, 1991). It also has been used to define the real-time semantics of programming languages (Zhou *et al.*, 1991b; He & Bowen, 1992; Hansen *et al.*, 1993a), to specify real-time scheduling policies (Zhou *et al.*, 1991b; Zhang & Zhou, 1994) and to specify the real-time behaviour of circuits (Hansen *et al.*, 1992). Applications of the extended duration calculus to hybrid systems can be found in Hansen *et al.* (1993b) and in Yu *et al.* (1994a; 1994b).

7.10 Exercises

Exercise 7.1 Prove the following useful formulas:

1. $(\textit{true} \; ; \; \textit{true}) \Leftrightarrow \textit{true}$
2. $(\lceil P_1 \rceil \; ; \; \textit{true}) \wedge (\lceil P_2 \rceil \; ; \; \textit{true}) \Leftrightarrow (\lceil P_1 \wedge P_2 \rceil \; ; \; \textit{true})$
3. $(\mathcal{F} \Rightarrow \mathcal{G}) \Rightarrow (\Diamond \mathcal{F} \Rightarrow \Diamond \mathcal{G})$
4. $\Diamond \Diamond \mathcal{F} \Leftrightarrow \Diamond \mathcal{F}$
5. $\Diamond (\mathcal{F} \wedge \mathcal{G}) \Leftrightarrow \Diamond \mathcal{F} \wedge \Diamond \mathcal{G}$
6. $\Diamond (\mathcal{F} \; ; \; \mathcal{G}) \Rightarrow \Diamond \mathcal{F} \wedge \Diamond \mathcal{G}$
7. $(\mathcal{F} \Rightarrow \mathcal{G}) \Rightarrow (\Box \mathcal{F} \Rightarrow \Box \mathcal{G})$

Exercise 7.2 For each formula with $\Diamond$ in Exercise 7.1 find and prove a dual formula using $\Box$.

Exercise 7.3 For the abbreviation $\lceil \mathcal{F} \rceil \stackrel{t}{\longrightarrow} \lceil P \rceil$ defined in Section 7.2, prove the following formulas:

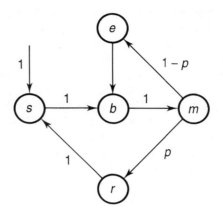

Figure 7.8 A protocol over an unreliable medium

1. $\lceil P\rceil \xrightarrow{t} \lceil\neg P\rceil \Leftrightarrow \Box(\lceil P\rceil \Rightarrow \ell \le t)$
2. $(\lceil P_1\rceil \xrightarrow{t} \lceil P_2\rceil) \wedge t \le t' \Rightarrow \lceil P_1\rceil \xrightarrow{t'} \lceil P_2\rceil$
3. $(\lceil P_1\rceil \xrightarrow{t_1} \lceil P_2\rceil) \wedge (\lceil P_1 \wedge P_2\rceil \xrightarrow{t_1} \lceil P_3\rceil) \Rightarrow \lceil P_1\rceil \xrightarrow{t_1+t_2} \lceil P_2 \wedge P_3\rceil$
4. $(\lceil P\rceil \xrightarrow{c} \lceil\neg P\rceil) \wedge ((\lceil P\rceil \; ; \; \lceil\neg P\rceil) \xrightarrow{\le t-c} \lceil\neg P\rceil) \Rightarrow \Box(\ell \le t \Rightarrow \int P \le c)$

Exercise 7.4 Specify a scheduling policy that has an overhead of δ time units whenever a process has to be either placed on a processor for execution or removed from a processor.

Exercise 7.5 Figure 7.8 illustrates a protocol over an unreliable medium which transmits a message from a process called Sender to a process called Receiver through a buffer. s, b, m and r are states when the sender, the buffer, the medium and the receiver, respectively, are active; e represents the error state of the medium. Calculate the following probabilities using the PDC rules:

1. $\mu(\int r > 0)[t]$
2. $\dfrac{\mu(D_1 \wedge D_2)[t]}{\mu(D_2)[t]}$, where $\begin{aligned} D_1 &\triangleq (\textit{true}; \lceil e\rceil) \wedge (\ell = k); \lceil\neg e\rceil \wedge (\ell = k_1); \lceil e\rceil; \textit{true} \\ D_2 &\triangleq (\textit{true}; \lceil e\rceil) \wedge (\ell = k); \textit{true} \end{aligned}$

Exercise 7.6 Use matrix-based theorems to calculate the probabilities of Exercise 7.5.

Chapter 8

Real-time Systems and Fault-tolerance

Henk Schepers

Introduction

When a component of a computer system fails, it will usually produce some undesirable effects and it can be said to no longer behave according to its specification. Such a breakdown of a component is called a *fault* and its consequence is called a *failure*. A fault may occur sporadically, or it may be stable and cause the component to fail permanently. Even when a fault occurs instantaneously, a fault such as a memory fault may have consequences that manifest themselves after a considerable time.

Fault-tolerance is the ability of a system to function correctly despite the occurrence of faults. Faults caused by errors (or 'bugs') in software are *systematic* and can be reproduced in the right conditions. The formal methods described in previous chapters address the problem of errors in software and, while their use does not guarantee the absence of software errors, they do provide the means of making a rigorous, additional check. Hardware errors may also be systematic but in addition they can have random causes. The fact that a hardware component functions correctly at some time is no guarantee of flawless future behaviour; in Chapter 7, the formal treatment of random faults was described using the probabilistic duration calculus. Note that hardware faults often affect the correct behaviour of software. One of the reasons for introducing dynamic scheduling (see Chapter 4) is to deal with the unexpected computational load imposed when faults do occur.

Of course, it is not possible to tolerate every fault. A *failure hypothesis* stipulates how faults affect the behaviour of a system. An example of a failure hypothesis is the assumption that a communication medium might corrupt messages. With triple modular redundancy, a single component is replaced by three replicas and a voter that determines the outcome, and the failure hypothesis is that at any time at most one replica is affected by faults. A failure hypothesis divides abnormal behaviour, i.e. behaviour that does not conform to the specification, into *exceptional* and *catastrophic* behaviours. Exceptional behaviour conforms to the failure hypothesis and must be tolerated, but no attempt need be made to handle catastrophic behaviour (and, indeed, no attempt may be possible). For example, if the communication medium mentioned earlier repeatedly sends the same message, then this may be catastrophic for a given fault-tolerance scheme. It is important to note that 'normal' behaviour does not mean 'perfect' behaviour: after a time-out occurs, the retransmission of a message by a sender is normal but it may result in two copies of the same message reaching its destination. Exceptional and normal behaviours together form the *acceptable* behaviour that the system must tolerate. This chapter is concerned with the following question: can we reason about acceptable behaviour in the same way that we reason about normal behaviour?

We shall use the compositional proof method of Chapter 5 for reasoning about acceptable behaviour, and the failure hypothesis of a system will be formalized as a relation between its normal and acceptable behaviour. Such a relation will allow us to abstract from the precise nature and occurrence of faults and focus on the abnormal behaviour that might be caused. This will lead us to a proof rule by which a specification of the acceptable behaviour can be obtained from the specification of the normal behaviour and a predicate characterizing the failure hypothesis. Given a failure hypothesis χ, $P \wr \chi$ stands for 'P under χ' and means execution of process P under the assumption χ. The acceptable behaviour of process P under the failure hypothesis χ is the normal behaviour of the failure prone process $P \wr \chi$.

Use of the method will be demonstrated on the mine pump problem. We shall describe how each component can be affected by malfunctions and then devise ways to tolerate the failures. Because we have to be particularly careful, shifts might be missed unnecessarily. However, we shall prove that the resulting system is safe, i.e. it will not cause an explosion.

8.1   Assertions and correctness formulae

Let R be a special variable referring to the timed occurrence function (see Section 5.1.2) which denotes the observable behaviour of a real-time system. Let *MVAR* be a set of logical variables with typical element M ranging over timed occurrence functions. The boolean primitive $O @ texp$ will be considered as an abbreviation of $O \in R(texp)$. In addition, the boolean primitive $O @_M texp$ will be used as an abbreviation of $O \in M(texp)$ and similarly we shall use $P \text{ during}_M I \equiv \forall t \in I \cdot P @_M t$, and $P \text{ in}_M I \equiv \exists t \in I \cdot P @_M t$.

Since R refers to all observables, the unrestricted occurrence of R in assertions leads to problems when trying to apply the parallel composition rule.

Definition 8.1   (*Event projection*) If E is a set of observable events and ρ is a mapping, the restriction $\rho \downarrow E$ of ρ to E at time τ is

$$(\rho \downarrow E)(\tau) = \rho(\tau) \cup E$$

$\diamond$

Define $obs(R \downarrow E) = E$.

Definition 8.2   (*Interval projection*) For an interval $I \subseteq TIME$ and a mapping ρ, $\rho \downarrow I$ is the restriction of ρ with respect to I and is defined as

$$(\rho \downarrow I)(\tau) = \left\{ \begin{array}{ll} \rho(\tau) & \text{if } \tau \in I \\ \emptyset & \text{if } \tau \notin I \end{array} \right\}$$

$\diamond$

Let x_0 denote the initial state value of a variable x and let now now_0 denote the starting time. Then instead of

$$\langle\langle x = v \geq 0 \wedge now = t < \infty \rangle\rangle \; \text{SQRT} \; \langle\langle x = \sqrt{v} \wedge t + 3 \leq now < t + 5 \rangle\rangle$$

we may write, using now_0 to refer to the starting time

$$\langle\langle x_0 \geq 0 \wedge now_0 < \infty \rangle\rangle \; \text{SQRT} \; \langle\langle x = \sqrt{x_0} \wedge now_0 + 3 \leq now < now_0 + 5 \rangle\rangle$$

Let $var(\varphi)$ denote the program variables in φ and $var_0(\varphi)$ the variables $x \in VAR$ such that x_0 appears in ϕ. An assertion will be interpreted with respect to a 4-tuple $(\sigma_0, \sigma, \rho, \gamma)$. The state σ_0 gives now_0 and the terms x_0 their value; the state σ, the mapping ρ and the environment γ are as defined in Chapter 5. The most important cases are:

- $\mathcal{V}[\![now_0]\!](\sigma_0, \sigma, \rho, \gamma) = \sigma_0(now)$
- $\mathcal{V}[\![x_0]\!](\sigma_0, \sigma, \rho, \gamma) = \sigma_0(x)$
- $\mathcal{V}[\![R]\!](\sigma_0, \sigma, \rho, \gamma) = \rho$
- $\mathcal{V}[\![M]\!](\sigma_0, \sigma, \rho, \gamma) = \gamma(M)$ for $M \in MVAR$

Furthermore,

- $(\sigma_0, \sigma, \rho, \gamma) \models \exists M \cdot \varphi$ iff there is some $\hat{\rho}$ such that $(\sigma_0, \sigma, \rho, (\gamma : M \mapsto \hat{\rho})) \models \varphi$

and if $var_0(\varphi) = \emptyset$ then $(\sigma_0, \sigma, \rho, \gamma) \models \varphi$ iff $(\sigma, \rho, \gamma) \models \varphi$ according to the definition (Section 5.2.3).

These additions lead to a slightly different definition of the validity of a correctness formula.

Definition 8.3 (*Valid correctness formula*) If $X \in VAR^*$ is the list of all variables $x \in var(A)$ and X_0 is the corresponding list of terms x_0, the correctness formula $\langle\langle A \rangle\rangle \; \text{P} \; \langle\langle C \rangle\rangle$ is *valid*, $\models \langle\langle A \rangle\rangle \; \text{P} \; \langle\langle C \rangle\rangle$, iff for all γ and σ_0 and any σ and ρ with $(\sigma, \rho) \in \mathcal{M}[\![P]\!](\sigma_0)$:

$$(\sigma_0, \sigma, \rho, \gamma) \models A[X_0/X, now_0/now] \rightarrow C$$

$\diamond$

If $var_0(C) = \emptyset$ then this reduces to the original definition. In this chapter, all program variables are assumed to be local.

8.2   Formalizing a failure hypothesis

A failure hypothesis χ of program P is a predicate relating the normal and acceptable executions of P. To define such a predicate, we extend the assertion language with the special variables now_{nml} and R_{nml}, and associate with each term x the term x_{nml}.

R, *now* and x refer to an observation of P, possibly afflicted by faults. Since our task is to show that a system tolerates the abnormal behaviour of its components to the extent expressed by the failure hypothesis, R, *now* and x refer to an observation of P that is *acceptable* with respect to χ.

On the other hand, R_{nml}, now_{nml} and x_{nml} refer to a normal observation of P. For example, x_{nml} refers to the value of the program variable x in the final state of a normal execution, while x denotes its value in the final state of an acceptable execution. Note that the state in which an execution is started is not affected by faults occurring later in the execution.

For instance, consider the program $INC : x := x + 1$, which may be subject to a stuck-at-zero-fault in the hardware which does not affect the execution time (i.e. $now = now_{nml}$) but causes the final value of x to be zero (i.e. $x = x_{nml} \lor x = 0$). This is defined in the failure hypothesis *StuckAtZero*.

$$StuckAtZero \equiv (x = x_{nml} \lor x = 0) \land now = now_{nml} \land R = R_{nml}$$

Note: This formalization does not depend on what the final value of x ought to be. $\diamond$

If the mapping R has x as an observable, the clause $R = R_{nml}$ will be unrealistic. In such a case, the failure hypothesis should show that there may be a time during the execution at which x becomes and remains zero. As mentioned before, in this chapter program variables are not observable.

Note: We shall assume that communication channels and lines are not prone to failure and that the axiomatization of their properties, given in Chapter 5, still applies. $\diamond$

Sentences of the extended assertion language are called transformation expressions, typically denoted by ψ. Let $var_{nml}(\psi)$ denote those variables $x \in VAR$ for which there is a corresponding x_{nml} in ψ. A transformation expression is interpreted with respect to a tuple:

$$(\sigma_0, \sigma_{nml}, \sigma, \rho_{nml}, \rho, \gamma)$$

where the state σ_{nml} is used to evaluate the terms x_{nml}, the mapping ρ_{nml} gives R_{nml} its value and, as before, the state σ_0 is used to evaluate the terms x_0, the state σ interprets the terms x, the mapping ρ gives R its value and the environment γ interprets the logical variables:

- $\mathcal{V}[\![x_{nml}]\!](\sigma_0, \sigma_{nml}, \sigma, \rho_{nml}, \rho, \gamma) = \sigma_{nml}(x)$ for $x \in VAR$
- $\mathcal{V}[\![x]\!](\sigma_0, \sigma_{nml}, \sigma, \rho_{nml}, \rho, \gamma) = \sigma(x)$ for $x \in VAR$
- $\mathcal{V}[\![R_{nml}]\!](\sigma_0, \sigma_{nml}, \sigma, \rho_{nml}, \rho, \gamma) = \rho_{nml}$

- $\mathcal{V}[\![R]\!](\sigma_0, \sigma_{nml}, \sigma, \rho_{nml}, \rho, \gamma) = \rho$

$O @_{nml} t$ will be used as an abbreviation for $O \in R_{nml}(t)$, etc.

Since R_{nml}, now_{nml}, and x_{nml} do not appear in assertions, the following lemma is trivial.

Lemma 8.1 (*Correspondence*) For an assertion φ,

$$(\sigma_0, \sigma_{nml}, \sigma, \rho_{nml}, \rho, \gamma) \models \varphi \text{ iff } (\sigma_0, \sigma, \rho, \gamma) \models \varphi$$

$\square$

Definition 8.4 (*Valid transformation expression*) A transformation expression ψ is *valid*, $\models \psi$, iff for all σ_0, σ_{nml}, σ, ρ_{nml}, ρ and γ, it is the case that $(\sigma_0, \sigma_{nml}, \sigma, \rho_{nml}, \rho, \gamma) \models \psi$.

$\Diamond$

A *failure hypothesis* χ is a transformation expression which respects the communication and invariance properties defined in Chapter 5. Thus, a failure hypothesis will not allow the derivation of properties which violate those defined earlier, e.g. $send(c) @ 3 \wedge waitrec(c) @ 3$ or $now = \infty \rightarrow x = 5$.

Definition 8.5 (*Failure hypothesis*) A *failure hypothesis* χ guarantees that the normal behaviour is part of the acceptable behaviour and thus χ is a reflexive relation on the normal behaviour:

$$\models \chi \rightarrow \chi[X_{nml}/X, now_{nml}/now, R_{nml}/R]$$

where X is a list of the variables $x \in var(\chi)$ and X_{nml} is the corresponding list of terms x_{nml}.

No failure can occur before the program starts execution, or after its termination. So χ must ensure that R equals R_{nml} before the start of the execution and χ does not restrict the behaviour after termination:

$$\models \chi \rightarrow R \downarrow [0, now_0] = R_{nml} \downarrow [0, now_0]$$

and

$$\models \chi \rightarrow \forall M \cdot (M \downarrow [0, now] = R \downarrow [0, now] \rightarrow \chi[M/R])$$

$\Diamond$

$P \wr \chi$ represents the execution of program P under the assumption χ. The observations of the failure prone process $FP \wr \chi$ are those that are related by χ to the observations of FP:

$$\mathcal{M}[\![FP \wr \chi]\!](\sigma_0) = \{ (\sigma, \rho) \in MOD \mid \text{ there exists a } (\sigma_{nml}, \rho_{nml}) \in \mathcal{M}[\![FP]\!](\sigma_0)$$
$$\text{such that for all } \gamma$$
$$(\sigma_0, \sigma_{nml}, \sigma, \rho_{nml}, \rho, \gamma) \models \chi \}$$

The set $\mathcal{M}[\![FP \wr \chi]\!](\sigma_0)$ represents the acceptable behaviour of FP under the failure hypothesis χ, which is the *normal* behaviour of the failure prone program $FP \wr \chi$.

Transformation expressions can be functionally composed.

Definition 8.6   (*Composite transformation expression*) If $X \in VAR^*$ is the list of all $x \in$ *VAR* such that $x \in var(\chi_1) \cap var_{nml}(\chi_2)$, X_{nml} is the corresponding list of terms x_{nml} and *V* is a list of fresh logical value variables of the same length as X, then a composite transformation expression $\chi_1 \wr \chi_2$ is

$$\chi_1 \wr \chi_2 \equiv \exists t, V, M \cdot (\chi_1[V/X, t/now, M/R] \wedge \chi_2[V/X_{nml}, t/now_{nml}, M/R_{nml}])$$

$\diamond$

Thus $\chi_1 \wr \chi_2$ means the application of χ_1 and then χ_2.

Consider the transformation expressions $\chi_1 \equiv (x = x_{nml} \vee x = 0) \wedge (y = y_{nml} \vee y = 3)$ and $\chi_2 \equiv (y = y_{nml} \vee y = 1) \wedge (z = z_{nml} \vee z = 2)$. By definition,

$$\chi_1 \wr \chi_2 \equiv \exists v \cdot \quad (x = x_{nml} \vee x = 0) \wedge (v = y_{nml} \vee v = 3)$$
$$\wedge \quad (y = v \vee y = 1) \wedge (z = z_{nml} \vee z = 2)$$

that is, $\chi_1 \wr \chi_2 \equiv (x = x_{nml} \vee x = 0) \wedge (y = y_{nml} \vee y = 1 \vee y = 3) \wedge (z = z_{nml} \vee z = 2)$

The operator χ will also be used to compose assertions and transformation expressions, e.g. $\varphi \wr \chi$, in commitments. If $X \in VAR^*$ is a list of all $x \in var_{nml}(\chi)$, X_{nml} the corresponding list of terms x_{nml} and *V* is a list of fresh logical value variables of the same length as X, then the composite expression $\varphi \wr \chi$ is equivalent to

$$\exists t, V, M \cdot (\varphi[V/X, t/now, M/R] \wedge \chi[V/X_{nml}, t/now_{nml}, M/R_{nml}])$$

This replaces all terms x_{nml} that occur in χ by logical value variables. And since φ is an assertion, R_{nml}, now_{nml} and the terms x_{nml} do not appear in φ and the composite expression $\varphi \wr \chi$ is also an assertion.

Since the interpretation of assertions has not changed, the validity of a correctness formula $\langle\langle A \rangle\rangle$ FP $\langle\langle C \rangle\rangle$ remains as defined in Section 8.1.

8.3   A proof rule for failure prone processes

An assumption *A* may refer to actions that occur during the execution of a program. Since faults can affect those occurrences, assumptions should not place restrictions on observable events beyond the starting time. Let

$$NonProphetic(\varphi) \equiv \varphi \rightarrow \forall M \cdot (M \downarrow [0, now] = R \downarrow [0, now] \rightarrow \varphi[M/R])$$

Then the acceptable behaviour of a process is given in terms of its normal behaviour and a predicate representing the failure hypothesis.

Rule. 8.1   (*Failure hypothesis introduction*)

$$\frac{\langle\langle A \rangle\rangle \text{ FP } \langle\langle C \rangle\rangle , \; NonProphetic(A)}{\langle\langle A \rangle\rangle \text{ FP} \wr \chi \; \langle\langle C \wr \chi \rangle\rangle}$$

Soundness and completeness of this rule are proved in Section 8.5.

Example 8.1 If the program INC terminates after three and within at most five time units, it can be shown that it satisfies

$$\langle\langle now < \infty \rangle\rangle \text{ INC } \langle\langle x = x_0 + 1 \wedge now_0 + 3 < now < now_0 + 5 \rangle\rangle$$

Since *NonProphetic*($now < \infty$), the failure hypothesis introduction rule gives

$$\langle\langle now < \infty \rangle\rangle \text{ INC} \wr \textit{StuckAtZero} \langle\langle \exists t, v \cdot \quad v = x_0 + 1$$
$$\wedge\, now_0 + 3 < t < now_0 + 5$$
$$\wedge\, (x = v \vee x = 0) \wedge now = t \rangle\rangle$$

i.e.

$$\langle\langle now < \infty \rangle\rangle \text{ INC} \wr \textit{StuckAtZero} \langle\langle \quad x = x_0 + 1 \vee x = 0$$
$$\wedge\, now_0 + 3 < now < now_0 + 5 \rangle\rangle$$

Example 8.2 Consider the program F with specification

$$\langle\langle \texttt{true} \rangle\rangle \text{ F } \langle\langle \forall t < \infty, v \cdot rec(\texttt{in}, v) \,@\, t$$
$$\rightarrow (\neg waitsend(\texttt{out})) \textbf{ during } [t, t + T_{comp})$$
$$\wedge\, await\,send(\texttt{out}, f(v)) \,@\, t + T_{comp} \rangle\rangle$$

Suppose, due to faults, that the computation time increases by a factor Δ. For the sake of simplicity, let us assume that the individual inputs are far enough apart in time not to be influenced by this (i.e. $rec(\texttt{in}, v) \,@_{nml}\, t \leftrightarrow rec(\texttt{in}, v) \,@\, t$). Then, faults only affect the willingness of the process to perform an out communication, i.e.

$$(\neg waitsend(\texttt{out})) \textbf{ during }_{nml} [t_1, t_2) \leftrightarrow (\neg waitsend(\texttt{out})) \textbf{ during } [t_1, t_2 + \Delta)$$

and

$$await\,send(\texttt{out}, v) \,@_{nml}\, t \leftrightarrow await\,send(\texttt{out}, v) \,@\, t + \Delta$$

Formally,

$$\textit{Slow} \equiv \forall t < \infty, v \cdot (rec(\texttt{in}, v) \,@_{nml}\, t \leftrightarrow rec(\texttt{in}, v) \,@\, t)$$
$$\wedge\, \forall t_1, t_2 < \infty \cdot (\neg waitsend(\texttt{out})) \textbf{ during }_{nml} [t_1, t_2)$$
$$\leftrightarrow (\neg waitsend(\texttt{out})) \textbf{ during } [t_1, t_2 + \Delta)$$
$$\wedge\, \forall t < \infty, v \cdot await\,send(\texttt{out}, v) \,@_{nml}\, t$$
$$\leftrightarrow await\,send(\texttt{out}, v) \,@\, t + \Delta$$

Notice that this formalization is transparent to the original computation time and the computed function.

Since *NonProphetic*(true), the failure hypothesis introduction rule yields

$\langle\langle\text{true}\rangle\rangle$
$\text{F}\wr Slow$
$\langle\langle\exists M\cdot\forall t<\infty, v\cdot rec(\text{in},v)\,@_M t$
$\qquad\qquad \rightarrow(\neg waitsend(\text{out}))\;\textbf{during}\,_M[t,t+T_{comp})$
$\qquad\qquad\qquad \wedge\,await\,send(\text{out},f(v))\,@_M t+T_{comp}$
$\qquad \wedge\,\forall t<\infty, v\cdot(rec(\text{in},v)\,@_M t\leftrightarrow rec(\text{in},v)\,@\,t)$
$\qquad \wedge\,\forall t_1,t_2<\infty\cdot(\neg waitsend(\text{out}))\;\textbf{during}\,_M[t_1,t_2)$
$\qquad\qquad\qquad \leftrightarrow(\neg waitsend(\text{out}))\;\textbf{during}\,[t_1,t_2+\Delta)$
$\qquad \wedge\,\forall t<\infty, v\cdot await\,send(\text{out},v)\,@_M t$
$\qquad\qquad\qquad \leftrightarrow await\,send(\text{out},v)\,@\,t+\Delta\rangle\rangle$

or, equivalently,

$\langle\langle\text{true}\rangle\rangle\,\text{F}\wr Slow\,\langle\langle\forall t<\infty, v\cdot rec(\text{in},v)\,@\,t$
$\quad \rightarrow(\neg waitsend(\text{out}))\;\textbf{during}\,[t,t+T_{\text{comp}}+\Delta)$
$\quad \wedge\,await\,send(\text{out},f(v))\,@\,t+T_{\text{comp}}+\Delta\rangle\rangle$

8.4   Reliability of the mine pump

We shall now look more closely at the components of the mine pump system that are prone to failure:

. The sensors may provide incorrect readings or readings.
. The pump may break down.
. The pump controller may fail to switch the pump on when the water level is high, or off when the methane level reaches the danger threshold.
. The communication lines between various components may be broken.

Note that there is no observable difference between a component with a broken communication line and a non-responding component. (We do not consider here the communication errors that may occur in practice: see Exercises 8.3 and 8.4 for a number of fault models that apply to communication media.)

Given these sources of failure, the most important task is to make sure that explosions do not occur. Therefore, we have to guarantee that the pump is never working when the methane level is high, even if this means losing a shift. We will successively deal with unreliable sensors, unreliable pumps and unreliable pump controllers. Finally, we will demonstrate that with the measures taken the operation of the mine is indeed safe.

8.4.1   Unreliable sensors

A defective sensor may produce incorrect readings, or no readings at all. So the only means of failure detection is by replication and comparison. Let each sensor be replaced

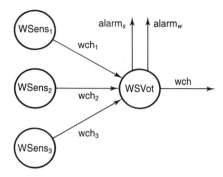

Figure 8.1 A triplicate water level sensor

by three sensors, using triple modular redundancy. A 'voter' component can then detect only that a single sensor or its line has failed since these failures will be indistinguishable.

Figure 8.1 shows the resulting system for a water level sensor. Assume that the line between the voter and the pump controller can be considered to be fault-free because of the short distance. For simplicity, assume that the voter never fails.

An *unreliable* sensor can:

1. send correct readings, and in time,
2. send incorrect readings, but in time, or
3. send no readings at all.

(3) occurs also when the sensor that produced incorrect readings is being replaced. Let the following abbreviations be used for each of these conditions. For $k = 1, 2, 3$:

$$SensOK(\mathtt{wch}_k) \,@\, t \;\equiv\; R \downarrow \{\mathtt{wch}_k\}(t) = R_{nml} \downarrow \{\mathtt{wch}_k\}(t)$$

$$SensFaulty(\mathtt{wch}_k) \,@\, t \equiv R \downarrow \{\mathtt{wch}_k\}(t) = \emptyset \wedge \neg send(\mathtt{wch}_k) \,@_{nml}\, t$$
$$\vee \, send(\mathtt{wch}_k) \,@\, t \wedge send(\mathtt{wch}_k) \,@_{nml}\, t$$

$$SensNC(\mathtt{wch}_k) \,@\, t \;\equiv\; R \downarrow \{\mathtt{wch}_k\}(t) = \emptyset$$

Note: These predicates do not exclude each other because it is not always possible to tell whether or not a device is in sound working order. $\diamond$

Then the failure hypothesis *UnRel* is

$$UnRel(\mathtt{wch}_k) \equiv \forall t < \infty \cdot \; SensOK(\mathtt{wch}_k) \,@\, t$$
$$\vee \, SensFaulty(\mathtt{wch}_k) \,@\, t$$
$$\vee \, SensNC(\mathtt{wch}_k) \,@\, t$$
$$\wedge \mathtt{wl}(t) = \mathtt{wl}_{nml}(t)$$

(Although this definition is sufficient for our purposes here, it can be easily adapted to express *quantitative* requirements, such as the mean time between failures and the mean time to repair.)

The voter should produce a reading at least once every Δ_{ws} time units. Since voting will take some time, we require the sensors to send a reading within the first δ_{ws} time units of each Δ_{ws} period, where $\delta_{ws} < \Delta_{ws}$:

$$WSensC_1(\texttt{wch}_k) \equiv \forall i \cdot send(\texttt{wch}_k) \textbf{ in } [i\Delta_{ws}, i\Delta_{ws} + \delta_{ws}]$$

As before, we assume that a correct reading does not differ too much from the actual level, i.e. that the error is bounded by some value ε_{ws}:

$$WSensC_2(\texttt{wch}_k) \equiv \forall t < \infty, v \cdot \ send(\texttt{wch}_k, v) @ t$$
$$\rightarrow v - \varepsilon_{ws} \le \texttt{wl}(t) \le v + \varepsilon_{ws}$$

Define $WSensC(\texttt{wch}_k) \equiv WSensC_1(\texttt{wch}_k) \wedge WSensC_2(\texttt{wch}_k)$. Then, for $k = 1, 2, 3$,

$$\langle\langle now = 0 \rangle\rangle \ \texttt{WSens}_k \ \langle\langle WSensC(\texttt{wch}_k) \rangle\rangle \tag{8.1}$$

Because no two sensors are identical, their readings may differ slightly, even when taken at the same time. Assume that the voter $\texttt{WSVot}$ takes the average of the two closest values (the so-called *inexact* voting). If the reading of one sensor differs substantially from those of the other two, the voter calls for maintenance on the channel $\texttt{alarm}_s$ by asynchronously sending the identification number of the faulty sensor. Notice that this method only works provided the voter receives at least two correct readings in time.

Failure of a sensor reading to arrive may be due to a defective sensor, or a broken line. Given $CWSens_1$, this absence can easily be detected. A call for maintenance can then be sent on the channel $\texttt{alarm}_{\overline{w}}$.

During the first δ_{ws} of each Δ_{ws} interval, the voter $\texttt{WSVot}$ is always willing to receive one reading from each sensor:

$$WSVotC_1 \equiv \forall i, k \in \{1, 2, 3\} \cdot waitrec(\texttt{wch}_k) \textbf{ during } [i\Delta_{ws}, i\Delta_{ws} + \delta_{ws}]$$
$$\vee \ \exists t, v \cdot i\Delta_{ws} \le t < i\Delta_{ws} + \delta_{ws}$$
$$\wedge waitrec(\texttt{wch}_k) \textbf{ during } [i\Delta_{ws}, t)$$
$$\wedge rec(\texttt{wch}_k, v) @ t$$
$$\wedge (\neg rec(\texttt{wch}_k)) \textbf{ during } (t, i\Delta_{ws} + \delta_{ws}]$$

We have to assume that there are at least two correct readings for each vote. Then inexact voting can be considered as applying a function *InexactVote* which takes three inputs. The *result* part of the outcome is the average of the two values that are closest to each another; the *dissent* part is either zero or identifies the value that differs substantially from the other two. Let the application of the function take $T_{InexactVote}$ time units which is small enough to guarantee that the voter can produce a reading before the end of the Δ_{ws} interval, i.e. $\delta_{ws} + T_{InexactVote}$ is smaller than Δ_{ws}. The voter produces output as soon as possible, i.e.

1. if all three readings get through in time, $T_{InexactVote}$ time units after the last vote is received, and

2. if only two readings get through in time, $T_{InexactVote}$ time units after the δ_{ws} window closes; in this case, by our assumption, these readings are correct. Let the distinguished value † stand for the missing value when applying *InexactVote*.

Thus:

$$
\begin{aligned}
WSVotC_2 \equiv{} & \forall i, t < \infty, v \cdot send(\texttt{wch}, v) \,@\, i\Delta_{ws} + t \\
& \leftrightarrow \exists t_1, t_2, t_3, v_1, v_2, v_3 \cdot \\
& \quad \wedge_{k=1}^{3}\, 0 \le t_k \le \delta_{ws} \\
& \quad \wedge_{k=1}^{3}\, rec(\texttt{wch}_k, v_k) \,@\, i\Delta_{ws} + t_k \\
& \quad \wedge v = result(InexactVote(v_1, v_2, v_3)) \\
& \quad \wedge t = max(t_1, t_2, t_3) + T_{InexactVote} \\
& \vee \exists t_1, t_2, v_1, v_2, k, l, m \cdot \\
& \quad \wedge_{k=1}^{2}\, 0 \le t_k \le \delta_{ws} \\
& \quad \wedge k \neq l \wedge k \neq m \wedge l \neq m \\
& \quad \wedge rec(\texttt{wch}_k, v_1) \,@\, i\Delta_{ws} + t_1 \\
& \quad \wedge rec(\texttt{wch}_l, v_2) \,@\, i\Delta_{ws} + t_2 \\
& \quad \wedge waitrec(\texttt{wch}_m) \textbf{ during } [i\Delta_{ws}, i\Delta_{ws} + \delta_{ws}] \\
& \quad \wedge v = result(InexactVote(v_1, v_2, \dagger)) \\
& \quad \wedge t = \delta_{ws} + T_{InexactVote}
\end{aligned}
$$

The voter calls for maintenance only when necessary, and then as soon as possible:

1. When one sensor's reading differs too much from the readings of the other two, the voter sends this sensor's identity along the channel $\texttt{alarm}_\texttt{s}$ in $T_{InexactVote}$ time units after the last vote is received.
2. When one sensor's reading does not get through, the voter sends this wire's identity along the channel $\texttt{alarm}_\texttt{w}$ in T_{NoVote} time units after the δ_{ws} window closes, where $T_{NoVote} < T_{InexactVote}$.

This is defined as follows:

$$
\begin{aligned}
WSVotC_3 \equiv{} & \forall i, t < \infty, v \cdot send(\texttt{alarm}_\texttt{s}, v) \,@\, i\Delta_{ws} + t \\
& \leftrightarrow \exists t_1, t_2, t_3, v_1, v_2, v_3 \cdot \\
& \quad \wedge_{k=1}^{3}\, 0 \le t_k \le \delta_{ws} \\
& \quad \wedge_{k=1}^{3}\, rec(\texttt{wch}_k, v_k) \,@\, i\Delta_{ws} + t_k \\
& \quad \wedge v = dissent(InexactVote(v_1, v_2, v_3)) \neq 0 \\
& \quad \wedge t = max(t_1, t_2, t_3) + T_{InexactVote} \\
& \wedge send(\texttt{alarm}_\texttt{w}, v) \,@\, i\Delta_{ws} + t \\
& \quad \leftrightarrow waitrec(\texttt{wch}_v) \textbf{ during } [i\Delta_{ws}, i\Delta_{ws} + \delta_{ws}] \\
& \quad \wedge t = \delta_{ws} + T_{NoVote}
\end{aligned}
$$

Define $WSVotC \equiv WSVotC_1 \wedge WSVotC_2 \wedge WSVotC_3$ Then,

$$\langle\langle now = 0 \rangle\rangle \;\texttt{WSVot}\; \langle\langle WSVotC \rangle\rangle \tag{8.2}$$

It can be shown, after the manner of Chapter 5, that there does indeed exist a voter $\texttt{WSVot}$ for which $\langle\langle now = 0 \rangle\rangle \;\texttt{WSVot}\; \langle\langle WSVotC \rangle\rangle$; we leave this as an exercise (Exercise 8.6).

Readings are available from at least two of the three sensors for each vote:

$$UnRel^{\leq 1} \equiv \wedge_{k=1}^{3} UnRel(\mathtt{wch}_k)$$
$$\wedge \forall i \cdot \exists k \neq l \in \{1,2,3\}.$$
$$SensOK(\mathtt{wch}_k) \textbf{ during } [i\Delta_{ws}, i\Delta_{ws} + \delta_{ws}]$$
$$\wedge SensOK(\mathtt{wch}_l) \textbf{ during } [i\Delta_{ws}, i\Delta_{ws} + \delta_{ws}]$$

Note: If one sensor has already been reported as faulty, it would be possible also to tolerate incorrect readings from another sensor if, for example, the voter selects the more pessimistic of the readings of these two sensors (for the methane level, for instance, this is the higher reading). ◇

The term *now* does not occur in $WSensC(\mathtt{wch}_k)$, $k = 1, 2, 3$, so by applying the proof rule for parallel composition we obtain from (8.1):

$$\langle\!\langle now = 0 \rangle\!\rangle \, \mathtt{WSens}_1 \|\mathtt{WSens}_2\|\mathtt{WSens}_3 \, \langle\!\langle \wedge_{k=1}^{3} WSensC(\mathtt{wch}_k) \rangle\!\rangle$$

Clearly, $NonProphetic(now = 0)$. Hence, by the rule for failure hypothesis introduction, we may conclude that

$$\langle\!\langle now = 0 \rangle\!\rangle \, (\mathtt{WSens}_1 \|\mathtt{WSens}_2\|\mathtt{WSens}_3) \wr UnRel^{\leq 1} \, \langle\!\langle UnrelWSensC \rangle\!\rangle \qquad (8.3)$$

where

$$UnrelWSensC \equiv \exists N \cdot \quad (\wedge_{k=1}^{3} WSensC(\mathtt{wch}_k))[N/R]$$
$$\wedge UnRel^{\leq 1}[N/R_{nml}]$$

We can now prove that, even in the presence of faults, at least two correct readings are produced every Δ_{ws} time units.

Lemma 8.2 $UnrelWSensC \quad \rightarrow \quad \forall i \cdot \exists k \neq l \cdot (WSC(\mathtt{wch}_k) \wedge WSC(\mathtt{wch}_l))$ where

$$WSC(\mathtt{wch}_k) \equiv \quad send(\mathtt{wch}_k) \textbf{ in } [i\Delta_{ws}, i\Delta_{ws} + \delta_{ws}]$$
$$\wedge \forall t \in [i\Delta_{ws}, i\Delta_{ws} + \delta_{ws}] \cdot \quad send(\mathtt{wch}_k, v) @ t$$
$$\rightarrow v - \varepsilon_{ws} \leq \mathtt{wl}(t) \leq v + \varepsilon_{ws}$$

Proof: Assume $UnrelWSensC$, i.e. assume that there exists an N such that

$$(\wedge_{k=1}^{3} WSensC(\mathtt{wch}_k))[N/R] \wedge UnRel^{\leq 1}[N/R_{nml}] \qquad (8.4)$$

By $(\wedge_{k=1}^{3} WSensC(\mathtt{wch}_k))[N/R]$, we obtain

$$\forall k \in \{1,2,3\} \cdot \quad \forall i \cdot send(\mathtt{wch}_k) \textbf{ in}_N [i\Delta_{ws}, i\Delta_{ws} + \delta_{ws}] \qquad (8.5)$$
$$\wedge \forall t < \infty, v \cdot \quad send(\mathtt{wch}_k, v) @_N t$$
$$\rightarrow v - \varepsilon_{ws} \leq \mathtt{wl}(t) \leq v + \varepsilon_{ws}$$

By $UnRel^{\leq 1}[N/R_{nml}]$, we know that

$$\forall i \cdot \exists k \neq l \cdot \forall \; t \in [i\Delta_{ws}, i\Delta_{ws} + \delta_{ws}], v \cdot \qquad (8.6)$$
$$send(\mathtt{wch}_k, v) @_N t \quad \leftrightarrow \quad send(\mathtt{wch}_k, v) @ t$$
$$\wedge send(\mathtt{wch}_l, v) @_N t \quad \leftrightarrow \quad send(\mathtt{wch}_l, v) @ t$$

The lemma follows from (8.4), (8.5), and (8.6). $\square$

By the rule for parallel composition, and (8.3) and (8.2), we know that for

$$\texttt{TripleWSens} \equiv ((\texttt{WSens}_1 \| \texttt{WSens}_2 \| \texttt{WSens}_3) \wr UnRel^{\leq 1}) \| \texttt{WSVot}$$

it is the case that

$$\langle\!\langle now = 0 \rangle\!\rangle \texttt{ TripleWSens } \langle\!\langle UnrelWSensC \wedge WSVotC \rangle\!\rangle$$

The next step is to prove that $\texttt{TripleWSens}$ still produces output at least once every Δ_{ws} time units, but that the time taken for voting causes the δ_{ws} window to increase by $\text{T}_{InexactVote}$ time units.

Lemma 8.3 $\langle\!\langle now = 0 \rangle\!\rangle \texttt{ TripleWSens } \langle\!\langle WSensC_1(\texttt{wch})[\delta_{ws} + \text{T}_{InexactVote}/\delta_{ws}] \rangle\!\rangle$

Proof: By the consequence rule, we need to prove that

$$(UnrelWSensC \wedge WSVotC) \quad \rightarrow \quad WSensC_1(\texttt{wch})[\delta_{ws} + \text{T}_{InexactVote}/\delta_{ws}]$$

Therefore, assume that $UnrelWSensC \wedge WSVotC$, or, consequently,

$$UnrelWSensC \wedge WSVotC_1 \wedge WSVotC_2 \tag{8.7}$$

By $UnrelWSensC$ and Lemma 8.2, we obtain

$$\forall i \cdot \exists k \neq l \cdot \quad \begin{aligned} send(\texttt{wch}_k) &\quad \textbf{in} \quad [i\Delta_{ws}, i\Delta_{ws} + \delta_{ws}] \\ \wedge\, send(\texttt{wch}_l) &\quad \textbf{in} \quad [i\Delta_{ws}, i\Delta_{ws} + \delta_{ws}] \end{aligned}$$

By $WSVotC_1$ from (8.7), this leads to

$$\forall i \cdot \exists k \neq l \cdot \quad \begin{aligned} rec(\texttt{wch}_k) &\quad \textbf{in} \quad [i\Delta_{ws}, i\Delta_{ws} + \delta_{ws}] \\ \wedge\, rec(\texttt{wch}_l) &\quad \textbf{in} \quad [i\Delta_{ws}, i\Delta_{ws} + \delta_{ws}] \end{aligned} \tag{8.8}$$

Independently of whether or not

$$\wedge_{k=1}^{3}\, rec(\texttt{wch}_k)\, \textbf{in}\, [i\Delta_{ws}, i\Delta_{ws} + \delta_{ws}]$$

holds for a particular i, we know from $WSVotC_2$ in (8.7) and (8.8) that there exists a $t \leq \delta_{ws} + \text{T}_{InexactVote}$ such that $send(\texttt{wch}) @ i\Delta_{ws} + t$ Consequently,

$$\forall i \cdot send(\texttt{wch})\, \textbf{in}\, [i\Delta_{ws}, i\Delta_{ws} + \delta_{ws} + \text{T}_{InexactVote}]$$

$\square$

The following lemma states that due to delays caused by the voting, the reading error can increase by as much as $\widehat{\varepsilon_{ws}} = \lambda_{in}^{max}(\frac{3}{2}\delta_{ws} + \text{T}_{InexactVote})$.

Lemma 8.4 $\langle\!\langle now = 0 \rangle\!\rangle \texttt{ TripleWSens } \langle\!\langle WSensC_2(\texttt{wch})[\varepsilon_{ws} + \widehat{\varepsilon_{ws}}/\varepsilon_{ws}] \rangle\!\rangle.$

Proof: We leave this as an exercise (Exercise 8.7).

Hence, by Lemmas 8.3 and 8.4:

$$\langle\!\langle now = 0 \rangle\!\rangle \texttt{ TripleWSens } \langle\!\langle WSensC(\texttt{wch})[\ \delta_{ws} + \text{T}_{InexactVote}/\delta_{ws}, \tag{8.9}$$
$$\varepsilon_{ws} + \widehat{\varepsilon_{ws}}/\varepsilon_{ws}] \rangle\!\rangle$$

One effect of triple modular redundancy is that it results in less accurate readings. Since the original requirement is for at least one reading every Δ_{ws} time units, the increase of the δ_{ws} window is not a problem.

8.4.2   An unreliable pump

If the pump breaks down while running, the outflow drops to zero within some δ_{bd} time units. For simplicity, let us assume that δ_{bd} equals δ_p (see Chapter 5). Malfunctioning of the pump may also mean that there is no outflow when the pump is activated. Suppose that, due to the space limitations in the mine shaft, the pump cannot be replicated and that a defective pump must be replaced. During such a replacement, work can continue in the mine until the water level rises above a limit.

One way to monitor the proper functioning of a pump is to look for a reduction in the water level. But, in practice, the feedback would be too slow to be of much use. So to detect a defective pump we add a water flow sensor to monitor the pump's outflow. This sensor is also triplicated.

Failure of the pump to start, or to stop, can be due to a broken control channel. A pump that will not stop is a hazard as it can burn out if there is no water to pump, or cause an explosion if the methane level is critical. A broken control channel can be detected indirectly using the water flow sensors.

Typically, a pump is switched on by energizing a relay. To model this, we replace the channel pch by the line pln (see Section 5.4.3). Let pln(*texp*) represent the voltage level of the line pln at time *texp*. Assume that the line pln is either *high* (i.e. pln = 1), or *low* (i.e. pln = 0). Assume also that the voltage level drops to zero if the wire is broken. This provides a *fail-safe* system: if the wire is broken, the relay is not energized and the pump stops within δ_p time units.

Let the maximum outflow of the pump be λ_{out}^{max} (see Chapter 5):

$$PumpC_1 \equiv \forall t < \infty \cdot 0 \leq \texttt{outflow}(t) < \lambda_{out}^{max}$$

The delays in switching the relay on or off are usually insignificant when compared to the pump's reaction time of δ_p. Consequently, we can safely assume that the pump starts within δ_p time units of the line pln becoming high:

$$PumpC_2 \equiv \forall t_1, t_2 < \infty \cdot \ \texttt{pln} = 1 \textbf{ during } (t_1, t_2]$$
$$\rightarrow \texttt{outflow} \geq \lambda_{out}^{min} \textbf{ during } [t_1 + \delta_p, t_2]$$

Similarly, assume that the pump stops within δ_p time units after the line pln becomes low:

$$PumpC_3 \equiv \forall t_1, t_2 < \infty \cdot \ \texttt{pln} = 0 \textbf{ during } (t_1, t_2]$$
$$\rightarrow \texttt{outflow} = 0 \textbf{ during } [t_1 + \delta_p, t_2]$$

We specify that no explosion will occur if the methane level is below the critical level CML, or if the pump has been switched off (see Chapter 5):

$$PumpC_4 \equiv \forall t < \infty \cdot \ \texttt{ml}(t) < \texttt{CML} \vee \exists t_0 \leq t - \delta_p \cdot \texttt{pln} = 0 \textbf{ during } [t_0, t]$$
$$\rightarrow \neg \texttt{expl} @ t$$

Let $PumpC \equiv PumpC_1 \wedge PumpC_2 \wedge PumpC_3 \wedge PumpC_4$. The perfect pump is then defined as

$$\langle\langle now = 0 \rangle\rangle \ \texttt{Pump} \ \langle\langle PumpC \rangle\rangle \tag{8.10}$$

The following lemma, which is easily proved by *reductio ad absurdum*, states that the pump does not start spontaneously.

Lemma 8.5 $\models PumpC \rightarrow \forall t < \infty \cdot$ $\text{outflow}(t) > 0$
$$\rightarrow \neg (\text{pln} = 0 \ \textbf{during} \ (t - \delta_p, t])$$

Define

- $PumpOK @ t \equiv \text{outflow}(t) = \text{outflow}_{nml}(t)$
- $PumpNotOK @ t \equiv \text{outflow}(t) < \text{outflow}_{nml}(t) \lor \text{outflow}(t) = 0$

The way in which specification (8.10) is weakened due to the possible occurrence of faults must be defined in a failure hypothesis, and this appears below as *NoFlow*. First, when a pump breaks down its outflow becomes zero within δ_p time units. Then, failure detection and replacement of a defective pump takes at least T_{Repair} time units and the new pump produces the same outflow as a normal pump within δ_p time units:

$$
\begin{aligned}
NoFlow \equiv \forall t < \infty \cdot\ & (PumpOK \lor PumpNotOK) @ t \\
& \land \text{outflow}(t) = \text{outflow}_{nml}(t) \\
& \rightarrow \exists t_1 > t \cdot \text{outflow} < \text{outflow}_{nml} \ \textbf{during} \ (t, t_1) \\
& \quad \rightarrow \text{outflow} = 0 \ \textbf{during} \ [t + \delta_p, t + \delta_p + \text{T}_{Repair}) \\
& \land \exists t_1 < t \cdot \text{outflow} < \text{outflow}_{nml} \ \textbf{during} \ (t_1, t) \\
& \quad \rightarrow \text{outflow} = 0 \ \textbf{during} \ (t - \delta_p - \text{T}_{Repair}, t - \delta_p] \\
& \land \text{pln}(t) = \text{pln}_{nml}(t) \land \text{expl}(t) = \text{expl}_{nml}(t)
\end{aligned}
$$

Thus, $obs(NoFlow) = \{\text{expl}, \text{outflow}, \text{pln}\}$.

Note: This formalization holds for *all* behaviours, so it may not be illuminating in respect of specific behaviours. For example, the pln signal does not change, but there is no indication that a defective or disconnected pump reduces the water level. expl does not change because a pump, whether or not it is defective, can cause an explosion if pln is high, indicating that it has not been switched off. $\diamond$

Since *NonProphetic*($now = 0$), the failure hypothesis introduction rule yields

$$\langle\!\langle now = 0 \rangle\!\rangle \, \text{Pump} \, \langle \, NoFlow \, \langle\!\langle UnrelPumpC \rangle\!\rangle \tag{8.11}$$

where

$$UnrelPumpC \equiv \exists N \cdot (PumpC[N/R] \land NoFlow[N/R_{nml}])$$

Although the parameters δ_p and λ_{out}^{min} have little significance for an unreliable pump, the outflow is still bounded by λ_{out}^{max}.

Lemma 8.6 $\models UnrelPumpC \rightarrow \forall t < \infty \cdot 0 \leq \text{outflow}(t) < \lambda_{out}^{max}$

Proof: Suppose *UnrelPumpC*, i.e. suppose that there is an N such that

$$PumpC[N/R] \wedge NoFlow[N/R_{nml}] \tag{8.12}$$

Since $NoFlow[N/R_{nml}]$, we may conclude that

$$\forall t < \infty \cdot 0 \leq \texttt{outflow}(t) \leq \texttt{outflow}_N(t) \tag{8.13}$$

From (8.12), $PumpC[N/R]$, we know $PumpC_1[N/R]$, that is,

$$\forall t < \infty \cdot 0 \leq \texttt{outflow}_N(t) < \lambda_{out}^{max} \tag{8.14}$$

The lemma follows from (8.13) and (8.14). □

A more important property to establish is that even an unreliable pump does not start spontaneously.

Lemma 8.7
$$\models UnrelPumpC \rightarrow \forall t < \infty \cdot (\texttt{outflow}(t) > 0) \rightarrow \neg(\texttt{pln} = 0 \textbf{ during } (t - \delta_p, t])$$

Proof: Assume *UnrelPumpC*, i.e. assume that there exists an N for which

$$PumpC[N/R] \wedge NoFlow[N/R_{nml}] \tag{8.15}$$

Consider any $\widehat{t}$ such that

$$\texttt{outflow}(\widehat{t}) > 0 \tag{8.16}$$

Since, by (8.15), $NoFlow[N/R_{nml}]$, we may conclude that

$$\forall t < \infty \cdot \texttt{outflow}(t) \leq \texttt{outflow}_N(t) \tag{8.17}$$

and

$$\forall t < \infty \cdot \texttt{pln}(t) = \texttt{pln}_N(t) \tag{8.18}$$

By (8.16) and (8.17),

$$\texttt{outflow}_N(\widehat{t}) > 0 \tag{8.19}$$

By (8.15), $PumpC[N/R]$. Consequently, by (8.19) and Lemma 8.5, we may conclude that $\neg(\texttt{pln} = 0 \textbf{ during }_N (\widehat{t} - \delta_p, \widehat{t}])$, which, by (8.18), yields

$$\neg(\texttt{pln} = 0 \textbf{ during } (\widehat{t} - \delta_p, \widehat{t}])$$

□

Since faults affect only the outflow, the following lemma is obvious.

Lemma 8.8 $\quad UnrelPumpC \rightarrow PumpC_4$

8.4.3 An unreliable pump controller

The pump controller must monitor the pump's yield to detect a fault in the pump. Assume that a sensor `FSens` sets a line `flow` to one if there is some outflow from the pump, and to zero otherwise:

$$FSensC \equiv \forall t < \infty \cdot (\texttt{flow}(t) = 1 \;\leftrightarrow\; \texttt{outflow}(t) > 0)$$

Assume further that whenever a flow sensor breaks down, the value of the corresponding line drops to zero without delay:

- $FSensOK @ t \equiv \texttt{flow}(t) = \texttt{flow}_{nml}(t)$
- $FSensNotOK @ t \equiv \texttt{flow}(t) = 0$

The failure hypothesis *SensStuckAtZero* for the sensor is defined as follows:

$$SensStuckAtZero \equiv \forall t < \infty \cdot (FSensOK \vee FSensNotOK) @ t$$
$$\wedge \, \texttt{outflow}(t) = \texttt{outflow}_{nml}(t)$$

For reliability, the sensor is triplicated, $FSens_i \equiv FSens[\texttt{flow}_i/\texttt{flow}], i = 1, 2, 3$. A voter `FVot` sets the value of the line `flow`. Assume that the voting takes exactly T_{Vote} time units:

$$FVotC_1 \equiv \texttt{flow} = 0 \textbf{ during } [0, T_{Vote})$$
$$\wedge \, \forall t < \infty \cdot \texttt{flow}(t + T_{Vote}) = Majority(\{\texttt{flow}_j(t) \mid j = 1, \ldots, 3\})$$

The value of the line `flow` is either zero or one and, provided that at any time at most one sensor is defective, a line value differing from the majority indicates a defective sensor or a broken wire:

$$FVotC_2 \equiv \forall t < \infty, i \in \{1, 2, 3\} \cdot send(\texttt{alarm}_\texttt{f}, i) @ t$$
$$\leftrightarrow \texttt{flow}_i \neq Majority(\{\texttt{flow}_j(t) \mid j = 1, \ldots, 3\}) @ t$$
$$\wedge \, t > 0 \rightarrow \exists t_1 < t \cdot$$
$$\texttt{flow}_i = Majority(\{\texttt{flow}_j(t) \mid j = 1..3\}) \textbf{ during } [t_1, t)$$

As before, assume that the voter never fails and that at most one sensor is defective at any time:

$$SensStuckAtZero^{\leq 1} \equiv \wedge_{k=1}^{3} SensStuckAtZero[FSens_k/FSens, \texttt{flow}_k/\texttt{flow}]$$
$$\wedge \forall t < \infty \cdot \exists k \neq l \cdot$$
$$FSensOK[\texttt{flow}_k/\texttt{flow}] @ t \wedge FSensOK[\texttt{flow}_l/\texttt{flow}] @ t$$

In contrast with a single flow sensor `FSens`, the triple modular redundant flow sensor `TripleFSens` $\equiv ((FSens_1\|FSens_2\|FSens_3) \wr SensStuckAtZero^{\leq 1}) \| FVot$ is subject to a delay T_{Vote} for the time taken for voting, whether or not faults occur.

Lemma 8.9 $\langle\langle now = 0 \rangle\rangle \texttt{TripleFSens} \langle\langle \varphi_{TFS} \rangle\rangle$
where

$$\varphi_{TFS} \equiv \texttt{flow} = 0 \textbf{ during } [0, T_{Vote})$$
$$\wedge\, \forall t < \infty \cdot (\texttt{flow}(t + T_{Vote}) = 1 \;\leftrightarrow\; \texttt{outflow}(t) > 0)$$

Proof: By the rule for parallel composition, we need to show that

$$(\wedge_{i=1}^{3} FSensC[\texttt{flow}_i/\texttt{flow}]) \wr SensStuckAtZero^{\leq 1}$$
$$\to \forall t < \infty \cdot (Majority(\{\texttt{flow}_j(t) \mid j = 1..3\}) = 1 \;\leftrightarrow\; \texttt{outflow}(t) > 0)$$

Therefore, assume $(\wedge_{i=1}^{3} FSensC[\texttt{flow}_i/\texttt{flow}]) \wr SensStuckAtZero^{\leq 1}$, i.e. that there exists an N such that $(\wedge_{i=1}^{3} FSensC[\texttt{flow}_i/\texttt{flow}])[N/R] \wedge SensStuckAtZero^{\leq 1}[N/R_{nml}]$ Consequently,

$$\forall t < \infty \cdot \texttt{outflow}_N(t) > 0 \tag{8.20}$$
$$\leftrightarrow \wedge_{i=1}^{3}(\texttt{flow}_i)_N(t) = 1 \wedge \wedge_{i=1}^{3}\texttt{flow}_i(t) = (\texttt{flow}_i)_N(t)$$
$$\vee\, \exists k, l, m \cdot k \neq l \neq m$$
$$\wedge\, \texttt{flow}_k(t) = (\texttt{flow}_k)_N(t) \wedge \texttt{flow}_l(t) = (\texttt{flow}_l)_N(t) \wedge \texttt{flow}_m(t) = 0\,,$$

and

$$\forall t < \infty \cdot \texttt{outflow}(t) = \texttt{outflow}_N(t) \tag{8.21}$$

Now consider any $\widehat{t}$ such that $Majority(\{\texttt{flow}_i(\widehat{t}) \mid i = 1, \ldots, 3\}) = 1$, which, by definition, is the case iff

$$\exists k \neq l \cdot (\texttt{flow}_k(\widehat{t}) = 1 \wedge \texttt{flow}_l(\widehat{t}) = 1) \tag{8.22}$$

By *reductio ad adsurdum* we conclude from (8.20) and (8.22) that $\texttt{outflow}_N(\widehat{t}) > 0$, which, by (8.21), leads to

$$\texttt{outflow}(\widehat{t}) > 0$$

$\square$

The methane level sensors must also be triplicated. This means that we have also to take into account the possible increase of the methane level during the delay T_{Vote} caused by voting:

$$MSensC \equiv \forall t < \infty \cdot (\texttt{mOK}(t) = 1 \;\leftrightarrow\; \texttt{ml}(t) < \texttt{SML} - T_{Vote}\lambda_{ml}^{max})$$

Let $\texttt{MSens}_i \equiv \texttt{MSens}[\texttt{mOK}_i/\texttt{mOK}]$ for $i = 1, 2, 3$. Since, apart from the names of the communication lines and channels, the voters MVot and FVot behave identically, define

$$\texttt{MVot} \equiv \texttt{FVot}[\texttt{mOK}_i/\texttt{flow}_i]_{i=1}^{3}[\texttt{alarm}_\texttt{m}/\texttt{alarm}_\texttt{f}]$$

It is likely that faults affect the sensors MSens *and* FSens in the same way, i.e.

$$MSensStuckAtZero^{\leq 1} \equiv SensStuckAtZero^{\leq 1}[\texttt{FSens}_i/\texttt{MSens}_i, \texttt{mOK}_i/\texttt{flow}_i]_{i=1}^{3}$$

Then the triple modular redundant methane level sensor,

$$\texttt{TripleMSens} \equiv ((\texttt{MSens}_1 \| \texttt{MSens}_2 \| \texttt{MSens}_3) \wr MSensStuckAtZero^{\leq 1}) \| \texttt{MVot}$$

conforms to the original specification in Chapter 5.

Lemma 8.10 $\langle\langle now = 0 \rangle\rangle \, \texttt{TripleMSens} \, \langle\langle \forall t < \infty \cdot (\texttt{mOK}(t) = 1 \leftrightarrow \texttt{ml}(t) < \texttt{SML}) \rangle\rangle$

Proof: Exercise 8.8.

For the component $\texttt{MContr}$ we shall copy with the appropriate changes the commitments CMC_1 through CMC_6 from Section 5.5.2. For instance, CMC_6 becomes

$$
\begin{aligned}
CMC_6 \equiv\ & \forall t_0, t_1 \cdot t_0 + \delta_{ml} \leq t_1 \\
& \wedge\, read(\texttt{mOK}, 0)\, @\, t_0 \wedge (\neg read(\texttt{mOK}, 1))\ \textbf{during}\ [t_0, t_1] \\
& \rightarrow \exists t_2 \leq t_0 + \delta_{ml} \cdot \texttt{pln} = 0\ \textbf{during}\ [t_2, t_1]
\end{aligned}
$$

In addition, $\texttt{MContr}$ reads the line $\texttt{flow}$ at least once every Δ_{read} time units:

$$
CMC_7 \equiv \forall t < \infty \cdot read(\texttt{flow})\, \textbf{in}\, [t, t + \Delta_{read})
$$

If the controller finds that the line $\texttt{flow}$ is low while the line $\texttt{pln}$ has been high for the last $\delta_p + \text{T}_{Vote}$ time units, maintenance is notified (by asynchronously sending the value one along the channel $\texttt{alarm}_\texttt{p}$) after T_{NoFlow} time units, but only once for each period that the pump is activated:

$$
\begin{aligned}
CMC_8 \equiv\ & \forall t \cdot send(\texttt{alarm}_\texttt{p}, 1)\, @\, t + \text{T}_{NoFlow} \\
& \leftrightarrow \exists t_1 \cdot t_1 < t - (\delta_p + \text{T}_{Vote}) \\
& \qquad \wedge\, \texttt{pln}(t_1) = 0 \wedge \texttt{pln} = 1\ \textbf{during}\ (t_1, t] \\
& \qquad \wedge\, read(\texttt{flow}, 0)\, @\, t \wedge (\neg send(\texttt{alarm}_\texttt{p}))\ \textbf{during}\ (t_1, t]
\end{aligned}
$$

Despite the use of the excellent techniques propagated in this book, it is still possible that the pump controller software has errors! It is also possible that the processor executing the software fails. This can have serious consequences, as a defective pump controller may not activate the pump when it should begin pumping out water and it may not switch the pump off when the methane level is critical. This means that incorrect functioning of the pump controller should be detected and dealt with as soon as possible.

One way to do this is to duplicate the controller and compare the outputs: the pump can then be activated only if both controllers agree on the action. For better fault location, it is more sensible to *tri*plicate the controller and use voting to decide on the action.

Assume that the controller software is sufficiently small and simple to be formally verified and checked, and that the processor failure rate is not very high. It may then be acceptable to select a cheaper solution and to use a *watchdog timer* (cf. Exercise 5.9) which switches the pump off unless it is regularly restarted by the controller (see Figure 8.2). This provides a good low-level check for *run-away* software and provides a fail-safe system:

$$
CMC_9 \equiv \forall t < \infty \cdot send(\texttt{restart}, 1)\, \textbf{in}\, [t, t + \text{T}_{Restart})
$$

Once again we see that, in comparison with the pump controller presented in Chapter 5, taking the water flow sensor and the watchdog timer into account results in an altogether new component; the restarting of the timer, for instance, is not the consequence of a fault, but is normal behaviour.

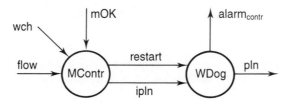

Figure 8.2 A watchdog for the pump controller

`WDog` has to enable communication through `restart` sufficiently often:

$$WDogC_1 \equiv minwait(\texttt{restart}, \texttt{Init}, \texttt{Period}) \textbf{ during } [0, \infty)$$

`WDog` restarts its timer whenever a one is received on channel `restart`. It sets the line `pln` low when this timer expires (for which a reaction time of δ_{WDog} is allowed) and notifies maintenance (by asynchronously sending a one along the channel `alarm`$_{\texttt{ctrl}}$):

$$
\begin{aligned}
WDogC_2 \equiv \forall t_1, t_2 &< \infty \cdot t_2 > t_1 + T_{Restart} \\
\wedge\, t_1 &= 0 \vee rec(\texttt{restart}, 1) @ t_1 \\
\wedge\, (\neg rec&(\texttt{restart}, 1)) \textbf{ during } (t_1, t_2) \\
\rightarrow \texttt{pln} &= 0 \textbf{ during } [t_1 + T_{Restart} + \delta_{WDog}, t_2 + \delta_{WDog}) \\
&\wedge send(\texttt{alarm}_{\texttt{ctrl}}, 1) \textbf{ in } [t_1 + T_{Restart}, t_1 + T_{Restart} + \delta_{WDog})
\end{aligned}
$$

As long as the timer is restarted at least every $T_{Restart}$ time units, the lines `ipln` and `pln` have the same value.

$$
\begin{aligned}
WDogC_3 \equiv \texttt{pln} = \texttt{ipln} &\textbf{ during } [0, T_{Restart} + \delta_{WDog}) \\
\wedge\, \forall t < \infty \cdot rec&(\texttt{restart}, 1) @ t \\
\rightarrow \texttt{pln} = \texttt{ipln} &\textbf{ during } [t + \delta_{WDog}, t + T_{Restart} + \delta_{WDog})
\end{aligned}
$$

This means that provision must be made to restart the timer at time $t = 0$.

We must assume that the component `WDog` never fails. And from the failure hypothesis *NoRestarts* it can be seen that the pump controller never restarts the watchdog timer and, most important, does not let `ipln` become high when this is not allowed. Define

$$
\begin{aligned}
MContrOK @ t &\equiv R \downarrow \{\texttt{restart}, \texttt{ipln}\}(t) = R_{nml} \downarrow \{\texttt{restart}, \texttt{ipln}\}(t) \\
MContrNotOK @ t &\equiv \neg (send(\texttt{restart}) @ t) \\
&\quad \wedge \texttt{ipln}(t) = \texttt{ipln}_N(t) \vee \texttt{ipln}(t) = 0
\end{aligned}
$$

Then

$$
\begin{aligned}
NoRestarts \equiv \forall t < \infty \cdot (MContrOK \vee MContrNotOK) &@ t \wedge \texttt{flow}(t) = \texttt{flow}_{nml}(t) \\
\wedge \texttt{wch}(t) = \texttt{wch}_{nml}(t) &\wedge \texttt{mOK}(t) = \texttt{mOK}_{nml}(t)
\end{aligned}
$$

Let $\texttt{SML} \equiv \texttt{CML} - (\Delta_{read} + \delta_{ml} + T_{Restart} + \delta_{WDog} + \delta_p)\lambda_{ml}^{max}$ From the following lemma `FailSafeContr` $\equiv (\texttt{MContr} \langle NoRestarts) \| \texttt{WDog}$ sets the voltage level on the line `pln` to low within at least $\Delta_{read} + \delta_{ml} + T_{Restart} + \delta_{WDog}$ time units after the methane level is reported to have exceeded `SML`.

Lemma 8.11 $\langle\langle now = 0 \rangle\rangle$ FailSafeContr $\langle\langle \varphi_{FSC} \rangle\rangle$, where

$$\begin{aligned} \varphi_{FSC} \equiv \forall t_0, t_1 < \infty \cdot\ & t_0 + \Delta_{read} + \delta_{ml} + T_{Restart} + \delta_{WDog} \leq t_1 \\ & \wedge \mathtt{mOK} = 0 \ \textbf{during} \ [t_0, t_1] \\ & \rightarrow \mathtt{pln} = 0 \ \textbf{during} \ [t_0 + \Delta_{read} + \delta_{ml} + T_{Restart} + \delta_{WDog}, t_1] \end{aligned}$$

Proof: There are two cases to consider:

(i) If *MContrOK* **during** $[t_0, t_0 + \Delta_{read} + \delta_{ml}]$ then, according to CMC_1, there exists t_2 ($t_0 \leq t_2 \leq t_0 + \Delta_{read}$) such that $read(\mathtt{mOK}, 0) @ t_2$, which, by CMC_6 (with appropriate changes), implies that there exists t_3 ($t_0 \leq t_3 \leq t_0 + \Delta_{read} + \delta_{ml}$) such that

$$\mathtt{pln} = 0 \ \textbf{during} \ [t_3, t_0 + \Delta_{read} + \delta_{ml}]$$

Using CMC_6 once more, $\mathtt{pln}$ normally remains low up to and including t_1, so we may conclude, based on *NoRestarts*, that

$$\mathtt{pln} = 0 \ \textbf{during} \ [t_3, t_1]$$

(ii) According to the worst case scenario, *MContrOK* **during** $[t_0, t_0 + \Delta_{read} + \delta_{ml}]$ does not hold because MContr fails at $t_0 + \Delta_{read} + \delta_{ml}$. Also, the timer may not expire before $t_0 + \Delta_{read} + \delta_{ml} + T_{Restart}$, and, consequently, $\mathtt{pln}$ is not set low before

$$t_0 + \Delta_{read} + \delta_{ml} + T_{Restart} + \delta_{WDog}$$

$\square$

Taking account of the maximum increase in the methane level in the time $\Delta_{read} + \delta_{ml} + T_{Restart} + \delta_{WDog}$ gives the following lemma.

Lemma 8.12
$$\langle\langle now = 0 \rangle\rangle \text{ FailSafeContr} \langle\langle \forall t < \infty \cdot \mathtt{ml}(t) \geq \mathtt{CML} - \delta_p \lambda_{ml}^{max} \rightarrow \mathtt{pln}(t) = 0 \rangle\rangle$$

8.4.4 A safe mine

In the presence of faults, it can no longer be guaranteed that the water level stays in between the specified lower and higher bounds LWL and HWL, even if the methane level never rises above its safe level SML. Let

$$\begin{aligned} \text{SafeMine} \equiv (\text{Pump} \wr NoFlow) \| \text{TripleWSens} \| \text{TripleFSens} \\ \| \text{TripleMSens} \| \text{FailSafeContr}) \end{aligned}$$

Then it is obviously *not* true that

$$\begin{aligned} \langle\langle now = 0 \rangle\rangle \text{ SafeMine} \langle\langle \forall t < \infty \cdot \mathtt{ml} < \text{SML} \ \textbf{during} \ [0, t] \\ \rightarrow \text{LWL} < \mathtt{wl}(t) < \text{HWL} \rangle\rangle \end{aligned}$$

But although a number of work-shifts may be lost because the pump fails to operate when it should, it can be proved that SafeMine is indeed safe.

Theorem 8.1 $\langle\langle now = 0\rangle\rangle$ SafeMine $\langle\langle \forall t < \infty \cdot \neg \, \texttt{expl} \, @ \, t \rangle\rangle$

Proof: Two cases need examination:

  (i) If $\texttt{ml}(t) <$ CML, then, by Lemma 8.8, not even an unreliable pump can cause an explosion at time t.

  (ii) If $\texttt{ml}(t) \geq$ CML, then, considering that the methane level increase is at most λ_{ml}^{max} in unit time, there exists a $t_0 \leq t - \delta_p$ such that $\texttt{ml} \geq$ CML $- \delta_p \lambda_{ml}^{max}$ **during** $[t_0, t]$ Hence, by Lemma 8.12, $\texttt{pln} = 0$ **during** $[t_0, t]$, which, by Lemma 8.8, allows us to conclude that $\neg \, \texttt{expl} \, @ \, t$.

$\square$

8.5   Soundness and completeness of the new proof rule

In this section we show that the failure hypothesis introduction rule is sound: in other words, if the correctness formula $\langle\langle A \rangle\rangle$ FP $\langle\langle C \rangle\rangle$ is derivable, then it is valid. We show also that the rule is complete: if the correctness formula $\langle\langle A \rangle\rangle$ FP $\langle\langle C \rangle\rangle$ is valid, then it is derivable.

Theorem 8.2 (Soundness)   The failure hypothesis introduction rule is sound.

Proof: Assume *NonProphetic*(A), that is,

$$\models A \;\; \rightarrow \;\; \forall M \cdot (M \downarrow [0, now_0] = R \downarrow [0, now_0] \;\; \rightarrow \;\; A[M/R]) \tag{8.23}$$

and

$$\models \langle\langle A \rangle\rangle \, \text{FP} \, \langle\langle C \rangle\rangle \tag{8.24}$$

Consider any σ_0. Let $(\sigma, \rho) \in \mathcal{M}[\![\text{FP} \wr \chi]\!](\sigma_0)$. Then, from the definition of the semantics, there exists a $(\sigma_{nml}, \rho_{nml}) \in \mathcal{M}[\![\text{FP}]\!](\sigma_0)$ such that, for all γ,

$$(\sigma_0, \sigma_{nml}, \sigma, \rho_{nml}, \rho, \gamma) \models \chi \tag{8.25}$$

Since χ is a failure hypothesis,

$$\rho \downarrow [0, \sigma_0(now)] = \rho_{nml} \downarrow [0, \sigma_0(now)] \tag{8.26}$$

We must prove $\langle\langle A \rangle\rangle$ FP $\wr \chi$ $\langle\langle C \wr \chi \rangle\rangle$. Assume that, for any γ,

$$(\sigma_0, \sigma, \rho, \gamma) \models A[X_0/X, now_0/now]$$

i.e. by (8.23),

$$(\sigma_0, \sigma, \rho, \gamma) \models \forall M \cdot \;\; M \downarrow [0, now_0] = R \downarrow [0, now_0]$$
$$\rightarrow A[X_0/X, now_0/now][M/R]$$

Let $\widehat{\gamma} = (\gamma : M \mapsto \rho_{nml})$. By (8.26),

$$(\sigma_0, \sigma, \rho, \widehat{\gamma}) \models A[X_0/X, now_0/now][M/R]$$

By the substitution lemma, we obtain $(\sigma_0, \sigma, \rho_{nml}, \gamma) \models A[X_0/X, now_0/now]$. Since neither *now* nor any term x appears in $A[X_0/X, now_0/now]$, this leads to, e.g.

$$(\sigma_0, \sigma_{nml}, \rho_{nml}, \gamma) \models A[X_0/X, now_0/now]$$

Consequently, by (8.24) and the fact that $(\sigma_{nml}, \rho_{nml}) \in \mathcal{M}[\![FP]\!](\sigma_0)$,

$$(\sigma_0, \sigma_{nml}, \rho_{nml}, \gamma) \models C$$

Define $\widehat{\gamma} = (\gamma : V \mapsto \sigma_{nml}(X), t \mapsto \sigma_{nml}(now), M \mapsto \rho_{nml})$. By the substitution lemma $(\sigma_0, \widehat{\sigma}, \widehat{\rho}, \widehat{\gamma}) \models C[V/X, t/now, M/R]$ for any $\widehat{\sigma}$ and $\widehat{\rho}$, for instance

$$(\sigma_0, \sigma, \rho, \widehat{\gamma}) \models C[V/X, t/now, M/R] \tag{8.27}$$

By (8.25), we know $(\sigma_0, \sigma_{nml}, \sigma, \rho_{nml}, \rho, \widehat{\gamma}) \models \chi$. By the substitution lemma, this obviously leads to $(\sigma_0, \sigma_{nml}, \sigma, \rho_{nml}, \rho, \widehat{\gamma}) \models \chi[V/X_{nml}, t/now_{nml}, M/R_{nml}]$. Since R_{nml}, now_{nml} or any x_{nml} are not in $\chi[V/X_{nml}, t/now_{nml}, M/R_{nml}]$, the correspondence lemma yields

$$(\sigma_0, \sigma, \rho, \widehat{\gamma}) \models \chi[V/X_{nml}, t/now_{nml}, M/R_{nml}] \tag{8.28}$$

By (8.27) and (8.28),

$$(\sigma_0, \sigma, \rho, \widehat{\gamma}) \models C[V/X, t/now, M/R] \wedge \chi[V/X_{nml}, t/now_{nml}, M/R_{nml}]$$

Consequently,

$$(\sigma_0, \sigma, \rho, \gamma) \models \exists t, V, M \cdot (C[V/X, t/now, M/R] \wedge \chi[V/X_{nml}, t/now_{nml}, M/R_{nml}])$$

i.e.

$$(\sigma_0, \sigma, \rho, \gamma) \models C \wr \chi$$

□

As usual when proving completeness, we assume that we can prove any valid formula of the underlying logic. Thus, using $\vdash \varphi$ to denote that assertion φ is derivable, we add the following axiom to our proof theory.

Axiom 8.1 (Relative completeness assumption) For an assertion φ,

$$\vdash \varphi \text{ if } \models \varphi$$

□

Definition 8.7 (Strongest commitment) An assertion C is called a *strongest commitment* of the assertion A and the failure prone process FP if, and only if,

(i) $\models \langle\!\langle A \rangle\!\rangle$ FP $\langle\!\langle C \rangle\!\rangle$, and

(ii) $\forall \varphi \cdot (\models \langle\!\langle A \rangle\!\rangle \, \mathrm{FP} \, \langle\!\langle \varphi \rangle\!\rangle \Rightarrow \models C \to \varphi)$.

Using the definition of validity, assertion C is a strongest commitment of A and FP if, and only if,

(i) $\forall \sigma_0, \sigma, \rho, \gamma \cdot \ (\sigma_0, \sigma, \rho, \gamma) \models A[X_0/X, now_0/now] \wedge (\sigma, \rho) \in \mathcal{M}[\![\mathrm{FP}]\!](\sigma_0)$
$\quad\quad\quad\quad \Rightarrow (\sigma_0, \sigma, \rho, \gamma) \models C$, and

(ii) $\forall \varphi \cdot \ \forall \sigma_0, \sigma, \rho, \gamma \cdot \ (\sigma_0, \sigma, \rho, \gamma) \models A[X_0/X, now_0/now] \wedge (\sigma, \rho) \in \mathcal{M}[\![\mathrm{FP}]\!](\sigma_0)$
$\quad\quad\quad\quad\quad\quad \Rightarrow (\sigma_0, \sigma, \rho, \gamma) \models \varphi$
$\Rightarrow \models C \to \varphi$

Suppose that an assertion $sc(A, \mathrm{FP})$ satisfies

$\forall \sigma_0, \sigma, \rho, \gamma \cdot \ (\sigma_0, \sigma, \rho, \gamma) \models A[X_0/X, now_0/now] \wedge (\sigma, \rho) \in \mathcal{M}[\![\mathrm{FP}]\!](\sigma_0)$
$\quad\quad\quad \Leftrightarrow (\sigma_0, \sigma, \rho, \gamma) \models sc(A, \mathrm{FP})$

This stronger version of (i) also satisfies (ii), because for all ψ,

$\forall \sigma_0, \sigma, \rho, \gamma \cdot ((\sigma_0, \sigma, \rho, \gamma) \models \psi \Rightarrow (\sigma_0, \sigma, \rho, \gamma) \models \varphi) \Rightarrow \models \psi \to \varphi$

We extend the class of assertions from Section 8.1 to a class of conditions that contains the strongest commitments. The truth value of a condition with respect to $(\sigma_0, \sigma, \rho, \gamma)$ is an extension of the interpretation of assertions with the additional clause

$(\sigma_0, \sigma, \rho, \gamma) \models sc(A, \mathrm{FP})$ iff $(\sigma_0, \sigma, \rho, \gamma) \models A[X_0/X, now_0/now]$
$\quad\quad\quad\quad\quad\quad$ and $(\sigma, \rho) \in \mathcal{M}[\![\mathrm{FP}]\!](\sigma_0)$

The next lemma, which follows directly from the definitions, states that $sc(A, \mathrm{FP})$ is a semantic characterization of the strongest commitment of A and FP.

Lemma 8.13   For all φ, if $\models sc(A, \mathrm{FP}) \leftrightarrow \varphi$ then φ is a strongest commitment of A and FP. $\qquad\qquad\square$

Observe that a strongest commitment must be an assertion, and hence $sc(A, \mathrm{FP})$ itself is not a strongest commitment. The following lemma shows how the strongest commitment of A and $\mathrm{FP} \wr \chi$ can be expressed in the case of *NonProphetic(A)*.

Lemma 8.14   If *NonProphetic(A)* then $\models sc(A, \mathrm{FP} \wr \chi) \leftrightarrow sc(A, \mathrm{FP}) \wr \chi$.

Proof: Consider any σ_0, σ, ρ and γ and any A such that *NonProphetic(A)*. By the definition of sc, $(\sigma_0, \sigma, \rho, \gamma) \models sc(A, \mathrm{FP} \wr \chi)$ iff

$(\sigma_0, \sigma, \rho, \gamma) \models A[X_0/X, now_0/now] \wedge (\sigma, \rho) \in \mathcal{M}[\![\mathrm{FP} \wr \chi]\!](\sigma_0)$

From the definition of the semantics of $\mathrm{FP} \wr \chi$, we obtain $(\sigma_0, \sigma, \rho, \gamma) \models sc(A, \mathrm{FP} \wr \chi)$ iff

$(\sigma_0, \sigma, \rho, \gamma) \models A[X_0/X, now_0/now] \wedge \exists \sigma_{nml}, \rho_{nml} \cdot$
$\quad\quad\quad (\sigma_{nml}, \rho_{nml}) \in \mathcal{M}[\![\mathrm{FP}]\!](\sigma_0) \wedge (\sigma_0, \sigma_{nml}, \sigma, \rho_{nml}, \rho, \gamma) \models \chi$

Equivalently, $(\sigma_0, \sigma, \rho, \gamma) \models sc(A, \mathrm{FP} \wr \chi)$ iff

$$\exists \sigma_{nml}, \rho_{nml} \cdot \quad (\sigma_0, \sigma, \rho, \gamma) \models A[X_0/X, now_0/now]$$
$$\wedge (\sigma_{nml}, \rho_{nml}) \in \mathcal{M}[\![\text{FP}]\!](\sigma_0) \wedge (\sigma_0, \sigma_{nml}, \sigma, \rho_{nml}, \rho, \gamma) \models \chi$$

Observe that

(a) since neither *now* nor any term x appears in $A[X_0/X, now_0/now]$,

$$(\sigma_0, \sigma, \rho, \gamma) \models A[X_0/X, now_0/now]$$

implies that, for all $\widehat{\sigma}$,

$$(\sigma_0, \widehat{\sigma}, \rho, \gamma) \models A[X_0/X, now_0/now]$$

(b) by the definition of a failure hypothesis, $(\sigma_0, \sigma_{nml}, \sigma, \rho_{nml}, \rho, \gamma) \models \chi$ implies that

$$\rho \downarrow [0, \sigma_0(now)] = \rho_{nml} \downarrow [0, \sigma_0(now)]$$

(c) since *NonProphetic(A)*, and hence *NonProphetic(A[X_0/X, now_0/now])*,

$$(\sigma_0, \sigma, \rho, \gamma) \models A[X_0/X, now_0/now]$$

implies

$$(\sigma_0, \sigma, \widehat{\rho}, \gamma) \models A[X_0/X, now_0/now]$$

provided $\widehat{\rho} \downarrow [0, \sigma_0(now)] = \rho \downarrow [0, \sigma_0(now)]$.

Consequently, $(\sigma_0, \sigma, \rho, \gamma) \models sc(A, \text{FP} \wr \chi)$ iff

$$\exists \sigma_{nml}, \rho_{nml} \cdot \quad (\sigma_0, \sigma_{nml}, \rho_{nml}, \gamma) \models A[X_0/X, now_0/now]$$
$$\wedge (\sigma_{nml}, \rho_{nml}) \in \mathcal{M}[\![\text{FP}]\!](\sigma_0)$$
$$\wedge (\sigma_0, \sigma_{nml}, \sigma, \rho_{nml}, \rho, \gamma) \models \chi$$

Then, by the definition of sc, $(\sigma_0, \sigma, \rho, \gamma) \models sc(A, \text{FP} \wr \chi)$ iff

$$\exists \sigma_{nml}, \rho_{nml} \cdot (\sigma_0, \sigma_{nml}, \rho_{nml}, \gamma) \models sc(A, \text{FP})$$
$$\wedge (\sigma_0, \sigma_{nml}, \sigma, \rho_{nml}, \rho, \gamma) \models \chi$$

Hence, $(\sigma_0, \sigma, \rho, \gamma) \models sc(A, \text{FP} \wr \chi)$ if, and only if, $(\sigma_0, \sigma, \rho, \gamma) \models sc(A, \text{FP}) \wr \chi$.

$\square$

Now we can establish relative completeness.

Theorem 8.3 (Completeness) The failure hypothesis introduction rule is relatively complete.

Proof: Assume that *NonProphetic(A)*. Assume also that

$$\vdash \langle\!\langle A \rangle\!\rangle \text{ FP } \langle\!\langle C_S \rangle\!\rangle \text{ with } sc(A, \text{FP}) \leftrightarrow C_S$$

Then, by the failure hypothesis introduction rule, we obtain $\vdash \langle\!\langle A \rangle\!\rangle \text{ FP} \wr \chi \langle\!\langle C_S \wr \chi \rangle\!\rangle$.

Suppose $\models \langle\langle A \rangle\rangle \, \mathrm{FP} \wr \chi \, \langle\langle C \rangle\rangle$. From $sc(A, \mathrm{FP}) \leftrightarrow C_S$ and Lemma 8.14, we obtain

$$\models sc(A, \mathrm{FP} \wr \chi) \leftrightarrow C_S \wr \chi$$

Consequently, by Lemma 8.13 and the definition of a strongest commitment,

$$\models \langle\langle A \rangle\rangle \, \mathrm{FP} \wr \chi \, \langle\langle C \rangle\rangle \text{ leads to } \models C_S \wr \chi \to C$$

Then, by the relative completeness assumption, $\vdash C_S \wr \chi \to C$.

From $\vdash \langle\langle A \rangle\rangle \, \mathrm{FP} \wr \chi \, \langle\langle C_S \wr \chi \rangle\rangle$ and $\vdash C_S \wr \chi \to C$ we obtain, using the consequence rule,

$$\vdash \langle\langle A \rangle\rangle \, \mathrm{FP} \wr \chi \, \langle\langle C \rangle\rangle$$

$$\square$$

The next lemma states that $sc(A, \mathrm{FP} \wr \chi)$ does not impose restrictions on the observable behaviour after termination; the proof is left as an exercise (Exercise 8.9).

Lemma 8.15

$$\models sc(A, \mathrm{FP} \wr \chi) \to \forall M \cdot (M \downarrow [0, now] = R \downarrow [0, now] \to sc(A, \mathrm{FP} \wr \chi)[M/R])$$

8.6   Historical background

Fault-tolerance is the ability of a system to keep functioning correctly, despite faults occurring or having occurred (Laprie, 1985). An elaborate overview of many techniques to achieve fault-tolerance can be found in Lee and Anderson (1990). For the greater part, the account in this chapter of the ways of adding to the reliability of the mine pump are taken from Laprie (1991).

A number of formal methods for dealing with fault-tolerance have been proposed in the literature. Much of the earlier work on this formalization is state based: in the state machine approach, the output of several instantiations of a program, each running on a distinct processor, is compared. Lamport's original description (1978) dealt with fault-free environments only; for a survey of the efforts to generalize the state machine approach to deal with faults see Schneider (1990a). A well-known application of the state machine approach is the implementation of fail-stop processors (Schlichting & Schneider, 1983).

In layered architectures, the exception handling concept (see, e.g. Lee and Anderson, 1990) is popular: a layer that provides a service to some higher level layer raises an exception to signal to that layer when a problem is detected that prevents the completion of the requested service, and the higher level layer contains handlers to deal with such exceptions. In a proof system based on Hoare triples, $\{p\}S\{q\}$, correctness requires the final state to satisfy q and Cristian (1985) used Hoare logic to make the normal and exceptional domains of execution explicit by partitioning the initial state space (specified by p) into disjoint subspaces for normal and exceptional behaviour by providing a separate specification for each part. Started in the normal subspace the program terminates normally, but started in the exceptional subspace the program terminates by raising an exception. In Lodaya and Shyamasundar (1991), a proof system is proposed for exception handling in a concurrent program, such as in Ada-like languages.

This kind of fault-tolerance accounts for processor crashes and the effects of faults that occur before the invocation of the program. The resulting specifications are often trivially satisfied by any process that just raises an exception. In Coenen (1993) deontic logic was proposed to overcome this 'lazy programmer paradox'. All the same, an unreliable communication medium, for instance, does not raise an exception if a message becomes corrupted and simply delivers the bad message.

In the formalisms of Joseph *et al.* (1987) and He and Hoare (1987) the execution of a process restarts as soon as a fault occurs. Hence, a failure prone execution of a process P consists of a number of partial executions of P that end in failure followed by a final and complete execution. Liu (1991) and Liu and Joseph (1992) describe a framework for reasoning about programs in the presence of faults and show how program transformations can be used to derive fault-tolerant behaviour by composing specifications of the fault environment and recovery actions with the program. The incorporation of checkpointing and backward recovery into a program have been investigated in Liu and Joseph (1993; 1994) which also contain laws for fault-refinement; Peled and Joseph (1994) contains an extended study of specification and recovery transformations using linear temporal logic.

Processes that crash are studied in Peleska (1991): more precisely, a dual computer system is proved correct. Such a system contains two replicas of the crash prone process, a 'master' and a 'slave' which shadows the operation of the master and takes over if and when the master crashes. The failure hypothesis in this case stipulates that at least one replica remains active.

The formalism proposed in Cau and de Roever (1993) allows a program to exhibit arbitrary behaviour after a fault occurs. This approach results in conditional specifications: a process behaves according to its specification as long as no faults have occurred. Fault-tolerance is proved by virtue of the system's failure hypothesis and the available redundancy. This approach is not adequate for dealing with the effects of faults that cannot be masked. For instance, when verifying a system or protocol which employs an error detecting code it is crucial to be certain that one valid codeword has not been changed into another.

The effects of faults are taken into account by Weber (1989), where he introduces fault scenarios which are traces that include, besides records of the system's input and output operations, a description of the faults that have occurred. A fault-tolerance property is expressed as an equivalence between a fault scenario, from which the fault events have been removed, and a fault-free trace; this tolerance relation is not elaborated.

In Nordahl (1993), the normal behaviour $S_{original}$ of a system S is distinguished from its exceptional 'failure mode' behaviour S_f. However, it is not possible to derive S_f from $S_{original}$ and once in failure mode there is no way back. A similar treatment of normal and exceptional behaviour can be found in Coenen and Hooman (1993).

The idea of formalizing a failure hypothesis as a relation between the normal and the acceptable process behaviour was introduced in Schepers (1993). The early attempts towards the compositional specification and verification of distributed fault-tolerant systems abstract from the internal state of a process as well as the timing of its actions (Schepers & Hooman, 1994; Schepers & Coenen, 1995). Consequently, they do not include rules for atomic statements or sequential composition and such proof theories are called network proof theories. Network proof theories for distributed real-time fault-tolerant systems are given in Schepers and Gerth (1993), where maximal parallelism is assumed and in Schepers (1994), where the limited resources are shared. The proof theory presented in this chapter extends these approaches in that it does take the internal state of a process into account.

8.7   Exercises

Exercise 8.1   For a process SORT, where

$$\langle\langle now = 0 \rangle\rangle \ \text{SORT} \ \langle\langle x = min(x_0, y_0) \wedge y = max(x_0, y_0) \wedge now < \Delta_{Sort} \rangle\rangle$$

which of the following transformation expressions do not qualify as a failure hypothesis, and why?

(a) $x_0 = 0 \wedge y_0 = 0$
(b) $now = now_0$
(c) $O @ now_0 - 1$
(d) $x = y_{nml} \wedge y = x_{nml}$
(e) $now > now_{nml} \wedge O @ now_{nml} + 5$

Exercise 8.2   For a continuously observable variable x, formalize stuck-at-zero memory faults.

Exercise 8.3   Consider a transmission medium MEDIUM that waits to (synchronously) accept an input message from a set *MSG* via a channel in, and within Δ_{Medium} time units enables its delivery through the synchronous channel out. Fresh input cannot be accepted until the previous message has been delivered.

(a) Specify the normal behaviour of MEDIUM.
(b) Formalize omission.
(c) Formalize corruption. (Hint: if the failure hypothesis does not restrict the output values, they are arbitrary.)

Exercise 8.4   Consider the communication medium of Exercise 8.3. In practice, an encoding function is used to transform a dataword into a codeword which contains some redundant bits. Thus the set of datawords is mapped into a small part of a much larger set of codewords. Codewords to which a dataword is mapped are called valid, and the encoding ensures that it is very unlikely that due to corruption one valid codeword is changed into another. Formalize this *detectable* corruption hypothesis. You may assume that the functions *Encode*, *Decode* and *Valid* are given.

Exercise 8.5 Consider Figure 8.1. Assume that the channels wch_1, wch_2 and wch_3 are replaced by media that are prone to detectable corruption, such as the one discussed in the previous exercise. Design a failure hypothesis that allows that, per vote, at most either one sensor or one wire fails.

Exercise 8.6 Show, in the style of Chapter 5, that there exists a voter WSVot such that $\langle\langle now = 0 \rangle\rangle$ WSVot $\langle\langle WSVotC \rangle\rangle$. You may assume that the function *InexactVote* is given.

Exercise 8.7 Prove Lemma 8.4. Remember to take into account the effect of a missing or incorrect reading. (Hint: because the voter allows each sensor to communicate at most one reading for each vote and because channels do not buffer messages, the average of two correct readings differs at most by $\varepsilon_{ws} + \frac{1}{2}\delta_{ws}\lambda_{in}^{max}$ from the water level to which the most recently received reading corresponds. This occurs when the two readings arrive at the start and the end of the window, respectively, and either both readings are ε too high while the water level drops maximally during the interval, or both readings are ε too low while the water level rises maximally.)

Exercise 8.8 Prove Lemma 8.10. (Hint: the proof is similar to that of Lemma 8.9.)

Exercise 8.9 Prove Lemma 8.15.

Exercise 8.10 Show as in Section 8.5, soundness and completeness of the proof rules of Chapter 5. (Hint: for atomic statements, the strongest commitments follow directly from the relevant axioms and rules, and the non-termination axiom.)

References

Abadi, M., & Lamport, L. 1994. An old-fashioned recipe for real-time. *ACM Trans. on Prog. Lang. & Syst.*, **16**, 1543–1571.

Alur, R., & Henzinger, T. 1990. Real-time logics: complexity and expressiveness. *Pages 390–401 of: Proc. Symp. on Logic in Comp. Sc.*

Alur, R., Courcoubetis, C., & Dill, D.L. 1990. Model-checking for real-time systems. *Pages 414–425 of: Proc. Symp. on Logic in Comp. Sc.*

Apt, K.R. 1981. Ten years of Hoare's logic: a survey – part I. *ACM Trans. on Prog. Lang. & Syst.*, **3**, 431–483.

Apt, K.R. 1984. Ten years of Hoare's logic: a survey – part II: nondeterminism. *Th. Comp. Sc.*, **28**, 83–109.

Apt, K.R., Francez, N., & de Roever, W.-P. 1980. A proof system for communicating sequential processes. *ACM Trans. on Prog. Lang. & Syst.*, **2**, 359–385.

Audsley, N.C. 1993. *Flexible scheduling in hard real-time systems.* Ph.D. thesis, Dept. of Comp. Sc., University of York, UK.

Audsley, N.C., Burns, A., Richardson, M.F., & Wellings, A.J. 1991. Hard real-time scheduling: the deadline monotonic approach. *Pages 127–132 of: Proc. 8th IEEE Workshop on Real-Time Op. Syst. and Softw.*

Audsley, N.C., Burns, A., Richardson, M.F., Tindell, K.W., & Wellings, A.J. 1993a. Applying new scheduling theory to static priority pre-emptive scheduling. *Softw. Eng. J.*, **8**(5), 284–292.

Audsley, N.C., Burns, A., & Wellings, A.J. 1993b. Deadline monotonic scheduling theory and application. *J. Control Eng. Pr.*, **1**(1), 71–78.

Audsley, N.C., Burns, A., Davis, R.I., Tindell, K.W., & Wellings, A.J. 1995. Fixed priority scheduling: an historical perspective. *J. Real-Time Syst.*, **8**, 173–198.

Baker, T.P. 1990. A stack-based resource allocation policy for realtime processes. *In: Proc. 11th IEEE Real-Time Syst. Symp.*

Baker, T.P. 1991. Stack-based scheduling of real-time processes. *J. Real-Time Syst.*, **3**(1).

Barringer, H., Kuiper, R., & Pnueli, A. 1984. Now you may compose temporal logic specifications. *Pages 51–63 of: Proc. 16th ACM Symp. on Theory of Comp.*

259

Baruah, S., & Rosier, L.E. 1991. Limitations concerning on-line scheduling algorithms for overloaded systems. *Pages 128–132 of: 8th IEEE Workshop on Real-Time Op. Syst. and Softw.*

Baruah, S., Koren, G., Mao, D., Mishra, B., Rosier, A.R.L., Shasha, D.E., & Wang, F. 1992. On the competitiveness of on-line real-time tasks scheduling. *J. Real-Time Syst.*, **4(2)**.

Bate, G. 1986. Mascot3: an informal introductory tutorial. *Softw. Eng. J.*, **1**(3), 95–102.

Bernstein, A.J. 1987. Predicate transfer and timeout in message passing. *Inf. Proc. Letts.*, **24**, 43–52.

Bernstein, A.J., & Harter, Jr., P.K. 1981. Proving real-time properties of programs with temporal logic. *Pages 1–11 of: Proc. 8th Annual ACM Symp. on Op. System Principles.*

Berry, G., & Gonthier, G. 1992. The ESTEREL synchronous programming language, design semantics, implementation. *Sc. of Comp. Progr.*, **19(2)**, 87–152.

Biyabani, S., Stankovic, J.A., & Ramamritham, K. 1988.. The integration of deadline and criticalness in hard real-time scheduling. *In: Proc. 9th IEEE Real-Time Syst. Symp.*

Bjørner, D., Langmaack, H., & Hoare, C.A.R. 1993. *ProCos I final deliverable.* Tech. rept. ID/DTH DB 13/1. Dept. of Comp. Sc., Technical University of Denmark.

Blake, B.A., & Schwan, K. 1991. Experimental evaluation of a real-time scheduler for a multiprocessor system. *IEEE Trans. Softw. Eng.*, **17(1)**.

Blazewicz, J., Cellary, W., Slowinski, R., & Weglarz, J. 1986. Scheduling under resource constraints – deterministic models. *Annals of Op. Res.*, **3**.

Bondavalli, A., Stankovic, J.A., & Strigini, L. 1993. *Adaptable fault-tolerance for real-time systems.* Tech. rept. ESPRIT BRA 6362 Predictably Dependable Comp. Syst. 2.

Brookes, S.D., & Roscoe, A.W. 1985. An improved failures model for communicating sequential processes. *In: Proc. Pittsburgh Seminar on Concurrency.* LNCS 197. Springer-Verlag.

Brookes, S.D., Hoare, C.A.R., & Roscoe, A.W. 1984. A theory of communicating sequential processes. *J. ACM*, **31**(7).

Burns, A. 1994. Preemptive priority-based scheduling: an appropriate engineering approach. *Pages 225–248 of:* Son, S.H. (ed), *Advances in Real-Time Systems.* Prentice Hall.

Burns, A., & Lister, A.M. 1991. A framework for building dependable systems. *Comp. J.*, **34**(2), 173–181.

Burns, A., & Wellings, A.J. 1994. HRT-HOOD: a design method for hard real-time systems. *J. Real-Time Syst.*, **6**(1), 73–114.

Burns, A., Lister, A.M., & Wellings, A.J. 1987. *A review of Ada tasking.* LNCS 262. Springer-Verlag.

Burns, A., Wellings, A.J., Bailey, C.M., & Fyfe, E. 1993. The Olympus attitude and orbital control system: a case study in hard-real-time system design and implementation. *Pages 19–35 of: Ada sans frontieres: Proc. 12th Ada-Europe Conf.* LNCS 688. Springer-Verlag.

Butazzo, G., & Stankovic, J.A. 1993. RED: Robust earliest deadline scheduling. *In: Proc. 3rd Intl. Workshop on Resp. Comp. Syst.*

Cau, A., & de Roever, W.-P. 1993. Specifying fault-tolerance within Stark's formalism. *Pages 392–401 of: Proc. 23rd Symp. on Fault-Tolerant Comp.* IEEE Comp. Society Press.

Chetto, H., & Chetto, M. 1989. Some results of the earliest deadline scheduling algorithm. *IEEE Trans. on Softw. Eng.*

Coenen, J. 1993. Top-down development of layered fault-tolerant systems and its problems – A deontic perspective. *Annals of Maths. and AI*, **9**, 133–150.

Coenen, J., & Hooman, J. 1993. Parameterized semantics for fault-tolerant real-time systems. *Pages 51–78 of:* Vytopil, J. (ed), *Formal Tech. in Real-Time and Fault-Tolerant Syst.* Kluwer Academic Publishers.

Coffman, E.G. (ed). 1976. *Computer and Job-shop Scheduling Theory.* John Wiley & Sons.

Cristian, F. 1985. A rigorous approach to fault-tolerant programming. *IEEE Trans. on Softw. Eng.*, **SE-11**(1), 23–31.

Cristian, F., Aghili, H., Strong, R., & Dolev, D. 1989. *Atomic broadcast: from simple message diffusion to Byzantine agreement.* Research Report RJ 5244. IBM Almaden Research Center.

Davies, J.W. 1993. *Specification and Proof in Real-Time Systems.* Cambridge University Press.

Davies, J.W., & Schneider, S.A. 1990. Factorising proofs in timed CSP. *In: Proc. 5th Intl. Conf. on the Mathematical Foundations of Prog. Semantics.* LNCS 442. Springer-Verlag.

Davies, J.W., & Schneider, S.A. 1993. Recursion induction for real-time processes. *Formal Asp. of Comp.*, **5**(6).

Davies, J.W., & Schneider, S.A. 1995. Real-time CSP. *In:* Rus, T., & Rattray, C. (eds), *Theories and Experiences for Real-Time System Development.* AMAST Series in Comp., vol. 2. World Scientific.

Davies, J.W., Jackson, D.M., & Schneider, S.A. 1992. Broadcast communication for real-time processes. *In:* Vytopil, J. (ed), *Proc. Symp. on Real-Time and Fault-Tolerant Syst.* LNCS 571. Springer-Verlag.

de Bakker, J. 1980. *Mathematical Theory of Program Correctness.* Prentice Hall International.

de Roever, W.-P. 1985. The quest for compositionality – A survey of assertion-based proof systems for concurrent programs, Part I: Concurrency based on shared variables. *Pages 181–207 of: Proc. IFIP Working Conf. 1985: The role of abstract models in computer science.* North-Holland.

Dertouzos, M.L., & Mok, A.K.-L. 1989. Multiprocessor on-line scheduling of hard-real-time tasks. *IEEE Trans. on Softw. Eng.*, **15**(12).

Dijkstra, E.W. 1976. *A Discipline of Programming.* Prentice Hall.

Emerson, E., Mok, A.K.-L., Sistla, A.P., & Srinivasan, J. 1989. *Quantitative temporal reasoning.* Workshop On Automatic Verification Methods for Finite State Syst., Grenoble, France.

Engel, M., & Rischel, H. 1994. *Dagstuhl seminar specification problem – a duration calculus solution.* Personal communication.

Engel, M., Kubica, M., Madey, J., Parnas, D.L., Ravn, A.P., & van Schouwen, A.J. 1993. A formal approach to computer systems requirements documentation. *Pages 452–474 of:* Grossman, R.L., Nerode, A., Ravn, A.P., & Rischel, H. (eds), *Hybrid Systems.* LNCS 736. Springer-Verlag.

Francez, N., Lehman, D., & Pnueli, A. 1984. A linear history semantics for distributed programming. *Th. Comp. Sc.,* **32**, 25–46.

Furht, B., Grostick, D., Gluch, D., Rabbat, G., Parker, J., & Roberts, M. 1991. *Real-time Unix Systems.* Kluwer Academic Publishers.

Gerber, R., & Lee, I. 1989. Communicating shared resources: a model for distributed real-time systems. *Pages 68–78 of: Proc. 10th IEEE Real-Time Syst. Symp.*

Gerber, R., & Lee, I. 1990. CCSR: a calculus for communicating shared resources. *Pages 263–277 of: CONCUR 90.* LNCS 458. Springer-Verlag.

Gibbins, P., Kay, A., & Schneider, S.A. 1993. *Asynchronous perceptrons in real-time CSP.* ESPRIT CONCUR2 project deliverable.

Goli, P., Kurose, J., & Towsley, D. 1990. *Approximate minimum laxity scheduling algorithms for real-time systems.* Tech. rept. University of Massachusetts, Amherst, Dept. of Comp. and Inf. Sc.

Goodenough, J.B., & Sha, L. 1988. The priority ceiling protocol: A method for minimizing the blocking of high priority Ada tasks. *Chap. 8(7), pages 20–31 of: Proc. 2nd Intl. Workshop on Real-Time Ada Issues, ACM Ada Letts.*

Gudmundsson, O., Mose, D., Ko, K., Agrawala, A., & Tripathi, S. 1992. Maruti, an environment for hard real-time applications. *In:* Agrawala, A., Gordon, K., & Hwang, P. (eds), *Mission Critical Operating Systems.* IOS Press.

Haase, V.H. 1981. Real-time behaviour of programs. *IEEE Trans. on Softw. Eng.,* **SE-7**(5), 494–501.

Hammer, D., Luit, E., van Roosmalen, O., van der Stok, P., & Verhoosel, J. 1994. Dedos: A distributed real-time environment. *IEEE Parallel & Distr. Technology, Syst. & Applications,* **2**(4), 32–47.

Hansen, M.R., & Zhou, C.C. 1992. Semantics and completeness of the duration calculus. *Pages 209–225 of:* de Bakker, J.W., Huizing, K., de Roever, W.-P., & Rozenberg, G. (eds), *Real-time: Theory in Practice, 1991.* LNCS 600. Springer-Verlag.

Hansen, M.R., Zhou, C.C., & Staunstrup, J. 1992. A real-time duration semantics for circuits. *In: Proc. 1992 ACM/SIGDA Workshop on Timing Issues in Specification and Synthesis of Digital Systems.* Princeton, NJ, March 18–20.

Hansen, M.R., Olderog, E.-R., Schenke, M., Fränzle, M., v. Karger, B., Müller-Olm, M., & Rischel, H. 1993a. *A duration calculus semantics for real-time reactive systems.* Tech. rept. OLD MRH 1/1. Oldenburg Universität.

Hansen, M.R., Pandya, P.K., & Zhou, C.C. 1993b. *Finite divergence.* Tech. rept. Rep. 15. UNU/IIST, Macau.

Hansson, H., & Jonsson, B. 1989. A framework for reasoning about time and reliability. *Pages 102–111 of: Proc. IEEE Real-Time Syst. Symp.*

Harel, D. 1987. Statecharts: a visual formalism for complex systems. *Sc. Comp. Prog.*, **8**, 231–274.

Harel, E. 1988. *Temporal analysis of real-time systems*. Master's Thesis. The Weizmann Institute of Sc., Rehovot, Israel.

Harel, E., Lichtenstein, O., & Pnueli, A. 1990. Explicit clock temporal logic. *Pages 402–413 of: Proc. Symp. on Logic in Comp. Sc.* IEEE.

Harter Jr., P.K. 1987. Response times in level structured systems. *ACM Trans. Comp. Sys.*, **5(3)**, 232–248.

He, J., & Bowen, J. 1992. Time interval semantics and implementation of a real-time programming language. *In: Proc. 4th Euromicro Workshop on Real-Time Syst.* IEEE Comp. Society Press.

He, J., & Hoare, C.A.R. 1987. Algebraic specification and proof of a distributed recovery algorithm. *Distr. Comp.*, **2**, 1–12.

He, J., Hoare, C.A.R., Fänzle, M., Müller-Olm, M., Olderog, E., Schenke, M., Hansen, M.R., Ravn, A.P., & Rischel, H. 1994. Provably correct systems. *Pages 288–335 of:* Langmaack, H., de Roever, W.-P., & Vytopil, J. (eds), *Proc. Symp. on Formal Tech. in Real-Time and Fault-Tolerant Syst.* LNCS 853. Springer-Verlag.

Hehner, E.C.R. 1989. Real-time programming. *Inf. Proc. Letts.*, **30**, 51–56.

Hoare, C.A.R. 1969. An axiomatic basis for computer programming. *Comm. ACM*, **12**(10), 576–580, 583.

Hoare, C.A.R. 1978. Communicating sequential processes. *Comm. ACM*, **21**(8).

Hoare, C.A.R. 1985. *Communicating Sequential Processes*. Prentice Hall International.

Holmes, V.P., Harris, D., Piorkowski, K., & Davidson, G. 1987. *Hawk: An operating system kernel for a real-time embedded multiprocessor*. Tech. rept. Sandia National Labs.

Hong, J., Tan, X., & Towsley, D. 1989. A performance analysis of minimum laxity and earliest deadline scheduling in a real-time systems. *IEEE Trans. on Comp.*, **C-38(12)**.

Hong, K.S., & Leung, J.Y-T. 1988. On-line scheduling of real-time tasks. *In: Proc. 9th IEEE Real-Time Syst. Symp.*

Hooman, J. 1987. A compositional proof theory for real-time distributed message passing. *Pages 315–332 of: Parallel Architectures and Languages Europe.* LNCS 259. Springer-Verlag.

Hooman, J. 1990. Compositional verification of distributed real-time systems. *Pages 1–20 of: Proc. Workshop on Real-Time Syst. – Theory and Applications.* North-Holland.

Hooman, J. 1991. *Specification and Compositional Verification of Real-Time Systems.* LNCS 558. Springer-Verlag.

Hooman, J. 1993. Specification and verification of a distributed real-time arbitration protocol. *Pages 284–293 of: Proc. 14th IEEE Real-Time Syst. Symp.*

Hooman, J. 1994a. Compositional verification of a vistributed real-time arbitration protocol. *J. Real-Time Syst.*, **6**(2), 173–205.

Hooman, J. 1994b. Correctness of real-time systems by construction. *Pages 19–40 of:* Langmaack, H., de Roever, W.-P., & Vytopil, J. (eds), *Proc. Formal Tech. in Real-Time and Fault-Tolerant Syst.* LNCS 863. Springer-Verlag.

Hooman, J., & de Roever, W.-P. 1986. The quest goes on: a survey of proof systems for partial correctness of CSP. *Pages 343–395 of: Current Trends in Concurrency.* LNCS 224. Springer-Verlag.

Hooman, J., & de Roever, W.-P. 1990. Design and verification in real-time distributed computing: an introduction to compositional methods. *Pages 37–56 of: Protocol Specification, Testing and Verification, IX.* North-Holland.

Hooman, J., & Widom, J. 1989. A temporal-logic based compositional proof system for real-time message passing. *Pages 424–441 of: Parallel Architectures and Languages Europe.* LNCS 366. Springer-Verlag.

Hooman, J., Kuiper, R., & Zhou, P. 1991. Compositional verification of real-time systems using explicit clock temporal logic. *Pages 110–117 of: Proc. 6th Intl. Workshop on Softw. Specification and Design.* IEEE.

Howles, F. 1993. *Distributed arbitration in the Futurebus protocol.* M.Sc. thesis, Oxford University.

Huizing, C., Gerth, R., & de Roever, W.-P. 1987. Full abstraction of a real-time denotational semantics for an OCCAM-like language. *Pages 223–237 of: Proc. 14th ACM Symp. on Principles of Prog. Languages.*

Hung, D.V., & Zhou, C.C. 1994. *Probabilistic duration calculus for continuous time.* Tech. rept. UNU/IIST Report 25. UNU/IIST, Macau.

IEEE. 1988. *Standard backplane and bus specification for multiprocessor architectures: Futurebus.* IEEE.

Jackson, D.M. 1989. *The specification of aircraft engine control software in timed CSP.* M.Sc. thesis, Oxford University.

Jackson, D.M. 1990. *Specifying timed communicating sequential processes using temporal logic.* Tech. rept. TR–5–90. Programming Research Group, Oxford University.

Jackson, D.M. 1992. *Logical verification of reactive software systems.* D.Phil thesis, Oxford University.

Jahanian, F., & Mok, A.K.-L. 1986. Safety analysis of timing properties in real-time systems. *IEEE Trans. on Softw. Eng.,* **SE-12**(9), 890–904.

Jensen, D. 1992. The kernel computational model of the Alpha real-time distributed operating system. *In:* Agrawala, A., Gordon, K., & Hwang, P. (eds), *Mission Critical Operating Systems.* IOS Press.

Joseph, M., & Pandya, P.K. 1986. Finding response times in a real-time system. *Comp. J.,* **29(5)**, 390–395.

Joseph, M., Moitra, A., & Soundararajan, N. 1987. Proof rules for fault-tolerant distributed programs. *Sc. Comp. Prog.,* **8**, 43–67.

Kay, A., & Reed, J.N. 1990. *A specification of a telephone exchange in timed CSP.* Tech. rept. TR–19–90. Programming Research Group, Oxford University.

Klein, M.H., Ralya, T.A., Pollak, B., Obenza, R., & Harbour, M.G. 1993. *A Practitioner's Handbook for Real-time Analysis: a guide to rate monotonic analysis for real-time systems.* Kluwer Academic Publishers.

Koymans, R. 1990. Specifying real-time properties with metric temporal logic. *J. Real-Time Syst.*, **2**(4), 255–299.

Koymans, R. 1992. *Specifying Message Passing and Time-Critical Systems with Temporal Logic.* LNCS 651. Springer-Verlag.

Koymans, R., & de Roever, W.-P. 1985. Examples of a real-time temporal logic specification. *Pages 231–252 of: The Analysis of Concurrent Systems.* LNCS 207. Springer-Verlag.

Koymans, R., Vytopyl, J., & de Roever, W.-P. 1983. Real-time programming and asynchronous message passing. *Pages 187–197 of: Proc. 2nd ACM Symp. on Principles of Distr. Comp.*

Koymans, R., Shyamasundar, R.K., de Roever, W.-P., Gerth, R., & Arun-Kumar, S. 1988. Compositional semantics for real-time distributed computing. *Inf. & Comp.*, **79**(3), 210–256.

Kramer, J., Magee, J., Sloman, M.S., & Lister, A.M. 1983. CONIC: an integrated approach to distributed computer control systems. *Proc. IEE (Part E)*, **180**(1), 1–10.

Lamport, L. 1978. Time, clocks, and the ordering of events in a distributed system. *Comm. ACM*, **21**(7), 558–565.

Lamport, L. 1983. Specifying concurrent program modules. *ACM Trans. on Prog. Lang. & Syst.*, **5**(2), 190–222.

Lamport, L. 1993. Hybrid systems in TLA$^+$. *Pages 77–102 of: Workshop on Theory of Hybrid Systems.* LNCS 736. Springer-Verlag.

Lamport, L. 1994. The temporal logic of actions. *ACM Trans. on Prog. Lang. & Syst.*, **1**(3), 872–923.

Lamport, L., & Merz, S. 1994. Specifying and verifying fault-tolerant systems. *Pages 41–76 of:* Langmaak, H., de Roever, W.-P., & Vytopil, J. (eds), *Proc. Formal Tech. in Real-Time and Fault-Tolerant Syst.* LNCS 863. Springer-Verlag.

Laprie, J.C. 1985. Dependable computing and fault-tolerance: concepts and terminology. *Pages 2–11 of: Proc. 15th Symp. on Fault-Tolerant Comp.* IEEE Comp. Society Press.

Lee, P.A., & Anderson, T. 1990. *Fault-Tolerance: Principles and Practice.* Springer-Verlag.

Lehoczky, J. 1990. Fixed priority scheduling or periodic task sets with arbitrary deadlines. *Pages 201–209 of: Proc. 11th IEEE Real-Time Syst. Symp.*

Lehoczky, J., Sha, L., & Ding, Y. 1989. The rate-monotonic scheduling algorithm: exact characterisation and average case behavior. *Pages 261–270 of: Proc. 10th IEEE Real-Time Syst. Symp.*

Levin, G.M., & Gries, D. 1981. A proof technique for communicating sequential processes. *Acta Inf.*, **15**, 281–302.

Lincoln, P., & Rushby, J. 1993. The formal verification of an algorithm for interactive consistency under a hybrid fault model. *Pages 292–304 of: Comp. Aided Verif. 93.* LNCS 697. Springer-Verlag.

Liu, C.L., & Layland, J.W. 1973. Scheduling algorithms for multiprogramming in a hard-real-time environment. *J. ACM*, **20(1)**, 40–61.

Liu, J.W.S., Lin, K., Shih, W., Yu, A., Chung, J., & Zhao., W. 1991. Algorithms for scheduling imprecise calculations. *IEEE Comp.*, **24(5)**, 58–68.

Liu, J.W.S., Shih, W.K., Lin, K.J., Bettati, R., & Chung, J.Y. 1994a. Imprecise computations. *In: Proc. IEEE.*

Liu, Z. 1991. *Fault-tolerant programming by transformations*. Ph.D. thesis, University of Warwick.

Liu, Z., & Joseph, M. 1992. Transformation of programs for fault-tolerance. *Formal Asp. Comp.*, **4**, 442–469.

Liu, Z., & Joseph, M. 1993. Specification and verification of recovery in asynchronous communicating systems. *Pages 137–165 of:* Vytopil, J. (ed), *Proc. Formal Tech. in Real-Time and Fault-Tolerant Syst.* Kluwer Academic Publishers.

Liu, Z., & Joseph, M. 1994. Stepwise development of fault-tolerant reactive systems. *Pages 529–546 of:* Langmaak, H., de Roever, W.-P., & Vytopil, J. (eds), *Proc. Formal Tech. in Real-Time and Fault Tolerant Syst.* LNCS 863. Springer-Verlag.

Liu, Z., Nordahl, J., & Sørensen, E.V. 1993a. Composition and refinement of probabilistic real-time systems. *Pages 31–40 of:* Górski, Janusz (ed), *Proc. 12th Intl. Conf. on Comp. Safety, Reliability and Security.* Springer-Verlag.

Liu, Z., Nordahl, J., & Sørensen, E.V. 1993b. Compositional design and refinement of probabilistic real-time systems. *In: IMA Conf. on Maths. of Dependable Syst.*

Liu, Z., Ravn, A.P., Sørensen, E.V., & Zhou, C.C. 1993c. A probabilistic duration calculus. *Pages 29–52 of:* Kopetz, H., & Kakuda, Y. (eds), *Responsive Comp. Syst.* Dep. Comp. and Fault-Tol. Syst., vol. 7. Springer-Verlag.

Liu, Z., Ravn, A.P., Sørensen, E.V., & Zhou, C.C. 1994b. Towards a calculus of systems dependability. *High Integrity Syst.*, **1**(1), 49–75.

Liu, Z., Joseph, M., & Janowski, T. 1995. Verification of schedulability for real-time programs. *Formal Asp. of Comp.*, **7**.

Locke, C.D. 1985. *Best-effort decision making for real-time scheduling.* Ph.D. thesis, Carnegie-Mellon University, Pittsburgh, PA.

Lodaya, K., & Shyamasundar, R.K. 1991. Proof theory for exception handling in a tasking environment. *Acta Inf.*, **28**, 7–41.

Lowe, G. 1993. *Probabilities and priorities in timed CSP.* D.Phil thesis, Oxford University.

Mahony, B.P., & Hayes, I.J. 1992. A case-study in timed refinement: a mine pump. *IEEE Trans. on Softw. Eng.*, **18**(9), 817–826.

Manna, Z., & Pnueli, A. 1982. Verification of concurrent programs: a temporal proof system. *Pages 163–255 of: Foundations of Comp. Sc. IV, Distr. Syst.: Part 2.* Mathematical Centre Tracts, vol. 159.

Mislove, M.W., Roscoe, A.W., & Schneider, S.A. 1995. Fixed points without completeness. *Th.Comp. Sc.*, **138**.

Mok, A.K.-L. 1983. *Fundamental design problems of distributed systems for the hard real-time environment.* Ph.D. thesis, Dept. of Electrical Eng. and Comp. Sc., M.I.T, Cambridge, MA.

Mok, A.K.-L., & Dertouzos, M.L. 1978. Multiprocessor scheduling in a hard real-time environment. *In: Proc. 7th Texas Conf. on Comp. Syst.*

Moszkowski, B. 1985. A temporal logic for multi-level reasoning about hardware. *IEEE Comp.*, **18**(2).

Nassor, E., & Bres, G. 1991. Hard real-time sporadic task scheduling for fixed priority schedulers. *Pages 44–47 of: Proc. Intl. Workshop on Responsive Comp. Syst.*

Nguyen, V., Demers, A., Gries, D., & Owicki, S. 1986. A model and temporal proof system for networks of processes. *Distr. Comp.*, **1**(1), 7–25.

Nordahl, J. 1993. Design for dependability. *Pages 65–89 of: Proc. 3rd IFIP Intl. Working Conf. on Dependable Comp. for Critical Applications, Vol. 8.* Springer-Verlag.

Olderog, E.R. 1985. Process theory: semantics, specification and verification. *Pages 509–519 of: ESPRIT/LPC Advanced School on Current Trends in Concurrency.* LNCS 194. Springer-Verlag.

Ostroff, J. 1989. *Temporal Logic for Real-Time Systems.* Advanced Softw. Development Series. Research Studies Press.

Owicki, S., & Gries, D. 1976. An axiomatic proof technique for parallel programs. *Acta Inf.*, **6**, 319–340.

Owicki, S., & Lamport, L. 1982. Proving liveness properties of concurrent programs. *ACM Trans. on Prog. Lang. & Syst.*, **4**(3), 455–495.

Owre, S., Rushby, J., & Shankar, N. 1992. PVS: A prototype verification system. *Pages 748–752 of: 11th Conf. on Automated Deduction.* LNAI 607, Springer-Verlag.

Pandya, P.K. 1994. *Weak chop inverses and liveness in duration calculus.* Tech. rept. Computer Science Group, TIFR, India,. TR-95-1.

Panwar, S.S., & Towsley, D. 1988. *On the optimality of the step rule for multiple server queues that serve customers with deadlines.* Tech. rept. COINS 88-81. University of Massachusetts Amherst, Dept. of Comp. and Inf. Sc.

Panwar, S.S., Towsley, D., & Wolf, J.K. 1988. Optimal scheduling policies for a class of queues with customer deadlines until the beginning of service. *J. ACM*, **35(4)**.

Peled, D., & Joseph, M. 1994. A compositional framework for fault-tolerance by specification transformation. *Th. Comp. Sc.*, **128**, 99–125.

Peleska, J. 1991. Design and verification of fault-tolerant systems with CSP. *Distr. Comp.*, **5**, 95–106.

Pnueli, A. 1977. The temporal logic of programs. *Pages 46–57 of: Proc. 18th Symp. on Foundations of Comp. Sc.*

Pnueli, A., & Harel, E. 1988. Applications of temporal logic to the specification of real-time systems. *Pages 84–98 of:* Joseph, M. (ed), *Proc. Formal Tech. in Real-Time and Fault-Tolerant Syst.* LNCS 331. Springer-Verlag.

Ramamritham, K., & Stankovic, J.A. 1984. Dynamic task scheduling in distributed hard real-time systems. *IEEE Softw.*, **1**(**3**), 65–75.

Ramamritham, K., Stankovic, J.A., & Zhao, W. 1989. Distributed scheduling of tasks with deadlines and resource requirements. *Pages 1110–23 of: IEEE Trans. on Comp.*, vol. 38(8).

Ramamritham, K., Stankovic, J.A., & Shiah, P. 1990. Efficient scheduling algorithms for real-time multiprocessor systems. *IEEE Trans. on Parallel and Distr. Syst.*, **1**(**2**), 184–94.

Ravn, A.P. 1994. *Design of embedded real-time computing systems.* Tech. rept. ID/DTH.

Ravn, A.P., & Rischel, H. 1991. Requirements capture for embedded real-time systems. *Pages 147–152 of: Proc. IMACS-MCTS'91 Symp. on Modelling and Control of Techn. Syst., Villeneuve d'Ascq, France 7–10, 1991*, vol. 2. IMACS.

Ravn, A.P., Rischel, H., & Hansen, K.M. 1993. Specifying and verifying requirements of real-time systems. *IEEE Trans. Softw. Eng.*, **19**(1), 41–55.

Ready, J. 1986. VRTX: A real-time operating system for embedded microprocessor applications. *IEEE Micro*, 8–17.

Reed, G.M. 1988. *A uniform mathematical theory for distributed computing.* D.Phil thesis, Oxford University.

Reed, G.M. 1990. A hierarchy of models for real-time distributed computing. *In: Proc. 5th Intl. Conf. on the Mathematical Foundations of Prog. Semantics.* LNCS 442. Springer-Verlag.

Reed, G.M., & Roscoe, A.W. 1986. A timed model for communicating sequential processes. *Pages 314–323 of: Proc. 13th Intl. Coll. on Automata, Languages and Prog.* LNCS 226. Springer-Verlag.

Reed, G.M., & Roscoe, A.W. 1987. Metric spaces as models for real-time concurrency. *In: Proc. Workshop on the Mathematical Foundations of Prog. Languages Semantics.* LNCS 298. Springer-Verlag.

Reed, G.M., & Roscoe, A.W. 1991. A study of nondeterminism in real-time concurrency. *In: Proc. 2nd UK–Japan CS Workshop.* LNCS 491. Springer-Verlag.

Roscoe, A.W. 1994. Model-checking CSP. *In:* Roscoe, A.W. (ed), *A Classical Mind: Essays in Honour of C.A.R. Hoare.* Prentice Hall International.

Rushby, J. 1993. A fault-masking and transient-recovery model for digital flight-control systems. *Pages 109–136 of:* Vytopil, J. (ed), *Formal Tech. in Real-Time and Fault-Tolerant Syst.* Kluwer Academic Publishers.

Rushby, J., & von Henke, F. 1993. Formal verification of algorithms for critical systems. *IEEE Trans. on Softw. Eng.*, **19**(1), 13–23.

Scattergood, B. 1990. *The description of a laboratory robot in timed CSP.* M.Sc. thesis, Oxford University.

Schepers, H. 1993. Tracing fault-tolerance. *Pages 91–110 of: Proc. 3rd IFIP Intl. Working Conf. on Dependable Comp. for Critical Applications, Vol. 8.* Springer-Verlag.

Schepers, H. 1994. Compositional reasoning about responsive systems with limited resources. *J. Real-Time Syst.*, **7**(3), 291–313. Reprinted in M.Malek (Ed.), *Responsive Computing*, Kluwer Academic, 1994, 65-87.

Schepers, H., & Coenen, J. 1995. Trace-based compositional refinement of fault-tolerant distributed systems. *Pages 309–324 of: Dependable Computing and Fault-tolerant Systems* **9**.

Schepers, H., & Gerth, R. 1993. A compositional proof theory for fault-tolerant real-time distributed systems. *Pages 34–43 of: Proc. 12th Symp. on Reliable Distr. Syst.* IEEE Comp. Society Press.

Schepers, H., & Hooman, J. 1994. A trace-based compositional proof theory for fault tolerant distributed systems. *Th. Comp. Sc.*, **128**, 127–158.

Schlichting, R.D., & Schneider, F.B. 1983. Fail-stop processors: an approach to designing fault tolerant computing systems. *ACM Trans. on Comp. Syst.*, **1**(3), 222–238.

Schneider, F.B. 1990a. Implementing fault-tolerant services using the state machine approach: A tutorial. *ACM Comp. Surveys*, **22**(4), 299–319.

Schneider, F.B., Bloom, B., & Marzullo, K. 1992. Putting time into proof outlines. *Pages 618–639 of: Workshop on Real-Time: Theory in Practice*. LNCS 600. Springer-Verlag.

Schneider, S.A. 1990b. *Correctness and communication of real-time systems*. D.Phil thesis, Oxford University.

Schneider, S.A. 1991. *Unbounded non-determinism in timed CSP*. ESPRIT SPEC project deliverable.

Schneider, S.A. 1993. *Fischer's protocol in timed CSP*. ESPRIT CONCUR2 project deliverable.

Schneider, S.A. 1994. Timewise refinement for communicating processes. *In: Proc. 9th Intl. Conf. on the Mathematical Foundations of Prog. Semantics*. LNCS 802. Springer-Verlag.

Schneider, S.A. 1995. An operational semantics for timed CSP. *Inf. & Comp.*, **116**(2).

Scholfield, D.J., Zedan, H.S.M., & He, J. 1994. A specification-oriented semantics for real-time systems. *Th. Comp. Sc.*, **131**, 219–241.

Schwan, K., Geith, A., & Zhou, H. 1990. From $Chaos^{base}$ to $Chaos^{arc}$: A family of real-time kernels. *Pages 82–91 of: Proc. 11th IEEE Real-Time Syst. Symp.*

Scott, B.G.O. 1994. Translating timed CSP processes to occam2. *In: Proc. 1994 World Transputer Congress*. IOS Press.

Sha, L., Rajkumar, R., & Lehoczky, J.P. 1990. Priority inheritance protocols: An approach to real-time synchronisation. *IEEE Trans. on Comp.*, **39**(9), 1175–1185.

Shankar, A.U., & Lam, S.S. 1987. Time-dependent distributed systems: proving safety, liveness and real-time properties. *Distr. Comp.*, **2**, 61–79.

Shankar, N. 1993. Verification of real-time systems using PVS. *Pages 280–291 of: Comp. Aided Verif. '93*. LNCS 697. Springer-Verlag.

Shasha, D.E., Pnueli, A., & Ewald, W. 1984. Temporal verification of carrier-sense local area network protocols. *Pages 54–65 of: Proc. 11th ACM Symp. on Principles of Prog. Languages*.

Shen, C., Ramamritham, K., & Stankovic, J.A. 1993. Resource reclaiming in multiprocessor real-time systems. *IEEE Trans. on Parallel and Distr. Syst.*, **4(4)**, 382–397.

Skakkebæk, J.U. 1994. Liveness and fairness in duration calculus. *Pages 283–298 of:* Jonsson, B., & Parrow, J. (eds), *CONCUR '94: Concurrency Theory*. LNCS 836. Springer-Verlag.

Skakkebæk, J.U., & Shankar, N. 1994. Towards a duration calculus proof assistant in PVS. *Pages 660–679 of:* Langmaack, H., de Roever, W.-P., & Vytopil, J. (eds), *Proc. Formal Tech. in Real-time and Fault-Tolerant Syst.* LNCS 863. Springer-Verlag.

Skakkebæk, J.U., Ravn, A.P., Rischel, H., & Zhou, C.C. 1992. Specification of embedded real-time systems. *In: Proc. Euromicro Workshop on Real-time Syst.* IEEE Comp. Society Press.

Stamper, R. 1990. *The specification of AGV control software in timed CSP*. M.Sc. thesis, Oxford University.

Stankovic, J.A., & Ramamritham, K. 1988. *Hard Real-Time Systems: Tutorial Text.* IEEE Comp. Society Press.

Stankovic, J.A., & Ramamritham, K. 1991. The Spring kernel: A new paradigm for hard real-time operating systems. *IEEE Softw.*, **8(3)**, 62–72.

Stankovic, J.A., & Ramamritham, K. 1993. *Advances in Hard Real-Time Systems.* IEEE Comp. Society Press.

Stankovic, J.A., Ramamritham, K., & Cheng, S. 1985. Evaluation of a flexible task scheduling algorithm for distributed hard real-time systems. *IEEE Trans. on Comp.*, **C-34(12)**, 1130–43.

Superville, S. 1991. *Specifying complex systems with timed CSP: a decomposition and specification of a telephone exchange system which has a central controller.* M.Sc. thesis, Oxford University.

Tindell, K.W. 1993. *Fixed priority scheduling of hard real-time systems.* Ph.D. thesis, Dept. of Comp. Sc., University of York, UK.

Turski, W.M. 1988. Time considered irrelevant for real-time systems. *BIT*, **28**, 473–486.

Venema, Y. 1991. A modal logic for chopping intervals. *J. Logic of Comp.*, **1**(4), 453–796.

Wallace, A.R. 1991. *A TCSP case study of a flexible manufacturing system.* M.Sc. thesis, Oxford University.

Wang, F. 1993. *Issues Related to Dynamic Scheduling in Real-Time Systems.* Ph.D. thesis, University of Massachusetts.

Weber, D.G. 1989. Formal specification of fault-tolerance and its relation to computer security. *ACM Softw. Eng. Notes*, **14**(3), 273–277.

Wirth, N. 1977. Towards a discipline of real-time programs. *Comm. ACM*, **20**(8), 577–583.

Yu, H., Pandya, P.K., & Sun, Y. 1994a. A calculus for hybrid sampled data systems. *Pages 716–737 of:* Langmaack, H., de Roever, W.-P., & Vytopil, J. (eds), *Proc. Formal Tech. in Real-time and Fault-Tolerant Syst.* LNCS 863. Springer-Verlag.

Yu, X., Wang, J., Zhou, C.C., & Pandya, P.K. 1994b. A formal design of hybrid systems. *Pages 738–755 of:* Langmaack, H., de Roever, W.-P., & Vytopil, J. (eds), *Proc. Formal Tech. in Real-time and Fault-Tolerant Syst.* LNCS 863. Springer-Verlag.

Zhang, Y., & Zhou, C.C. 1994. A formal proof of the deadline driven scheduler. *Pages 756–775 of:* Langmaack, H., de Roever, W.-P., & Vytopil, J. (eds), *Proc. Formal Tech. in Real-time and Fault-Tolerant Syst.* LNCS 863. Springer-Verlag.

Zhao, W., & Ramamritham, K. 1987. Simple and integrated heuristic algorithms for scheduling tasks with time and resource constraints. *J. Syst. & Softw.*, **7**, 195–205.

Zhao, W., Ramamritham, K., & Stankovic, J.A. 1987a. Preemptive scheduling under time and resource constraints. *IEEE Trans. on Comp.*, **C-36(8)**, 949–60.

Zhao, W., Ramamritham, K., & Stankovic, J.A. 1987b. Scheduling tasks with resource requirements in hard real-time systems. *IEEE Trans. on Softw. Eng.*, **SE-12(5)**, 567–77.

Zhou, C.C. 1993. Duration calculii: An overview. *Pages 256–266 of:* Bjørner, D., Broy, M., & Pottosin, I.V. (eds), *Proc. Formal Methods in Prog. and Their Application.* LNCS 735. Springer-Verlag.

Zhou, C.C., & Xiaoshan, L. 1994. A mean-value duration calculus. *Pages 431–451 of:* Roscoe, A. W. (ed), *A Classical Mind: Essays in Honour of C. A. R. Hoare*. Prentice Hall International.

Zhou, C.C., Hoare, C.A.R., & Ravn, A.P. 1991a. A calculus of durations. *Inf. Proc. Letts.*, **40**(5).

Zhou, C.C., Hansen, M.R., Ravn, A.P., & Rischel, H. 1991b. Duration specifications for shared processors. *Pages 21–32 of:* Vytopil, J. (ed), *Proc. Symp. on Formal Tech. in Real-time and Fault-Tolerant Syst.* LNCS 571. Springer-Verlag.

Zhou, C.C., Hansen, M.R., & Sestoft, P. 1993a. Decidability results for duration calculus. *Pages 58–68 of:* Enjalbert, P., Finkel, A., & Wagner, K.W. (eds), *Proc. STACS 93.* LNCS 665. Springer-Verlag.

Zhou, C.C., Ravn, A.P., & Hansen, M.R. 1993b. An extended duration calculus for hybrid real-time systems. *Pages 36–59 of:* Grossman, R.L., Nerode, A., Ravn, A.P., & Rischel, H. (eds), *Hybrid Systems.* LNCS 736. Springer-Verlag.

Zhou, C.C., Zhang, J., Yang, L., & Li, X. 1994. Linear duration invariants. *Pages 86–109 of:* Langmaack, H., de Roever, W.-P., & Vytopil, J. (eds), *Proc. Formal Tech. in Real-time and Fault-Tolerant Syst.* LNCS 863. Springer-Verlag.

Zhou, C.C., Dang, V. H., & Li, X. 1995. A duration calculus with infinite intervals. *Pages 16–41 of:* Reichel, H. (ed), *Fundamentals of Computation Theory.* 10th Intl. Conf., Dresden, Germany. LNCS 965. Springer-Verlag.

Zhou, P., & Hooman, J. 1995. Formal specification and compositional verification of an atomic broadcast protocol. *J. Real-Time Sys.*, **9**(6), 119–145.

Zlokapa, G. 1993. *Real-time systems: well-timed scheduling and scheduling with precedence constraints.* Ph.D. thesis, University of Massachusetts.

Zwarico, A., & Lee, I. 1985. Proving a network of real-time processes correct. *Pages 169–177 of: Proc. 6th IEEE Real-Time Syst. Symp.*

Zwiers, J. 1989. *Compositionality, Concurrency and Partial Correctness.* LNCS 321. Springer-Verlag.

Index

C.A.R. Hoare, Series Editor

PEYTON JONES, S.L., *The Implementation of Functional Programming Languages*
PEYTON JONES, S. and LESTER, D., *Implementing Functional Languages*
POMBERGER, G., *Software Engineering and Modula-2*
POTTER, B., SINCLAIR, J. and TILL, D., *An Introduction to Formal Specification and Z*
REYNOLDS, J.C., *The Craft of Programming*
ROSCOE, A.W. (ed.), *A Classical Mind: Essays in honour of C.A.R. Hoare*
RYDEHEARD, D.E. and BURSTALL, R.M., *Computational Category Theory*
SHARP, R., *Principles of Protocol Design*
SLOMAN, M. and KRAMER, J., *Distributed Systems and Computer Networks*
SPIVEY, J.M., *The Z. Notation: A reference manual (2nd edn)*
TENNENT, R.D., *Principles of Programming Languages*
TENNENT, R.D., *Semantics of Programming Languages*
WATT, D.A., *Programming Language Concepts and Paradigms*
WATT, D.A., *Programming Language Processors*
WATT, D.A., WICHMANN, B.A. and FINDLAY, W., *ADA: Language and methodology*
WELSH, J. and ELDER, J., *Introduction to Modula 2*
WELSH, J. and ELDER, J., *Introduction to Pascal (3rd edn)*
WELSH, J., ELDER, J. and BUSTARD, D., *Sequential Program Structures*
WELSH, J. and HAY, A., *A Model Implementation of Standard Pascal*
WELSH, J. and McKEAG, M., *Structured System Programming*
WIKSTRÖM, Å., *Functional Programming Using Standard ML*